Auditing, Trust and Governance
Regulation in Europe

The reputation of corporate reporting has been in crisis. Trust in the process of financial accounting and auditing has been undermined by a series of high profile scandals involving major corporations, including Enron, Parmalat, Ahold, and Worldcom. In response, regulators and practitioners world-wide have put forward a series of initiatives to repair the damage and restore faith in corporate governance.

In this important new book, the European Auditing Research Network analyzes how that response has developed in Europe, with particular emphasis on the field of auditing. Leading international academics review how regulation has been revised in specific European countries to help restore confidence in the contribution of auditing to corporate governance. Various themes are analyzed, including the growing trend of internationalization in regulation, ethics and auditing, professional liability, and professional education. Additional chapters place trends in Europe in the context of broader international developments and consider both the overall pattern of regulatory change and the future of auditing and governance.

Auditing, Trust and Governance is a timely appraisal of the regulatory environment in Europe. It will be an invaluable volume for students, researchers, and professionals working in the fields of auditing, accountancy, and corporate governance, and will provide a useful basis for further research on the effects of the increased regulation.

The European Auditing Research Network (EARNet) was formed in April 2000 to foster research and exchange ideas among auditing scholars and researchers at a European level. Its objectives are to promote new research in auditing in Europe and to contribute to European policy making.

Reiner Quick is Professor of Accounting and Auditing at Darmstadt University of Technology, Germany.

Stuart Turley is Professor of Accounting at Manchester Business School, UK.

Marleen Willekens is Professor of Auditing at Tilburg University, the Netherlands.

Auditing, Trust and Governance

Regulation in Europe

Edited by Reiner Quick,
Stuart Turley and Marleen Willekens
on behalf of
European Auditing Research Network

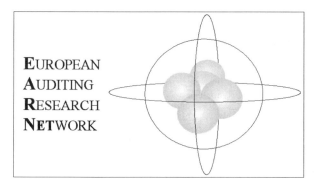

EUROPEAN
AUDITING
RESEARCH
NETWORK

Routledge
Taylor & Francis Group

LONDON AND NEW YORK

First published 2008
by Routledge
2 Park Square, Milton Park, Abingdon, Oxon OX14 4RN

Simultaneously published in the USA and Canada
by Routledge
270 Madison Avenue, New York, NY 10016

*Routledge is an imprint of the Taylor & Francis Group,
an informa business*

© 2008 Reiner Quick, Stuart Turley and Marleen Willekens

Typeset in Times New Roman by
Rosemount Typing Services, Auldgirth, Dumfriesshire
Printed and bound in Great Britain by
Cromwell Press, Trowbridge, UK

British Library Cataloguing in Publication Data
A catalogue record for this book is available from the British Library

Library of Congress Cataloging in Publication Data
A catalog record for this book has been requested

ISBN13: 978–0–415–44889–5 (hbk)
ISBN13: 978–0–415–44890–1 (pbk)
ISBN13: 978–0–203–93601–6 (ebk)

Contents

Figures

Tables

Contributors

C. Richard Baker is Professor and Chair of Accounting, Finance and Economics in the School of Business at Adelphi University, Garden City, New York. Prior to joining Adelphi University, he was Professor and Chair of Accounting and Finance at the University of Massachusetts-Dartmouth. He has also been a professor at Columbia and Fordham universities in New York City. His research interests focus on the regulatory, legal, disciplinary and ethical aspects of the public accounting profession. He is the author of over 90 academic papers, books and other publications. He holds a PhD from the School of Management at UCLA and he is also a certified public accountant in New York State.

Jean Bédard is Professor of Accounting at the Business School of Université Laval in Quebec City. He holds a PhD in Business Administration from the University of Southern California. He has been visiting professor at the University of Pittsburgh, London School of Economics, Université de Grenoble, Université de Bordeaux, and the University of New South Wales. He is the authors of several articles in the field of auditing that have been published in academic as well as professional journals, including: *Accounting, Organization and Society*, *Contemporary Accounting Research*, and *Auditing: A Journal of Practice and Theory*. He is a member of the editorial board of *Contemporary Accounting Research*, *Canadian Perspective on Accounting*, and *International Journal of Auditing* and associate editor of *Auditing: A Journal of Practice and Theory*. He has served as associate editor for *Contemporary Accounting Research*.

Mara Cameran is an assistant professor of financial accounting at the Università Bocconi, Milan. She also holds a PhD from the Università Bocconi. She has carried out mainly empirical auditing studies, including research on topics such as audit pricing, the quality of external auditing and the reputation of audit firms and has published in academic journals including the *International Journal of Auditing*. She currently serves as a referee for the *International Journal of Auditing* and is a member of the Scientific Committee for the European Accounting Association (Lisbon 2007 and Rotterdam 2008).

Aasmund Eilifsen is a professor and the Director of the Graduate Auditing Program at the Norwegian School of Economics and Business Administration. He serves on the Norwegian Auditing Standards Committee and is on the editorial boards of *Auditing: A Journal of Practice & Theory*, *European Accounting Review*, and *International Journal of Accounting*. He has published numerous articles in journals and books, including the recent co-authored textbook *Auditing and Assurance Services International Edition*.

Jere R. Francis is Curator's Professor at the University of Missouri where he also holds the Robert J. Trulaske Sr Chair of Accountancy. He has published widely on the auditing industry around the world and on the role of external audits in the production of credible financial reports. He currently serves on a number of editorial boards including the *Accounting Review* and *Review of Accounting Studies*, and is co-editor of the *International Journal of Accounting* and an associate editor at *Auditing: A Journal of Practice and Theory*.

Cristina de Fuentes Barberá, PhD in Business and Finance, is a lecturer at the Universidad de Valencia (Spain), specializing in the areas of auditing and financial statement analysis. She has been involved in the management of the Facultad de Economicas as Vice-Dean and is currently the assistant editor of the *Revista de Contabilidad-Spanish Accounting Review*. Her main research interests are in the areas of auditing and corporate governance. She has conducted several research projects resulting in books, monographs and academic articles published in journals including *Corporate Governance: An International Review*, *European Accounting Review*, *European Journal of Finance* and the *International Journal of Auditing*.

María Antonia García-Benau is Professor of Accounting and Auditing at the University of Valencia (Spain). She belongs to the Auditing Commission in the Spanish Ministry of Economy. She is also the editor of the academic journal *Revista de Contabilidad-Spanish Accounting Review*.

Claus Holm is an associate professor in accounting and auditing at Aarhus School of Business, University of Aarhus (Denmark). His academic background includes a PhD in auditing, MSc in accounting and auditing, and MSc in business administration. He is the head of the accounting research group at the Department of Business Research, Aarhus School of Business. Currently he is conducting research in the fields of corporate governance, auditing and financial reporting.

Christopher Humphrey is Professor of Accounting in Manchester Business School, University of Manchester. He has previously worked at both Leeds University Business School and Sheffield University Management School and has also had visiting academic positions at universities in Japan, Spain and New Zealand. His current research projects include studies of the nature and status of contemporary auditing practice and the historical development of the International Federation of Accountants (IFAC). He is an associate editor of the *European Accounting Review* and is also on the editorial board of a number of international accounting journals. He is a qualified chartered accountant and is currently a co-opted academic member of the Council of the Institute of Chartered Accountants in England and Wales (ICAEW).

Annette G. Köhler is Professor of Accounting and Auditing at the University of Duisburg-Essen. She earned her PhD from the University of Cologne and her professional dissertation from the University of Ulm. Her research work is focused on auditing, financial reporting, and corporate governance issues, and she has published widely on these topics. She is a member of several bodies and boards and is General Secretary of the European Auditing Research Network (EARNet).

Kai-Uwe Marten is Professor of Accounting and Auditing at Ulm University. Since October 2004 he has held the position of Dean of Studies in Economics. He earned his PhD from the University of Augsburg. Prior to joining Ulm University he was a *locum tenens* for the Chair of Accounting and Auditing at the Technical University of Berlin and a professor at the University of Wuppertal. His research interests are in the fields of auditing, especially quality assurance, public oversight, audit market research, and the internationalization of accounting. Professor Marten is a member of the SG – Forum for Dialogue between Science and Business and the German Academic Association for Business Research (VHB). Since the beginning of 2005 he has been the deputy chairman of the Auditor Oversight Commission (AOC) in Germany. He has been engaged as an observer on the Public Interest Oversight Board at the International Federation of Accountants (IFAC) for the EU Commission since October 2005.

Roger Meuwissen is Professor of Control and Auditing at the University of Maastricht and Director of the Maastricht Accounting, Auditing and Information Management Research Center (MARC). He received his PhD from the University of Maastricht. He teaches courses in auditing and accounting information systems and his research interests lie primarily in the areas of audit markets, earnings management, and audit regulation. He has conducted several research projects on the market for audit services and audit regulation at MARC and is the author of several articles in academic journals such as *Contemporary Accounting Research*, the *European Accounting Review*, and *Accounting Education*. Currently, he is also a member of the editorial board of *Auditing: A Journal of Practice and Theory*.

Peter Moizer was a chartered accountant with Price Waterhouse and became a professor at Leeds University in 1989, after ten years at Manchester University. He has been a Council member of the Institute of Chartered Accountants in England and Wales and is one of two senior moderators for its professional stage examination. He is a reporting member of the Competition Commission and has been involved in three inquiries: the economic regulation of Heathrow, Gatwick and Stansted, the ITV merger and the home credit market. He is a strategy advisor to the Greater Manchester Pension Fund (assets of approx. 14 billion euros).

Lasse Niemi is an assistant professor in auditing in the Helsinki School of Economics, Finland. His research focuses mainly on auditing and on the markets for auditing services. He has published several articles in academic, refereed journals including the *European Accounting Review*, the *International Journal of Accounting*, and the *International Journal of Auditing*. He is actively involved in supervisory bodies for the auditing profession in Finland: as a member of the Finnish Board for Chartered Public Finance Auditors and a deputy member of the Auditing Board of the Central Chamber of Commerce. He teaches auditing and financial accounting courses for bachelors and masters students, and auditing research courses for international doctoral students.

Christian Prat dit Hauret is Professor of Auditing at Bordeaux University. He earned his PhD from Bordeaux University and conducts mainly empirical studies, including research on topics such as ethics, the quality of external auditing, and audit regulation. Dr Prat dit Hauret has published in national journals including *Comptabilité-Contrôle-Audit* and *Finance-Contrôle-Stratégie*.

Reiner Quick is Professor of Accounting and Auditing at Darmstadt University of Technology (DUT). He earned his PhD from the University of Mannheim. Prior to joining DUT he was a professor at the University of Essen and the University of Muenster. He has been visiting professor at the Norwegian School of Management, the Norwegian School of Economics and Business Administration and the University of Southern Denmark. His research interests focus on auditor liability, auditor independence, audit methodology, and value reporting. He is the author of over 200 academic papers, books, and other publications published in journals including *Accounting, Organizations and Society*, *International Journal of Auditing*, and *European Accounting Review*. He is currently a member of the editorial board of *Auditing: A Journal of Practice & Theory*, the *International Journal of Auditing*, and *Accounting in Europe*.

Klaus Ruhnke is Professor of Accounting and Auditing at the Free University in Berlin. He is the author/co-author of two textbooks oin auditing and financial accounting and has published more than 70 articles. His main research interests are positive and normative research in international financial accounting and auditing. Another field of particular interest is research in and development of cluster-based eLearning systems in accounting. He also acts as a consultant and outside expert on IFRS and is a member of the board of examiners of the German Chamber of Public Auditors.

Anna Samsonova is a lecturer in accounting in the Manchester Business School, University of Manchester. She joined Manchester in 2006 after obtaining her Doctor of Science degree from Åbo Akademi University (Turku, Finland), having conducted a comprehensive study of the transformation of auditing in Russia. Her research employs qualitative approaches to examine the process of the professionalizsation of auditing and the manner in which global trends in audit regulation are interpreted locally in the context of transitional economies.

Stefan Sundgren is Professor in Accounting and Auditing at Umeå School of Business in Sweden. His main teaching areas are financial accounting and financial statement analysis and his main research interests are financial reporting, auditing, and law and economics. He has published articles in, for example, *European Accounting Review*, *Accounting & Business Research*, *European Journal of Law and Economics* and the *Journal of Financial Economics*. He is also the co-author of a financial accounting textbook (written in Swedish) and has done contract research for the Swedish bankruptcy priority committee as well as other governmental bodies.

Jürgen Tiedje works in the Directorate-General, Internal Market and Services of the European Commission. He is a lawyer educated in Germany and started with the European Commission in 1992. Since October 2005 he has been head of the unit responsible for audit regulation in the European Union, which is overseeing the successful implementation of the Statutory Audit Directive, including issues concerning relations with the United States and other third countries, the European Group of Auditor Oversight Bodies, the possible introduction of international standards on auditing and auditors' liability.

Stuart Turley is Professor of Accounting at the Manchester Business School, University of Manchester. He is also a member of the Auditing Practices Board, the body which sets both practice and ethical standards for auditors in the United Kingdom and Ireland. His research work is focused on auditing, financial reporting regulation, and related aspects of corporate governance structures, and he has published widely on these topics in many academic journals. He is a past editor of both the *British Accounting Review* and the *International Journal of Auditing* and is currently a member of the editorial boards of several journals.

Ann Vanstraelen is Professor of Accounting and Assurance Services at Maastricht University and has a part-time position at the University of Antwerp. Her research interests primarily relate to financial reporting quality, auditing and assurance services. She has been involved in several research projects, including commissioned research by the International Federation of Accountants (IFAC) in the field of assurance services. Ann has published in national and international journals including *Auditing: A Journal of Practice and Theory*, the *Journal of Accounting, Auditing and Finance*, *Accounting and*

Business Research, European Accounting Review, International Journal of Auditing, and *Journal of International Financial Management and Accounting*. Since January 2007 she has been an associate editor for *European Accounting Review*.

Antonio Vico-Martínez is a senior lecturer in accounting and auditing and Dean of the Faculty of Economics at the University Jaume I of Castellón (Spain). His main research area is concerned with the independence of auditors.

Philip Wallage is Professor of Auditing at the University of Amsterdam and a partner at KPMG Accountants in Amsterdam. He studied business economics (1984), received his CPA exam in 1986, and completed his PhD in economics in 1991. His dissertation was entitled "Methodology and Degree of Structure: A Dissertation on the Audit Process". He has authored many papers on financial auditing and corporate governance in Dutch and international academic journals. Dr Wallage is currently a member of the editorial board of *Maandblad voor Accountancy en Bedrijfseconomie* and *Handboek Accountancy*. He is also a member of the editorial board of *Current Issues in Auditing* (American Accounting Association) and a research fellow at the Amsterdam Centre of Law and Economics.

Bent Warming Rasmussen, PhD, is associate professor in auditing at the University of Southern Denmark. His research focuses on audit quality, auditors' liability, audit regulation, and ethics. He has published 48 articles in national and international journals. He is a member of the Aarhus Business School research network in accounting and auditing. Bent Warming-Rasmussen's teaches Auditing and Business Ethics in the master programmes at the University of Southern Denmark. He has also been a guest professor at several Danish and German universities and at Griffith University, Queensland, Australia.

Marleen Willekens is Professor of Auditing at Tilburg University. She earned her PhD from Warwick University (UK) and conducts mainly empirical but also analytical auditing studies, covering topics such as audit pricing, the quality of external auditing, business risk auditing, auditor regulation and liability, and earnings management. Dr Willekens has published in various international journals including *Auditing: A Journal of Practice and Theory*, *Accounting and Business Research*, *Journal of Business Finance and Accounting*, *European Accounting Review*, and many others. She is currently associate editor of *Auditing: A Journal of Practice and Theory* and holds positions on various editorial boards.

Foreword

A well functioning economy relies on sound financial statements. Accounting by companies serves not only management but also the wider public interest, including financial stability. Statutory auditors play a pivotal role in this respect as they are gatekeepers for the benefit of users of such financial statements. The quality of the auditors' work should allow users to build trust and to decide whether to invest or to divest in companies. If users cannot trust financial statements, companies will no longer have access to the capital they need.

A few years ago, accounting scandals on both sides of the Atlantic not only demonstrated the importance of this gatekeeper function, but also made clear that the concept of self-regulation of the audit profession is no longer sustainable. Instead, independent public oversight, external quality assurance systems, and – possibly – endorsement of international auditing standards at the level of the European Union would offer safeguards to strengthen the auditors' role as independent gatekeepers.

It is a surprise that the United States and the European Union have at the international level taken the lead in this regard. The US abandoned self-regulation under the 2002 Sarbanes-Oxley Act. The EU followed suit with the new Directive on Statutory Audit which came into force in 2006 and which the EU member states should implement by 2008.

The two reforms have a common feature: they no longer focus on the qualifications of auditors. Instead, a comprehensive framework clarifies how auditors should carry out their activities. In addition, both instruments take account of the international dimension of audit activity. This is a result not only of more and more international audit networks, but primarily of the growing independence of capital markets on both sides of the Atlantic. There are also differences. For instance, it has been argued that the reform in the US has been more rules-based, whereas that in the EU is more principles-based. Another example is the extent to which audits should be carried out on the basis of domestic or international standards on auditing.

Divergences will therefore persist and always require close cooperation between jurisdictional and public oversight bodies. Divergences will remain a challenge inside the EU as the new directive only offers a minimum level of harmonization among 27 member states.

This volume makes a valuable contribution to the compilation and critical discussion of the regulatory developments currently taking place in Europe. It is useful for educators, researchers, and regulators in the field of auditing as it brings together a broad collection of descriptions and commentaries on selected regulatory systems and related issues. The scope as well as the variety of the national approaches toward enhancing trust in the audit function make clear how important it is to know what audit regulations cover in different European countries. I look forward to seeing further research which allows us to follow the – hopefully converging – paths the different countries will be taking in future.

Jürgen Tiedje, European Commission

1 In the name of trust

Some thoughts about trust, audit quality and audit regulation in Europe

Aasmund Eilifsen and Marleen Willekens

1 Introduction

In this book stock is taken of the wave of regulatory changes and initiatives that took place in Europe in the post-Enron era and that relate to the statutory audit function. In many countries auditor independence rules have become tighter, more precisely specified, and the auditing activity has been put under the supervision of public company oversight boards. These and other related regulatory changes exhibit close resemblance to initiatives that have been taken in the US, and are often seen as responses to the public trust crisis of the capital markets which (supposedly) existed in the aftermath of a number of corporate fraud scandals such as Enron and Parmalat.

One often quoted rationale for the expansion of auditing regulations has been to restore public trust in audited financial information such that trust in the capital markets could be regained. Trust in capital markets is a necessary condition to enable those markets to allocate capital efficiently. This rationale, however, is based on (at least) three (implicit) assumptions. First, that trust in the capital markets had been eroded below an acceptable level. Second, that the external audit function had failed or was at least a major reason why this trust had been eroded. And third, that regulation is the answer, implying that increased regulation is able to restore trust.

Given these observations, we aim to focus on a number of issues in this introductory chapter. First, we briefly elaborate on the concept of a "trust crisis," and question whether there is/has been evidence of a trust crisis in Europe in the aftermath of the accounting scandals (section 2). Second, we take stock of the empirical evidence on audit quality from European audit research contributions (section 3). We find that this evidence is fragmented and the results are mixed and highly country specific. This in itself triggers a number of interesting questions for future audit quality research in (and outside) Europe. Third, given that audit regulations have been increased in Europe, we draw from economic theory and welfare economics and elaborate on different types of regulations and their pros and cons and position the audit regulation debate within the broader framework of corporate governance regulation and recent evolutions therein (section 4). Finally, based on the reflections discussed in this chapter, throughout the text we provide some ideas for future research in auditing in (and perhaps outside) Europe. Note that our thoughts are very clearly biased by our own research backgrounds and preferences.

2 A trust crisis – really?

According to Webster's dictionary, *trust* is defined as: "(the) assured reliance on the character, ability, strength, or truth of someone or something." From this definition, it follows that the concept of trust in general is associated with the concepts of *assurance* and *reliability* (reliance). When trust is related to *capital markets*, reliance on the character, ability, strength, and truth of the capital market mechanisms is what is meant. To get that kind of assured reliability, various assuring mechanisms exist or are thinkable, one of which is an external audit of the financial information provided by the corporation. Indeed, an independent audit of financial statements leads to or should lead to reasonable *assurance* about the reliability of the financial statements. The latter are used as a source of information by capital market participants.

A further question is whether trust in capital markets was in a crisis. Webster's definition of crisis is as follows:

1 a the turning point for better or worse in an acute disease or fever
  b a paroxysmal attack of pain, distress, or disordered function
  c an emotionally significant event or radical change of status in a persons' life <a midlife *crisis*>
2   the decisive moment (as in a literary plot)
3 a an unstable or crucial time or state of affairs in which a decisive change is impending; *especially*: one with the distinct possibility of a highly undesirable outcome <a financial *crisis*>
  b a situation that has reached a critical phase <the environmental *crisis*>.

Clearly from these definitions it seems that a crisis is associated with change or, stated alternatively, with discontinuity. Also, a crisis very often has a negative connotation as the possibility of a highly undesirable outcome is suggested. Applied to capital markets, a crisis could refer to discontinuity of certain capital market attributes. And if trust is defined by attributes such as character, ability, strength, and truth, a capital market trust crisis implies a discontinuity (for worse) regarding these attributes. Finally, a trust crisis also suggests that assurance in these attributes has failed.

Given this simple analysis of the concept of trust crisis, it would be interesting to investigate whether indeed the "necessary conditions" for a trust crisis did hold at the time that the new regulations were installed. That is, is there evidence of discontinuity in the character, ability, strength, or truth of *European* capital markets around and after the time of the Enron-Andersen collapse? For only if this is the case, can a trust crisis be used as the rationale for stricter regulations of the assurance mechanisms, including the audit. A huge challenge is to specify how these attributes are to be measured. Questions that could be addressed include: did the relative importance of alternative financing mechanisms, such as bank lending, increase in Europe as a result of the Enron debacle (character)? Were there significant drops in market capitalization in the European capital markets (ability)? What happened to market volumes and stock market performance in the different European markets (strength)? And what about the value relevance of the accounting numbers? Did it change as a result of the Enron debacle (truth)?

3 Empirical audit quality evidence from Europe

In the auditing literature audit quality is often related to the *ability* of the auditor to detect material misstatements in the financial statements (competence) and his/her *willingness* to issue an appropriate audit report based on the audit findings (independence). A standard reference is DeAngelo (1981: 186), who defines audit quality as the "market-assessed joint probability that a given auditor both discover (a) breach in the client's accounting system, and (b) report the breach." Audit quality is in most cases *unobservable* for parties not involved in the audit, including regulators. Details of the audit (production) process, such as audit planning, risk assessments, performed audit procedures, and evaluation of audit evidence, are not publicly disclosed. Normally the audit report is the *only* observable outcome of a statutory audit, and in most cases this is an unmodified (clean) report.

Serious audit quality deficiencies may result in an "audit failure." One may state that an audit failure occurs when the auditor fails to issue a modified report when appropriate. Audit quality and audit failure rates are negatively correlated. Given this specification of audit failure, two distinct circumstances are associated with an audit failure. First, the auditor may have violated professional standards and regulations. Second, the auditor may have complied with professional standards and regulations, but still fail to detect all material misstatements. The latter reflects that an audit never will perfectly reveal the true state of the financial statements. Reducing the risk of not detecting all material misstatements to zero to obtain absolute assurance that the financial statements are free of all material misstatements is rarely attainable or cost beneficial (Eilifsen *et al.* 2006: 635). This is recognized in fundamental audit concepts such as "audit risk" and "reasonable assurance" and is communicated in the audit report.[1]

As indicated above, audit quality is largely unobservable. Evidence from the US suggests that known audit failures with material consequences are relatively infrequent for publicly listed companies (Francis 2004). We are not aware of systematic European evidence on audit failure rates (as indicated by, for example, business failure rates, litigation cases, findings from inspections of auditors, and disciplinary cases against auditors). As audit working papers and "audit production" data in general are not accessible for research purposes, it is difficult to evaluate the quality of audit engagements. Even in the US, where a rich body of audit quality research has emerged since the 1980s, the evidence is rather limited in scope for that reason. Audit quality has typically been investigated through proxy measures. An important development in audit quality research is based on the premise that "differences" in audit quality exist and can be inferred by comparing different groups or classes of auditors and audit firms (Francis 2004: 352). In other words, it is assumed that audit quality is constant for a particular group of auditors. Most audit quality research builds its theoretical arguments on DeAngelo (1981), who posits that audit-firm size affects audit quality and that larger audit firms provide higher audit quality because they have more to lose from acting opportunistically (i.e. failing to report detected breaches). As audit-firm size is a tangible measure, it has served as a surrogate for audit quality in many studies. According to other more recently researched audit quality proxies auditor groupings are specified in different ways, for example by identifying industry specialist audit firms (partners) as higher-quality auditors (Ferguson *et al.* 2003, Francis *et al.* 2005).

Whether the specified auditor groupings indeed relate to higher audit quality has been typically tested by looking at whether audits performed by such auditors are related to (1) higher audit fee premiums (Simunic 1980, Ireland and Lennox 2002), (2) less earnings management in client financial statements (Becker *et al.* 1998, Francis *et al.* 1999), (3) higher likelihood of issuing a going-concern opinion for distressed firms (Ireland 2003), (4) fewer regulatory sanctions against such auditors (Feroz *et al.* 1991), and (5) fewer litigation cases against such auditors (Palmrose 1988). The US evidence that follows this research approach is quite rich (see Francis 2004 for a review of the US evidence). Due to institutional differences between US and European countries, and across European countries, not all designs are equally relevant in a European setting. For example, due to the lack of litigation cases in Europe there are no studies that tested audit-firm size proxies against occurrence of litigation. European studies typically focus on audit pricing, earnings management, and audit reporting. We therefore concentrate on European evidence from selected studies,[2] using one of these three common approaches toward audit quality. Note that not all European countries have been equally subject to audit quality research.

Before we discuss the European audit quality evidence, we would like to emphasize that other specifications of audit quality (than those discussed above) exist or are thinkable. Other dimensions of audit quality, for example, relate to the number of misstatements that are detected (see Eilifsen and Messier 2000), or the number of restatements of financial statements demanded by the auditor (see Kinney *et al.* 2004).

3.1 Quality differentiation inferred from audit fee studies

Following the seminal audit fee study by Simunic (1980), numerous audit fee studies have been executed worldwide (see Hay *et al.* 2006 for an overview). The vast majority of studies are performed on samples of publicly held client firms and report higher audit fees for Big N audit firms. The latter result may reflect higher audit quality, but, given the high level of supplier concentration in the audit market, it may also be an indication of oligopolistic rents earned by the Big N audit firms. The European evidence indicates that audit fee differentiation between Big N and non-Big N audit firms, and even within the group of Big N firms, is country specific. Further, European evidence on the effect of auditor specialization on audit fees is not conclusive.

Although the private client segment of the audit market is quite significant in Europe, most European studies investigate audit pricing based on samples of publicly held clients. The evidence for the latter segment deviates from the US findings, and is not unilaterally consistent with significantly higher fees charged by Big N audit firms. There is evidence of Big N premia in the UK (see, for example, Taffler and Ramalinggam 1982, Chan *et al.* 1993, Pong and Whittington 1994, Ireland and Lennox 2002,[3] Pong 2004), Ireland (Simon and Taylor 2002), and Italy (Cameran 2005); but *not* in Denmark (Thinggaard and Kiertzer 2005, unpublished), the Netherlands (Langendijk 1997), and Norway (Firth 1997). Further, the observed Big N premium was attributed to PwC[4] in Ireland and KPMG in Italy. In addition, Langendijk (1997) does find a premium attributed to KPMG in the Netherlands; Thinggaard and Kiertzer (2005) a PwC fee premium for small companies and a PwC fee discount for large companies in Denmark; and Firth (1997) reported weak evidence of a fee premium for Arthur Andersen in Norway.

Audit fee premiums, and thus potentially audit quality, may also be related to audit firms' and auditors' *industry expertise.* Langendijk's (1997) findings suggest that industry specialist audit firms in the financial services industry in the Netherlands do not earn a higher fee than non-specialists. In contrast, Basioudis and Francis (2006, unpublished) find that city-specific industry leaders in the UK earn a premium relative to other Big Four auditors, while no premium for national industry leadership is present in their data.

Another relevant question in a European context is whether price differentiation is observed in the *private client market segment*?[5] Willekens and Achmadi (2003) investigate the private client segment of the Belgian audit market. They report that audit pricing is significantly positively associated with the incumbent auditor's market share. They also report a drop in the Big N audit fee premium between 1989 and 1997. A study of the Finnish audit market by Niemi (2004) also reports a positive relationship between audit pricing and auditor size for small audit firms.

Based on a rich dataset of all audit engagements in Belgium, Willekens and Gaeremynck (2005) provide further evidence on audit fee premia for Big N firms in the private client segment of the Belgian audit market. They also report that other audit-firm and partner characteristics are significantly associated with the level of the audit fee. For example, the number of years of partner experience is negatively associated with the level of the audit fee, and the number of employees at the audit firm is positively associated with the audit fee.

On the contrary, Chaney *et al.* (2004) provide evidence that private companies in the UK do not pay a Big Five audit fee premium, after controlling for the existence of a self-selection bias in the clients' choice of auditors.

3.2 Quality differentiation inferred from earnings management studies

The abnormal accounting accrual paradigm (Jones 1991) has been popular in accounting research investigating earnings management.[6] Schipper (1989: 92) defines earnings management as "a purposeful intervention in the external financial reporting process, with the intent of obtaining some private gain (as opposed to, say, merely facilitating the neutral operation of the process)." When abnormal accounting accruals represent earnings management, lower abnormal accounting accruals may indicate higher audit quality, i.e. the auditors detect earnings management attempts and require the client to make appropriate adjustments. Therefore, it is predicted that earnings management in firms audited by higher-quality auditors is smaller. For example, it is commonly hypothesized that Big N auditors tolerate less earnings management than non-Big N auditors.

Vander Bauwhede *et al.* (2003) investigated whether Big Six audit firms constrain earnings management more than non-Big Six firms for a (matched) sample of publicly held and privately held Belgian firms of similar size. They find that Belgian companies manage earnings opportunistically to meet the benchmark target of prior-year earnings. In the private client market Big Six auditors constrain income-decreasing earnings management more than non-Big Six auditors. No difference by audit-firm type is found in constraining income-increasing earnings management, even in the public client market. Vander Bauwhede *et al.*'s results differ from US findings indicating a general Big N constraining effect on earnings management for samples of public companies. Vander Bauwhede *et al.* attribute their results to the Belgian institutional environment. In a follow-up study of the entire private client segment of the Belgian audit market, Vander Bauwhede and Willekens (2004) used alternative continuous measures of audit firm size in addition to the dichotomous Big Six/non-Big Six variable. They report that the smaller and larger auditors do not differ systematically in constraining discretionary accruals management in privately held companies, suggesting that audit quality differentiation is not present in the private client segment of the market.

In a study on a sample of listed and non-listed Spanish firms Rodrígues and Torres (2005) find that Big Six audited firms have lower income smoothing (suggesting higher audit quality) than firms audited by non-Big Six firms. They report no clear difference between income smoothing practices in listed and non-listed firms, indicating that the constraining effect of using Big Six auditors extends to the private client market. Van Tendeloo and Vanstraelen (2005) analyze data from six European countries (Belgium, Finland, France, the Netherlands,

Spain, and the UK), and report evidence supporting audit quality differentiation in the private client market, with Big Six audit firms constraining earnings management more than non-Big Six audit firms.

3.3 Quality differentiation inferred from audit reporting studies

Although mixed, a majority of the European evidence indicates that large audit firms report more accurately on going-concern problems, suggesting that large audit firms provide superior audit quality. In a UK study, Ireland (2003) observes that large auditors are more conservative (i.e. more likely to detect problems) in going-concern reporting. Lennox (1999b) also shows that large audit firms give more accurate signals of financial distress in their audit reports. Keasey *et al.* (1988) observe, without directly testing reporting accuracy, that in the small company sector UK companies that were audited by large audit practices were more likely to receive a qualified audit report.

Vanstraelen (2002) examines the relationship between auditor economic incentives and the propensity to issue going-concern reports in Belgium. No evidence was found that the auditor's going-concern report decision is significantly influenced by auditor type. Likewise, Gaeremynck and Willekens (2003) find no differences between Big Six and non-Big Six audit firms in going-concern reporting when a client's financial difficulties are obvious (i.e. the company is about to go bankrupt). For less apparent financial difficulties (i.e. voluntary liquidation), however, Big Six audit firms are more likely to issue going-concern reports than non-Big Six audit firms.

Ruiz-Barbadillo *et al.* (2004) demonstrate for a sample of public Spanish companies that the likelihood of a going-concern report is positively associated with audit-firm size. Additionally, they report that the auditor's competence as measured by auditor tenure and specialization does not affect the propensity to issue a going-concern report. In Finland, Sundgren (1998) finds that there are no differences in the propensity to issue a going-concern report between auditors with the higher and lower professional qualification.

For a sample of listed UK companies Lennox (1999a) shows that a bankruptcy model could be more accurate than auditors' going-concern reports in predicting bankruptcy. Further, he does not find that audit reports signal useful incremental information about the probability of bankruptcy. Lensberg *et al.* (2006) find that, in a bankruptcy classification model (a genetic programming model) applied to a sample of both public and private Norwegian companies, the most significant variable was the content of the prior auditor report. Their results also suggest that accounting information, including the auditor's evaluation of it, is more important in bankruptcy prediction for larger than smaller companies. For a sample of private Belgian firms, Gaeremynck and Willekens (2003) report that a modified going-concern report is typically issued when a client faces financial difficulties.

3.4 Some lessons from the European evidence

To summarize, the evidence on audit quality differentiation in Europe is mixed and highly country specific. A number of studies in Europe report audit firm fee premia for Big N audit firms, but the evidence is mixed across countries. Likewise, the European studies performed on earnings management report mixed results. And even though most European audit reporting evidence indicates that large audit firms report more accurately on going-concern problems, suggesting that large audit firms provide superior audit quality, some studies report no differences. Note that, overall, the European evidence is not exhaustive in the sense that many countries or segments have not yet been subject to much research. Europe does not constitute a homogenous audit market, and significant differences in audit quality may exist between market segments, even within countries. The existing national auditing regulations presumably affect audit quality. Auditors' legal liability and exposure to litigation are considered to be a prime driver of audit quality. We are currently far from having a unified legal liability and enforcement regime for auditors in Europe. Competence differences among auditors are likely to exist throughout Europe and may translate into differences in audit quality. Thus, it is highly questionable whether it is meaningful at all to talk about a consistent (or common) audit quality level at a pan-European level.

Finding such mixed evidence on quality differentiation in Europe triggers many interesting questions and a very challenging future research agenda. The obvious question is "why"? Why is the evidence so different in Europe as compared to the US or Australia? For example, across Europe we found mixed evidence on whether or not Big N firms charge fee premia. But what does that mean? Does it mean that there is no quality differentiation in those countries? And is this a problem at all? Audit fee studies only provide indirect evidence on audit quality differentiation, and hence various explanations are possible. Another argument is that the absence of large audit firm fee premia does not refute the hypothesis that large audit firms provide superior audit quality, as large audit firms may enjoy economies of scale which could be passed on as lower audit fees. Still another argument is that the absence of fee premia in some European countries constitutes evidence of the absence of monopoly rents charged by Big N firms in Europe because the audit markets are less concentrated there.

Furthermore, in some countries (Belgium, for example) there is strong evidence of fee premia charged by Big N audit firms, whilst the evidence on earnings management tolerance and audit reporting provides no support for the quality differentiation hypothesis. Such evidence could be an indication that other audit quality attributes are priced in Europe (or some market segments there). An interesting avenue for future European auditing research would be to specify audit quality attributes that are relevant in the European auditing and financial reporting setting. Privately held firms are very significant players in the European economy, and the role of accounting (and hence auditing) is not the same as in the US and differs across European countries. Other governance mechanisms and corporate financing models are prevalent. A logical question is whether it is valid to use (largely unmodified) North American research models to investigate European data. What can we learn from using the American models whilst investigating European data? Is audit quality differentiation (only) a function of audit-firm size at all in Europe? Shouldn't, perhaps or at least, a distinction be made between the public client segment and the private client segment of the audit market? What is the impact of mandatory audit requirements for privately held firms on competition in the audit market? Do audit firms compete differently in the private client segment of the market? Is demand for audit quality different in the private versus the public client segment? These are just a few of the many interesting questions that follow from the mixed evidence that we found in Europe.

4 Auditing regulation

Audit failures are typically associated with two conditions: first, when the auditor does not deliver the implicit audit quality set by the regulations, and second when audit quality achieved from following the regulations fails to reveal all material misstatements in the financial statements. Although both situations relate to an audit quality deficiency, the former is a failure caused by the auditor's misconduct, whereas the latter is a result of a regulatory decision on the tolerable level of "accidental" audit failures. From a regulatory point of view it is important to draw a distinction between these two causes of audit failures since different regulatory measures should be used to deal with each of the two situations.

If the implicit minimum audit quality level set by audit regulation causes an unacceptable level of audit failures, there is a case for more restrictive regulation of the performance of the audit. Society and the profession have found it desirable to intervene in the audit market to secure some minimum level of quality for all audits. Occasionally, a revision of the minimum level of audit quality is considered warranted. For example, the International Auditing and Assurance Board's (IAASB) project to develop more comprehensive international standards on auditing and the EU's decision to endorse these standards for statutory audits within its member states are motivated by the desire to enhance and establish a common minimum level of audit quality.

Audit firms (and auditors) may deliver audit quality above the regulatory minimum, for example to protect their reputation or attract clients. However, firms may also be tempted to deliver the minimum regulatory audit quality level or even audit quality below this minimum, for example because of intense competition for clients combined with a low litigation risk. If an audit firm violates auditing standards or other regulations of audit performance, it is the behaviour of the firm and not necessarily insufficient auditing standards that is the problem. Stricter monitoring and enforcement of the rules, through for example tougher disciplinary actions and increased legal liability exposure, may be appropriate regulatory measures in this situation.

4.1 Arguments for auditing regulation

According to the economic theory of regulation, there is a prima facie case for regulatory intervention when there is market failure that is accompanied by private law failure (Ogus 1994).[7] Market failures are usually caused by lack of adequate information, lack of competition, or externalities, and exist when the quantity or quality of a good supplied differs from the (socially) efficient outcome. In such cases, government regulation that moves the private output of a good closer to the socially efficient solution can improve social welfare (efficiency) in a Pareto sense. Applied to the market for audited financial information, market failure exists if the output of audited information in annual reports (or distributed via other corporate communication channels) is non-optimal in a Pareto sense in the absence of audit regulation.

An early rationale for audit regulation was to protect the users of financial information (i.e. the investors), as they were presumed not to have perfect access to company information (see, for example, Watts and Zimmerman 1986). Disclosure choices of accounting information might create negative external effects or externalities[8] to users of this information. In general, an externality exists where an action of one economic agent affects the utility of another in a way that is not reflected in the marketplace (Just *et al.* 1982: 269). Losses to financial statement users due to resource allocation decisions based on defects in *audited* financial statements which the auditor did not detect or report could be seen as an "externality." Directors and the external auditors can thus be considered as *jointly* responsible for hazardous financial reporting. The externality is aggravated by informational asymmetry. Directors and external auditors have more information about the value of the firm than external parties. In addition, the delivered audit quality by auditors cannot be observed by clients and third party users of financial statements. The social objective of audit regulations and liability could be seen as to correct for externality-generating financial reporting behavior (by directors) *and* audit behavior (by external auditors) in such a way that total social utility is improved. Policies adopted to correct for hazardous financial reporting behavior – that is the behavior of the directors – will necessarily have an impact on audit demand (since the directors are the ones who acquire audit services). Policies adopted to correct for externality-generating audit behavior will necessarily affect audit production – or the behavior of the auditor.

4.2 Different types of regulation in the audit context

Ex ante regulation and *ex post* liability are two very different approaches to control for activities (such as the production of audit services) that create risks of harm to third parties or externalities. From its beginnings the literature on optimal regulation has focused on alternative types of *ex ante* policies, such as safety standards, Pigouvian taxes, and transferable permits. *Ex ante* policy instruments modify behavior in an immediate way through requirements that are imposed *before*, or at least independently of, the actual occurrence of harm, and that are *public* in nature (Shavell 1984a). *Ex ante* rules can be pronounced directly by the state through civil servants, or the state can delegate its authority to another body. In the context of audit regulation, an e*x ante* policy which applies to the auditee is the statutory audit requirement. For the auditor, professional auditing standards (GAAS) could be seen as an e*x ante* policy. Auditing standards (as opposed to disclosure standards) are, however, very general in the sense of stressing objectives rather than the means of reaching those objectives. Also, their power as a legal defense of "due care" in litigation is uncertain as they are advisory and do not have the same authoritative and enforcing character as standards set by statute. Therefore they may be considered as a "weak" form of *ex ante* policy. The recently launched audit regulations include a number of additional *ex ante* rules set by statute. The various auditor independence rules are examples of *ex ante* rules. By setting more precise *ex ante* standards, auditing standards become less vague and less at risk of being mis-specified.

The second policy instrument, namely liability in tort, works through the deterrent effect of damage actions that may be brought *after* harm has occurred, and hence is *private* in nature (Shavell 1984a). The threat of a lawsuit causes the potential injurer to internalize the expected social harm and hence to take optimal precautions. In the audit case this would imply that audit liability is an incentive for the auditor to produce an optimal level of audit quality. It is only since the 1980s that researchers have also analyzed the ability of exposure to *ex post* liability to correct for externalities.[9] The basic premise of law and economics is that legal rules create implicit prices on behavior and that responses of individuals and organizations to those prices can be analyzed in exactly the same way that responses to explicit prices can be analyzed (Ulen 1993). The threat of litigation to audit firms can thus be expected to affect audit production behavior, and the potential liability on the part of corporate management (that is, the directors) to third parties might affect the demand for auditing services and other monitoring mechanisms. It is, however, important to realize that alternative liability regimes[10] may affect the behavior of auditors and auditees differently and may result in alternative resource allocations, some of which might not be socially efficient. A similar remark holds for alternative legal environments, such as common-law systems versus civil-law systems. An obvious question is which enforcement mechanisms work as a deterrent against unwanted auditor behavior in environments where *ex post* liability is less prevalent, as is the case in various European countries.

Willekens *et al.* (1996) analyze the joint use of *ex ante* standards and *ex post* liability in the auditing setting. They also study the impact of uncertainty (or vagueness) about auditor due care (negligence) on audit quality, and the role of (*ex ante*) professional auditing standards (GAAS) in such a setting. They show that the vagueness of legal negligence standards can have either a positive or a negative effect on audit quality, and that this depends on the level of vagueness (or precision). Relatively small (large) vagueness will have a positive (negative) impact on audit quality as compared to the situation where negligence standards are clear. It is shown that *clear* GAAS accompanying a *vague* legal negligence standard have a positive impact on audit quality or effort. As the precision of audit regulations and the importance of *ex post* liability are not constant across countries, the impact of audit regulation and *ex post* liability on audit behavior can be expected to vary greatly across the globe. Why then are the new auditor independence rules so similar in most countries?

4.3 Auditing and governance: not isolated phenomena

The trust crisis led not only to more audit regulations but also to more governance regulations in general. Throughout this book we consider external auditing as one important element in a corporation's governance and reporting system. In other words, the external audit function is in constant interaction with other governance mechanisms. An important question is how the joint impact of all the new governance and auditing rules affects audit and financial reporting quality, and whether the increased regulations are indeed socially efficient. Various stakeholders can demand different control and auditing mechanisms to keep their risks under control. In an analytical paper, Knechel *et al.* (2007) show that in situations where multiple stakeholders with conflicting incentives have shared decision rights over one or more control mechanisms, there is a net overinvestment in control relative to a Pareto efficient solution. Their result highlights the need to evaluate demand effects when considering the production and pricing of control mechanisms. They also show that the regulation of control can exacerbate this overinvestment in controls. Further research is needed to investigate the welfare impact of the new auditing and control regulations in specific (European as well as non-European) environments.

Not only auditing but also corporate (governance) structures in general around the world differ. For example, the degree of separation between ownership and control is quite different in France as compared to the United States. And so is the degree of labor influence very different in both countries. In recent years a strong theory has emerged that the quality of technical corporate law in protecting distant shareholders determines whether securities markets will arise, whether ownership will separate from control, and whether the modern corporation will prosper. La Porta *et al.* (1997) present evidence that seems to suggest that countries with poor investor protection, measured by the character of legal rules and law enforcement, have smaller and narrower capital markets. This theory, however, does not explain why many continental European corporations have been just as successful as their American competitors.[11] Nor does it explain why major corporate governance failures have also happened in the US.

It looks as though not only legal and economic factors affect corporate structures around the world, but also political factors. Roe (2003) argues that corporate structures differ very significantly between conservative (more right wing) democracies and social (more left wing) democracies. He emphasizes the correlation between economic and political elements in this context, and identifies two packages of industrial organization, democratic macro-politics, and corporate ownership structure: one that has weakly competitive markets, fitting social democratic politics, and concentrated ownership; and another that is characterized by fierce competitive markets, conservative politics, and diffuse ownership. Note that many (continental) European countries fit the first package, but not all. Furthermore, there are many differences among European countries. Future research that investigates the quality of auditing and monitoring using variables that fit the European models is warranted.

5 Ideas for future (European) studies

The regulation of auditors and auditing, as well as many corporate governance arrangements (e.g. the establishing of an audit committee), are typically driven by concerns about audit quality. Regulatory reforms of the auditing sector are often initiated as a result of corporate scandals such as those involving Enron, WorldCom, Ahold, and Parmalat. In such situations, political expediency rather than insight into the status of audit quality and the effectiveness of regulatory measures to promote audit quality may dominate the regulatory process (DeFond and Francis 2005).

In this introductory chapter we focused on a number of questions that we believe require further investigation in future (European) research studies. First, we very briefly analyzed the concept of a "trust crisis" and questioned whether such a crisis was really present in Europe and warranted the wave of regulation it triggered. Future research could investigate whether, indeed, the character, ability, strength, and truth of the European capital markets was in crisis.

Second, we provided an overview of the mixed evidence on quality differentiation in Europe. From this limited survey it is revealed that the institutional environment matters. We therefore strongly believe that the design of future audit quality studies should take this into consideration. Privately held firms are very significant players in the European economy, and the role of accounting (and hence auditing) is not the same as in the US. Is audit quality differentiation (really and only) a function of audit-firm size in Europe (and even beyond Europe)? What are the drivers of audit quality and what is the role of audit demand and supply variables in this setting? Instead of assuming audit quality to be constant per audit firm, an alternative approach could be to assume that audit quality is the outcome of a constrained optimization problem that audit firms solve per engagement. Shouldn't, perhaps or at least, a distinction be made between the public client segment and the private client segment of the audit market? What is the impact of mandatory audit requirements for privately held firms on competition in the audit market? Do audit firms compete differently in the private client segment in the market? Is the demand for audit quality different in the private versus the public client segment? These are just a few of the many interesting questions that follow from the mixed audit quality evidence that we found in Europe.

Third, we provided a very brief and general (incomplete) discussion of some regulatory aspects of the auditing scene. We believe that, worldwide, more analytical research is necessary to investigate the effects of the new regulations in specific environments. In this book each chapter provides detailed information on the new regulations for a selected European country (as well as the US). As such, the book can provide a basis for more precisely designed analytical papers.

Notes

1 Audit risk is the risk that the auditor expresses an inappropriate audit opinion when the financial statements are materially misstated. Reasonable assurance means that the engagement assurance risk is reduced to an acceptably low level in the circumstances of the engagement.

2 It is beyond the ambition of this text to give a comprehensive presentation of European research that relates to audit quality. For example, we do not discuss the research that has investigated audit quality related to audit committees (see Turley and Zaman 2004, and Köhler 2005) and audit quality related to auditor and audit firm rotation (see Cameran *et al.* 2006). Furthermore, we also do not discuss European audit quality perception studies (see, for example, Warming-Rasmussen and Jensen 1998, Quick and Warming-Rasmussen 2005 and 2006).

3 As argued by Ireland and Lennox (2002) and Copley *et al.* (1995), the actual auditor choice is likely to be endogenous, and it is probable that clients self-select their incumbent auditors based upon firm characteristics, private information, or other unobservable characteristics. For example, Big N auditors may invest more in technology, training, and facilities and as a result carry out audits more efficiently for large, relatively complex clients. The costs of these investments result in a relatively high fixed component of audit fees, which may be unattractive for small and less complex clients. Ireland and Lennox (2002) find that, after controlling for self-select bias in public company audits in the UK, the Big Five audit fee premium increased twice.

4 In their sample either the former Price Waterhouse or Coopers & Lybrand.

5 In the private client market monitoring needs due to agency costs (including because of more closely held firms), and possibly the risk of litigation, are expected to be lower than for publicly listed companies. On the other hand, accounting information may actually play a relatively more important role in the evaluation of managerial performance of private firms for the very reason that these firms lack market measures of firm value (Chaney *et al.* 2004).

6 Estimated discretionary accruals are typically used to measure abnormal accruals. Inferences drawn from the tests of earnings management critically depend on the researcher's ability to accurately estimate discretionary accruals (see Dechow *et al.* 1995, and Kothari *et al.* 2005).

7 Note that it is only a prima facie, and not a conclusive, case for such intervention. The reason is that the regulatory solution may be no more successful in correcting the inefficiencies than the market or private law, or that any efficiency gains to which it does give rise may be outweighed by increased transaction costs or misallocations created in other sectors of the economy.

8 Although "market failure" and "externality" are related concepts, and sometimes used interchangeably, they are not synonyms. Market failure can be caused by externalities,

but can also be caused by other factors, such as monopoly situations, public goods, and informational asymmetry (see, for example, Cooter and Ulen 1993, unpublished).

9 Cooter (1991), for example, points that the elaboration of price theory by mathematical economists in the twentieth century took the legal framework for granted. Liability law is, however, an important mechanism for allocating resources. Nowadays, economic theories tend to understand liability law as a search for efficiency in incentives and risk-bearing.

10 Such as strict liability versus a negligence standard, or joint and several liability versus proportionate liability.

11 Other determinants that cannot fully explain corporate differences around the world include a nation's size and development level.

References

Basioudis, I.G. and Francis, J.R. (2006) "Big Four Audit Fee Premiums for National and Office-Level Industry Leadership in the United Kingdom," Paper presented at the Audit Quality Workshop, Milan, 24–5 November 2006.

Becker, C.L., Defond, M., Jiambalvo, J., and Subramanyam, K.R. (1998) "The Big Effect of Audit Quality on Earnings Management," *Contemporary Accounting Research*, 15: 1–24.

Cameran, M. (2005) "Audit Fees and the Large Auditor Premium in the Italian Market," *International Journal of Auditing*, 9(2): 129–46.

Cameran, M., Di Vincenzo, D., and Merlotti, E. (2006) "The Audit Firm Rotation Rule: A Review of the Literature," Paper presented at the Audit Quality Workshop, Milan, 24–5 November 2006.

Chan, P., Ezzalmel, M., and Gwilliam, D. (1993) "Determinants of Audit Fees for Quoted UK Companies," *Journal of Business Finance and Accounting*, 20(6): 765–86.

Chaney, P.K., Jeter, D.C., and Shivakumar, L. (2004) "Self-Selection of Auditors and Audit Pricing in Private Firms," *The Accounting Review*, 79(1): 51–72.

Committee on Basic Auditing Concepts (1973) *A Statement of Basic Auditing Concepts*, Sarasota, FL: American Accounting Association.

Cooter, R.D. (1991) "Economic Theories of Legal Liability," *Journal of Economic Perspectives*, 5(3, summer): 11–30.

Cooter, R.D., and Ulen, T.S. (1993) *Law and Economics*, Glenview, IL: Scott, Foresman and Co.

Copley, P., Gaver, J., and Gaver, K. (1995) "Simultaneous Estimation of the Supply and Demand of Differentiated Audits: Evidence from Municipal Audit Market," *Journal of Accounting Research*, 33 (spring): 137–55.

DeAngelo, L. (1981) "Auditor Size and Audit Quality," *Journal of Accounting and Economics*, (December): 183–99.

Dechow, P.M., Sloan, R.G., and Sweeny, A.P. (1995) "Detecting Earnings Management," *The Accounting Review*, 70(2): 195–221.

DeFond, M.L. and Francis, J.R. (2005) "Audit Research after Sarbanes-Oxley," *Auditing: A Journal of Practice and Theory*, 24 (Supplement): 5–30.

Eilifsen, Aa. and Messier Jr., W.F. (2000) "The Incidence and Detection of Misstatements: A Review and Integration of Archival Research," *Journal of Accounting Literature*, 19: 1–43.

Eilifsen, Aa., Messier Jr., W.F., Glover, S.M., and Prawitt, D.F. (2006) *Auditing and Assurance Services International Edition*, London: McGraw-Hill.

Ferguson, A., Francis, J.R., and Stokes, D. (2003) "The Effects of Firm-Wide and Office-Level Industry Expertise on Audit Pricing," *The Accounting Review*, 78(2): 429–48.

Feroz, E.H., Park, K., and Pastena, V. (1991) "The Financial and Market Effects of the SEC Accounting and Auditing Enforcement Releases," *Journal of Accounting Research*, (Supplement) 107–42.

Firth, M. (1997) "The Provision of Non-Audit Services and the Pricing of Audit Services," *Journal of Business and Finance and Accounting*, 23(3, 4): 511–24.

Francis, J.R. (2004) "What Do We Know about Audit Quality?" *The British Accounting Review*, 36(4): 345–68.

Francis, J.R., Maydew, E.L. and Sparks, H.C. (1999) "The Role of Big 6 Auditors in the Credible Reporting of Accruals," *Auditing: A Journal of Practice and Theory*, 18: 17–34.

Francis, J.R., Reichelt, K., and Wang, D. (2005) "The Pricing of National and City-Specific Reputations for Industry Expertise in the US Audit Market," *The Accounting Review*, 80(1): 113–36.

Francis, J.R. and Wilson, E. (1988) "Auditor Changes: A Joint Test of Theories Relating to Agency Costs and Auditor Differentiation," *The Accounting Review*, LXII (October): 663–82.

Gaeremynck, A. and Willekens, M. (2003) "The Endogenous Relationship between Audit-Report Type and Business Termination: Evidence on Private Firms in a Non-Litigious Environment," *Accounting and Business Research*, 33(1): 65–79.

Hay, D.C, Knechel, W.R., and Wong, N. (2006) "Audit Fees: A Meat-Analysis of the Effect of Supply and Demand Attributes," *Contemporary Accounting Research*, 23(1, spring): 141–91.

Ireland, J. (2003) "An Empirical Investigation of Determinants of Audit Reports in the UK," *Journal of Business Finance and Accounting*, 30(7, 8): 975–1016.

Ireland, J. and Lennox, C. (2002) "The Large Audit Firm Fee Premium: A Case of Selectivity Bias?," *Journal of Accounting, Auditing and Finance*, 17(1): 73–91.

Jones, J. (1991) "Earnings Management during Import Relief Investigations," *Journal of Accounting Research*, 29(2): 193–228.

Just, R.E., Hueth, D.L., and Schmitz, A. (1982) *Applied Welfare Economics and Public Policy*, Englewood Cliffs, NJ: Prentice Hall.

Keasey, K., Watson, R., and Wynarczyk, P. (1988) "The Small Company Audit Qualification: A Preliminary Investigation," *Accounting and Business Research*, 18(72): 323–33.

Kinney, W., Palmrose, Z.-V., and Scholz, S. (2004) "Auditor Independence, Non-Audit Services, and Restatements: Was the US Government Right?" *Journal of Accounting Research* 42(3): 561–88.

Knechel, W.R., Suijs, J., and Willekens, M. (2007) "A Stakeholder Model of Competing Demands for Control and Auditing," unpublished working paper.

Knechel, W.R. and Willekens, M. (2006) "The Role of Risk Management and Governance in Determining Audit Demand," *Journal of Business Finance and Accounting*, 33(9–10): 1344–67.

Köhler, A.G. (2005) "Audit Committees in Germany – Theoretical Reasoning and Empirical Evidence," *Schmalenbach Business Review*, 57 (July): 229–52.

Kolstadt, C.D., Ulen, T.S., and Johnson, G.V. (1990) "*Ex Post* Liability for Harm vs. Ex Ante Safety Regulation: Substitutes or Complements?" *American Economic Review*, 80(4, September): 888–901.

Kothari, S.P., Leone, A.J., and Wasley, C.E. (2005) "Performance Matched Discretionary Accrual Measures," *Journal of Accounting and Economics*, 39(1): 163–97.

Langendijk, H. (1997) "The Market for Audit Services in the Netherlands," *European Accounting Review*, 6(2): 253–64.

La Porta, R., Lopez-de-Silanes, F., Shleifer, A., and Vishny, R.W. (1997) "Legal Determinants of External Finance," *Journal of Finance*, LII(3): 1131–50.

Lennox, C. (1999a) "The Accuracy and the Incremental Information Content of Audit Reports in Predicting Bankruptcy," *Journal of Business Finance and Accounting*, 26(5, 6): 757–78.

Lennox, C. (1999b) "Are Large Auditors More Accurate Than Small Auditors?" *Accounting and Business Research*, 29(3): 217–27.

Lensberg, T., Eilifsen, Aa., and McKee, T.E. (2006) "Bankruptcy Theory Development and Classification via Genetic Programming," *European Journal of Operational Research*, 169(2): 677–97.

Niemi, L. (2004) "Auditor Size and Audit Pricing: Evidence from Small Audit Firms," *European Accounting Review*, 13(3): 541–60.

Ogus, A.I. (1994) *Regulation: Legal Form and Economic Theory*, Oxford: Clarendon Press.

Palmrose, Z.-V. (1988) "An Analysis of Auditor Litigation and Audit Service Quality," *The Accounting Review*, 73(1): 55–73.

Pong, C.K.M. (2004) "A Descriptive Analysis of Audit Price Changes in the UK 1991–95," *European Accounting Review*, 13(1): 161–78.

Pong, C.K.M. and Whittington, G. (1994) "The Determinants of Audit Fees: Some Empirical Models," *Journal of Business Finance and Accounting*, 21(8): 1071–95.

Posner, R.A. (1986) *Economic Analysis of Law*, Boston, MA: Little, Brown.

Quick, R. and Warming-Rasmussen, B. (2005) "The Impact of MAS on Perceived Auditor Independence – Some Evidence from Denmark," *Accounting Forum*, 29(1): 137–68.

Quick, R. and Warming-Rasmussen, B. (2006) "Auditor Independence and the Provision of Non-Audit Services – Perceptions by German Investors," Paper presented at the Audit Quality Workshop, Milan, 24–25 November 2006.

Rodrígues, M.C. and Torres, P.A. (2005) "Audit Quality Differentiation in the Absence of Incentives for Providing High Quality Audits," Paper presented at the Symposium of the European Auditing Research Network, Amsterdam, 28–29 October, 2005.

Roe, M.J. (2003) *Political Determinants of Corporate Governance*, Oxford: Oxford University Press.

Ruiz-Barbadillo, E., Gómez-Aguilar, N., De Fuentes-Barberá, C. and García-Benau, M.A. (2004) "Audit Quality and the Going-Concern Decision-Making Process: Spanish Evidence," *European Accounting Review*, 13(4): 597–620.

Schipper, K. (1989) "Commentary on Earnings Management," *Accounting Horizons*, (December): 91–102.

Shavell, S. (1984a) "Liability for Harm versus Regulation of Safety," *Journal of Legal Studies*, 13 (June): 357–74.

Shavell, S. (1984b) "A Model of the Optimal Use of Liability and Safety Regulation," *Rand Journal of Economics*, 15 (summer): 271–80.

Shavell, S. (1987) *Economic Analysis of Accident Law*, Cambridge, MA: Harvard University Press.

Simon, D.T. and Taylor, M.H. (2002) "A Survey of Audit Pricing in Ireland," *International Journal of Auditing*, 6: 3–12.

Simunic, D.A. (1980) "The Pricing of Audit Services: Theory and Evidence," *Journal of Accounting Research*, 18(1): 161–90.

Sundgren, S. (1998) "Auditor Choices and Auditor Reporting Practices: Evidence from Finnish Small Firms," *European Accounting Review*, 7(3): 441–65.

Taffler, R. and Ramalinggam, K. (1982) "The Determinants of the Audit Fee in the UK: An Explanatory Study," unpublished manuscript, City University Business School, London.

Thinggaard, F. and Kiertzer, L. (2005) "The Effect of Two Auditors and Non-Audit Services on Audit Fees: Evidence from a Small Capital Market," working paper, Aalborg University, Denmark.

Turley, S. and Zaman, M. (2004) "Corporate Governance Effects of Audit Committees: An Evaluation of the International Evidence," *Journal of Management and Governance*, 8(3): 305–32.

Ulen, T.S. (1993) "Cognitive Imperfections and the Efficiency of Legal Rules," working paper, University of Illinois at Urbana-Champaign.

Van Tendeloo, B.A. and Vanstraelen, A. (2005) "Earnings Management and Audit Quality in Europe: Evidence from Private Client Segment Market," Paper presented at the Symposium of the European Auditing Research Network, Amsterdam, 28–29 October 2005.

Vander Bauwhede, H. and Willekens, M. (2004) "Evidence on (the Lack of) Audit-Quality Differentiation in the Private Client Segment of the Belgium Market," *European Accounting Review*, 13(3): 501–22.

Vander Bauwhede, H., Willekens, M., and Gaeremynck, A. (2003) "Audit Firm Size, Public Ownership, and Firms' Discretionary Accruals Management," *The International Journal of Accounting*, 38(1): 1–22.

Vanstraelen, A. (2002) "Auditor Economic Incentives and Going-Concern Opinions in a Limited Litigious Continental European Business Environment: Empirical Evidence from Belgium," *Accounting and Business Research*, 32(3): 171–86.

Warming-Rasmussen, B. and Jensen, L. (1998) "Quality Dimensions in External Audit Services – An External User Perspective," *European Accounting Review*, 7(1): 65–82.

Watts, R.L. and Zimmerman, J.L. (1986) *Positive Accounting Theory*, Englewood Cliffs, NJ: Prentice Hall.

Willekens, M. (1995) "Economic Aspects of Audit Standards and Auditor Liability," PhD dissertation, University of Warwick.

Willekens, M. and Achmadi, C. (2003) "Pricing and Supplier Concentration in the Private Client Segment of the Audit Market: Market Power or Competition?" *International Journal of Accounting*, 38(4): 431–55.

Willekens M. and Gaeremynck, A. (2005) *Prijszetting in de Belgische auditmarkt,* IBR – Die Keure.

Willekens, M., Steele, A., and Miltz, D. (1996) "Audit Standards and Auditor Liability: A Theoretical Model," *Accounting and Business Research*, 26(3, summer): 249–64.

2 Audit regulation in Belgium

Overregulation in a limited capital market oriented country?

Ann Vanstraelen and Marleen Willekens

1 Introduction

Unlike most other industrialized countries such as the Netherlands, the UK, and the US, the Belgian auditing profession is fairly young. It only developed during the second half of the twentieth century after the creation – by law in 1953 – of the Institute of Registered Auditors (Instituut der Bedrijfsrevisoren, IBR/Institut des Réviseurs d'Entreprises, IRE). Since then, however, audit-related regulatory initiatives have accelerated and audit activity in Belgium has become extremely regulated.

In Belgium, as elsewhere in Europe, legal provisions covering the supervision and independence of the statutory auditor had been in existence for many years before the wave of financial scandals that characterized the start of the new millennium. Contrary to the US, Belgium did not have a purely self-regulatory system for registered auditors and many non-audit services were already prohibited due to independence reasons. The Belgian system is and has always been a multi-tier system including external parties, such as the High Council for Economic Professions and the existing disciplinary bodies (which include magistrates alongside auditors). However, most regulatory principles have been established by the profession, which was granted regulatory authority through the law of 22 July 1953.

It was definitely not only because of the corporate scandals characterizing the new millennium that auditor regulation accelerated in Belgium and Europe. The harmonization of policies covering audits in European Union member states has been a very important driver in this context as well. However, the financial scandals may have triggered some "overregulation" (sometimes duplication), and this in a setting where most auditees are relatively small non-listed firms. Note that only 0.7 percent of Belgian statutory audit mandates relate to listed companies. The median audit fee earned on a statutory audit mandate for an individual company (not at group level) in Belgium is only about €5,000, and the average is about €10,000 (Willekens and Gaeremynck 2005). For listed companies the average fee for the group paid for statutory audit services (for all group members) is €210,000 (Knechel and Willekens 2006). Furthermore, the risk of litigation in Belgium is low. Without a proper enforcement of the regulations in place, auditors may be tempted to produce below-standard quality and to issue more clean opinions than appropriate. Empirical support for this is provided by Vanstraelen (2002), who studied auditor economic incentives and the incidence of going-concern opinions to failing companies in Belgium.

In this chapter we describe audit regulation and the functioning of the audit profession in Belgium before the new millennium (sections 2, 5 and 6). Given the importance of the subject, we also provide some descriptive statistics regarding audit demand and supply in Belgium (section 3). Although regulation of auditing in Belgium stems from legislation, in many instances the Institute of Registered Auditors plays a central role in quality control, the enforcement of regulations, and in disciplinary sanctioning. We therefore devote a separate section to the role and functioning of the Institute of Registered Auditors (section 4). We also examine the enforcement of regulation in Belgium (section 5). Next, we focus on the major new regulations and initiatives that were launched since the new millennium (sections 7 and 8) and put Belgian auditing regulation in a broader corporate governance framework (section 9). Some concluding thoughts are also presented (section 10).

2 Audit demand and supply regulations

As in many other countries, both the parties that demand auditing and those that are allowed to supply audit services in Belgium are influenced by regulation. Demand is regulated through a mandatory audit requirement for relatively small companies (see section 2.1) and supply by entry regulations (see section 2.2).

2.1 Statutory audit requirement and auditor appointment regulations

Financial statement auditing became mandatory for certain companies in Belgium by the statute of 21 February 1985. Before 1985 auditing was voluntary. Every company (i.e. legal entity) that meets specific legal form and size criteria is required to have its financial statements audited by a member of the Institute of Registered Auditors. These criteria are such that relatively small and unlisted firms are required to appoint a statutory auditor. In particular, if a company meets more than one of the following criteria, the requirement holds: (1) average number of employees on an annual basis is 50; (2) annual turnover, exclusive of VAT, is equal to €7,300,000; (3) balance sheet total is €3,650,000 (KB 25/05/2005; BS 04/06/2005). If the average number of employees during the period exceeds 100, a statutory auditor must always be appointed, irrespective of the other size variables. Note that these criteria are applied at company group level, but auditors are appointed per legal entity (individual group member). Hence, numerous rather small individual accounts and unlisted company accounts are subject to a mandatory audit in Belgium.

The statutory auditor examines the company's financial situation and its financial statements, consisting of the balance sheet, the profit and loss account, and the notes. Subsequently, the auditor has to form an opinion as to whether the financial statements convey a true and fair view of the company's shareholders' equity and financial position at the balance sheet date, and whether the results are in accordance with the legal and administrative requirements. The audit has to be conducted in accordance with the generally accepted auditing standards promulgated by the Institute of Registered Auditors.

Statutory auditors are appointed by the general assembly of shareholders based on a recommendation of the corporate board of directors. The term of appointment is three years, which can subsequently be renewed without limitation for further three-yearly periods. Where the company has a works council, it has the right to veto the appointment of the nominee auditor and defend this position in court. Note that works councils are mandatory in all Belgian companies and institutions that employ on average more than 100 employees. The works council is a body with parity representation of employers and employees. Its purpose is to implement social legislation. The works council is entitled to adequate financial and economic information about the entity.[1]

A statutory auditor can only be dismissed under very exceptional circumstances (for example, physical incapacity or negligence resulting in a loss of confidence). Resignation by the auditor during her/his mandate is likewise restricted. Barring grave personal reasons, the statutory auditor is not permitted to resign during her/his assignment, except before the general assembly after having informed the members in writing of the reasons for resignation. The resignation of the auditor is required to be approved by the works council, if established, or by the supervisory body for companies under prudential control.

2.2 Regulations regarding entry to the profession

Entry requirements to the auditing profession are governed by the law of 22 July 1953, as adjusted by the statute of 21 February 1985. In order to be recognized as an auditor in Belgium, one must: be Belgian, or resident in Belgium; be at least twenty-five years of age and no older than sixty-five; never have been deprived of civil and political rights; hold a university diploma or a diploma of higher education of at least four years of study, or be registered for two years on the roll of chartered accountants; have successfully passed an admission examination; have completed a three-year training period with a professional auditor; have passed an aptitude exam at the end of the training period; and have made an oath before the President of the Commerce Tribunal. In Belgium, auditors have to continue practicing in order to keep their licence. They also have to fulfill continuous practice education requirements.

3 Characteristics of the Belgian audit market: demand, supply and pricing

3.1 Demand side statistics of the Belgian audit market

In a study that covers almost all statutory audit engagements performed in 2001 in Belgium, Willekens and Gaeremynck (2005) report the size characteristics given in Table 2.1 for Belgian audit clients. The average (median) total assets of Belgian auditees in the study is about €60 million (€5.67 million), the average (median) turnover is about €34 million (€7 million). On average (median), Belgian auditees employ 95 (21) people. Note further that only 0.7 percent of all audit mandates are for companies that are listed on the stock exchange. Table 2.1 also provides an insight into the different size characteristics of Big N clients versus non-Big N clients. As expected Big N clients are significantly larger than non-Big N clients along all defined size criteria.

Willekens and Gaeremynck (2005) also provide data on the industries to which Belgian audit clients belong. Details are provided in Table 2.2. Inspection of column (2) in Table 2.2 reveals that about two-thirds of audit mandates[2] (clients) are active in the service industry, whereas one-third are active in production related industries. Most audit clients are active in manufacturing (24.83 percent), wholesale and retail trade (30.07 percent), or real estate, renting and business activities (21.58 percent). From columns (4) and (5) in Table 2.2 it also appears that the market share of the Big N and non-Big N audit firms is equal, when expressed in terms of the number of mandates (49.88 percent vs. 50.12 percent). Market shares computed on the basis of audit fees earned provide a different picture, with a Big N market share of about 70 percent (Willekens and Gaeremynck 2005).

3.2 Supply side statistics of the Belgian audit market

Overall, it is clear that Big N market concentration is quite low in Belgium compared to Anglo-Saxon and other European countries (see also Willekens and Achmadi 2003, Weets and Jegers 1997, Schaen and Maijoor 1997). For example, in the public client segment of the Anglo-Saxon audit market, Big N audit firms typically have about 90-95 percent (or more) of the market share (compared to 50 percent [based on number of mandates] or 70 percent [fee based in Belgium]). The large international accounting firms originally established their presence in the Belgian audit services market by following their multinational clients, which had head offices in the US and UK. Before the early 1990s they were not allowed to operate under their own brand name, so operated through local practices.

Willekens and Gaeremynck (2005) also provide statistics regarding other audit-firm characteristics, including the average number of years' experience that auditors in a firm have, the number of mandates the firm has, and the number of offices. The average (median) number of mandates a Belgian audit firm has is 41.42 (9), with a very significant difference between Big N and non-Big N firms

Table 2.1 Size characteristics of the demand side of the Belgian audit market

	Mean	Min.	Q1	Median	Q3	Max.	Big 5	Non-Big 5	p-value
Listed companies	0.7%						1%	0.5%	0.0026
Total assets (€1,000)	60,185	3	2,221	5,670	16,227	16,713,009	91,050	29,466	<0.0001
Turnover (€1,000)	34,040	1	1,716	7,001	18,551	13,990,888	47,356	20,786	0.0084
Number of employees	95	0	4	21	58	39,902	116	76	0.0091

Source: Willekens and Gaeremynck (2005)

Table 2.2 Statutory audit clients per NACE 2-digit group of industries

Industry (NACE digits) (1)	% of all mandates (2)	Total mandates (3)	% by non-Big 5 (4)	% by Big 5 (5)
Production	32.27	3,969	56.51	43.49
Mining and quarrying (10–14)	1.17	144	58.33	41.67
Manufacturing (15–37)	24.83	3,054	53.70	46.30
Electricity, gas and water supply (40–41)	0.59	73	65.75	34.25
Construction (45)	5.67	698	67.48	32.52
Services	67.73	8,332	47.07	52.93
Wholesale and retail trade (50–52)	30.07	3,699	50.99	49.01
Hotels and restaurants (55)	0.89	110	53.64	46.36
Transport, Storage and communication (60–64)	8.83	1,086	45.76	54.24
Financial intermediation (65–67)	3.55	437	39.82	60.18
Real estate, renting and business activities (70–74)	21.58	2,654	42.73	57.27
Miscellaneous (75–99)	2.81	346	49.71	50.29
Total	100.00	12,301	50.12	49.88

Source: Based on Willekens and Gaeremynck (2005: Table 5, p. 28)

(1227.4 vs. 21.12, $p = 0.0001$). The median number of offices that a Belgian audit firm has is one, and again there is a significant difference between the Big N and non-Big N group (6.2 vs. 1.28, $p < 0.0001$). The average experience of auditors in Belgium is 14.84 years and there is no significant difference between Big N and other firms regarding experience.

However, from Willekens and Gaeremynck (2005) it is clear that there is significant variation within the non-Big N group. Therefore, dichotomization of the supply side of the Belgian audit market into Big N and non-Big N firms hardly does justice to the large differences that exist among the non-Big N group. Willekens and Gaeremynck (2005) identify five clusters at the supply side of the Belgian audit market. The cluster analysis was performed based on audit-firm size, office, and auditor experience variables. The five clusters include: 1) the Big N group of audit firms, 2) the second tier audit firms, and 3) three clusters of small audit firms. The latter three clusters differ from one another by the average number of years of experience the auditors in the firm have. Figure 2.1 shows the location of the audit firms in the Belgian market in five clusters, along a size (vertical axis) and an experience (horizontal axis) dimension.

From Figure 2.1 it is clear that the Big N in Belgium (cluster 5) distinguish themselves from all other clusters by the number of employees. Cluster 4, which contains the second tier audit firms, has more employees than the small firms but fewer than the Big N firms. The average experience in the second tier firms is greater than in the Big N firms. Clusters 1, 2, and 3 are the small audit firms, with only a small number of employees. They distinguish themselves from one

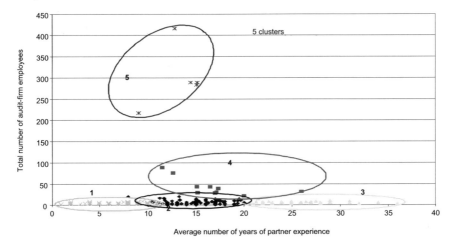

Figure 2.1 Clusters on the supply side of the Belgian audit market

Source: Willekens and Gaeremynck 2005

another through the average number of years' experience their auditors have in the firm. Note that Willekens and Gaeremynck (2005) also report the results of an audit fee analysis that indicates that audit fees significantly differ among the five types of audit firms, *ceteris paribus*. Table 2.3 contains further statistics for each of the five types of Belgian audit firms.

4 The Institute of Registered Auditors: role and structure

Unlike other (European) countries, such as the Netherlands, the external auditing profession did not spontaneously develop as a consequence of the economic activity in the nineteenth century. This is mainly due to the nature of business financing in Belgium, which was characterized by large family holdings and hence by very concentrated and closely held ownership structures. The first audit-related regulations in Belgium can be found in the law of 22 July 1953. It was actually by this law that the Institute of Registered Auditors (IBR-IRE) was founded. It is remarkable that the Institute was not founded as a result of the development of the auditing activity in Belgium, but rather in order to further organize and develop the external audit function in Belgium. Since 1953 several laws and royal decrees have been issued to further refine and develop auditing in Belgium. An important law is the Act of 21 February 1985 which was issued to comply with the Fourth and Eighth EU directives, and which specified among other things the statutory audit requirement in Belgium, to be performed by

Table 2.3 Descriptive statistics regarding audit-firm and portfolio characteristics

	Cluster 1		Cluster 2		Cluster 3		Cluster 4		Cluster 5	
	Av.	Med	Av.	Med	Av.	Med	Av.	Med	Av.	Med
Audit firm turnover										
Turnover statutory audit engagements (€)	65,304	39,914	181,903	103,228	139,560	90,307	1,609,821	1,381,243	28,063,758	25,823,345
Turnover from other statutory engagements (€)	43,700	27,952	52,051	34,996	36,171	19,339	581,266	212,202	779,641	436,817
Turnover other professional activities (€)	199,684	47,722	90,783	50,561	60,184	31,799	1,673,777	930,756	8,511,237	10,042,629
Turnover from activities for other audit firms (€)	7,081	0	9,904	0	5,951	0	0	0	2,372,024	0
Turnover statutory audit engagements (%)	35	27	49	46	60	61	52	52	70	72
Turnover other statutory engagements (%)	24	22	19	14	16	12	15	15	2	2
Turnover other professional activities (%)	37	35	28	25	23	18	33	30	24	27
Turnover activities for other audit firms (%)	5	0	4	0	2	0	0	0	5	0
Audit firm characteristics										
Years' experience of auditors in the firm	7.35	8	15.17	15	25.96	25.5	16.8	16.8	13.39	14.53
Number of offices in the firm	1.10	1	1.26	1	1.20	1	3.2	2.5	6.2	5
Number of partners in the firm	1.23	1	1.52	1	1.26	1	7.3	7	35.2	37
Client profile per cluster										
Audit fee (€)	4,747	4,044	5,517	4,619	8,845	4,803	6,802	6,663	15,145	16,420
Total fee (€)	5,333	4,581	6,226	5,054	9,176	5,093	8,640	9,045	16,842	17,687
Total assets (€1,000)	9,609	6,977	18,965	9,007	187,901	9,039	41,852	26,640	96,262	96,503
Turnover (€1,000)	15,595	10,782	15,833	12,736	109,290	15,895	25,572	21,680	48,785	52,339
Number of employees	47	36	52	38	532	43	78	61	119	124

Source: Willekens and Gaeremynck 2005

members of the Institute of Registered Auditors. Before 1985 financial statement audits were not mandatory in Belgium.

The Institute of Registered Auditors is a public (royal since 2003) institute under the authority of the Ministry of Economic Affairs and is assisted by the High Council for Auditing and Accounting. All statutory auditors in Belgium are required to be members of the Institute of Registered Auditors. Currently, the Institute of Registered Auditors has about 1,000 members. The mission of the Institute of Registered Auditors is: "to guard over the education and to provide in the permanent organization of a team of specialists capable of fulfilling the function of an auditor with all the required guarantees in terms of authority, independence and professional ethics (and monitor the appropriate performance of the assignments entrusted to its members)." To accomplish this mission, the Institute has the following working structures: a general assembly, a board of the Institute, an executive committee, and a number of committees with a specific purpose.

The general assembly of the Institute of Registered Auditors consists of all member-auditors. Each member is entitled to one vote in the assembly. The assembly meets at least once a year and its function consists of electing the president, vice-president, the members of the Board of the Institute, and the auditors who sit on the Appeal Committee (see section 5.3).

The Board of the Institute governs the Institute of Registered Auditors. The Board consists of a president, a vice-president, and 12 members (i.e. six Dutch speaking and six French speaking members). The Board is responsible for the functioning and representation of the Institute. In particular, the Board monitors the membership list, provides permission for the formation of audit firms, enrols auditor-candidates, sets the auditing standards, and can file cases with the Disciplinary Committee.

The Executive Committee is responsible for the daily management of the Institute of Registered Auditors and is governed by the president. This committee deals with the current operations, monitors the financial position of the Institute of Registered Auditors, and governs its personnel.

The Belgian legislator has delegated the authority to supervise and monitor Belgian registered auditors to the Institute of Registered Auditors. In this context the Board of the Institute has established two committees, i.e. the Supervisory Committee and the Quality Control Committee. Until 2001 both committees functioned as subcommittees of the same committee. Since 2001 the committees have functioned autonomously and separately from each other.

The Quality Control Committee (before 2002 this committee was named "peer review committee") is responsible for establishing and executing a procedure of peer review applicable to all Belgian auditors. The Board of the Institute of Registered Auditors decided in 1991 that every member of the Institute is required to undergo a peer review at least once every five years. In 2002 the Belgian quality control and peer review standards were updated. A peer review focuses on the auditors' working papers and office organization in general. The report with the findings from the peer review is signed by the auditor and the peer reviewer and sent to the Quality Control Committee. The latter committee in turn reports to the Board of the Institute. Where serious deficiencies are reported, the Board can send the file to the Supervisory Committee, which can start an independent investigation. In 2005, for example, 104 quality controls were performed by the Quality Control Committee. This resulted in 47 cases which were investigated more thoroughly by the committee. Examples of the main problems identified by the committee in these cases included:

- the audit activity of the auditor cannot be considered as his main activity (an auditor needs to perform a minimum number of audits to keep his title);
- independence problems;
- insufficient monitoring of individual auditors' application of manuals used in the audit firm;
- insufficient tailoring of the general audit program to the specifics of the audited company;
- non-existent or insufficient risk management.

The Supervisory Committee monitors the quality of the statutory audit activities executed by the members of the Institute and compliance with rules with respect to independence and competence. In this context every Belgian registered auditor and audit firm has to make an annual declaration of all statutory audit engagements performed that year, as well as the corresponding fee that has been charged and some other information. This information is used by the committee to detect low balling. If discrepancies are detected, the Supervisory Committee makes recommendations to the auditor for improvement. In the event of serious deficiencies, the committee can file a report with the Board of the Institute, which can subsequently file it with the Disciplinary Committee (see section 5.3). The Supervisory Committee opened 163 new cases in 2005 for investigation, of which 34 related to audit firms and 129 related to individual auditors. The majority of the cases in 2005 related to a technical failure, followed by problems of the auditor's main activity, legal procedure, independence, and ethics.

In addition to the Supervisory Committee and Quality Control Committee, the Institute of Registered Auditors has also established a number of other committees with a specific purpose, such as the Committee of Practice (responsible for the education and training of the candidate-auditors), the Legal Committee (dealing with, for example, specific legal questions of auditors), and the Standard Setting Committee (which develops the auditing standards). The organizational structure of the Institute of Registered Auditors is represented in Figure 2.2.

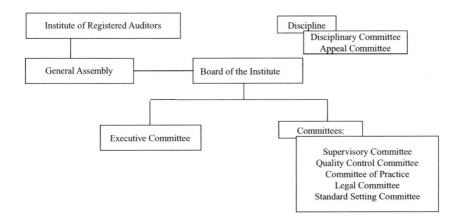

Figure 2.2 Organizational structure of the Institute of Registered Auditors

5 Enforcement of audit-related regulations in Belgium

Enforcement of auditing standards and regulations is theoretically possible through four different channels. First, the auditors are subject to tort law, and hence legally responsible for potential damage if their services are not executed with due professional care (see section 5.1). Second, auditors can also be held criminally liable in certain circumstances (see section 5.2). Third, auditors are subject to a disciplinary code (see section 5.3). And fourth, since 2003 auditor independence rules have also been enforceable by the Advisory and Supervisory Committee on the Independence of the Statutory Auditor (see further section 7.1c).

5.1 Liability from tort law

The auditor's report and the financial statements have to be filed with the Belgian National Bank and are publicly available. Legal action against an auditor in Belgium can be undertaken by the client company, its shareholders, or any interested third party. The liability allocation regime adopted in Belgium is the proportional liability system. This system is characterized by the fact that liability is placed upon the defendants according to their contribution to the damage. Since 2005 (law of 23 December 2005), there has been a cap on liability: €3 million for non-listed firms and €12 million for listed firms. This limitation is not applicable if the breach was made by the auditor deliberately or with the intent to mislead. Belgian statutory auditors are required to maintain professional indemnity insurance. Legal action against a statutory auditor in Belgium can be undertaken until five years after the issue of the auditor's report.

It should be noted that litigation rates in Belgium are low. This is typical for countries which have government-prescribed accounting standards that are rather conservative, with banks or the government being the major providers of capital.

5.2 Criminal liability

Belgian registered auditors are also criminally liable if they violate certain ethical principles, such as the confidentiality principle.

5.3 Disciplinary sanctions

The Institute of Registered Auditors plays a central role in the maintenance of discipline. Maintenance of discipline is organized by the Disciplinary Committee. The Disciplinary Committee consists of a president who is a judge in the Court of Commerce, and two auditors appointed by the Board of the Institute. On appeal, disciplinary cases appear before the Appeal Committee, which consists of five members: three magistrates and two auditors. These two auditors are appointed by the general assembly of the Institute of Registered Auditors.

A disciplinary case can be filed with the Disciplinary Committee by the Board of the Institute, by the High Council of Auditors and Accountants, and also (since 2003) by the Advisory and Supervisory Committee on the Independence of the Statutory Auditor. Any party involved (that is, any stakeholder) can lodge a complaint with the Board. The Board will first investigate the case itself, through the Supervisory Committee. Ultimately, it is the Disciplinary Committee which decides whether or not to issue a sanction. Disciplinary sanctions encompass a warning, reprimand, prohibition to accept or continue assignments, suspension for a maximum of one year, and removal from the member list of auditors.

The number of disciplinary sanctions issued against auditors in 2005 was 18 by the Disciplinary Committee and 4 by the Appeal Committee. The types of disciplinary sanctions for 2005 are tabulated in Table 2.4.

Table 2.4 Disciplinary sanctions against auditors in 2005

	Disciplinary committee	Appeal committee
Warning	5	0
Reprimand	2	1
Suspension	10	3
Removal	1	0
Total	18	4

Source: Annual Report Institute of Registered Auditors 2005

6 Auditor independence regulations before the new millennium

The statutory auditor in Belgium is subject to a strict code of ethics. Many of the regulations are aimed at protecting the auditor's independence, as this is considered to be of central importance to the auditor's assignment. Noteworthy is that a fair number of auditor independence rules were already effective in Belgium before the new rules were specified in 2002 and 2003. The main principles of ethics were incorporated into the "Law of 21 February 1985 on the reform of the audit profession," while more specific and stringent regulations were specified in the Royal Decree of 10 January 1994. This Royal Decree of 1994 is considered to be the cornerstone of the Belgian Code of Ethics. The recent auditor independence regulations included in the Corporate Governance Law of 2 August 2002, and the Royal Decree of 4 April 2003 (see section 7), are to be considered as additional regulations, since the regulations of the Royal Decree of 1994 remain in force.

The principal regulations included in the Royal Decree of 1994 with respect to auditor independence are the following:

- auditors are not allowed to accept an engagement if they have a personal or commercial relationship with the client;
- except for the audit fee received for delivered services, the auditor is not allowed to have any financial interest in the client;
- except for the remuneration determined in compliance with the law, the auditor is not entitled to any remuneration or other benefit that would constitute a direct or indirect reward for the auditing assignment, or that might inspire him to assume a benevolent attitude;
- auditors are not allowed to accept an engagement if they have been a director or manager in the client enterprise during the past three years;
- with the exception of representation in the context of other statutory assignments, or assignments that are inextricably linked with his statutory auditing assignment or follow from it, the statutory auditor is not permitted to accept any other position, mandate, or assignment that might lead to his involvement in the management of the entity;
- audit firms are not allowed to provide other services to an audit client within the same legal entity. In particular, tax, legal services, consulting, investment and financial advisory services, and corporate recovery are not allowed to be supplied by an audit firm to a statutory client within the same legal entity. The provision of bookkeeping and accounting services is allowed on an *ad hoc* and non-recurring basis;
- if any person with whom the statutory auditor cooperates professionally performs services to the company, then the auditor is to make sure that the nature and scale of these services do not compromise his own independence. Company law stipulates that the nature of services provided by persons with whom the auditor collaborates professionally and the remuneration paid for these services should be mentioned in the annual report;

- auditors must not restrict their activities to such an extent that they become financially dependent on a very limited number of assignments or positions, nor should their assignments and positions all depend on a single interest group or authority.

Note that the Royal Decree of 10 January 1994 also includes an "audit fee rule" formulated as follows:

The audit fee must depend on the complexity of the assignment and the nature, the scope, and the scale of the activities that are required in accordance with the standards set forth by the Institute of Registered Auditors. The fees must not depend on the benefits that the client may reap from the auditor's activities, and the auditors may neither receive nor grant commissions or other benefits.

Auditors are required to report to the Institute of Registered Auditors the audit fee charged to each of their clients. Furthermore, all forms of advertising and solicited offerings of services to the public in general are forbidden. Note also that auditors are not allowed to be employed full-time outside the auditing profession. If so, they lose their licence.

7 New auditor independence regulations

It was not only financial scandals that inspired the analysis of the necessity for further auditor regulation in Belgium (and Europe). The harmonization of policies covering audits in European Union member states has been studied since 1996 (see Buijink *et al.* 1996) and a lead on corporate governance legislation in Belgium had already been given in 1998. This resulted in new regulations that were included in the Corporate Governance Law of 2 August 2002 (voted only two days after Sarbanes-Oxley) and the Royal Decree of 4 April 2003 concerning activities that may impair auditor independence. In addition, the Institute of Registered Auditors has issued a recommendation on the independence of statutory auditors following the European recommendation on the independence of the statutory auditor of 16 May 2002. We will now discuss each of these new regulations.

7.1 Corporate Governance Law (2 August 2002)

The Corporate Governance Law of 2 August 2002 emerged in a broader corporate governance context, and hence contains not only regulations which should further strengthen auditor independence, but also regulations relating to the responsibilities and liability of corporate directors, the establishment of an Executive Committee, the constitution of advisory committees (including audit committees), the holding of annual general meetings, conflicts of interest, and the publication of significant shareholdings. The new regulations relating to auditor independence are as follows:

(a) Cooling-off period

The cooling-off period rule says that an auditor is not allowed to take up a mandate as director, manager or other function within the company, or related company, that was subject to his/her audit within a period of two years after the end of the audit mandate. Note that the Belgian cooling-off period rule is similar to the one included in the recommendation of the European Commission on the independence of the statutory auditor.

(b) One-to-one rule

Auditors are allowed to provide other services as long as they do not compromise their independence. Examples of services which are considered to be compatible with auditor independence include:

- educational activities;
- performing the function of director within own audit firm;
- consulting services to, for example, lawyers, solicitors, receivers;
- executor of a will;
- liquidator;
- public functions not in a subordinate position: representative, senator, mayor or magistrate.

However, these services can only be provided in second order. In this respect, the Corporate Governance Law of 2 August 2002 introduced the so-called "one-to-one" rule. This rule implies that fees received from non-audit services, either by the auditor or other persons with whom the auditor has a professional relation of cooperation, must not exceed the fees received for audit services. The European Commission did not include this rule in its recommendation on the independence of the statutory auditor. As a result, Belgium's one-to-one rule is unique in the EU.

Application of the one-to-one rule has serious (even extraterritorial) consequences for the Belgian audit profession. The reason is that – according to the 2002 law – the ratio of audit fees to non-audit fees is to be computed on the basis of fees earned by the entire (international) audit-firm network and for all client group members. The Institute of Registered Auditors therefore suggests amending the Corporate Governance Law by redefining what constitutes a professional network. They point out the extraterritorial effects of the Belgian rules and demand that services rendered by the foreign network of the statutory auditor to the foreign subsidiaries of the audit client not be included.

Finally, note that the Corporate Governance Law specifies three cases where deviation from the one-to-one rule is allowed:

1   after positive advice from the audit committee of the audited company;
2   after positive advice from the Advisory and Supervisory Committee on the Independence of the Statutory Auditor (see below);
3   if the audited company has established a *team* of independent auditors.

*(c) Advisory and Supervisory Committee on the Independence
      of the Statutory Auditor*

The Corporate Governance Law provides for the establishment of an Advisory and Supervisory Committee on the Independence of the Statutory Auditor, which consists of members who are independent of the auditing profession. The committee is appointed by the King for a renewable period of five years. The responsibilities of the committee include:

- to provide – at the auditor's request – preliminary advice concerning the compatibility of a non-audit service with auditor independence (see above);
- to file a case with respect to auditor independence with the Disciplinary Committee (see above).

To this end, the Advisory and Supervisory Committee on the Independence of the Statutory Auditor can demand all relevant information from the Institute of Registered Auditors.

(d) Disclosure of fees

Belgian Company Law already required companies to declare in their annual reports the fees for additional assignments or extraordinary activities paid to the auditor or to a person with whom the auditor has a collective agreement or a professional relation of cooperation. In this respect, the Corporate Governance Law further clarifies for which companies and persons (different from the audited firm) the fees for extraordinary activities should be reported. In particular, this relates to:

- extraordinary activities or special assignments performed by the auditor within the audited firm, or for a Belgian firm or Belgian person that is related to his firm, or for a foreign subsidiary of a Belgian company that is subject to a financial statement audit;
- the tasks, mandates or assignments performed by 1) a person with whom the auditor has a collective agreement, or 2) persons with whom he has a professional relationship of cooperation, or 3) a company or person related

to the auditor. These tasks, mandates, or assignments are performed within the audited company, or for a Belgian company or a Belgian person that is related to this company, or for a foreign subsidiary of a Belgian company that is subject to a financial statement audit.

It is important to note that the Corporate Governance Law does *not* prescribe public disclosure of audit fees.

(e) New tasks of the statutory auditor under the Corporate Governance Law

The Corporate Governance Law has also granted new responsibilities to the statutory auditor, in particular with respect to the procedure for the resolution of conflicts of interest within the Executive Committee.

7.2 Royal Decree of 4 April 2003

The Royal Decree of 4 April 2003 provides a list of activities that are considered to impair auditor independence and are as a result forbidden. These activities are the following:

- taking decisions in the audited company or intervening in the decision process;
- assisting or participating in the preparation of or doing the bookkeeping or preparing the financial statements (individual or consolidated) of the audited company;
- the preparation, development, implementation, and monitoring of financial information systems in the audited company;
- the valuation of elements of the financial statements (individual or consolidated) of an audited company if these constitute significant elements of the financial statements;
- participating in the internal audit function;
- representing the audited company for the settlement of tax or other disputes;
- intervening in the recruitment of persons who become members of a board of or are involved in directing an audited company.

Note that this list is in line with the recommendation of the European Commission on the independence of the statutory auditor (16 May 2002).

It is important to note that these activities are not only forbidden for the auditor but also for any other person with whom the auditor has a collective agreement, or other persons with whom the auditor has a professional relation of cooperation (i.e. belongs to the auditor's network). Furthermore, these activities are restricted not only to the audited company but also to the companies or persons that are related in Belgium to this audited company, and to the Belgian and foreign subsidiaries of this audited company.

Finally, the Royal Decree of 4 April 2003 also contains regulations concerning the composition, organization, functioning, and financing of the Advisory and Supervisory Committee on the Independence of the Statutory Auditor.

7.3   Recommendation of the Institute of Registered Auditors on the independence of the statutory auditor

The Institute of Registered Auditors is currently finalizing a recommendation on the independence of the statutory auditor. The purpose of this recommendation is to comply with the recommendation of the European Commission on auditor independence (16 May 2002), since certain elements of the European recommendation are not yet included in Belgian law. In particular, Belgian law does not contain requirements on audit partner rotation, and on a maximum fee dependence limit of 20 percent.

7.4   New Eighth EU Directive

The Board of the Institute of Registered Auditors has started an investigation into the consequences for Belgium of the implementation of the new Eighth EU Directive. The main consequences are the following. First, the International Standards on Auditing (ISAs) are likely to become mandatory under the new Eighth EU Directive. Second, the new Eighth EU Directive requires listed firms to install an internal audit committee. Finally, the role of public oversight and quality control will be further strengthened.

8   Other relevant regulatory developments in the new millennium

The start of the new millennium, and especially 2002, will be remembered for some unfortunate financial scandals that happened in different parts of the world and have triggered reflection on the role and integrity of the different parties involved in financial reporting, and also affected audit independence regulation worldwide and in Belgium. However, other important audit-related initiatives have been taken by the Institute of Registered Auditors that are not related to auditor independence issues. We list only the most pertinent initiatives here.

First, a new standard on quality control was issued by the IBR-IRE in 2002 (see also our discussion on the Quality Control Committee in section 4). This standard matches the relevant European recommendation. The fact that a relatively small number of modifications have been made to the existing standards (before 2002) on peer review shows that the Belgian profession was at the leading edge in this respect.

Second, major efforts have been undertaken by the IBR-IRE to ensure that Belgian auditing standards are in total conformity with the structure in the

International Standards on Auditing (ISAs). Furthermore, the Institute has started a translation project of the ISAs into both French and Flemish (Dutch). To establish international consistency regarding translation, cooperation with the French CNCC exists for the French translation of the ISAs, and cooperation with the Dutch NIVRA for the Dutch translation. The major impact of the application of the ISAs in Belgium is expected to come from the implementation of the audit risk model, for example as described in ISA 315 (*Understanding the entity and its environment and assessing the risks of material misstatement*) and ISA 330 (*The auditor's procedures in response to assessed risks*). Furthermore, current regulations with respect to fraud and audit planning are limited compared to the requirements of ISA 240 (*The auditor's responsibilities to consider fraud in an audit of financial statements*) and ISA 300 (*Planning an audit of financial statements*). While in most countries ISA 700 (*The auditor's report on financial statements*) will have a major impact, this is not the case for Belgium since this format of reporting has been in use since 1997. It is expected that the implementation of the International Standards on Quality Control (ISQs) will have a larger impact in Belgium than the ISAs. The ISQs require audit firms to formally lay down their policies and procedures. Furthermore, there has to be a quality control reviewer for every auditor. These practices do not yet exist in Belgium. Finally, the documentation requirements are much higher under the international standards. It appears from the annual reports of the Belgian Institute of Registered Auditors that lack of documentation is always in the first or second position in the top-10 problems with quality control.

9 Auditing and corporate governance in Belgium

External financial statements auditing is one (important) element within a broader corporate governance context. Good governance requires more than independent financial statement auditing alone. In addition to provisions governing the independence of the statutory auditor (see above), the Corporate Governance Law of 2 August 2002 includes, as mentioned, other governance provisions on the liability of corporate directors, the establishment of an Executive Committee, the constitution of advisory committees (including audit committees), the holding of annual general meetings, conflicts of interest, and the publication of significant shareholdings. However, the Corporate Governance Law does not include a best practice code on corporate governance.

In Belgium, best practice codes on corporate governance have been in place for listed companies since 1998, but no provision in these codes could be interpreted as derogating from Belgian law. In 1998 the Brussels Exchanges (i.e. the Commission Cardon), the Banking and Finance Commission (CBF), as well as the Federation of Belgian Enterprises (CEB-VBO) issued *recommendations* on good corporate governance. The recommendations of the CBF related to disclosure on corporate governance, whereas the recommendations of the Brussels Exchanges and CEB-VBO described good corporate governance practice.[3] In particular, the latter pertain to the responsibilities, size, composition, and working procedures of the board of directors (BOD). The Brussels Exchanges recommended in 1998, for example, that the board should not consist of more than 12 directors, and that the majority of the directors be non-executives. Another recommendation was that some of the non-executive directors be independent of management as well as of the majority shareholders, and that the company establish an audit committee.[4]

On the initiative of the same parties that were involved in the 1998 corporate governance recommendations – that is, the Banking, Finance, and Insurance Commission (BFIC, formerly BFC), Euronext Brussels (formerly Brussels Exchanges), and the Federation of Belgian Enterprises [CEB-VBO]) – a committee was established to draft a new code of best practice on corporate governance for all listed companies. This new code (i.e. Code Lippens) was launched in December 2004 and became effective as of 2005; it is aligned with OECD principles and EU recommendations. It has a high degree of built-in flexibility as it is based on the "comply or explain" system. Disclosure leading to transparency is an essential ingredient of the code. Transparency is to be obtained through two different documents: the corporate governance charter (on the corporate website) and the corporate governance chapter (included in the annual report). The code contains three types of rules: principles, provisions, and guidelines.[5] According to the Corporate Governance Committee, the nine principles form the pillars of good governance. Provisions are recommendations describing how to apply the principles, and guidelines provide guidance as to how the company should implement or interpret the provisions. The new rules in the code relate to best practice board characteristics (like independence, size, leadership, and remuneration) and audit committee membership characteristics, and explicitly recommend the installation of an internal audit function within the company. Note that the code is complementary to Belgian legislation, but BFIC recommends that listed companies disclose relevant information about their corporate governance rules and practices in accordance with provisions of the code. The Lippens code does not contain specific rules about the external audit function. However, audit quality remains a very important dimension of corporate monitoring and control.

Willekens and Sercu (2005) published a study regarding the implementation and effectiveness of various governance mechanisms in Belgium which indicates that, before the Lippens code was constructed, a lot of Belgian listed companies already complied with some basic rules concerning what (supposedly) is good governance. However, they also reported that this did not lead to effective monitoring in all dimensions. There is no univocal evidence that the typical "good board" characteristics have led to better monitoring. Also, the mere presence of audit committees did not yield effective monitoring. However, to judge from the scarce Belgian evidence (Willekens *et al.* 2005), the installation of an internal audit function seems to be very effective as it is clearly associated with more corporate transparency. Further, Knechel and Willekens (2006) found for a sample of listed Belgian companies that different types of governance mechanisms are complementary to each other (instead of being substitutes). In particular, the presence of audit committees and independent directors is associated with a higher demand for external audit services (in terms of a willingness to pay higher audit fees).

Note that, in 2005, a best practice code on corporate governance for non-listed companies was also published in Belgium (i.e. Code Buysse). Currently, Belgium is the only EU country to have developed a corporate governance code for non-listed firms. Non-listed firms in Belgium can take many forms, ranging from small starting firms to large multinationals. Code Buysse contains recommendations for good management related to the position of the company in its life cycle. Code Buysse consists of three main parts.[6] The first part contains recommendations for all non-listed firms, relating to the role of the board of directors, management, and shareholders. The second part deals with family owned companies. A noteworthy recommendation is the establishment of a family forum through which communication, information, and consultation should take place (for example, what is the role of the family within the company?; compensation of family members working within the company; how to deal with a potential take-over). The third part of Code Buysse relates to small companies and contains recommendations relating to stakeholders such as suppliers, customers, employees and government.

10 Concluding thoughts

From the discussion of audit-related regulations in Belgium in this chapter it is clear that even before the new independence rules were issued in 2002 and 2003, Belgian auditing was already heavily regulated. Since 2002 the Corporate Governance Law of 2 August 2002 and the European recommendation of 16 May 2002 have been of vital importance for registered auditors in Belgium, in particular in their role of statutory auditor, and have led to what some call "overregulation" of Belgian practice. The specification of the one-to-one rule is an example of "unique" Belgian regulation which – although not required by the European Union recommendation and directive – has greatly complicated audit practice and required a tremendous amount of effort and cost to implement.

One can question whether more was really necessary in an environment where only 0.7 percent of statutory audits relates to listed companies, and the median (average) audit fee is only about €5,000 (€10,000). Perhaps the focus should be on enforcement rather than more regulation. Note that Maijoor and Vanstraelen (2006) found that there is no evidence of an international Big Four audit differentiation effect in Europe. Hence, they argue that for the comparability of earnings not only the standardization of financial reporting is important but also the standardization of enforcement mechanisms, as embodied in the national audit environment and the quality of audit firms. Furthermore, Willekens and

Sercu (2005) found that the mere presence of good corporate governance practice in Belgian listed firms does not guarantee their effectiveness.

We therefore see two major challenges for the Belgian (European?) legislator in the future. A first challenge is to formulate a different set of rules for audits of listed versus non-listed clients. After all, the economic theory of regulation suggests that regulation only improves social efficiency in certain situations, for example when there are externalities and information asymmetries. It may well be that the regulatory cost exceeds the benefit, especially in cases where audit risks are relatively low and information asymmetries between management and stakeholders are limited. The Belgian corporate governance code is also different for listed and unlisted firms. So why couldn't audit regulations be better adjusted to the type of firms they relate to?

A second challenge relates to enforcement of regulation in Belgium (and Europe). It is true that the Corporate Governance Law of August 2002 has established the Advisory and Supervisory Committee on the Independence of the Statutory Auditor, which consists of non-auditors. Also, the Institute of Registered Auditors has firmed up its supervisory and quality control standards and activities. Future disciplinary actions will depend on the activities of these committees. Given that the Belgian tort system is not litigious, the true deterrent for unwanted auditor behavior will have to come from these actions. And if the rules are enforced, no additional rules will be needed in the future.

The new Eighth EU Directive approved on 11 October 2005, which includes principles relating to the profession, quality control, independence, ethics, auditing standards, discipline, and appointment, will have a further impact on the audit profession in the EU member states, including Belgium. The implementation of the directive should be such that the benefits outweigh the cost.

Notes

1 Statutory auditors in Belgium are required to provide specific information to the works council. This is done in the so-called part II of the (Belgian) audit report.
2 An audit mandate relates to the individual accounts of the audited company. Each company is identified by a company number.
3 These are recommendations and in no way mandatory regulations. The regulation of the internal audit function within credit banks is an exception.
4 Other recommendations related to the responsibilities and remuneration of non-executive directors, remuneration of management, and reporting and control.
5 For an overview of all principles, rules, and provisions in the code, see http://www.corporategovernancecommittee.be.
6 The full text of Code Buysse is available at http://www.codebuysse.be.

References

Buijink, W., Maijoor, S., Meuwissen, R., and van Witteloostuijn, A. (1996) *The Role, Position, and Liability of the Statutory Auditor within the European Union,* Study commissioned by DG XV of the European Commission, Luxembourg: ECSC-EC-EAEC.

Dries, R., Van Brussel, L., and Willekens, M. (2004) *Handboek Auditing*, 2nd ed., Antwerp, Oxford; Intersentia Publishers.

Instituut der Bedrijfsrevisoren – Institut des Réviseurs d'Entreprise. Jaarverslag 2005 – Rapport Annuel 2005.

Knechel, R. and Willekens, M. (2006) "The Role of Risk Management and Governance in Determining Audit Demand," *Journal of Business Finance and Accounting*, 33(9–10): 1344–67.

Maijoor, S. and Vanstraelen, A. (2006) "Earnings Management within Europe: the Effect of Member State Audit Environment, Audit Firm Quality and International Capital Markets," *Accounting and Business Research*, 36(1): 33–52.

Schaen, M. and Maijoor, S. (1997) "The Structure of the Belgian Audit Market: the Effects of Client Concentration and Capital Market Activity," *International Journal of Auditing*, 1(2): 151–62.

Vanstraelen, A. (2002) "Auditor Economic Incentives and Going-Concern Opinions in a Limited Litigious Continental European Business Environment: Empirical Evidence from Belgium," *Accounting and Business Research*, 32(3): 171–86.

Weets, V. and Jegers, M. (1997) "Are the 'Big Six' 'Big' in Belgium?" *The European Accounting Review*, 6(4): 773–89.

Willekens, M. and Achmadi, C. (2003) "Pricing and Supplier Concentration in the Private-Client Segment of the Audit Market," *International Journal of Accounting*, 38(4): 431–56.

Willekens, M., Bruynseels, L., and Heiremans, A. (2005) "Corporate Governance en Risicomanagement: empirische evidentie voor België," *Accountancy & Bedrijfskunde*, March.

Willekens, M. and Gaeremynck, A. (2005) *Prijszetting in de Belgische Auditmarkt*, Brussels, Bruges: Instituut der Bedrijfsrevisoren & die Keure.

Willekens, M. and Sercu, P. (2005) *Corporate Governance at the Crossroads*, Antwerp, Oxford: Intersentia Publishers.

3   An account of accountants

Audit regulation and the audit profession in Denmark

Claus Holm and Bent Warming-Rasmussen

1 Introduction

In Denmark, as in the rest of Europe, audits by independent auditors became required by law as a consequence of the Industrial Revolution. Denmark had been a distinctly agricultural country, and trade and industry had primarily consisted of small craft businesses. The growth of industry, which used external capital in the form of loans and stock, caused the need for a competent and independent audit.

Serious political initiatives to ensure a law-required (statutory) audit and the foundation of the audit profession were therefore first taken around the turn of the nineteenth century. For a few years the implementation of a law was blocked by Minister of Justice Alberti, who later turned out to be an accomplice in Denmark's, until then, largest business scandal. The minister was convicted by a State Court and sentenced to eight years in prison for fraud amounting to 20 percent of the yearly state revenues at that time. After the Alberti scandal, legislation was quickly prepared, so that the first Danish act exclusively concerning auditors (LAR 1909) came into effect on 14 May 1909 (Christensen 2000: 17).

The 1909 act was fairly brief and consisted of requirements for an auditor's integrity, competency, and independence, plus some penal provisions. An authorized auditor should be of age, his estate could not be under legal restraint, and he should have led an "honest course of life" (integrity). To become an authorized auditor one was required to work for an authorized auditor for at least three years and to pass an oral and a written exam given by the Accountancy Committee[1] (competence). An authorized auditor was not allowed to take public office or any other paid public employment. Furthermore, in 1913 it was added that the auditor could not be employed in certain branches of business that were deemed incompatible with the audit profession (independence). Already at that time the penal provisions authorized the courts to revoke an auditor's right to exercise his profession.

The 1909 act came about in the wake of an extensive business scandal and as an answer to the demand for independent and competent control of a company's financial statements, in order to regain the public's trust in those statements. Auditing for fraud and embezzlement was not made an explicit requirement under the act, even though the business scandal involving Minister Alberti had concerned just that.

The audit profession developed *pari passu* with the spreading of the Industrial Revolution in Denmark. During the first two years after the implementation of the 1909 act, 21 auditors were authorized by a transitional provision. In 1924 there were some 37 practicing authorized auditors, spread over 31 audit firms. Altogether, these firms employed a staff of 93 people. In the 1950s there were about 400 practicing authorized auditors, in approximately 240 firms. The firms employed about 1,200-1,400 people (Christensen 2000: 19).

In 1930 the status of the authorization had been tied to the state through the Act on State Authorized Public Accountants (LSR 1930), i.e. identifying the official title of the "state authorized auditor" (SR: Statsautoriseret Revisor). The lifespan of the 1930 act was very short (one year); the requirements were lifted into other laws. An exclusive auditor law was not re-established until 1967 with the Act on State Authorized Public Accountants (LSR 1967). In the 1960s the need for auditors increased so rapidly that the traditional education system could no longer meet the demand for State Authorized Public Accountants (because of the very strict competency requirements). The Danish government therefore introduced a second protected profession with fewer educational requirements. By establishing another protected title, the Certified Public Accountant (RR: Registreret Revisor), the 1970 act (LRR 1970) implemented the two-tier system that still exists in Denmark. Both categories of auditors grew in number and by the year 2000 there were approximately 2,000 practicing State Authorized Public Accountants, spread over some 450 firms, employing a staff of about 9,000 people. In the same year Certified Public Accountants numbered approximately 4,400, in 1,140 certified public accountancy firms, employing a staff of about 4,000 people (Christensen 2000: 18). Since then, the number of SR-auditors has been stable, while the number of RR-auditors fell to approximately 2,670 in 2004.[2]

The foreign reader might be surprised by the large number of auditors with protected titles, given the relatively small size of the country with only 5.3 million inhabitants. The primary reason for this large number is that all limited companies were required by law to be subjected to statutory audits of their financial statements (see Table 3.1). Denmark had until 2006 required statutory audits for all "small enterprises." Apart from Denmark, Malta and Sweden, all other EU member countries had to some extent utilized the exemption possibility in the EU Annual Accounts Directive. The Danish Commerce and Companies Agency (DCCA) estimates that some 90 percent of small companies in the EU are exempt from statutory auditing (DCCA 2005: 3).

Another distinctive characteristic was implemented in Danish audit laws in 1994: the auditor is considered to be a "confidential agent of the community" (Johansen *et al.* 2003: 64). This role of the auditor applies to any statement or report the auditor is required by law to sign or to any statement or report which is not just meant for the principal's own use (Erkl.bek. 1996: § 1). The new broader responsibility was implemented as a direct result of the 1990 bankruptcy of

Table 3.1 Annual report reporting classes, number of enterprises and audit
requirements

	Class A Single proprietorships and certain very small enterprises	Class B Small enterprises	Class C Medium-sized enterprises	Class C Large enterprises	Class D Listed companies and state-owned enterprises
Balance sheet total	DKK0–6m	DKK0–29m	DKK29–119m	>DKK119m	
Revenue	DKK0–12m	DKK0–58m	DKK58–238m	>DKK238m	All irrespective of size
Average no. of full-time employees	0–10	0–50	50–250	> 250	
Approximate no. of enterprises (2005)	300,000	130,000	6,500		250
Annual report	Voluntary	Mandatory	Mandatory	Mandatory	Mandatory
Audit	Voluntary	Mandatory*	Mandatory	Mandatory	Mandatory

Sources: DCCA (2005) and AARL (2004).

Note: €1 = DKK7.5.
    * From 1 January 2006 approximately 7,500 small enterprises were exempt from audits.

Nordic Feather Inc. (Nordisk Fjer), the biggest Danish business scandal in recent
history. The unexpected bankruptcy sent shock waves through Danish business
life, and several auditors and audit firms were involved. The explicit goal of the
amendment to the 1994 act was to re-establish the public's trust in financial
statements and in auditors. In combination with stricter rules on independence,
the amendment was an expression of the idea that "auditing is a necessary
function for society and its results are not just in the auditor's client's own
interests, but also have substantial interest for a long line of other parties" (own
translation from Langsted 2000: 91). An auditor shall therefore take into account
the users' reasonable information needs when auditing/issuing an audit report on
a company's financial statements, or when issuing reports on written materials
meant for people other than the principal.

By the end of the 1990s the public was increasingly demanding that Denmark
adopt the international accounting and auditing standards. Since 2005 listed
companies in Denmark have been required to issue financial reports at group
level in compliance with International Financial Reporting Standards (IFRSs).
The International Standards on Auditing (ISAs) will be implemented gradually in
Denmark from 2002 to 2006, concurrent with their translation into Danish.

The debate about and the recognition of the necessity of following the
international trend in audit regulation have brought about another update. In the
Danish Act on State Authorized and Certified Public Accountants (LBR 2003),
laws for the two groups of auditors in Denmark were for the first time combined
in one single law. A remarkable change is that auditors are now allowed to be

active in business other than auditing and related consultancy activities. The especially stringent rules, originating in the first Danish act on authorized auditors from 1909, forbidding an auditor to take public office or to work in other lines of business, such as the real estate business, have thereby been repealed. At the same time, auditing firms were allowed to engage in any consultancy business for which they had/could obtain the necessary competence, although they naturally had to observe the independence rules. The new act states: "An auditor is not allowed to perform tasks (to issue reports not limited to the principal's own use) if there are circumstances that may raise doubts about his independence in the eyes of a well-informed third party" (LBR 2003: § 11).

An auditor's consultancy services used to be limited by law to consultancy work on audits and related disciplines. The liberalization of the Act on State Authorized and Certified Public Accountants happened simultaneously with the Enron scandal in the US and the subsequent demise of audit firm (Arthur) Andersen. The resulting public debate meant that certain limitations were reimplemented. The rules of independence relating to a specific client were made stricter for companies that are considered to have a special interest for society.[3] This means, for example, that internal auditor rotation within the audit firm is required every seven years, just as it is now forbidden for an auditor to participate in the client's bookkeeping or in the drawing up of documents on which the auditor (or a member of his team) is to issue a report. Furthermore, the auditor or any other member of the audit firm is not allowed to sign a company's financial statements, when they have compiled a list of candidates for recruiting purposes for crucial financial and administrative management positions in that company.[4]

The question is whether liberalizing the strict independence rules in the former Danish acts on State Authorized and Certified Public Accountants for the sake of internationalization will improve the Danish user's trust in a company's financial statements and in the auditor's report. An empirical study eliciting opinions on the independence issue from key financial statement users in Denmark indicates that the level of trust does diminish when an auditor performs non-audit services for the same client for whom he audits (Warming-Rasmussen and Jensen 2001, Quick and Warming-Rasmussen 2004).

2 Education and training

The Danish Company Accounts Act (AARL 2004: § 135.2) states that *only* a State Authorized Public Accountant (SR-auditor) or a Certified Public Accountant (RR-auditor) is allowed to perform a statutory audit on a company's financial statements in Denmark. Both titles are protected by law (LBR 2003: § 8) and both require a theoretical as well as a practical education (LBR 2003:§§ 3 and 9).

State Authorized Public Accountant (SR-auditor)

The normal way to complete the theoretical part is as follows (see Figure 3.1). After obtaining a General Certificate of Education at an Advanced Level, a bachelor's degree in business economics is required (Danish: HA, normally three years). An equivalent to the latter demand is obtained by many students through participation in four-year part-time study (Danish: HD), which is supplemented at the end by a proficiency test. Finally, the theoretical audit part is obtained through a two-year full-time master's degree (Danish: cand.merc.aud.[CMA]).

The bachelor's and master's degree are at university level; the master's degree CMA is offered by four Danish universities: the Copenhagen Business School, the University of Southern Denmark, the Aarhus School of Business, and Aalborg University. Approximately 500 new students are enrolled in CMA programs each year, but because of the strict requirements (every subject has to be passed separately) only about 350 students graduate. The CMA study consists of four main majors: auditing, accountancy, tax law, and business law. On top of these a student has to choose two elective minors within the business economics discipline. These minors can be either specializations within one of the four majors, for instance family and inheritance/succession law, or a wider orientation

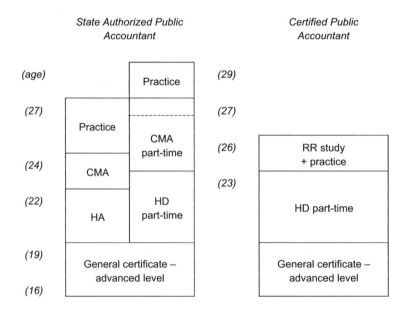

Figure 3.1 Educational optimal route for SR- and RR-auditors

Note: The optimal route is more often than not extended in time due to delays during the theoretical and/or the practical part, i.e. reflecting strict requirements for passing the exams (Holm and Steenholdt 2003).

with special modules in, for instance, marketing or organizational science. Finally, the student has to write a master's thesis within the field of business economics. To obtain the master's degree the student has to pass all the subjects separately and must score a passing grade for his thesis.

In addition to this theoretical education, the student must obtain at least three years' work experience within an audit firm. At least two out of these three practical years have to be completed after obtaining the theoretical degree. In parallel with this, the Institute for State Authorized Public Accountants (FSR)[5] offers a series of practically oriented courses, in which the auditor candidate solves a number of complicated practical cases, such as auditing financial statements in bankruptcy, auditing groups, auditing financial institutions, and so on. These courses are offered in order to ensure the necessary wide practical experience.

Finally, the auditor candidate appears before the Accountancy Committee for the practical examinations. The exam consists of both a written and an oral exam; passing the written exam gives access to the oral exam (Executive Order on Examination [Ex.bek. 2004]). This exam is also very demanding, and only about 40 percent of the students pass the exam at the first attempt. The candidate has a maximum of three chances to pass the exam. The total percentage of candidates passing the exam for SR-auditor is on average 70 percent.[6]

Certified Public Accountant (RR-auditor)

The theoretical part comprises a business economics education (Danish: HD, normally four years of part-time study). Thereafter the student follows the education for Certified Public Accountant at university level. In recent years, this education has been offered in conjunction with the CMA program, as the students have to pass the same four majors of the CMA study and finally also have to write a thesis within the field of these majors. Note that at the RR level the thesis is somewhat shorter than at the CMA levels, and that the candidates are not required to take elective minors.

The requirements for the theoretical part were implemented in 1992 with the purpose of adapting the education of Certified Public Accountants to the demands for qualified auditors as listed in the European Union's Eighth Directive. The numbers graduating as Certified Public Accountants in the wake of the new requirements have been relatively modest (about 30 students per year). The reason for this has not been researched, but it is assumed that the explanation is to be found in the increased requirements, which are now almost at the same level as the CMA program. The new rules have divided the potential candidates into three camps: those who think the theoretical level is too high and exceeds their ambitions within the audit field; those who think they might as well pursue the fullest theoretical education, if there is no real difference anyway; and finally those who think that the theoretical level is fine and conform to it.

To become a Certified Public Accountant the candidate also has to go through a period of three years working in a Certified Public Accountancy firm (or in a State Authorized Public Accountancy firm),[7] after which the candidate has to pass the exam for Certified Public Accountant set by the Accountancy Committee. The exam consists of a written and an oral test; passing the written exam gives access to the oral exam. This new intensified system turns out a mere 15 new Certified Public Accountants per year, which raises the question about the long-term viability of this group of the profession.

In spite of the overlap between the two educations, the two professions are still separate, mainly because the Institute of State Authorized Public Accountants claims that SR-auditors have significantly deeper and broader theoretical and practical skills than RR-auditors.

Gender division

Women make up about 30 percent of the students enrolling in the studies in question at commercial colleges or universities today. The proportion of female students studying for a CMA was approximately 5 percent in 1986, but rose continuously from 1986 until 1990. Since 1990 the percentage of female students has been relatively stable at about 25-30 percent (Rindom 2001: 6). Strangely enough, this increase cannot be seen to the same degree in the Accountancy Committee's examination for State Authorized Public Accountant, and it is even less evident in the number of female partners in audit firms. The first female SR-auditor passed her practical exam in 1934, and it took another 17 years before the second woman passed the exam. In the 1960s the annual number of female SR-auditors rose to an average of 10, which was about 3–7 percent of the total number of students passing the exam. In the period 1990 to 2000 the percentage has been relatively stable at 12 percent.

In-service training

Both the Institute for State Authorized Public Accountants and the Institute for Certified Public Accountants (FRR)[9] offer a wide range of in-service training. These courses are voluntary. The big audit firms offer their employees their own in-service training programs that are more or less compulsory.

3 Audit firm structure and services provided

In recent years the concentration of audit firms in Denmark has been rather stable. Audit firm concentration for the period 1998–2004 is compared in Table 3.2 using revenue for all services provided as a size measure. The rank and combined rank are compared to the total revenue for the top one to twenty audit firms. The table indicates that the concentration of the total market has increased for the top one to four from 67 percent to 72 percent over the period. However,

Table 3.2 Audit firm revenues for all services (Index Top 1–20 = 100)

Firm	1998	1999	2000	2001	2002	2003	2004
1	21	21	23	24	26	26	27
2	18	20	19	19	20	20	20
3	17	17	19	19	16	17	16
4	11	10	9	9	10	9	9
Top 1–4	67	68	71	71	72	71	72
Top 1–6	81	82	81	81	83	82	82
Top 1–10	91	91	90	91	91	91	91
Top 1–20	100	100	100	100	100	100	100

Source: Compiled from BN (2000), BN (2002), BN (2003) and BN (2005)

the percentages are rather stable both the audit firms in the top one to six (approx. 82 percent) and for those in the top one to ten (approx. 91 percent).

Over the period, revenue has increased steadily as demonstrated in Table 3.3. Considering the audit firm revenue development for the period 1998–2004, it is clear that the increase in revenue has been bigger for the top one to four than for the top one to twenty audit firms. This phenomenon is further emphasized by the fact that, in 2002, PwC Management Consulting was sold. The effect on the 2001 revenue would be a drop in absolute amounts from DKK1,549 million to DKK991 million. In Table 3.3, the effect is a break in the revenue development for the following years when looking at the top one to four companies.

The most recent overview of the structure of the Danish audit market is provided in Table 3.4, which ranks the twenty largest audit firms by revenue for all services provided in 2004. In Denmark, Deloitte became the largest audit firm after the merger with (Arthur) Andersen in 2002. The number of employees in audit firms has actually decreased in recent years, contributing to a higher revenue per employee ratio. Two audit firms have reached the magical one million DKK per employee, namely KPMG and Grant Thornton. Both revenue and the number of SR-auditors in the largest audit firms stand out for Deloitte, KPMG,

Table 3.3 Audit firm revenues: development 1998–2004 (Index 2004 = 100)

Firm	1998	1999	2000	2001	2002	2003	2004
1	64	71	82	90	94	94	100
2	72	90	90	98	97	97	100
3	85	94	109	117	97	99	100
4	94	102	95	95	99	98	100
1–4	75	85	92	99	96	97	100
1–6	78	89	92	100	96	97	100
1–10	80	90	93	100	96	97	100
1–20	80	89	93	101	96	97	100

Source: Source: Compiled from BN (2000), BN (2002), BN (2003) and BN (2005)

Table 3.4 Audit firm structure 2004: the twenty largest audit firms by revenue

	Audit firm	Revenue (DKKm)	Revenue per empl. (DKK 1,000)	No. of employees	No. of SR aud.	No. of partners	No. of cities	No. of public limited co. clients	No. of listed clients
1	Deloitte	1,718	900	1,908	317	248	19	5,188	85
2	KPMG	1,272	1,027	1,239	228	176	19	na	100
3	PricewaterhouseCoopers	1,046	827	1,265	230	157	18	4,500	64
4	Ernst & Young	592	841	704	126	99	8	2,505	35
5	BDO ScanRevision	438	665	658	105	45	29	na	23
6	Mortensen & Beierholm	238	710	335	56	40	13	1,350	13
7	Kommunernes Revision	183	579	316	41	0	17	na	na
8	Grant Thornton	156	1,040	150	40	19	2	556	32
9	RSM plus	129	611	211	30	27	9	384	3
10	H. Martinsen	89	639	140	20	18	6	na	na
11	AP Statsautoriserede Revisorer	77	752	102	15	9	2	350	3
12	Partner Revision	74	623	119	15	14	9	na	na
13	Revisionsinstituttet	72	655	110	12	12	5	104	0
14	Nielsen & Christensen	72	640	112	25	19	5	432	5
15	Andersen Hübertz Kirkhoff	58	754	77	14	14	1	317	2
16	Leo Olsen & Dalgaard	55	665	83	12	14	5	289	1
17	Info:Revision	52	693	75	11	9	1	285	0
18	Brandt & Sigsten Pedersen	50	667	75	13	11	6	246	na
19	S.A. Christensen & W. Kjærulff	49	751	65	17	9	1	263	3
20	Kresten Foged	39	899	43	8	6	1	na	2
	Total – Top 20	6,458	829	7,787	1,335	946			

Source: Compiled from BN (2005)

and PricewaterhouseCoopers. This suggests a top three structure (rather than a top four structure) in the top tier of the Danish audit market. KPMG and Deloitte dominated the auditing of listed companies in 2004. The number of listed companies as audit clients should be considered in the light of the Danish requirement for two auditors on such engagements; in a sense this could be seen as counting double when looking at the actual number of listed companies. Historically, this requirement was considered part of the higher demands toward these public companies. However, the requirement was abolished for the year 2005 and forward. The arguments for the abolition were a matter of both price and quality. Presumably, having one auditor (audit firm) should allow for a more holistic approach, enhancing quality and thus trust in the audits. Nevertheless, a number of listed companies chose to continue this practice for the year 2005. Whether this will be the case only in a transition phase remains to be seen.

As indicated above, Denmark is a comparatively large audit market and regional differences do exist (see Table 3.5). The Copenhagen area is home to a considerable number of the enterprises in Denmark, i.e. 43 percent of the entire

Table 3.5 Number of clients and market shares by percentage of clients

	Number of clients			Small client market share (percentage of small clients)		Large client market share (percentage of large clients)
	Small enterprises (< 100 employees)	*Large enterprises (> 100 employees)*	*Total*	*By top 5 audit firms (%)*	*By top 20 audit firms (%)*	*By top 5 audit firms (%)*
Copenhagen area	50,684	1,385	52,069	27.5	45.0	70.8
Rest of the country	68,170	1,967	70,137	43.6	70.6	76.1
Total	118,854	3,352	122,206	36.7	59.7	73.9

Source: Compiled from BN (2005)

Note: In this table "Top five" and "top 20" audit firms include national audit firm networks. The enterprises in this table consist of public limited and private limited companies.

population of public limited and private limited companies. Table 3.5 also indicates that small clients to a large extent are serviced by smaller audit firms. In this table, a "small" company is classified as having fewer than 100 employees and a "large" company as having more than 100 employees. The market share for small clients is 27.5 percent in the Copenhagen area, while the market share for large clients is 70.8 percent. The composition of the top five audit firms actually differs across different regions in Denmark (not shown in the table). When comparing the Copenhagen area with the rest of the country as a whole, it is obvious that the top five audit firms hold a larger market share of clients (both small and large clients) outside the Copenhagen area.

In Denmark a possible abolition of statutory audits on small enterprises has been considered at the moment. Small companies are primarily private limited companies and limited liability companies which for two consecutive years do not exceed two of the following criteria: (a) a balance sheet total of DKK29 million, (b) a net revenue of DKK58 million, and (c) an average number of full-time employees of 50. These companies fall within reporting class B of the Danish Financial Statements Act, which comprises a total of 130,000 companies. Of these, 80,000 have actual operating activities, while 50,000 are holding companies, brass-plate companies, etc. without independent operating activities (DCCA 2005: 2). In a report on the auditing requirement for B Enterprises (Small Companies), the Danish Commerce and Companies Agency has estimated the total cost (in terms of aggregated audit fees) at DKK1.7 billion (DCCA 2005: 2). Apart from the political aim of reducing the costs and paperwork of smaller enterprises, the question was also raised as to whether it makes sense to let the strengthened requirements of the new auditing standards be applied to small enterprises.

In the report by DCCA (2005: 6) four alternatives were considered:

(1) Introduce limits for net revenue, balance sheet total, and number of employees. If the companies are below two of these three limits, they are exempt from statutory auditing. This is the model used by the EU countries.
(2) Replace the statutory auditing requirement with a less extensive control by an auditor (e.g. a review).
(3) Abolish or relax the auditing requirement for private limited companies.
(4) A *quid pro quo* policy: the philosophy behind this alternative is that companies could be exempted from statutory auditing if they show a willingness and ability to keep their annual and tax accounts in order. On the other hand, if companies do not show this willingness and ability, their accounts will continue to be subject to control by an auditor.

In the report by DCCA (2005), the use of auditors by small enterprises was examined (see Table 3.6). Only 10 percent of small enterprises use the auditors exclusively for the purpose of statutory audits. The auditors provide a number of services, where assistance with the preparation of accounts is very predominant for small enterprises (83 percent on average). The companies were also asked whether the statutory audits should be abolished. As indicated in Table 3.7, 29 percent are against while 59 percent are for either a voluntary system or a relaxation of the current system. The answers provided in Table 3.7 suggest that company size does seem to matter within the population of small enterprises, i.e.

Table 3.6 Use of auditors by Class B small enterprises

Revenue (DKKm)	Only statutory audits (%)	Book-keeping (%)	Assistance with preparation of accounts (%)	Tax assistance (%)	Other advisory services (%)
Holding companies, etc.	12	18	83	62	23
<0.5	16	19	76	53	28
0.5–1.9	15	22	80	61	33
2–4.9	4	19	91	72	49
5–11.9	4	18	90	73	53
12–25	3	7	83	81	52
25>	5	8	75	78	70
Not stated	9	14	91	77	32
Total	10	18	83	66	43

Source: DCCA (2005: 20, N = 655)

Table 3.7 Should the auditing requirement be abolished or relaxed? The opinions of companies, percentage distribution

Revenue (DKKm)	No.	Should be voluntary	Relaxed	Don't know
Holding companies, etc.	27	35	30	9
<0.5	33	26	29	12
0.5–1.9	25	30	32	14
2–4.9	30	28	29	14
5–11.9	32	24	28	16
12–25	33	29	19	19
25>	48	23	20	10
Not stated	25	13	33	29
Total	29	30	29	13

Source: DCCA (2005: 23, N = 655)

48 percent of the "biggest" small enterprises are against the abolition of statutory audits. As can be seen, the number of statutory audits will shrink significantly if the requirement for small enterprise audits is abolished. The fee consequences will reflect the chosen alternative, i.e. the effect of part abolition with an exemption from audits for 7,500 small enterprises from 1 January 2006. However, the consequences for the total audit firm market might not be as harsh in the light of other services provided (see Table 3.6) and the new liberalizations related to other services.

4 Auditing standard setting

Historically, the standard setting process in Denmark has been inspired by national as well as international developments. As has been the case in other countries, the international element has been dominant in recent years, but national regulations and institutional particularities still influence the standard setting process.

Regarding the institutional background, the process has been driven by one of two private member organizations for the profession. The member organizations reflect the two-stringed qualification system for SR-auditors and RR-auditors. The standard setting process has been dominated by the Institute of State Authorized Public Accountants in Denmark (FSR). Although membership is voluntary, the SR-membership percentage is 95. At present both accounting guidelines and auditing standards are based on FSR activities, although the procedures are not the same for the two fields. For example, accounting guidelines must be submitted to a public hearing process, while this is not typical when implementing auditing standards.[9]

The development of auditing standards can be interpreted as a manifestation of an awareness of the professional responsibility to ensure and contribute to the fulfillment of general and specific audit obligations (FSR Statutes 2003: § 2).

With a high level of membership and an awareness of the responsibility to self-regulate, the Institute has acquired a proprietary role in the national context which it is maintaining in the new context of adopting international auditing standards as national standards.

Danish auditing standards (RSs)[10] are now based on the International Standards on Auditing (ISAs) issued by the International Federation of Accountants (IFAC) through the International Auditing and Assurance Standards Board (IAASB). The international standards are translated section by section and only special regulations in the Danish legislation are added. Hence most of the Danish standards and the international standards are directly comparable. In three distinct areas additional national auditing standards have been issued, i.e. RS 265 related to communication with the client through the use of long form audit reports ("audit protocols"), RS 585 related to the section in the annual report containing "the management report" or "Management's Discussion and Analysis," because of the special Danish requirement for the auditor to issue an opinion on the full set of information comprised by the annual report and not only the financial statements,[11] and, finally, RS 635 on "the cooperation between two appointed auditors," reflecting the possibility of having two auditors who have to issue a joint opinion on the full annual report.[12]

It is necessary to distinguish between regulation through law and regulation through standards. A private organization cannot issue legally binding regulations. It is, of course, possible to issue rules of conduct for members of an organization, but the aim and the practical application of audit guidelines go far beyond the statutory rules of the organization (Langsted *et al.* 2003: 82). The purpose of standards is, of course, "to set a standard." As such, the standard should be shared by the key stakeholders in order to serve the public interest. This perspective is an explicit objective for the standard setting process as stated in the mission statement by IAASB: "Establishing high quality auditing standards and guidance for financial statement audits that are generally accepted and recognized by investors, auditors, governments, banking regulators, securities regulators and other key stakeholders across the world" (IFAC 2004: 122).

In relation to regulating the expected work of the profession, a standard should also set a benchmark for good audit practice, i.e. enhancing the quality and uniformity of practice. As explained in an earlier section, audit regulation in Denmark has been founded in law since 1909. This regulation does not describe what the auditors should do, but the law sets forth certain requirements for the tasks handled by auditors. The present law stipulates that audits should be conducted with due consideration of "the care, precision and speed required by the task," and "in accordance with good auditor practice" (LBR 2003: § 2.2). Hence, "good auditor practice" is established as a legal requirement to be met not only by law and court rulings, but also by the profession. Thus audit regulation through standards is accepted (given relevance) as the profession is expected to self-regulate proactively through auditing standards.[13]

The timeline for the standard setting process in Denmark is shown in Table 3.8 below. The timeline indicates the major transitions in the process, and the three periods will be described in more detail below. From the first national guideline issued in 1978 until the decision in 2000 to change to international auditing standards, the process was influenced by national considerations. The change from a primarily national to an international context was decided at the general assembly meeting of FSR in May/June 2000. At the same time, the term "standards" (Danish: "standarder") was adopted instead of "guidelines" (Danish: "vejledninger"). The period up to 2000 is subdivided into two main parts, in order to get a sense of the pace and focus of prior contemplations.

One new audit guideline was typically issued every year in the period 1978-1990. Exceptions were 1981 with three and 1989 with four new guidelines. Three of the early guidelines (early 1980s) were inspired by Auditing Statements issued by the Auditing Statements Board of the "Union Européen des Experts Comptables Economiques et Financiers" (UEC). As a member of this organization, FSR was required to forward the statements to the membership body. In this period three of the statements were translated and provided with interpretive comments. The three statements were UEC AS number 2 (on the use of other auditors' work), number 4 (on going concern), and number 6 (on quality control).

Although the first Danish guideline was on the general principles of auditing, the later guidelines typically concentrated on special issues like the use of other auditors' work. In 1983 the membership of the International Federation of Accountants (IFAC) is mentioned for the first time in the preamble to the guidelines. From then on the wording was that FSR is a member of UEC[14] and of IFAC and is therefore required to publish the guidelines of these organizations. In contrast to the current situation, it was explicitly stated that the international guidelines should not be taken as an expression of good audit practice in Denmark.

In the period 1991–2000, the number of new guidelines decreased in favour of revising existing guidelines. This development partly reflected the general concern regarding the expectation gap. This awareness could be seen as a parallel

Table 3.8 Timeline for auditing standard setting in Denmark, 1978–2004

1978–1990	*1991–2000*	*2001–2004*
17 new audit guidelines (Revisionsvejledning 1-17)	4 new audit guidelines (Revisionsvejledning 18-21)	31 new national auditing standards 6 practice statements
1 revised audit guideline	10 revised audit guidelines	
		8 remaining audit guidelines (to be replaced in 2004/05)

to the issue of a set of expectation gap standards in the US. In addition, the development reflects the implementation of requirements as stated in changing audit laws (reflecting the implementation of directives). Most explicitly, this is seen in the rapid changes to the guideline on the audit report (guideline number 7). This guideline was first issued in 1982 and has been revised several times, i.e. in 1988, 1991, and again in 1996, to reflect new audit law and, of course, new developments in audit practice.

In the period 2001–4, the standard setting process has shifted direction and pace. With the FSR decision to adopt ISAs through translation, the direction was shifted from a primarily national to an international perspective on good audit practice. The pace has shifted compared to the prior periods too. A total of 28 new national auditing standards (Revisionsstandarder)[15] have been issued with implementation dates between 1 January 2003 and 30 June 2004. Fifteen of these are brand new standards in a Danish context, and 13 have replaced existing audit guidelines. In addition, six practice statements (Revisionsudtalelser)[16] have been issued between January 2001 and April 2004. As a natural consequence of the enormous workload, the task of translating the International Audit Practice Statements (IAPSs) has been given second priority to the auditing standards, although the work has been initiated. The status of the standard setting process in 2004 was that eight audit guidelines were still in force. In 2005 three additional auditing standards were implemented leaving 12 IASs to be translated. In addition the work on revising the already implemented standards in line with the audit risk standards has been done (i.e. having an effect on almost 20 standards [FSR Annual Report 2005]).

As mentioned above, FSR has taken a proprietary role in relation to the standard setting process. As an example of this role, the publication of auditing standards is postponed in relation to the public until one month after the annual general assembly of FSR. Even though the auditing standards are issued on behalf of both member organizations (FSR and FRR), the responsibility for developing and finally approving the standards is under the auspices of a committee of the FSR. Formally, the auditing standards are termed "the auditing standards of the technical audit committee" (Revisionsteknisk udvalg's revisionsstandarder). The board of FSR appoints this committee on technical audit matters. The committee has up to seven members and appoints its own chairman and vice-chairman (FSR Statutes 2003: § 23.1). Earlier the committee was directly elected by the annual general assembly of FSR. The need for ensuring a suitable composition of the committee and the required shift in pace of the auditing standard process may have influenced this change.

The declared purpose of issuing auditing standards (RSs) is that Danish audit practice should develop in accordance with international audit practice as embodied in the international auditing standards (ISAs) issued by the International Federation of Accountants (IFAC) through the International Auditing and Assurance Standards Board (IAASB). Through their IFAC membership, FSR and FRR are required to support IFAC in the ongoing efforts for development and enhancement of an audit profession with harmonized standards, capable of providing services of consistently high quality in the public interest.

On behalf of the Institute the committee submits auditing standards (RSs) which are based on the International Standards on Auditing (ISAs) issued by the International Federation of Accountants (IFAC) (FSR Statutes 2003: § 23.2.) The auditing standards are translated section by section and only in the case of more strict legal requirements are any special regulations in the Danish legislation added (and marked clearly in italics). Hence most of the Danish standards and the international standards are directly comparable. In addition, RSs are issued in areas not covered by ISAs. At the moment, RS 265, 585, and 635 are examples.

Auditing standard drafts are issued to each of the members of FSR and to FRR for a minimum hearing period of three months. The committee is allowed on its own judgment to submit the drafts for hearing among other interest groups (FSR Statutes 2003: § 23.3). At the end of the hearing period the committee evaluates the text of the draft in the context of the comments received during the hearing process (FSR Statutes 2003: § 23.4). The draft is approved by the members of the committee with a two-thirds majority vote (i.e. with a minimum of five of seven members) and is thereafter issued as the particular auditing standard of the committee (FSR Statutes 2003: § 23.5). In the case of revisions required by law or as a result of changes in ISAs (if not altering the real contents of the RS), the committee is granted the right to change the text with the same majority vote, but without adhering to the hearing and publication procedures for a new standard (FSR Statutes 2003: § 23.6.)

Both SR- and RR-auditors are expected not to violate the requirements set forth in the auditing standards. In cases of obvious violations the matter can be referred to the disciplinary system (see also sections 5 and 6). On the other hand, it is impossible to establish auditing standards for all situations and conditions that an auditor might face. In the preface to the Danish auditing standards, it is stated that the auditor should consider the approved standards as the fundamental principles to be applied. It is up to the individual auditor to use his professional judgment in order to decide exactly which procedures are necessary in order to apply these standards, because this will be contingent on the specific conditions of the individual engagement. This emphasis on professional judgment could be considered to be in contradiction to the strict rule of adherence to the standards. The translated section 17 of the preface to the set of auditing standards clearly states that:

> The nature of the IAASB's Standards requires professional auditors to exercise professional judgment in applying them. In exceptional circumstances, a professional auditor may judge it necessary to depart from a basic principle or essential procedure of an Engagement Standard to achieve more

effectively the objective of the engagement. When such a situation arises, the professional auditor should be prepared to justify the departure.

(IFAC 2004: 128)

Hence, a departure should be seen as exceptional and must be justified. However ,you may also view the emphasis put forth by FSR as having a wider scope reflecting a principle-based interpretation of the standards. In effect, the standards are seen as holding principles in relation to which the auditor has to meet the requirements by using his professional judgment regarding the choice of the specific procedures needed.

In 2004 the European Commission issued a proposal for a new and modernized Eighth Directive on Statutory Audit in the European Communities.[17] One of the central articles in the proposal states that member states shall require statutory auditors and audit firms to carry out statutory audits in accordance with the ISAs and that the Commission, under certain conditions, shall adopt the standards for application in the Community.[18] Member states are expected to adopt the provisions necessary to comply with the directive (some time within 2006–7).[19] Given the current status of the translation project, this will be without problems from a standard setting perspective. A remaining challenge in the standard setting process is to address small statutory audits in practice. Due to the new requirements in the auditing standards many small company audits may in reality be better suited for reviews instead. However, reviews cannot replace statutory audits as long as these are required by law. Is the profession ready to handle the challenge (including the issue of what should be the authoritative text) in small as well as large audits?

5 Ethics

Ethics is a philosophy which defines right and wrong behavior. As a consequence, the formulation of ethical rules for a profession, in this case the audit profession, is an attempt to regulate the behavior of the members of the profession.

In Denmark the rules for right auditor behavior are fundamentally formulated in the Act on State Authorized and Certified Public Accountants (LBR 2003). The act stipulates strict requirements in three areas, namely competence, integrity, and independence – as regards both being qualified for and being able to function as an SR- or RR-auditor. First, the requirements for competence are stated in § 3 and primarily list the demands for theoretical and practical education (see section 2). Second, the requirements for integrity are also stated in § 3 and primarily list the requirements for an auditor's standing, i.e. an auditor has to be of age, he cannot be under suspension of payments or be bankrupt, he cannot have a due debt of DKK50,000 or more to the state, and, finally, according to § 3.5, authorization can be denied if he does not have a clean criminal record[20] and he must have conducted his business in such a way that there is no reason to assume that he will perform his main tasks as an auditor in a reckless manner.

Third, the requirements for independence are mainly found in § 11 (LBR 2003).[21] This paragraph states that an auditor cannot perform audits and issue audit reports where there are circumstances that may raise doubts about the auditor's independence in the eyes of a well-informed third party. The 2003 act lists a number of cases where – according to the law – such circumstances exist. Mainly, it prohibits the auditor or members of his audit team from auditing a company's financial statements when named persons are closely related through family ties to the client company's management or to persons who have a controlling influence on the client company's economic affairs. Auditing is also prohibited where named persons have economic interests in the client company. The act further stipulates that the client company cannot have economic interests in the audit firm or have the right to appoint members of the board in the audit firm. A set of particularly strict rules has been drawn up for companies with a special interest for society[22] (FSR ethical code draft 2004: section 63), namely strict prohibitions against participating in the client's bookkeeping or similar records on which the statements or reports of the auditor are founded. Likewise, an auditor must refrain from auditing these companies if he has participated in recruiting employees for crucial financial and administrative management positions in the client company in the previous two years (LBR 2003: § 11.8).

Apart from the above, the 2003 act lists a series of circumstances that *could* cause independence problems (LBR 2003: § 11.3). Circumstances that *could* raise doubts exist when an auditor or a member of his audit team performs such tasks for the client company that in effect he or she is performing a self-review, or when he or she has performed an advocating role for the client within the previous two years. The audit firm has to implement guidelines to ensure that an auditor always has to consider, before taking on an audit task, whether there are any circumstances which could raise doubts about the independence of the people involved (LBR 2003: § 11.4).

As mentioned in section 1, rotation of auditors internally in the audit firm is required no later than seven years after the appointment of the responsible auditor in the case of companies with a special interest for society (LBR 2003: § 10.2). For at least two years following the rotation, the auditor is not allowed to provide any services for this client (cooling down period). Further, §§ 13.1 and 13.2 (LBR 2003) state that the total audit fee from any individual client cannot exceed 20 percent of the audit firm's total turnover for more than three consecutive years. For tasks where the auditor has to issue a report that is meant not just for the principal's own use, he cannot demand a higher fee for his work than can be considered reasonable. Nor is he allowed to make the payment or size of his fee dependent on other circumstances than the work performed (no cure–no pay condition is not allowed).

As indicated, the material components of auditor ethics in Demark are regulated by law. In addition, FSR in May 2005 has adopted IFAC's Code of Ethics. The first draft of the Danish translation of the Code of Ethics (Retningslinjer for revisors etiske adfærd) was completed in May 2004. IFAC's ethical rules are toughened, though, where Danish law is more restrictive than international rules. The most characteristic example of this is § 21 in the new ethics code, which imposes a duty on auditors to report economic crimes directly to the Public Prosecutor for Special Economic Crimes (Statsadvokaten for Særlig Økonomisk Kriminalitet) where a majority of the board of directors and management of the audited company is involved or has knowledge of these economic crimes. This clause originates from the latest update to the Danish Act on State Authorized and Certified Public Accountants of 2003, whereby Parliament imposed a duty on auditors to counteract economic crime (LBR 2003: § 10.6).

Finally, since the foundation of the Institute, FSR has had a series of rules in its statutes aimed at creating and maintaining the good reputation of FSR members. Among other things these rules formerly prohibited advertising by the audit firm and a firm's uninvited soliciting of a colleague's employees or clients. These rules were repealed in 1994 as being out of date (Jensen and Warming-Rasmussen 2000: 216). Only the general rule is still valid, namely the one that prohibits members from causing "one's colleagues substantial economic or non-economic damage by improper behaviour, such as uttering false or misleading statements, or from causing an obvious danger of this...." (FSR Statutes 2003: §§ 3 and 4). The remaining statutes are therefore mainly meant to regulate ethics between colleagues.

6 Oversight system

The two sets of recommendations from the EU Commision on quality assurance[23] and on auditor independence,[24] respectively, were adopted through the revision in 2003 of the laws regulating auditing in Denmark. As explained earlier, the regulation of the two groups of auditors was combined in one single law (LBR 2003), which has had several implications for the supervision and control of the audit profession in Denmark. First, public oversight on quality control requirements has been introduced through a brand new institution, i.e. the Public Oversight Board (revisortilsynet). Second, the disciplinary system has been simplified. Third, transparency has been promoted through a new more public oriented registration of all licensed auditors[25] by the Danish Commerce and Companies Agency (DCCA).[26] The current institutional environment of auditors in Denmark is presented in Figure 3.2.

Public Oversight Board

The Public Oversight Board is required to monitor quality controls in all audit firms at least once every four years. Compared to the control procedures carried out by FSR and FRR, the public controls focus more explicitly on independence issues. It is the function of the Public Oversight Board to issue guidelines for the control process and to approve the controllers' performance of the actual quality

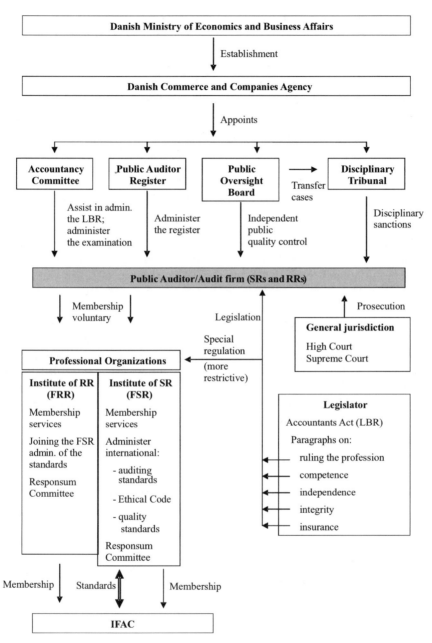

Figure 3.2 Institutional environment of auditors in Denmark

controls. In accordance with the EU recommendations, the nine members of the Public Oversight Board are predominantly non-auditors. However, it has been deemed important to have (four) auditor representatives due to their superior knowledge of the subject matter.

The new Danish system extends the EU demands for quality control from the public control of auditors of "public interest entities" (in other words, listed companies, banks, and insurance companies)[27] to all auditors interested in issuing an opinion. On the other hand, the original text of the proposal for a new directive required that only non-audit practitioners could participate in the governance of the system of public control of auditors of "public interest entities." Hence, an implementation of this proposal would demand a different composition of the Public Oversight Board or a particular composition for the quality control of audits tied to "public interest entities."

An overview of the number of accomplished quality controls in the first year of the Public Oversight Board is provided in Table 3.9. The emergence of the new public monitoring system has had immediate consequences in the form of weeding out a number of audit firms. As indicated in the table, 50 firms have decided not to continue and 27 firms have been excluded due to the lack of response to the audit firm registration system.

Table 3.10 gives an overview of the results of quality controls in 2004 by the Public Oversight Board. Of the 313 closed cases, 216 (69 percent) resulted in approval of the auditing quality system, whereas 97 cases in total carried sanctions. The harshest sanction required that the case be forwarded to the Disciplinary Tribunal together with a reprimand and a requirement for new quality control. Of the 23 cases brought to the Disciplinary Tribunal, 21 concerned audit firms with only one authorized RR-auditor.

Table 3.9 Number of quality controls accomplished in 2004 by the Public Oversight Board

Number of audit firms selected for quality control in 2004	435
- Of these, deleted from the Revireg list by the firms themselves	50
- Of these, deleted for lack of response (transferred to the DCCA authorities)	27
Number of received quality control declarations	358
- Of these, excluded due to being holding companies	17
Number of quality control declarations handled	341
- Of these, unclosed cases	28
Number of accomplished (closed) cases	313

Source: Public Oversight Board (2005: 8)

Table 3.10 Result of quality controls in 2004 by the Public Oversight Board

	Number of closed cases	*Approved*	*Sanctions*		
			Reprimand without new control	*Reprimand with new control*	*Reprimand with disciplinary tribunal and new control*
SR audit firms	72	57	4	9	2
RR audit firms	241	159	6	55	21
Total	313	216	10	64	23

Source: Public Oversight Board (2005: 8–9).

Note: The 72 SR audit firms represent 347 SR-auditors and the 241 RR firms represent 460 RR-auditors.

Quality controls by professional organizations

The new public oversight on quality control requirements must be seen as an addition to the existing quality control system for those in the profession who are State Authorized auditors. The members of FSR have for the past 11 years been subject to obligatory quality controls through their membership of the organization (see Table 3.11).

Table 3.11 Number of FSR-member audit firms subject to FSR quality control

Period	*Quality control declarations received*	*Of these, ordinary quality controls*	*Of these, renewed or supplementary controls*
First round			
June 94–May 95	75	75	–
June 95–May 96	100	100	–
June 96–May 97	188	162	26
June 97–May 98	93	41	52
Second round			
June 98–May 99	92	75	17
June 99–May 00	131	120	11
June 00–May 01	137	124	13
Third round			
June 01–May 02	116	112	4
June 02–May 03	110	101	9
June 03–May 04	113	109	4
Fourth round			
June 04–May 05	75	66	9

Source: FSR Annual Report (2005)

In accordance with the FSR statutes (2003: § 25.2), the members and the audit firms are required to submit to quality control. The FSR quality control is regulated through a set of internal guidelines and checklists. The result is summarized and publicly disclosed in a quality control report once a year. Table 3.11 gives an overview of the total number of FSR quality controls since they were initiated in 1994. During each round, all members have been subject to quality controls.

2004/05 was the first year of the fourth round. This was the first year in which the tasks related to issuing the opinion were subject to the legally required quality control by the Public Oversight Board, whereas other services provided by the audit firms were subject to the FSR quality control of member firms. The selection of audit firms for the 2004–5 FSR quality control was the same as the selection of firms for the legally required quality control by the Public Oversight Board, excluding of course a few SR firms not belonging to FSR (FSR Annual Report 2005).

The total number of audit firms belonging to FSR is 348 and the total number of State Authorized auditors belonging to FSR is 1,896 (FSR Annual Report 2005). Table 3.12 gives an overview of the results of the FSR quality control on 64 of these audit firms in 2004. The results show that for most firms (55) the quality of the professional services not covered by legal control is satisfactory. In seven audit firms (representing 11 SR-auditors) quality management was not satisfactory. Of these, six firms were requested to undergo new quality controls in 2005 due to considerable omissions. One firm was reprimanded (requested to get its quality management into full order before the next ordinary control). In two audit firms (representing two SR-auditors) supplementary information or

Table 3.12 Result of FSR quality controls 2004–5

	Total	Satisfactory	Reprimand	Renewed control	Supplementary control
Ordinary control as selected in 2004	64 firms (278 SR-auditors)	55 firms (265 SR-auditors)	1 firm (1 SR-auditor)	6 firms (10 SR-auditors)	2 firms (2 SR-auditors)
Ordinary control as selected in 2003	2 firms (2 SR-auditors)	1 firm (1 SR-auditor)	0 firms (0 SR-auditors)	0 firms (0 SR-auditors)	1 firm (1 SR-auditor)
Supplementary control as regards third round (2001–2003)	9 firms (14 SR-auditors)	6 firms (8 SR-auditors)	3 firms (6 SR-auditors)	0 firms (0 SR-auditors)	0 firms (0 SR-auditors)
Total	75 firms (294 SR-auditors)	62 firms (274 SR-auditors)	4 firms (7 SR-auditors)	6 firms (10 SR-auditors)	3 firms (3 SR-auditors)

Source: FSR Annual Report (2005)

supplementary control was requested before a final conclusion on the quality management could be issued. In addition, Table 3.12 gives an overview of the results of postponed quality controls from earlier years.

For RR-auditors quality control every five years was implemented for members of FRR in 1998.[28] With public oversight, the focus on quality control has clearly been strengthened at the audit firm level. Hence, the extension of the demand for quality control to all auditors is expected to increase quality awareness, especially among FRR firms (Seheim 2004).

Public disciplinary system

The new Public Oversight Board does not handle complaints. These are handled by the disciplinary system (see also section 7 on liability). The new audit law introduced one common tribunal for the two groups of auditors. This change can be seen as a logical conclusion to the series of adjustments to the disciplinary system.[29] Until 1967 there was no obligatory public disciplinary system in Denmark. FSR was active in supervising its members but, due to the fact that membership was not compulsory, the entire system of disciplinary observance was voluntary. With laws for the two groups of auditors, in 1967 (SR) and 1970 (RR) respectively, disciplinary committees were established. In the 1980s and at the beginning of the 1990s, strong public criticism was leveled against the disciplinary committees. The main points of criticism were that members of the profession were responsible for disciplinary observance, that sanctions against offending auditors were relatively light (e.g. the maximum penalty was only DKK5,000), and that only a select few groups were permitted to initiate disciplinary proceedings against an SR-auditor, i.e. the Danish Trade and Corporations Office, the Finance Minister, FSR, and FRR (Goldin 1997: 21).

From 1993 to 2002 a new disciplinary system consisting of two levels was implemented, reflecting the expressed points of criticism. The first level was the Disciplinary Tribunal (Disciplinærnævn), with a tribunal for each group of auditors. The second level was the Accountants Tribunal (Revisornævn). Guidelines were established to ensure that the majority was held by non-auditors at both levels. Furthermore, the legislators ensured that the penalties were made more severe and that any party with a legal interest could bring an auditor before a disciplinary court. In 2002 the disciplinary system was simplified from two levels to one. The Accountants Tribunal had functioned as a court of appeal and had had the right to revoke the auditing license. These responsibilities were now combined in the Disciplinary Tribunal. With the new 2003 act, the system was further simplified from a tribunal for each of the two groups of auditors to just one instance. With the new legal requirements, the tribunal is now also responsible for handling cases related to inappropriate quality controls. As a natural consequence of the new emphasis in the audit law on auditor tasks related to the issuing of opinions,[30] the competence of the tribunal is now focused specifically on these tasks (see Figure 3.2). The Disciplinary Tribunal handles complaints against auditors regarding inappropriate behavior, as judged against the responsibilities to be expected by auditors in particular situations (good practice). As such, the tribunal does not handle complaints about audit fees. Criminal and civil liability for damages must be determined by the court system as part of the general jurisdiction system. With the slimming down of the disciplinary system to one level, appeals against rulings made by the tribunal are also referred to general jurisdiction, i.e. to be decided at the High Court (Landsretten). A second appeal possibility to the Supreme Court (Højesteret) is theoretically available, but has never been used in the past.

The 13 members of the Disciplinary Tribunal are appointed by the DCCA, and the composition ensures a predominance of non-auditors, i.e. the chairman is a judge, six members represent the two groups of auditors, and six members represent the financial statement users.[31] In Denmark the disciplinary judgments should be made public if possible (Goldin 1997: 99–100). Traditionally the decision about publication has been made by the disciplinary courts. In recent years most cases were published (i.e. approximately 80 percent). In addition it is usual to publicize the names of the punished auditors in order to increase their punishment (Goldin 1997: 100).

The new audit act and the Disciplinary Tribunal came into force on 1 September 2003. Table 3.13 gives an overview of the cases handled by the Disciplinary Tribunal in the first periods since that date. According to the Annual Report, the total amount awarded in the first full year (2004) of the Disciplinary Tribunal was DKK390,000. In 2004 the fines ranged between DKK5,000 and DKK150,000. In comparison, the maximum fine which can be awarded by the Disciplinary Tribunal is DKK300,000 (LBR 2003: § 20.1).

Table 3.13 Cases handled by the Disciplinary Tribunal 2003–4

	New cases	Rejected cases	Cases with acquittal	Cases resulting in fines	Unclosed cases
1 September 2003–31 December 2003	10	1	1	8 (fines in total DKK200,000)	0
2004	59	8	9	35 (fines in total DKK390,000)	7

Source: Disciplinary Tribunal (2005)

Responsum and fee cases handled by the profession organizations

All disciplinary cases are handled by the courts, i.e. FSR and FRR do not have the opportunity or the means at their disposal to punish their members. The membership bodies can, however, expel members of the organization who violate quality standards (e.g. FSR statutes 2003: § 3.4). The expelled members are still able to practice because they are state authorized to do so. In relation to disciplinary complaints, the two organizations may, however, be asked to provide a "responsum," i.e. an expert opinion on good practice (audit practice, accounting practice, or auditor practice).[32] Table 3.14 gives an overview of the number of cases raised and handled by the FSR Responsum Committee in 2001–5. The year 2003 was exceptional in regard to the number of cases raised. In 2004 FSR decided to request from the complainant a charge of DKK500 for cases related to fees. The justification for this was the increased number of cases involving disagreements about fees, often regarding very small amounts (FSR Annual Report 2005). Most cases raised are related to fee issues. In the latter years approximately 30 percent of the cases have resulted in a reduction in the fee payable by the client.

Public Auditor Register

Due regard is now being given to the public interest in being able to identify potentially suspect or below-standard auditors. As mentioned above, a significant

Table 3.14 Number of cases raised and handled by the FSR Responsum Committee 2001–5

	Cases raised			Cases handled		
	Total cases	Responsum cases on good audit practice	Fee cases	Responsum cases on good audit practice	Fee cases	Of these fee decreased
March 01 –February 02	52 (100%)	13 (25%)	39 (75%)	20	41 (100%)	17 (41%)
March 02 –February 03	48 (100%)	12 (25%)	38 (75%)	11	48 (100%)	11 (23%)
March 03 –February 04	89 (100%)	27 (30%)	62 (70%)	18	34 (100%)	10 (29%)
March 04 –February 05	55 (100%)	18 (33%)	37 (67%)	15	43 (100%)	13 (30%)

Sources: FSR Annual Reports (2002, 2003, 2004 and 2005)

implication of the new audit law is the registration of all licensed auditors by DCCA. In addition to the practical purpose of keeping track of auditors in order to carry out the recurring quality controls, this facilitates transparency for potential users of the services offered by the auditors. In order to be able to offer the publicly supervised service of issuing opinions, each and every auditor is now required to be registered in the "Revireg" list, which is publicly disclosed on the DCCA website.

7 Liability

A fundamental element in the building of stakeholders' trust in professional auditors is the fact that they can be held legally accountable when they do not comply with the laws of the country (especially the ones concerning accountancy and consultancy). They also have to live up to good auditor practice, i.e. the behavioral rules stated in the auditing standards.

In Denmark an auditor can be held legally liable in three ways:

1 criminal liability (Straffeansvar);
2 civil liability (to pay damages; Erstatningsansvar);
3 disciplinary liability (disciplinær ansvar).

Criminal liability can, according to the Penal Code, result in a fine, imprisonment, or the revoking of the right to exercise a profession which requires special public authorization (STRL 2004: § 79), depending on which criminal paragraphs are broken. The main aim of criminal sanctions is to deter others from imitating the same behavior (general prevention), but also to deter the convicted party from repeating his actions (special prevention) (Langsted 2000: 194).

For a person to be convicted in a criminal court certain conditions have to be met: the auditor has to have 1) committed a criminal offence (i.e. an act that is forbidden by law), 2) with the necessary liability (which means intent or negligence), and 3) have been in a sane state of mind at the time of the offence, and there are no other circumstances exempting him from criminal liability. If the criminal offence has been committed with the intent to gain unjust profit for himself or for others, the punishment can be up to two years' imprisonment (STRL 2004: § 152).

A central criminal provision in the Penal Code concerns professional confidentiality, which forbids an auditor to use or pass on confidential client information unjustifiably (STRL 2004: § 152). Detailed rules on confidentiality can be found in the Company Act (AL 2002: § 160) and the Marketing Act (ML 2000: § 10). If these rules are broken, an auditor can be fined or imprisoned for up to six months. Confidentiality rules are suspended in a number of specific cases though, for example when a company changes auditor. In such a case the new auditor has the obligation to contact the retiring auditor and ask for the reasons why he discontinued his work for the client. The retiring auditor has the obligation to inform the new auditor of these reasons (LBR 2003: § 10.1). Another very important case is when the auditor suspects money laundering as a result of criminal offences within the company or when he suspects the financing of terrorism (Act on the Prevention of Money Laundering and the Financing of Terrorism: HVL 2004). When an auditor in good faith passes on such information to the police, confidentiality rules in the Penal Code are not considered to be broken (STRL 2004: § 152.2). Finally, there is an obligation on an auditor to report to the Public Prosecutor for Special Economic Crimes (see also section 4).

Civil action always results in a claim for financial compensation for any loss which the offender has caused the injured party. The primary goal is to settle the damage (Langsted 2000: 198). The fundamental conditions to be met for liability to pay damages are:

- there has to be a basis for liability, meaning the accused has to have acted culpably;
- there has to be necessary causality between the culpable behavior and the damage caused;
- the damage can be reasonably expected as a result of the culpable behavior;
- there has to be an economic loss, which it would be reasonable for the offender to make good.

If, for instance, an auditor breaks his oath of confidentiality, there is a possibility that the client will suffer an economic loss. First, it has to be determined that the act itself was culpable. This is the case when the auditor behaves in a way which is different from the way in which a good average auditor would behave in a similar situation; in other words, when the auditor does not act like a *"bonus pater auditor."* If the auditor has acted culpably, the next step is to determine whether there is causality between his behavior and the economic loss. The requirement for causality is not fulfilled if the damage would have occurred regardless of the auditor's behavior. The same rule applies to conditions three and four. When all four conditions are met, the auditor is liable to pay damages to the client.

Finally, one can take disciplinary action against an auditor, resulting in a warning, a reprimand, a fine, or the revoking of the right to work as an SR- or an RR-auditor. Sanctions can be a warning or a fine of up to DKK 300,000 if the case is brought against an auditor personally. If the case is brought against the audit firm as well, the firm can be fined up to DKK 750,000. Disciplinary sanctions require that the auditor has neglected the duties that accompany his profession according to the Act on State Authorized and Certified Public Accountants, hence indirectly also neglect of the requirements of auditing standards through the demand for behavior in accordance with good auditor practice. In deciding whether the auditor has neglected his duties, the Disciplinary Tribunal has to determine both whether the auditor objectively has acted differently from the way in which a good average auditor would have acted, and whether the auditor can be held accountable for acting with either intent or negligence. When deciding on the question of possible neglect, there is no condition stating that a party has to have suffered a loss of some kind because of the auditor's actions (see also section 5).

Guarantee provision and insurance

Trust in a State Authorized or Certified Public Accountant is of course not only based on the fact that one can sue for suffered economic losses. Trust is also based on a certain security that the auditor is actually capable of paying compensation for the economic losses of the clients as well as of third parties. Therefore, the Executive Order on Guarantee Provision and Liability Insurance (Gar.bek. 2003) requires the provision of a guarantee as well as liability insurance. The aim of the guarantee is that the auditor should always be able to cover financial claims as a surety if such claims are raised in relation to tasks performed as a State Authorized Accountant (Johansen *et al.* 2003: 95).

According to the Executive Order, the guarantee provision has to be at least DKK500,000 per State Authorized or Certified Public Accountant (Gar.bek. 2003: § 4), and the guarantor has to be an insurance company, a finance house, or another financial institution that provides equivalent security (Gar.bek. 2003: § 7). If the guarantee for a specific auditor is established as part of a collective agreement, then the guarantor can also be an independent fund or union. In such cases, permission has to be given by the DCCA, which reviews the security.

Furthermore, the Executive Order requires an SR- or an RR-auditor to have liability insurance for at least DKK two million (Gar.bek. 2003: § 8). Audit firms with fewer than six SR- or RR-auditors can sign individual insurance policies, where the insured amount is not accumulated. Other audit firms have to sign liability insurance with a total coverage of at least DKK two million per year, multiplied by the total number of SR- and RR-auditors in the firm. When the total number of SR- or RR-auditors in an audit firm is above 10, the liability insurance does not have to cover more than DKK 20 million.

8 Corporate governance

In line with developments around Europe, Denmark has decided on a soft-law approach to dealing with corporate governance issues. In 2001 the Danish Minister for Business and Industry sponsored an examination of the need for recommendations for good corporate governance in Denmark. The resulting report is generally referred to as the Nørby report[33] and the suggestions have since been adopted by the Copenhagen Stock Exchange as corporate governance recommendations for the companies listed on the Exchange. The Exchange appointed a committee consisting of a broad group of people to ensure the continued development of a management culture and management structures in listed companies. Based on an examination of the experience among companies, investors, auditors, and advisers, the Exchange committee published its "Report on Corporate Governance in Denmark" in January 2004. The report reflected on current international issues relating to risk management and the role of the auditor. While the (first) Nørby report did not list the latter as an explicit element, the 2004 report does include a number of recommendations related to the election of and cooperation with auditors. The suggestions of the second report have been through a hearing process, but they have not yet been adopted in the Stock Exchange recommendations. The revision of the code is awaiting a policy decision by the European Commission regarding the "comply or explain" rule.

The issues raised are not necessarily identical for all owing to the particular circumstances of Danish companies and, of course, the broader societal role (responsibility) of auditors in Denmark. Hence, current differences in Denmark can be attributed to 1) regulatory requirements in the company law, 2) the two-tier management structure, and 3) standardized communication between auditors and those charged with governance through long form audit reports (so-called protocols).

First, Danish company law has already addressed some of the problems that have attracted attention in certain other countries. Danish company law sets a framework for the tasks and responsibilities to be assigned to the supervisory board, including the chairman, and to the executive board respectively. According to company law (AL 2002: § 51), a majority of the members of the supervisory board cannot be executive officers of the relevant company, and the chairman of the supervisory board and the CEO may not be one and the same person.

Second, Danish companies have a two-tier management structure, where the supervisory board is appointed by the general assembly and must perform the role of a body supervising the activities of the executive board, while drawing up or addressing strategies, and appointing the executives (see Figure 3.3). Hence, the board independence issue has not been as strong (or as relevant) in the corporate governance debate in Denmark as in countries such as the USA and the United Kingdom. The use and function of supervisory board committees have been relevant issues in Denmark too, but because of the Danish management structure and its inherent traditions the supervisory boards of Danish companies are generally small, even in listed companies. Hence supervisory board committees such as audit committees, nomination committees, and remuneration committees are almost non-existent. Given the typical size of the supervisory board of a Danish listed company, the Nørby Committee generally recommended that no supervisory board committees be used (Nørby Report 2001). The current debate, which reflects international trends and increased focus on control, means that it cannot be ruled out that Danish companies with particularly complex accounting and auditing needs could profit from using an audit committee (Nørby Report 2004: 17).

Third, communication between the auditor and the supervisory board is regulated through the requirements of the special long form audit report (audit protocol).[34] The requirement for the auditors to make the audit protocol is based in the Act on State Authorized and Certified Public Accountants (LBR

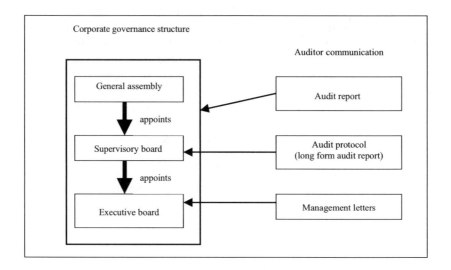

Figure 3.3 Corporate governance structure and auditor communication

2003: § 10.4), and the content is specified through the special national standard RS 265 (see also section 3). As indicated in Figure 3.3, communication with the supervisory board is distinct from the communication through management letters directed toward the executive board.[35] In the protocol, the auditor describes the nature and extent of the audit work performed and the conclusion thereof.[36] If the supervisory board and the auditor have made agreements on special investigations or detailed control, or if this is a legal requirement, the information about the execution and results thereof must be entered in the audit protocol. The auditor is required to make the following types of audit protocols: (1) protocol of initiation (in which the terms of the engagement are described), (2) entries during the year (typically on audit procedures performed during the year, including the assessment of internal controls), (3) protocol on the annual report, (4) entry of withdrawal (if relevant), (5) protocol about reports or statements in connection with counseling or assistance. The national standard RS 265 holds more detailed recommendations for each of these types of audit protocols. At every meeting of the supervisory board, the audit protocol must be shown to all its members. Every entry must be acknowledged by signing of the protocol by all members of the board. This requirement is stated in the company law (AL 2002: § 56.6) and is popularly referred to as lex Nordic Feather, as it was introduced as a result of the behavior of the chairman of that company, who chose to read aloud only "relevant" parts of the audit protocol at board meetings.

The special national issues should be considered in the light of the proposed EU Directive on Statutory Audits. The proposal addresses corporate governance aspects of audited entities that are closely interlinked with statutory audit, particularly matters concerning the appointment, the dismissal, and the resignation of the auditor as well as communication with the auditor. For public interest entities, the establishment of audit committees will be mandatory (EU 2004). It would be a paradox if effective national solutions to corporate governance issues were discarded in favor of common solutions across Europe. Anyhow, the aim is to enhance trust in the corporate governance of companies – including the role of the auditor.

9 Summary and conclusion

As indicated in this chapter, Danish legislation concerning auditors was initiated by the industrialization process, and has therefore been greatly inspired by English audit regulations. The birth of the law itself was delayed by the Alberti scandal. The exposure of the scandal had a big influence on the first act on authorized auditors, which was therefore already in 1909 relatively restrictive and durable. The period up to the 1980s was relatively stable and predominantly characterized by national adjustments of the audit norms.

In recent years Danish audit regulations have been marked by Denmark's joining the EU, starting with the EU's Fourth, Seventh, and Eighth Directives and later the EU's aim of combining and influencing the international audit norms, including IFAC's Code of Ethics. The biggest Danish business scandal of recent years (Nordic Feather in 1990) and the international Enron scandal have also influenced Danish audit regulations.

The most significant changes to audit regulations in the last few years have concerned the auditor's independence. Denmark has, for instance, repealed the demand for general independence, according to which auditors were not allowed to have other occupations than auditing and related tasks. The adaptations have resulted in a liberalization of an auditor's opportunities to offer non-audit services, just as they have opened up the possibility of starting other businesses, simultaneously with running an audit firm. Conversely, the adaptations have imposed more restrictive rules for independence in specific cases where an auditor signs written material for a third party.

Concurrently, stricter peer review has been implemented, the disciplinary system has been changed into a public legal system, and in 2003 the Public Oversight Board was established for quality control. This reflected a series of initiatives with the aim of strengthening the control of auditors and the sanctions against unacceptable quality in an auditor's work.

In the future, Danish accounting and audit regulation will be largely identical with international norms for the issuing of financial statements and the verification thereof, with the exception of situations where Danish law is considered to be more restrictive in its demands.

Notes

1 The Accountancy Committee is a public body, i.e. appointed by the Danish government. The tasks of the Committe are a) to assist the DCCA in administration of the audit law (LBR § 9.1), and b) to administer the yearly examination of the candidates wishing to become SR- and RR-auditors. See also Figure 3.2.
2 By 2004, 1,184 SR-auditors and 4,922 RR-auditors had given up their license to practice due to retirement or holding other jobs.
3 According to LBR 2003, § 10.2, these companies are: companies quoted on a stock exchange, state joint stock companies, companies under supervision of the Danish Financial Supervisory Authority (Finanstilsynet), and companies that for two consecutive years have fulfilled at least two of the following conditions: a balance sheet total of DKK5 billion, a net turnover of DKK5 billion, or 2,500 employees (€1 = ± DKK7.50).
4 See LBR 2003: § 11.2.8.
5 FSR: Abbreviation for "Foreningen af Statsautoriserede Revisorer."
6 In the period 1992–2002 an average of 73 persons per year actually passed the exam.
7 There is no requirement here that the practical period has to be after obtaining the theoretical degree for Certified Public Accountant.
8 FRR: Abbreviation for "Foreningen af Registrerede Revisorer."
9 Although auditing standards could be sent to selected interest groups for hearing, FSR Statutes (2003 § 23,3).
10 RS: Abbreviation for "Revisions Standard."
11 The Company Accounts Act distinguishes between the legally-required elements of the annual report (management report, explanation of accounting practices, and financial statements including notes) and supplementary reports containing voluntary information, e.g. environmental, ethics, social reports.
12 The two-auditor requirement for public companies in Denmark was no longer a mandatory requirement from the financial year starting 1 January 2005.
13 In contrast to reactive self-regulation in the form of good practice assessment through expert opinions (profession *responsa*).
14 In the preamble to guideline 12 from 1988, UEC is replaced with Fédération des Experts Comptables Européens (FEE).
15 In addition, the FSR committee has chosen to issue the "Preface" to the International Standards, to preserve the context, as a translation of the total set of standards.
16 Of the six, one is a draft to a practice statement.
17 Proposal for a directive of the European Parliament and of the Council on statutory audit of annual accounts and consolidated accounts and amending Council Directives 78/660/EEC [the Fourth Directive] and 83/349/EEC [the Seventh Directive] (EU [2004] 177).
18 Article 26.
19 Article 53, 1; currently national implementation of the directive is expected during 2006.
20 I.e. a clean record in relation to violations of the penal code (STRL § 78.2).
21 The requirements for independence have been revised to fulfill as a minimum the recommendations from the EU Commission in 2002.
22 See footnote 5 on companies with a special interest for society.
23 Commission Recommendation 2001/256/EC of 15 November 2000 on quality assurance for the statutory audit in the European Union: minimum requirements.
24 Commission Recommendation 2002/590/EC of 16 May 2002 – Statutory Auditors' Independence in the EU: A Set of Fundamental Principles.
25 A register of active auditors licensed as State Authorized or Certified Public Accountants.

26 DCCA is an agency under the Danish Ministry of Economic and Business Affairs with the responsibility for the administration of company and enterprise legislation and for the registration and disclosure of certain information and documents about companies, including company accounts.

27 Note that "public interest entities" does not comprise the same group of companies identified in footnote 5 as "companies with a special interest for society."

28 According to FRR coordinator Torben Bille, the decision to have a membership-based quality control for FRR was made in 1995, and the first quality controls were carried out in 1998.

29 For a closer examination of the historical development and a comparison of the Danish and German disciplinary systems up to 2001, see Quick and Warming-Rasmussen (2002).

30 LBR 2003: § 1.2.

31 LBR 2003: § 19.1.

32 The professional organizations have committees for this purpose, e.g. (FSR Statutes 2003: § 18). The Expert Opinion-committee will issue "responsa" on specific cases raised by their members, the government, the administrative court system or the general jurisdiction system.

33 "The Nørby Committee's Report on Corporate Governance in Denmark – Recommendations for Good Corporate Governance in Denmark" (2001) is available in English on the website of the Copenhagen Stock Exchange (http://www.cse.dk).

34 The audit protocol is made for the use of those charged with governance, cf. the definition hereof in ISA 260, paragraphs 5-9. The guidelines in ISA 260, including the timing and contents of the communication with those charged with governance, generally also apply to the keeping of the audit protocols.

35 RS 265 must be read together with RS (ISA) 260 "Communication of audit matters with those charged with governance" and RS (ISA) 210 "Terms of audit engagements."

36 The general recommendations for audit protocols are based in RS 265, sections 5–15.

References

AARL (2004) Lovbekendtgørelse nr. 196 af 23. marts 2004 om erhvervsdrivende virksomheders aflæggelse af årsregnskab m.v. (årsregnskabsloven).

AL (2002) Lovbekendtgørelse om aktieselskaber nr. 9 af 9. januar 2002.

Bærentsen, L. (2004) "Den nye revisorlov – 1 års fødselsdag," *Revision & Regnskabsvæsen*, 9: 6-10.

BN (2000) "Revisionsanalysen 2000," *Børsens Nyhedsmagasin*, No. 3.

BN (2002) "Revisionsanalysen 2002," *Børsens Nyhedsmagasin*, No. 2.

BN (2003) "Revisionsanalysen 2003," *Berlingske Nyhedsmagasin*, No. 3.

BN (2005) "Revisionsanalysen 2005," *Berlingske Nyhedsmagasin*, No. 2.

Christensen, M. (2000) "Revisors funktioner," in M. Christensen, K. Füchsel, L.B. Langsted, and A. Loft (eds) *Revision – koncept & teori*, 2nd ed., Copenhagen: Forlaget Thomson, pp. 11–38.

DCCA (2005) *Report on the Auditing Requirement for B Enterprises (Small Companies)*, English summary, the Danish Commerce and Companies Agency.

Disciplinary Tribunal (2005) *Årsberetning 2004*, Disciplinærnævnet for Statsautoriserede og Registrerede Revisorer.

DSR.bek. (2005) Bekendtgørelse nr. 130 af 28. februar 2005 om Disciplinærnævnet for Statsautoriserede og Registrerede Revisorer.

Erkl.bek. (1996) Bekendtgørelse om statsautoriserede og registrerede revisorers erklæringer mv. nr. 90 af 22. februar 1996.

EU (2001) Commission Recommendation 2001/256/EC of 15 November 2000 on quality assurance for the statutory audit in the European Union: minimum requirements.

EU (2002) Commission Recommendation 2002/590/EC of 16 May 2002 – Statutory Auditors' Independence in the EU: A Set of Fundamental Principles.

EU (2004) Commission of the European Communities, 2004: Proposal for a directive of the European Parliament and of the Council on statutory audit of annual accounts and consolidated accounts and amending Council directives 78/660/EEC and 83/349/EEC.

EU (2004) MEMO/04/60: European Commission proposal for a directive on statutory audit: frequently asked questions, Brussels, 16 March 2004.

Ex.bek. (2004) Bekendtgørelse om eksamen for statsautoriserede revisorer nr. 186 af 22. marts 2004.

FSR (2004) Retningslinjer for revisors etiske adfærd, FSRs etikudvalg og bestyrelse, maj 2004.

FSR Annual Report (2002) *Beretning 2001/2002*, Foreningen af Statsautoriserede Revisorer.

FSR Annual Report (2003) *Beretning 2002/2003*, Foreningen af Statsautoriserede Revisorer.

FSR Annual Report (2004) *Beretning 2003/2004*, Foreningen af Statsautoriserede Revisorer.

FSR Annual Report (2005) *Beretning 2004/2005*, Foreningen af Statsautoriserede Revisorer.

FSR Statutes (2003) Foreningen af statsautoriserede revisorers vedtægter af 3. november 2003.

Gar.bek. (2003) Bekendtgørelse nr. 740 af 21. august 2003 om statsautoriserede og registrerede revisorers garantistillelse og ansvarsforsikring.

Goldin, T. (1997) *Disciplinærsystemet for statsautoriserede og registrerede revisorer*, Copenhagen: Forlaget FSR.

Holm, C. and Steenholdt, N. (2003) "Measuring Learning Outcomes in Auditing Education," in N. Kærgaard (ed.) *Symposium i anvendt statistik*, Copenhagen: Den Kgl. Veterinær- og Landbohøjskole, pp. 81-92.

HVL (2004) Lovbekendtgørelse om forebyggende foranstaltninger mod hvidvaskning af penge og finansiering af terrorisme nr. 129 af 23. februar 2004.

International Federation of Accountants (IFAC) (2004) *Handbook of International Auditing, Assurance, and Ethics Pronouncements*, New York: IFAC.

Jensen, Ø.S. and Warming-Rasmussen, B. (2000) "Revisoretik," in M. Christensen, K. Füchsel, L.B. Langsted, and A. Loft (eds) *Revision – koncept & teori*, 2nd ed., Copenhagen: Forlaget Thomson, 209–261.

Johansen, A.R., Langsted, L., and Ring, N.A. (2003) *Revisorlovgivningen med kommentarer*, Copenhagen: Forlaget Thomson.

Langsted, L. (2000) "Revisorlovgivning," in M. Christensen, K. Füchsel, L.B. Langsted, and A. Loft (eds) *Revision – koncept & teori*, 2nd ed., Copenhagen: Forlaget Thomson, pp. 75-208.

Langsted, L., Andersen P.K., and Christensen M. (2003) *Revisoransvar*, 6th ed., Copenhagen: Forlaget Thomson.

LAR (1909) Lov nr. 117 af 14. maj 1909 om autoriserede revisorer.

LBR (2003), Lov nr. 302 af 30. april 2003 om statsautoriserede og registrerede (beskikkede) revisorer.

LRR (1970) Lovbekendtgørelse om registrerede revisorer nr. 220 af 27. maj 1970.

LSR (1967) Lov nr. 68 af 15. marts 1967 om statsautoriserede revisorer.

ML (2000) Lovbekendtgørelse nr. 699 af 17. juli 2000 om markedsføring.

Nørby Report (2001) *The Nørby Committee's Report on Corporate Governance in Denmark – Recommendations for Good Corporate Governance in Denmark*, Copenhagen: Stock Exchange.

Nørby Report (2004) *Report on Corporate Governance in Denmark – the Copenhagen Stock Exchange Committee on Corporate Governance*, Copenhagen: Stock Exchange.

Public Oversight Board (2005) *Revisortilsynets Redegørelse 2003-04*. Available at: www.revisortilsynet.dk/graphics/revisortilsynet/revisortilsynet_redegoerelse2005.pdf

Quick, R and Warming-Rasmussen, B. (2002) "Disciplinary Observance and Sanctions on German and Danish Auditors," *International Journal of Auditing*, 6(2): 133–53.

Quick, R. and Warming-Rasmussen, B. (2004) "The Impact of MAS on Perceived Auditor Independence – Some Evidence from Denmark," *Accounting Forum*, 29(2): 137–68.

Rindom, C. (2001) "Hvorfor er der så få kvindelige revisorer i Danmark?" *INSPI*, 4: 5–14.

Seheim, L.W. (2004) "Mens vi venter på kvalitetskontrollen," *Revisorbladet*, No. 3.

STRL (2004) Lovbekendtgørelse nr. 960 af 21. september 2004 om straffeloven.

Warming-Rasmussen, B. and Jensen, L. (2001) *Revisor som offentlighedens tillidsrepræsentant*, Copenhagen: Forlaget Thomson.

4 Developments in auditing regulation in Finland

From a national to an international framework

Lasse Niemi and Stefan Sundgren

1 Introduction

This chapter describes auditing regulation in Finland. The chapter has two objectives. First, by describing auditing regulation and its development over the years the chapter provides readers with the knowledge needed to analyze cross-country differences in auditing and its regulation. Second, the chapter attempts to address the question: what drives changes in audit regulaion? Are the changes in audit regulation stimulated by national scandals or by developments in regulation in other countries? To address this question and to provide a description of the development of audit regulation, we examined past and present legislation, recommendations and instructions of authorities, reports of working groups preparing proposals for regulatory changes, academic studies, as well as articles in professional journals describing and assessing the current state and history of auditing in Finland. To probe deeper into the issue we interviewed two people who have been following the development of regulation in auditing in Finland for decades (Riistama 2005, Troberg 2005).

We found that even though some high profile business failures at the end of the 1980s showed clearly that there was a *need* to change the regulation system, the structural changes in the economy are the underlying major force that has been driving the regulatory changes. For example, the internationalization process of Finnish companies that started in the latter half of the 1980s created a strong need to harmonize Finnish auditing rules with those in other countries. The harmonization process was speeded up as Finland joined the EU in 1995. The process still continues. The recently introduced new EU directive on auditing is the latest step in this process. In the foreseeable future new legislation will replace the current Auditing Act. The passage of the bill, as currently written, would remove the remaining Finnish idiosyncrasies in auditing regulation.

A pervasive feature underlying the regulation of auditing and financial reporting in Finland, as well as in the other Nordic countries, is the principle of transparency of the business entity. Consistent with this principle, all companies, regardless of their size, have to file their financial statements with the public Register of Companies (Kaupparekisteri), which means that financial statements are publicly available.[1] Furthermore, all companies are required to have their accounts audited too. Only small proprietorships are exempted from statutory audits. The consequence of this is that there is a wide range of different audit clients with varying needs for external auditing.

Four different types of auditor provide auditing services in Finland. First, there is a two-tier system of auditor certification similar to that in other Nordic countries and in some countries in continental Europe. The first-tier auditors, licensed by the Central Chamber of Commerce, have the training and competence to audit the largest corporations, while the second-tier auditors, licensed by regional chambers of commerce, concentrate on small and medium sized firms. In addition, there are also auditors specializing in audits of municipal organizations and other not-for-profit entities. A Finnish idiosyncrasy are laymen auditors, that is, auditors that are not licensed by any regulatory body or organization. Nevertheless, the Auditing Act requires that any person providing a statutory audit must have sufficient skills and knowledge to conduct the audit in accordance with good auditing practice. Moreover, legal liability is the same for persons having no license for auditing as for those who have.

The structure of this chapter is as follows. The next section provides a review of the history of auditing regulation and the profession in Finland, followed by a description of the current situation. After that, the anticipated changes are discussed. The chapter ends with a summary and our conclusions.

2 History of auditing regulation and the profession in Finland

2.1 Early days

The idea of increasing the credibility of accounting numbers through inspections conducted by independent outsiders is probably as old as accounting itself. In Finland the earliest records on auditing are from the tar trading and transporting business in the seventeenth century (Kosonen 2005: 36). Tar, which is a protective adhesive that was applied, for example, to ships to prevent them from leaking, was perhaps the most important export item at the time in Finland.

In the nineteenth century rapid industrial development boosted the need for capital. A company with limited liability and external investors became a common solution to this need, which increased significantly the demand for external audits. The legal basis for investor protection was laid down in the latter half of the nineteenth century as the Company Act of 1864 was introduced. Even though the act provided some investor protection, it contained no requirements for auditing. The mandatory audits for limited liability companies were introduced for the first time in the Company Act of 1895, which required that the accounts as well as the administration of all companies should be audited by one or more auditors. Perhaps not surprisingly, the new Company Act provided little guidance on auditing *per se*. The scarce guidance available was based more on the ideas of individuals than on any regulatory body. In the 1890s, when the first Finnish schools providing business education were established, the typical authorities in the auditing field were lecturers of those schools.

At that time, auditing was not a profession as we understand it now and, needless to say, auditing methods were very different from the ones we have today. The audit consisted of checking all documents and accounts thoroughly and its purpose was directed more against error detection than the examination of financial reporting (Kosonen 2005: 235). Apparently, an important factor influencing the choice of the auditor was the auditor's position in society. It may well be that in the early days of auditing the reputation capital of the auditor was an even more important factor in auditor choice than today.

2.2 The rise of the profession

It seems that users of financial statements have always been worried about audit quality. The first time the need for professional auditors was brought up was at the 1902 General Meeting of Merchants in Viipuri following some significant bankruptcies (Kosonen 2005: 95). The increasing calls for more credible audits were likely one of the reasons for the formation in 1911 of the first association of professional auditors – Suomen Tilintarkastajainyhdistys – Finska Revisors-föreningen (Auditors' Association of Finland).

To further increase the credibility of the profession, it was seen as vital that the supervision of the profession should be carried out by an outsider organization. At the turn of the decade the creation of the system of chambers of commerce made this possible. In 1924 the Central Chamber of Commerce (CCC), a private organization, took on the tasks of licensing and supervising professional auditors. It is still carrying out this task today.

The next year, in 1925, the current association of KHT (Keskuskauppakamarin hyväksymä tilintarkastaja) auditors – KHT-yhdistys – Föreningen CGR (the Institute of Authorised Public Accountants, hereafter the Institute of KHT auditors) was founded. In the same year, CCC authorized the first KHT auditors.

Figure 4.1 shows the numbers of KHT auditors from the birth of the Institute to 2005. In 1925 there were 35 KHT auditors, and over the next five decades the increase in the number was modest. One reason for this might be the relatively demanding educational prerequisites and other strict rules for becoming a KHT (Kosonen 2005: 104, 123). Because of the small number of KHTs, persons having no license typically audited small and medium sized firms.

At the beginning of the 1950s another tier of certified auditors (HTM, Kauppakamarin hyväksymä tilimies) was introduced when the rules for becoming an HTM auditor were approved. This led to a jump in the number of certified auditors; the number exceeded 400 in the early 1950s. The first HTM auditors formed their own professional organization – HTM-tilintarkastajat ry (the Association of Certified HTM Auditors, hereafter the Association of HTM auditors).

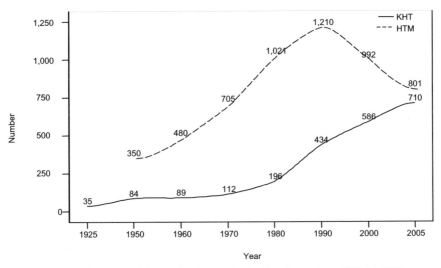

Figure 4.1 Development of the profession: authorized auditors from 1925 to 2005

Source: Central Chamber of Commerce (2005)

One reason for the relatively rapid increase in the number of HTM auditors, as opposed to KHTs, may be that becoming an HTM was considered much easier than becoming a KHT. For example, from 1950 to 1970 the evaluation of candidates for the HTM authorization was based solely on the educational background and the work experience of the HTM candidate. A similar kind of exam to that which KHTs had to pass before approval by CCC was introduced for HTMs only in 1970. However, the number of HTM auditors kept growing steadily even after that and exceeded 1,200 in the 1990s. The number has since been declining. At the beginning of 2005 there were only 801 HTM auditors and 24 firms of HTM auditors.

The number of KHT auditors follows a quite different pattern. Until 1980 the number of KHT auditors was relatively low, but since then the number has increased considerably from 196 in 1980 to 710 in 2005 (see Figure 4.1). During the same period of time the number of KHT auditors in relation to the total number of auditors has increased from 16 percent to 47 percent. This trend seems to be continuing since now the entrants to the profession are more often KHT than HTM auditors. For example, in 2004 there were 27 new KHT auditors and 16 HTM auditors. The structural changes underlying the increase in KHT auditors since the 1980s relate to the deregulation of capital markets[2] in Finland which created a strong demand for accounting and auditing that could be understood and accepted by foreign investors (Riistama 2005). Other reasons for the increase in the number of KHT auditors and the decrease in the number of HTM auditors are that auditing has become a more demanding profession and that the costs of staying in the profession have increased significantly over the years. Thus, it is less attractive to work as a part-time auditor doing just a small number of audits each year. According to the statistics prepared by the Central Chamber of Commerce in 2003, over 60 percent of HTM auditors are part-time auditors[3] and typically operate as sole practitioners. For comparison, less than 20 percent of the KHT auditors are part-time auditors and about 60 percent of KHT auditors work with the Big Four audit firms.

A third type of auditor certification was introduced in 1992, as the ordinance on specific municipal auditor certification, Julkishallinnon Tilintarkastaja (JHTT) (Chartered Public Finance Auditor), was issued, and in 1993 JHTT auditors founded their own association. The need for the JHTT certification was based on the assumption that entities owned by municipalities and other public sector organizations were so fundamentally different from other auditees that special skills and knowledge were needed to audit those entities. Currently, the Auditing Act (subsection 14 §) states that in those entities in which municipalities are controlling owners, a JHTT auditor can be chosen instead of an HTM auditor. However, if the law requires that a KHT auditor has to be chosen, a JHTT auditor cannot be chosen instead of a KHT. The possibility of choosing a JHTT instead of an HTM auditor will be likely removed in the new Auditing Act. The bill for a new act (subsection 6§) says that a JHTT can be chosen as a joint-auditor but not instead of an HTM or a KHT.

A fourth type of auditor – a person having no certification – may provide statutory audits for the smallest firms if he or she has sufficient skills and knowledge to conduct the audit following Good Auditing Practice. To put it another way, the current Auditing Act stipulates that an HTM or KHT auditor must be hired when the firm's size exceeds the threshold specified in the act (see Table 4.1). More specifically, a certified auditor has to be hired if two of the three following criteria are met: 1) total assets are over €0.34 million, 2) net sales are over €0.68 million, or 3) the firm employed more than 10 persons on average during the last financial year. Furthermore, the act stipulates that *only* a certified auditor can be hired (i.e. that a non-certified auditor cannot even be hired as a joint-auditor) if two of the following three criteria are met: 1) total assets are over €2.1 million, 2) net sales are over €4.2 million, or 3) the firm employed more than 50 persons on average during the last financial year. A KHT auditor has to be hired if a client is publicly held or if two of the following three criteria are met: 1) total assets are over €25 million, 2) net sales are over €50 million, or 3) the firm employed more than 300 persons on average during the last financial year.

2.3 Major changes in regulation during the twentieth century

The basic rules for the regulation of modern companies and their audits were laid down in the latter half of the nineteenth century. The Company Act of 1864 established the initial regulations for limited liability companies and investor protection. The Company Act of 1895 introduced a mandatory audit. However,

Table 4.1 Certified auditors according to the Auditing Act

	At least one HTM/KHT must be hired if two of the following three conditions are met	Only HTM/KHT auditors can be hired if two of the following three conditions are met	A KHT has to be hired if two of the following three conditions are met
Total assets	> €0.34 million	> €2.1 million	> €25 million
Net sales	> €0.68 million	> €4.2 million	> €50 million
Employees	> 10 persons	> 50 persons	> 300 persons

there was little guidance on accounting before the first Accounting Act was enacted in 1925. The act consisted of seven sections that provided some guidelines on bookkeeping and general valuation rules on company assets.

In 1945 a new Accounting Act replaced the old one. This act specified much more detailed rules with respect to the preparation of financial statements and required even cost accounting for some firms. Cost accounting was needed for some manufacturing firms, since the prices of many goods were controlled by the government due to a severe lack of raw materials and finished products during and after the Second World War. At the same time as the Accounting Act was issued, there was a proposal for the Council of the State to commission an auditing act. However, the Central Chamber of Commerce did not back up the proposal and it was eventually not accepted. The proposal was considered to be too detailed and inflexible (Kosonen 2005: 45–6).

A new era in accounting started in 1973 as the Accounting Act from 1945 was replaced by a new act. The new act was based on a framework called Meno-Tulo theory (cost-income theory; Saario 1959) that emphasized the measurement of earnings power (i.e. income statement approach) whereas the framework for the Accounting Act of 1945 and that of 1925 were based on a balance-sheet approach. Even the corporate income tax laws were changed to comply with the new framework for accounting.

A new Company Law, that included more detailed rules about auditing, was enacted in 1978. A major change for auditing was that the auditor's report became public. Shortly after this the Institute of KHT auditors advanced its recommendations for the contents of the standard audit report. Not surprisingly, the wording in the reports became much more homogeneous. Before that there were no common guidelines, and the audit reports often described the auditing work done and included an evaluation of how the management had run the company (Helenius 2004: 47). Together with the Accounting Act of 1973, the Company Law provided the legislation on statutory audits in Finland until the Auditing Act was enacted in 1995.

The general interest in auditing increased considerably during the 1980s as the capital markets were deregulated and Finnish companies were able to raise capital abroad (Riistama 1999: 18). Furthermore, a number of high profile bankruptcies during the deep recession at the turn of the decade raised serious doubts about audit quality and triggered changes in the auditing laws. The supervising bodies of the profession at the time, the Auditing Board of the Central Chamber of Commerce (i.e. the body responsible for the authorization and supervision of auditors, as described above) and the Oversight Board of the Auditing System (Tiintarkastusjärjestelmän valvontalautakunta), reacted to this situation by investigating thoroughly the most notorious bankruptcy cases of Mancon Oy and Wärtsilä Meriteollisuus Oy. They found no evidence of audit failures; however, they concluded that the prevailing auditing rules were insufficient.

The auditors of the state (Valtiontilintarkastajat) also investigated the Wärtsilä Meriteollisuus Oy case. They concluded that the auditors had issued an unqualified report, although the company's financial statements had provided a misleading picture about the future of the company. However, they concluded that the key problems were the prevailing accounting and auditing rules and not the auditors' reporting *per se*. Furthermore, they proposed that the oversight of the profession and the authorization of auditors should be moved from the Chambers of Commerce,[4] which are private organizations with companies as members, to a governmental body.

In 1992 the government responded to these relatively strong recommendations by setting up a working group to propose changes to the auditing system (Tilintarkastusjärjestelmän kehittämistoimikunnan mietintö; Komiteamietintö 1992: 14). It proposed that the Central Chamber of Commerce should continue as a supervisory body of the profession. A main conclusion also in their report was that the legislation but not the profession was to blame for the perceived audit quality problems.

An important change in auditing regulation took place in 1995, when the first Auditing Act came into effect. Before that, the rules on auditing were found mainly in the Company Law and the Accounting Act. The new law contained most of the proposals made by the working group described above (Sorsa 1997: 55). Thus, it is fair to say that the crises affected the regulation work via different working parties and authorities. The Wärtsilä Meriteollisuus Oy case in particular showed the inadequacy of audit regulation. It has been described as the detonator of the work leading to the birth of the Auditing Act (Riistama 2005). Still, the underlying structural changes in the Finnish economy were the forces that created the conditions that eventually revealed the need to update the Finnish system of auditing regulation.

Another event that had an impact on auditing regulation was that Finland entered the European Union in 1995, and, as a consequence, EU legislation was implemented through the Auditing Act. However, as the EU auditing regulations focused almost solely on the profession, e.g. the minimum criteria for becoming and being a professional auditor, and not on the auditing *per se*, there was little need to change the auditing rules, as Finnish systems of certification and training to become a professional auditor already closely resembled those in many EU countries.

In 2000 two changes in the Auditing Act lowered the entry barriers to the profession to the minimum level stipulated in the Eighth Directive. First, the requirement for five years of work experience before it was possible to take the exam was reduced to three years. Second, degrees from polytechnics were accepted as a sufficient educational background for the HTM (second-tier auditor) exam. Before that change a degree from a university was necessary. Now the minimum requirements for becoming a certified auditor in Finland are more in line with those in most other EU countries.

2.4 Summary

The history of auditing can be divided into three eras: the formation of the Finnish auditing institution (1895–1950), the period when the institution became established (1951–85), and the period of internationalization and publicity (from 1986) (Kosonen 2005). The shifts from one era into another were brought about by changes in the Finnish economy. In line with this, we found four examples of the interplay between changes in the economy and changes in audit regulation. First, the Industrial Revolution created a need for external finance and investor protection, which was reflected in the introduction of the Company Law and mandatory audits. Second, during and after the Second World War there were severe problems in the economy due to a lack of raw materials. The authorities gave instructions for companies to develop cost accounting that facilitated the price control of goods produced. Before that there were no mandatory rules on cost accounting for manufacturing firms (Kosonen 2005: 43–4). Third, the deregulation of the capital markets in Finland allowed Finnish firms and individuals to tap foreign capital markets, which created a strong demand for accounting and auditing rules understood by foreign investors. Fourth, the decision to join the EU transferred the regulation to EU level. Therefore, changes in the economy at the national level will hardly have the same impact on regulation as they had in the past century. Regulation now takes place at the EU level, and, as a consequence, events in the EU as a whole are much more likely to affect auditing regulation in Finland than those at the national level.

3 The regulatory environment

The regulatory environment of auditing typically consists of two elements: governmental regulation and the self-regulation of the profession. In Finland governmental regulation consists of legislation, interpretation guidance, as well as the supervision of the profession provided by the different regulatory bodies (see Figure 4.2). The Institute of KHT auditors and the Association of HTM auditors are responsible for self-regulation. The Institute of KHT auditors issues auditing standards that currently are translations of IFAC's ISA standards.

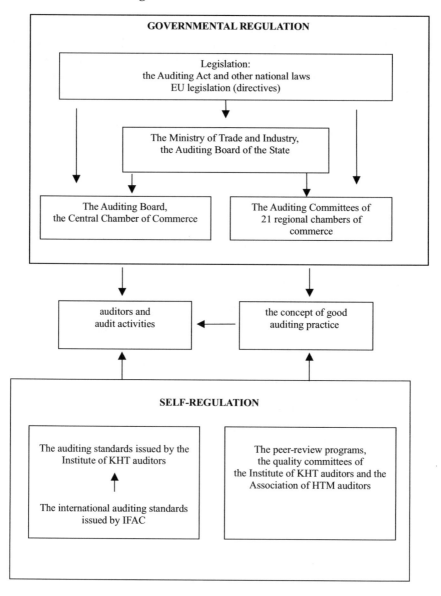

Figure 4.2 The regulatory environment of auditing in Finland

3.1 Governmental regulation

The major source of governmental regulation is the Auditing Act, which prescribes the scope of the statutory audit and auditors' reporting. The act also mandates regulatory bodies to authorize and supervise the members of the profession. The EU legislation on the minimum educational requirements, as well as other requirements for becoming a professional auditor, are implemented in Finland through the Auditing Act. Due to the new EU directive on auditing, the International Standards on Auditing issued by IFAC will become a vital part of the Finnish regulatory environment.

The regulation of auditing is also covered in the Auditing Ordinance and in decrees from the Ministry of Trade and Industry. These sources include regulation at a more detailed level than in the Auditing Act. Moreover, the Accounting Act and the Company Law include some rules mainly stipulating the requirement to have an auditor and the required authorization of auditors for public companies.

An important authority for governmental regulation is the Ministry of Trade and Industry. The ministry has a Business Law Division that participates in legislative work at both the national and the EU level. The Ministry of Trade and Industry maintains a register of authorized (i.e. certified) auditors. According to the Auditing Act (subsection 43§) it is a criminal offence for anyone not on that register to act as a KHT or HTM auditor by using the acronyms KHT or HTM.

The Auditing Act mandates the Auditing Board of the State (Valtion tilintarkastuslautakunta) to provide general guidance on interpreting the Auditing Act, to develop auditing in general, and to supervise the profession. The Board may also make proposals regarding audit regulation. However, the most important role of the Auditing Board of the State is that it is an appeal instance for disciplinary cases.

The Auditing Board of the Central Chamber of Commerce (Keskuskauppakamarin tilintarkastuslautakunta, for short TILA) and the Auditing Committees of the 21 regional Chambers of Commerce (Kauppakamarin tilintarkastusvaliokunta, for short TIVAs) are in charge of the more day-to-day supervision of the profession. TILA supervises and authorizes KHT auditors, whereas HTM auditors are supervised by the 21 regional TIVAs. These organizations, together with the Auditing Board of the State (VALA), are also the regulatory bodies that interpret the laws and, above all, ensure that the members of the profession follow the prevailing legislation.

3.2 Self-regulation

The key elements of self-regulation are the professional standards and the peer-review programs designed to ensure that auditors follow the standards as well as the other rules regulating auditing work. The Institute of KHT auditors issues auditing standards and both KHT and HTM auditors have to follow them. The development of auditing standards started in the 1970s. Before that, due to the lack of guidance, auditors had to rely on their own judgment and discussions with their colleagues regarding auditing work, and as a consequence audit quality varied a lot (Helenius 2004: 45). Development work started in the form of cooperation between auditors' professional associations in the Nordic countries.

The Nordic association "Nordiska Revisorförbundet" provided a forum for discussions, and the Institute of KHT auditors represented Finland.

The first recommendation was accepted by the Institute of KHT auditors in 1977, but it took many years before the individual recommendations formed a set of standards. The general meeting of the Institute of KHT auditors adopted the first set of auditing standards in 1992. From 1996 to 1999 the Institute carried out a significant harmonizing and translation project to harmonize the recommendations with the ISA standards.

Until the 1990s IFAC had little impact on auditing standards in Finland (Riistama 2005). From the 1980s to the 1990s there was a global shift from governmental intervention to more market-driven economies in many Western countries, including the US and the UK. In Finland the deregulation of the capital markets in the latter half of the 1980s created a demand for auditing and accounting rules that could be understood by foreign investors. As a consequence, the impact of Nordic cooperation has deteriorated since the 1990s, as the ISA standards have become a basis for professional standards (Troberg 2005). The current standards are based on translations of IFAC's ISA standards.

The Institute of KHT auditors and the Association of HTM auditors conduct peer-review programs that are based on ISA 220 (Quality Control for Audit Work). The programs also contain training and consulting elements that are aimed at helping auditors to ensure that they sufficiently plan and document their auditing work. The Institute of KHT auditors started its peer-review project in 1993, and the Association of HTM auditors initiated quality training programs and the development of working tools for quality control in 1995. The practice of monitored peer-review visits to KHT and HTM auditors started in 1998.

Auditors who do not comply with the quality program can be dismissed from their institute or association. The Institute of KHT auditors and the Association of HTM auditors make the proposals to dismiss auditors who do not comply with the quality program. The supervisory bodies of the programs, that is, TILA and the TIVAs, make the final dismissal decisions.

It is possible to work as an auditor without being a member of one of the professional organizations. Today 97 percent of KHT auditors are members of the Institute of KHT auditors and 93 percent of HTM auditors are members of the Association of HTM auditors. Those auditors who are not members also undergo peer-review programs; they are reviewed directly by TILA or the TIVAs.

The peer reviews are conducted at least once every five years. The participation in the program was voluntary until recently. However, the current quality assurance system in Finland complies with the minimum requirements of the European Commission's Recommendation of 15 November 2000 on quality assurance for the statutory auditor in the European Union (2001/256/EC).

3.3 The concept of good auditing practice

The Auditing Act (subsection 16§) states that auditors have to follow good auditing practice. However, the Auditing Act does not define the concept of good auditing practice; this task is left to the different regulatory bodies and to the profession. The Auditing Board of the Central Chamber of Commerce (TILA) provides some guidance, but the profession itself, through the Institute of KHT auditors and the Association of HTM auditors, has a key role in defining good auditing practice. One could say that governmental regulation sets the minimum level of audit quality, but it is the responsibility of the profession to provide instructions about *how* the minimum quality is to be achieved.

Today the most important sources of good auditing practice are the standards and recommendations that the Institute of KHT auditors has issued. The current standards, including the Code of Ethics, are based on the ISAs of the Council of the International Federation of Accountants (IFAC).

4 Current regulation

4.1 Education and training of auditors

Typically, persons wishing to become certified auditors in Finland follow a so-called educational route, though a so-called experience route is also possible. The detailed requirements for both routes are prescribed in regulations issued by the Ministry of Trade and Industry, and they comply with the Eighth Directive of the European Union. For KHT auditors, the educational prerequisites are a master's degree, including studies in accounting, auditing, law, as well as some other topics specified in a decree of the Ministry of Trade and Industry. It is necessary to have three years of work experience under the supervision of a KHT auditor before taking the KHT exam.

A bachelor's degree or an equivalent degree from a polytechnic is required for the HTM qualification. Furthermore, the requirements for the three years of practical experience are less demanding for the HTM qualification than for the KHT qualification (Keskuskauppakamari 2003). However, both the KHT and the HTM exams are difficult to pass. Between 1999 and 2004 the proportion that passed the KHT exam varied between 34 percent and 48 percent. The corresponding figures for the HTM exam were 28 percent and 52 percent. These figures, taken together with the facts that those taking the exam have at least three to five years of work experience in auditing and that the largest audit firms organize preparatory courses for their employees taking the exam, clearly illustrate that the KHT and HTM exams are a major challenge for those considering a career as a professional auditor in Finland.

4.2 Oversight and disciplinary actions

The Auditing Board of the Central Chamber of Commerce supervises KHT auditors, and the Auditing Committees of the regional chambers of commerce supervise HTM auditors. They check that auditors follow the rules, maintain their proficiency, and meet the other requirements for certification. For example, auditors are required to carry out a sufficient number of audits over a three-year period. If the number and nature of the engagements are insufficient, the auditor will have to give up his or her license. KHT and HTM auditors have to report their audit engagements and auditing hours to TILA.

TILA and the TIVAs investigate cases that may call for disciplinary action. Generally, the initiation of a case is based on complaints from an external party, but TILA or the TIVAs can also initiate cases themselves. This could, for example, be done if a claimed audit failure has brought about negative publicity. In essence, anyone can make a complaint to TILA or the TIVAs, but TILA and the TIVAs decide themselves whether the complaint provides sufficient grounds for an investigation.

The different types of sanction against authorized auditors are (a) a warning, (b) a remark, and (c) suspension or cancellation of the authorization. An auditor may appeal against these sanctions (see Figure 4.3). The appeal system includes one more instance for HTM auditors than for KHT auditors, since the appeal against a warning or remark issued by a regional Auditing Committee is first considered by the Auditing Board of the Central Chamber of Commerce. The following instances are the Auditing Board of the State and the Supreme Administrative Court for both types of auditors. Decisions to suspend or withdraw authorization are always made by the Auditing Board of the State. The maximum time of suspension is two years.

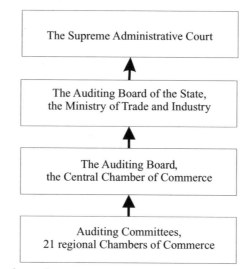

Figure 4.3 System of appeal

4.3 Auditor liability

An auditor is liable for damages that he or she has intentionally or by negligence of due care caused to the client or third parties (Auditing Act, subsection 44§). An important principle is that the auditor is not held liable unless negligence (that is, audit failure) can be shown. Thus, to succeed in an action against an auditor, the plaintiff must be able to show that there has been an audit failure and that there is a causal connection between the loss suffered by the plaintiff and the audit failure. Moreover, any liability is limited to the loss that can be attributed specifically to that audit failure. There is no cap on this liability though.

The risk of litigation is relatively small in Finland. The following four features of the Finnish legal system increase the threshold to sue the auditor (Niemi 2002). First, the awards have no punitive aspect, but are limited to the actual loss of the plaintiff. Second, regulations of the professional body of attorneys prohibit contingent fee-based billing. Third, class actions are not possible, and, fourth, the plaintiff is required to pay the defendant's (that is, the auditor's) legal costs if the auditor is not deemed liable.

The number of complaints concerning auditors' reporting is also very small in Finland. Complaints about auditors' reporting relate to business risk, since the auditor's reporting is at the heart of the examination of whether an audit failure has happened. According to Riistama (2005), KHT and HTM auditors have conducted approximately one million audits in the past ten years, but there have been only 37 complaints about auditor reporting for the same period. Moreover, the number of complaints leading to sanctions is even smaller than that.

4.4 Rules on auditor independence and ethics

The provision of rules on auditor independence and ethics has been left to the regulatory bodies, such as TILA, and the profession. The current law provides only a generic principle that the auditor has to refuse to audit a firm if the prerequisites for conducting an independent audit are missing (Auditing Act subsection 23§).

In the bill for a new Auditing Act, subsections 23 and 24 describe some situations and relationships where threats to auditor independence may arise. In these situations or relationships the auditor shall either forbear from carrying out an audit or apply safeguards to mitigate the threats. The proposed Auditing Act is in line with Article 22 (Independence and objectivity) of the new EU directive. If the auditor considers that it is possible to carry out an independent audit, despite the threats, the auditor must document in the working papers those threats and the safeguards undertaken to mitigate them. The proposed new subsection 23 also lists some situations where there is an apparent risk that independence could be threatened, including self-review, advocacy, familiarity, and intimidation.

The current professional standards of auditors include more detailed guidance on independence. These standards, issued by the Institute of KHT auditors, are based on the ISAs on ethics and auditor independence of the International Federation of Accountants (IFAC). The same standards apply to HTM auditors as to KHT auditors. The Institute of KHT auditors accepted the ISAs on auditor independence at the end of 2003. Before that, the professional standards were much less detailed.

It is fair to say that until recently there has been relatively little guidance on auditor independence. According to Saarikivi (1999), there have been two significant changes in auditor independence regulation: the Company Law of 1978 and the current Auditing Act. Before the Company Law of 1978 there was no guidance on auditor independence in the law. The Central Chamber of Commerce and its Auditing Board (TILA) issued general rules on auditor independence (Saarikivi 1999).

It seems that, even if there has been little ethical guidance, professional auditors' own reasoning and judgment have been adequate to guide them satisfactorily. Between 1980 and 1997 there were only 163 cases filed at TILA against KHT auditors. These cases exhibited a total of 274 alleged ethical violations. A study of these disciplinary cases has shown that alleged lack of auditor independence was a relatively common reason for complaints against auditors (Viitanen 2000). Around 30 percent of the cases investigated (81) concerned independence. Only cases of alleged violation of professional due care (50 percent) were more frequent. However, in a great majority of the cases (122; 70 percent), TILA's decision was acquittal. Only in one case did TILA cancel the license.

4.5 Auditing and corporate governance

4.5.1 Legislation

Corporate governance has been within the focus of a statutory audit in Finland from the early days of corporate regulation; the first Company Law of 1864 stipulated that the auditor has to audit the administration of the company in addition to the financial statements. The idea behind an administration audit is still the same. According to the current Auditing Act (subsection 17§), the main purpose of the administration audit is to determine whether the board members or the managing director have done anything that could give rise to claims for damages, and to investigate in general whether the Company Law or the company's bylaws have been violated. As investor protection is a central goal of corporate governance (Shleifer and Vishny 1997), the administration audit can be seen as part of the corporate governance system since it helps to assure that laws aimed at protecting creditors and equity investors are followed. A Finnish idiosyncrasy is that the auditor is also required to express his or her explicit opinion on whether the board and managing director can be discharged from liability for the financial year in the audit report.

4.5.2 *The Corporate Governance Recommendation of 2003*

For listed companies, a Best Practice Corporate Governance Recommendation issued in 2003 by a working group set up by the Helsinki Stock Exchange, the Central Chamber of Commerce, and the Confederation of Finnish Industry and Employers provides additional guidance. Recommendations from other countries have been used as the starting point for the recommendation. It provides explicit guidance on, among other things, audit committees, nomination committees, compensation committees, internal auditing, and risk management.

It is also recommended that audit fees as well as fees for non-audit services should be published. Furthermore, the recommendation stipulates that the board of directors, or the audit committee, shall inform the owners of their suggestion for an auditor before the annual general meeting is held.

5 Where are we going?

It seems that much of the legislative work in the area of auditing has been undertaken to harmonize Finnish audit regulation with EU legislation and the International Standards on Auditing. Consequently, it is likely that the remaining idiosyncrasies in Finnish auditing will disappear in the near future. More specifically, the Ministry of Trade and Industry started preparatory work for a new Auditing Act already in 2002 by appointing a working group to consider the need to amend the Auditing Act. The working group published its report in November 2003 (Ministry of Trade and Industry 2003). The report contained suggestions that would remove most of the Finnish idiosyncrasies in auditing. The working group suggested, for example, that persons holding no certification should no longer be allowed to conduct statutory audits. This would have a significant effect on the supply side of the audit market since these laymen auditors currently audit a large number of small firms. On the other hand, the working group also suggested that small firms should be exempted from mandatory audits. Taken together, these two suggestions would have a most significant effect on the structure of the audit market in Finland.

The other changes that the working group proposed relate to auditors' reporting. First, the current Auditing Act stipulates that the auditor's report shall include an opinion on (a) the financial statements, (b) the profit distribution, and (c) whether the board and managing director can be discharged from liability for the financial year. The working group suggested that the requirements that the auditor shall issue opinions in the report related to the profit distribution and discharge from liability should be removed from the Auditing Act altogether. However, the auditor should still report if certain laws have been violated. Second, the auditor is currently obliged to provide complementary information to the financial statements if it is considered to be necessary. The working group suggested that this requirement be dropped from the Accounting Act in order to emphasize that it is the role of the company to prepare the financial statements and of the auditor to audit the financial statements (Ministry of Trade and

Industry 2003: 143). In addition, the present Auditing Act states that the auditor shall include a confirmation that an audit has been done and that an audit report on the financial statements has been issued into the financial statements. This should also be dropped. Altogether, if the suggestions of the working group are implemented in the legislation, the Finnish idiosyncrasies in auditor reporting will cease to exist. Taken together, auditors would, as in most other countries, only give an opinion on the financial statements if the suggested rules come into effect.

6 Summary and conclusions

Auditing as a profession dates back to the beginning of the twentieth century in Finland. The first association of professional auditors was founded in 1910 and its successor, the current Institute of KHT auditors, was founded in 1925. Since 1895, the Company Law has stipulated that the accounts and administration of limited liability companies have to be audited. Due to the very small number of KHT auditors compared to the number of companies, small and mid-sized firms were typically audited by persons having no certification. At the start of the 1950s a second-tier HTM certification was introduced, which somewhat alleviated the lack of professional auditors. Today a majority of KHTs are employed by the Big Four, whereas most HTMs operate as sole practitioners, specializing in small and mid-sized firms. Still, many small firms hire a person having no certification as their auditor. A layman auditor can be hired unless an auditee is larger than a size threshold specified in law. However, this option is likely to be removed in the foreseeable future. According to the bill for a new Auditing Act, only professional auditors would be allowed to carry out statutory audits. However, the smallest firms would be exempt from mandatory audits. These two changes would have a most significant impact on the structure of the Finnish audit market.

The chapter has reviewed the changes in Finnish audit regulation, as well as its current state in order to answer the question: what drives changes in audit regulation? We found that some business failures were detonators of change in the early 1990s. However, when we probed deeper into the nature of the changes, we found that the underlying structural shifts in the economy were the ultimate drivers of the regulatory changes. In essence, the high profile business failures showed the need for change, but the structural changes in the economy showed *how* the regulation must be changed.

We found four such examples of changes in the economy. First, the Industrial Revolution created a need for investor protection, which resulted in the adoption of a Company Law and mandatory audits in the latter half of nineteenth century. Second, to facilitate governmental price regulation due to a severe lack of raw materials and products caused by the two wars between 1939 and 1945, the government issued instructions on cost accounting. Third, deregulation of capital markets in the mid-1980s allowed Finnish firms and individuals to tap the foreign capital markets, which resulted in a strong demand for accounting and auditing rules that could be understood by foreign investors. Fourth, the integration of the

Finnish economy into the Single Market of the EU has shifted the interplay between economy and regulation from the national level to the EU level.

Since 1995, when Finland joined the EU, the impact of national events on the public debate has clearly declined. It seems that now overseas crises have become the "detonators" of public debate on audit quality rather than national business failures. A good example of this is the proposal for a new auditing directive. The Commission of the EU explicitly mentioned some recent scandals, namely Parmalat and Ahold, in its press release of May 2004 on the Directive on Statutory Audits, as they motivate the need to change auditing rules. It is pointed out in the same document that the proposal for a new directive is not a knee-jerk reaction to recent corporate scandals. This statement is in line with our conclusion that business failures may serve as a stimulus for discussion on the need for change, but they seldom determine the nature of the change.

In our analysis we ran into a paradox concerning the costs and benefits of changes in regulation as the latter has shifted from the national to the international level. The current and forthcoming changes in regulation are based on international standards and probably have relatively little impact on international audit firms as they already have their own audit manuals, peer-review systems, and education programs. However, small local audit firms do not have their own quality assurance systems or education programs but are nevertheless obliged to follow the same standards and rules as their international counterparts. Consequently, the international developments have the strongest impact on local firms. Yet the clientele of these firms are not publicly held corporations but family businesses that have a quite different set of needs from accounting and auditing. While it is important to assess the value of a listed company every day, the main concern of a private firm is that there is enough cash for operations, which emphasizes the measurement of the earning power of the firm. As a consequence, there is a great risk that the costs of the international developments in audit regulation are much higher than the benefits for privately held companies. It is possible that cost-efficient auditing rules for private companies are of a quite different nature from the auditing rules for public companies.

7 Postscript

The new Auditing Act came into force in July 2007. The new law contains most of the changes proposed by the working group set up by the Ministry of Trade and Industry (see Section 5 for the anticipated changes). Now the new Auditing Act refers explicitly to "international standards" as auditing rules in addition to national legislation. Also the new EU directives are implemented to national legislation through the new Auditing Act. It is fair to say that the shift from a national to an international framework in audit regulation in Finland has reached the point where the international standards are as important a source of auditing rules as the Finnish legislation itself.

The market structure of auditing services will also change due to the two changes in the Auditing Act. First, under the new law only people holding approved professional certification may conduct statutory financial statement audits. Second, the very smallest firms will be exempted from mandatory audits. An audit is obligatory under the new act only when two of the following three criteria are met: assets are over €100,000, sales are over €200,000 or the number of employees is more than three. Together these changes will significantly reduce the number of players in the market.

Auditor reporting changes are also as anticipated. From now on an auditor gives an opinion only on financial statements. The other auditor opinions, the Finnish idiosyncrasies described earlier in this chapter, are now history.

Notes

1 Partnerships and small proprietorships whose assets, sales, or employees are below a certain size threshold are exempted from the obligation to file their financial statements with the public register.
2 Before deregulation, foreign equity and debt capital required the permission of the Bank of Finland.
3 Typical part-timers are accountancy teachers in universities or business schools, or accountants who offer their services to predominantly small and medium sized firms that have outsourced their accounting.
4 As the Auditing Act mandates the Chambers of Commerce to supervise the profession and authorize auditors, they can also be described as semi-governmental bodies.

References

Central Chamber of Commerce. Online. Available at <http://www.keskuskauppakamari. fi> (accessed July and August 2005).
Corporate Governance Recommendation for Listed Companies (2003). Online. Available at: <http://www.keskuskauppakamari.fi/kkk/julkaisut/en_GB/corporate_ governance> (accessed 4 August 2005).
Finnish Institute of Authorized Public Accountants. Online. Available at: <http:// www.kht.fi> (accessed July and August 2005).
Helenius, A. (2004) "Miten tilintarkastus on muuttunut 50 vuoden aikana – ja erityisesti millaista se oli 50 vuotta sitten," *Tilintarkastus – Revision*, 4: 45–52.
Keskuskauppakamari (2003) "Tilintarkastajien hyväksymisvaatimusten kehittäminen, työryhmämuistion," Helsinki: Central Chamber of Commerce.
Komiteamietintö (1992) '14. "Tilintarkastusjärjestelmän kehittämistoimikunnan mietintö," Helsinki: Kauppa-ja tiollisuusministeriö.
Kosonen, L. (2005) "Vaarinpidosta virtuaaliaikaan – Sata vuotta suomalaista tilintarkastusta (From paying heed to the virtual world – One hundred years of auditing in Finland)," doctoral thesis, Lappeenranta University of Technology.
Ministry of Trade and Industry (2003) *Tilintarkastuslakityöryhmän raportti* (Report of the Working Group on the Auditing Act) 12/2003, Helsinki: Kauppa ja teollisuusministeriö.

Ministry of Trade and Industry. Online. Available at: <www.ktm.fi> (accessed July and August 2005).

Niemi, L. (2002) "Do Firms Pay for Audit Risk? Evidence on Risk Premiums in Audit Fees after Direct Control for Audit Effort," *International Journal of Auditing*, 6(1): 37–51.

Registered Institute of Certified HTM Auditors. Online. Available at: <http://www.htm.fi> (accessed July and August 2005).

Riistama, V. (1999) *Tilintarkastuksen teoria ja käytäntö (The practice and theory of auditing)*, Porvoo: WSOY.

Riistama, V. (2005) Profile: KHT auditor from 1965, author of several books on accounting and auditing, worked with various audit firms including Price Waterhouse as a senior partner, served the profession and the regulation of it in many demanding tasks, e.g. was a member of the team that created the quality programs for HTM auditors, a member of several working groups making proposals for the development of legislation on accounting and auditing, including the working group that considered the need to amend the current Auditing Act. Interview 30 August.

Saarikivi, M.L. (1999) "Tilintarkastajan riippumattomuus," doctoral thesis A-155, Helsinki School of Economics.

Saario, M. (1959) "Kirjanpidon meno-tulo-teoria," doctoral thesis, Liiketaloudellisen tutkimuslaitoksen julkaisuja no. 28, Otava, Keuruu.

Shleifer, A. and Vishny, R. (1997) "A Survey of Corporate Governance," *Journal of Finance*, 52(2): 737–83.

Sorsa, E. (1997) "Tilintarkastustoiminnan historiaa ja tulevaisuutta – mikä on HTM-tilintarkastajan asema ensi vuosituhannella? (History and future of auditing – what will be the HTM auditor's position in the next millennium?)," *Tilintarkastus – Revision*, 1: 54–6.

Troberg, P. (2005) Profile: A member of the Auditing Board of the Central Chamber of Commerce (TILA) for ten years, professorships in auditing in the Swedish School of Economics and in international accounting in Helsinki School of Economics. Interview 30 August.

Viitanen, J. (2000) "Auditors' Professional Ethics and Factors Associated with Disciplinary Cases against Auditors," doctoral thesis (no. 88), Swedish School of Economics and Business Administration, Helsinki, Finland.

5   The regulatory response in France to accounting scandals

C. Richard Baker, Jean Bédard and Christian Prat Dit Hauret

In this chapter we examine the regulation of auditing in France and the initiatives to restore trust in auditing. First, we present a brief historical review of the regulation of auditing in France. Then we examine the following specific aspects of regulation: the institutions involved, licensing, professional liability, standards on auditing, ethics and independence, practice regulation, and audit committees.

1 Brief historical review[1]

While some form of auditing for companies had been present before 1860, the birth of auditing for companies in France was signaled by the Loi du 23 mai 1863, which created the Sociétés à Responsabilité Limitée (SARL). The 1863 Act and the subsequent Loi du 24 juillet 1867 regarding sociétés anonymes (SA) required the members of a SARL at the annual general meeting to designate one or more *commissaires* with the responsibility of preparing a report on the situation of the company, its balance sheet, and the accounts presented by the management.

The Décret de 1935 reiterated the Loi de 1867 requirement to designate a *commissaire de société*, but modified the requirement by restricting the choice to commissaires chosen from a list maintained by the Appeal Court. To appear on the court list, a person had to take a technical exam (Décret du 29 juin 1936). Commissaires on the court list were required to form an association, called a "Compagnie des commissaires agréés," which possessed disciplinary power. The Décret de 1935 also modified the Loi de 1867 by imposing requirements regarding independence and by establishing criminal penalties for confirming false information.

The Loi du 24 juillet 1966, regarding commercial companies, modernized the regulation of auditing. This law defined a rigorous legal framework for the exercise of auditing with a view to preventing conflicts of interests. "[I]ndependence was reinforced, entry to the profession was made conditional upon success in exams of a very high level and the object of the audit was defined" (Mikol 1993: 10). This law was supplemented by the Décret 69-810 du 12 août 1969 specifying the obligations of auditors and the rules of organization and operation of the profession. Over the years, a succession of laws has modernized the Loi du 24 juillet 1966 to take into account various European directives and changes in international standards. In 2000 the Loi du 24 juillet 1966 was integrated into the Code de commerce along with other commercial laws (Ordonnance 2000-912 du 18 septembre 2000).

The Loi 2003-706 du 1er août 2003 de sécurité financière, which modified the Code de commerce, was France's response to the confidence crisis created by financial scandals in the United States and other countries. In addition, there was some impetus for this law as a result of the financial problems of Crédit Lyonnais and Vivendi Universal. One of the main provisions of the law was the modernizing of the practice of statutory auditing. Contrary to the USA, where the profession lost its regulatory power due to the Sarbanes-Oxley Act, the Loi de sécurité financière did not revolutionize the regulation of auditing. The law retains the shared regulation model whereby auditors are governed by a legal framework conferring on them the status of a regulated profession, and where auditors self-regulate themselves by defining ethical rules and by installing monitoring mechanisms. The reform of auditing has been focused around three main axes: creating an external controlling authority for the profession (the Haut Conseil du Commissariat aux Comptes), clarification and reinforcement of independence rules, and new powers for the Garde des Sceaux (Minister of Justice) and the securities commission (Autorité des Marchés Financiers).

2 Institutions involved

In France the regulation of statutory auditing, as well as the regulation of the initial issue and trading of securities, is the responsibility of the French government. Pursuant to French law, companies with quoted shares must appoint two auditors, who are both engaged in auditing the company's accounts at the same time. As indicated in Figure 5.1, the members of the auditing profession (referred to collectively as *Commissariat aux Comptes*) are regulated by the French government with the assistance of various governmental and professional organizations created by the government. Figure 5.1 shows the regulatory structure before and after the Loi 2003-706 du 1er août 2003 de sécurité financière. The reform added two new institutions: the Haut Conseil du Commissariat aux Comptes (H3C) and the Autorité des Marchés Financiers (AMF), which replaced the Commission des Opérations de Bourse (COB). It also dissolved one, the Comité de Déontologie de l'Indépendance. The members of the H3C and the AMF are named by the government of France (through the Minister of Justice).

2.1 Compagnies des Commissaires aux Comptes[2]

Statutory auditors are organized at the regional level into Compagnies Régionales de Commissaires aux Comptes (CRCC) and at the national level into the Compagnie Nationale des Commissaires aux Comptes (CNCC). The CNCC operates under the supervision of the French Justice Minister (Garde des Sceaux).

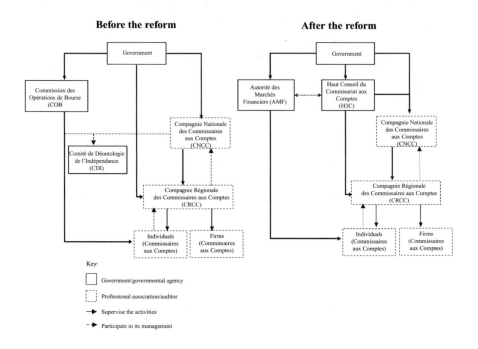

Figure 5.1 Regulatory structure of auditing in France

The mission of the CNCC is to assure the proper functioning of auditing practice and to supervise and defend the profession and the independence of its members (Décret du 12 août 1969, Art. 1). The CNCC is responsible for establishing the requirements for becoming a statutory auditor; for establishing auditing standards; and for establishing the disciplinary practices of the profession. The CNCC is administered by a national council whose members are elected by representatives from the regional CRCCs. The regional representatives are chosen according to a ratio of one representative per 200 members (Art. 51). Members of the CNCC include all statutory auditors as well as auditing firms (Art. 25). The CNCC also establishes the ethical standards for the auditing profession. The operations of the CNCC are financed primarily through membership fees. The day to day operations of the profession are conducted through 34 regional companies of statutory auditors (CRCCs), the membership of which includes individual auditors as well as auditing firms. The regional CRCCs are managed by councils composed of between six and 26 auditors elected by a secret ballot (Art. 30 and 31). The regional CRCCs are responsible for maintaining the list of members, supervising the practice of auditing, and determining the annual fees of members.

The Loi de sécurité financière modified the status of the CNCC. It is now a public corporation with legal personality instituted under the aegis of the Minister of Justice and directed to serve the public interest (Loi 2003-706 du 1er août 2003, Art. 100). This status does not change its mission or structure, but, as a public corporation, it has the power to defend the public interest by being a civil party against persons who commit infringements of rules or regulations.

2.2 Haut Conseil du Commissariat aux Comptes

In 2003 the Loi de sécurité financière created an external authority, the High Council for Auditors (H3C), to exercise supervision of the profession with the support of the CNCC and to ensure respect for professional ethics and the independence of auditors (Code de commerce, Art. L821-1). The H3C is composed of 12 members and includes legal experts and judges, persons qualified in the areas of economics and financial affairs, as well as representatives from the securities exchanges, along with some academic accountants. Statutory auditors are represented, but they constitute a minority of the members (three). The H3C is charged with reviewing and providing an opinion on the auditing standards issued by the CNCC prior to their approval by the Minister of Justice. The H3C has assumed the responsibility for audit quality reviews that was previously exercised by the Comité d'Examen National d'Activité (CENA). This program is directed toward the review of audit practices including: defining the scope of reviews; analysis of audit quality; conformity with ethical standards; and any other matters requested by the Minister of Justice in situations having public importance. The H3C also serves as an appeals authority for the disciplinary decisions of the regional chambers. The funds required to operate the H3C are charged to the budget of the Ministry of Justice.

2.3 Autorité des Marchés Financiers (AMF)

This entity was created by the Loi de sécurité financière du 1er août 2003, through a merger of the Commission des Opérations de Bourse (COB), the Conseil des Marchés Financiers (CMF), and the Conseil de Discipline de la Gestion Financière (CDGF). The mission of the AMF includes overseeing the functioning of the securities markets. The CNCC operates in close collaboration with the AMF. The work of these bodies is coordinated to improve the quality of the information provided by companies to the markets and to improve the practice of statutory auditing.

Like its predecessor, the AMF must be informed of proposals to appoint or reappoint the auditors of public companies and it may make a comment on such proposals. It may also request information on the auditees from auditors of public companies. The Loi de sécurité financière also gave the AMF the power to launch an inspection of an auditor of a public company and to request the assistance of the CNCC (Code de commerce, Art. L821-8).

2.4 Comité de Déontologie de l'Indépendance (CDI)

In 1999 the Commission des Opérations de Bourse (COB) and the CNCC established a consultative committee on independence, referred to by its French acronym as the CDI. The mission of the CDI was to provide advice and recommendations concerning the independence of statutory auditors, particularly with regard to auditors of companies with publicly traded securities, and also to enhance the objectivity of audit findings. The CDI was composed of 11 persons designated jointly by the CNCC and the AMF, of whom the majority cannot come from the auditing profession. Since 2003 the H3C has been the highest authority invested with the duty of monitoring the profession, whether or not the auditee is a public company.

3 Licensing

3.1 Licensed persons

In France the Code de commerce requires statutory auditing to be performed by one or more Commissaires aux Comptes (Code de commerce, Art. L225-218). An individual is not allowed to practice as an auditor unless he or she is enrolled in a Compagnie Régionale des Commissaires aux Comptes (CRCC) (Code de commerce, Art. L822-1). In 2005 the number of statutory auditors enrolled as members of the CNCC was approximately 14,500, with more than 3,000 firms also listed as members.

+ Joint Audit for firms issuing consolidated accounts !

3.2 Education and training

The requirements for becoming a statutory auditor were established by a French government decree (Décret 69-810 du 12 août 1969). This decree specified two different pathways to becoming a statutory auditor. The first was for the prospective auditor to obtain a higher education diploma approved by the CNCC, successfully pass several professional examinations, and then complete a three year internship (Art. 3). Following the second route, a person could first become an Expert Comptable and then complete an internship in the office of a registered Commissaire aux Comptes (CAC). During the internship the prospective auditor would be required to participate in several audit engagements.

To become an Expert Comptable, a candidate must complete a university level education, which involves taking a series of successively more advanced diplomas in accounting, finance, and business law. The candidate must also complete a professional internship of three years, write a memorandum on an accounting topic, and then pass a final examination. A large majority of statutory auditors in France become auditors by first becoming Experts Comptable. The examination to become a statutory auditor and the examination to become an Expert Comptable are both national examinations. The organization of these examinations (including the subject matter covered and the marking of the examination) is under the supervision of the French government through the Ministry of Education.

Any person who completes the educational and other preliminary requirements specified in the decree can request registration as a CAC by applying to a regional committee of the Cour d'Appel (Court of Appeal, a judicial arm of the French government). A committee composed of seven persons is then assigned to evaluate such applications. The committee is composed of: one judicial magistrate (who is the chairman); one member of the Chambre Régionale des Comptes; a professor of law, economics, or management; two persons qualified in law, economics, or finance; one representative of the Minister of the Economy (Code de commerce, Art. L822-2); and a representative of the CNCC. The members of the committee are designated by the Minister of Justice. The committee is charged with verifying whether the candidate has fulfilled the conditions necessary to become a statutory auditor (Décret 69-810 du 12 août 1969, art. 11).

3.3 Continuing education

Article 23 of the Code of Professional Ethics of the CNCC stipulates that "every Commissaire aux Comptes has the obligation to devote a sufficient number of hours annually to training, and must work with colleagues to see that the high level of competence that is required by the auditing profession is maintained." Practicing auditors must keep a record of the continuing education training that they have completed each year. They are obliged to have at least 20 hours per year of continuing education.

The Loi de la sécurité financière has introduced a legal requirement for continuing education. Thus, a commissaire who has not practised as an auditor for three or more years is now required to take a special part-time training course before accepting an auditing engagement (Code de commerce, Art. L822-4).

4 Standards

4.1 Auditing standards

The Code de commerce and the various other laws and regulations that regulate the practice of auditing do not define the principles or implementation aspects of auditing standards. The establishment of auditing standards has therefore been placed in the hands of the CNCC, which was created to assure the appropriate functioning of the practice of auditing and the surveillance of such practices (Décret 69-810 du 12 août 1969, art. 1–28 and 88). The CNCC is now in the process of developing a convergence between French auditing standards and the International Standards on Auditing (ISAs).

The Loi de sécurité financière did not change the CNCC's responsibility for setting auditing standards, but the standards now have to be approved by the

Minister of Justice, based on the advice of the H3C (Code de commerce, Art. L821-1).

Although the CNCC is the primary issuer of auditing standards, the Code de commerce also specifically defines the scope of the activities of statutory auditors in France in certain areas. These activities include:

- *Certification of annual accounts* – The primary function of the statutory auditor is to certify the "régularité," "sincérité," and "image fidèle" of annual accounts (Code de commerce, Art. L225-235).
- *Providing information about related party agreements* – Statutory auditors must give a report to the annual meeting of the shareholders regarding regulated agreements, generally those between related parties, such as agreements between a business entity and its executive management; agreements between business entities having a common management; and agreements between a business entity and any shareholders owning more than 10 per cent of the capital (Code de commerce, Art. L225-86, L225-88).
- *Notification procedure* – If, during the course of exercising the functions of a statutory auditor, the auditor becomes aware of conditions that cast doubt on the ability of the enterprise to continue as a going concern, the auditor must follow a notification procedure, which consists of informing the chairperson of the board of directors, the chairperson of the Commercial Court, and in certain cases notifying the general meeting of shareholders (Code de commerce, Art. L234-1).
- *Communication of irregularities or inaccuracies* – Auditors have to report to the next general meeting of shareholders any irregularities or inaccuracies they discover while performing their audit (Code de Commerce, Art. L225-240).
- *Reporting of criminal acts* – Auditors are required to report any criminal acts which they become aware of to the Public Prosecutor of the French government, e.g. fraud (Code de commerce, Art. L225-240).

The Loi de sécurité financière changed the requirements regarding the certification of annual accounts. Auditors are now required to justify their evaluations (Code de commerce, Art. L225-235). According to the Avis of the H3C (2004), this provision requires the auditor to add a justification of the opinion in a section following the opinion. The law also added a new reporting obligation.

- *Certification of internal control* – Auditors present their opinion regarding the chairman of the board of directors' report describing the internal control procedures related to the origination and processing of the accounting and financial information.

The Loi de sécurité financière also imposed new reporting obligations for auditors in relation to the AMF. Auditors must inform the AMF when they identify facts likely to compromise the continued operation of the company, or when they intend to refuse to certify the accounts, or report on discovered irregularities or inaccuracies that they will be presenting at the next general meeting (Code monétaire et financier, art. L621-22).

4.2 Ethics and independence standards

The CNCC has promulgated a Code of Professional Ethics which defines the ethical behavior expected of statutory auditors. The code was modified in 2004 to respond to the new requirements of the Loi de sécurité financière and IFAC. It establishes fundamental principles and general rules of ethical behavior for auditors.

The Code de commerce specifies certain activities which are deemed to be incompatible with the practice of statutory auditing. Article L822-10 of this code stipulates that the functions of statutory auditing are incompatible with any activity or any act that would impinge on the auditor's independence. Article 822-12 specifies that statutory auditors cannot be named as an administrator or executive, or member of the board of directors, of a company which they have audited for a period of five years after they cease their activities as statutory auditor. The same prohibition is applicable to shareholders or managers of a firm of auditors. Pursuant to Article L822-13, persons who have previously been executives, members of boards of directors, managers, or salaried employees of a company cannot be named as a statutory auditor for that company for at least five years after they have terminated their relationship with the company.

The Loi de sécurité financière re-emphasized the professional obligations of statutory auditors. The prohibition against taking, receiving, or maintaining any interest, direct or indirect, in an entity whose accounts the auditor certifies is reaffirmed. The law reaffirms the prohibition against auditors offering consulting advice to audit clients or their affiliates. This prohibition is likewise specified in the Code of Ethics. It is also prohibited for an auditor to audit an entity if the entity has received consulting advice from a member of a firm belonging to the same network of firms as the auditor (inserted in the Code de commerce, Art. L822-11). The law introduced a five-year cooling-off period for individual auditors and signing members of an auditing firm before they can be appointed as directors or employees of a company they have audited, and for directors or employees of a company before they can be appointed as auditors of that legal entity.

The definition of the incompatibilities related to personal, financial, or professional matters is left to the Code of Ethics. The code is intended to provide detailed assumptions and situations which were difficult to include in the law (Hyest 2003).

Whereas the CNCC is still responsible for professional ethics, the Loi de sécurité financière (Art. 104) now requires that the Code of Ethics be approved by a Conseil d'Etat decree based on the advice of the AMF (Code de commerce, Art. L-822-16).

5 Practice regulation

5.1 Quality control standards

There are no specific quality control standards for auditing in France.

5.2 External practice reviews

There are two levels of external practice reviews. The first level is the regional examination (l'examen régional d'activité [ERA]). The second level is a national examination (l'examen national d'activité [ENA]). A government decree (Décret 69-810 du 12 août 1969, Art. 66) requires statutory auditors to be examined at least once a year by the regional council and the national council. The purpose of these examinations is to maintain a uniform level of practice quality among auditors. The objectives of the regional examinations are to verify the correct application of professional norms and the appropriateness of the audit opinion and related conclusions based on the audit work papers; to contribute to a better assessment of risks inherent in auditing; and to reinforce the external credibility of the audit profession.

The national examination of audit quality, or ENA, focuses primarily on statutory auditors who audit companies subject to the jurisdiction of the AMF. The ENA is oriented toward assuring conformity with ethical norms, rigorous application of accounting standards, and establishing the reliability of the information issued to the financial markets.

Before the Loi de sécurité financière, control of the profession was primarily based on an internal inspection performed by the CRCC and the Comité d'Examen National d'Activité (CENA), which jointly defined the inspection program as well as the focus of the examination. The Loi de sécurité financière places the quality assurance function for audits of public companies under the responsibility of the H3C. The H3C is responsible for deciding on the extent of supervision, and determining the focus of investigations. The inspections are still carried out by practicing auditors. For public company auditors, the examinations are carried out by auditors appointed by the CNCC with the assistance of the AMF and, for the others, by auditors appointed by the regional companies. The H3C is also responsible for supervising the implementation and monitoring of the audit quality program (Code de commerce, Art. L821-1). Auditors may now be subject to a third category of inspection launched by the Minister of Justice or the AMF in situations involving a matter of public order or high interest (Code de commerce, Art. L821-7).

6 Audit committees

The corporate governance system in France is approximately the same as it is in the United Kingdom and in the United States. That is, there is a single board of directors elected by shareholders at an annual general meeting. As in other jurisdictions, best practice reports on corporate governance have been published over the years (e.g. Rapport Viénot 1, 1995, Rapport Viénot 2, 1999, Rapport Bouton 2002). These reports contain recommendations regarding audit committees.[3] However, the Code de commerce does not contain any provisions directly relating to audit committees. The legislative reforms imposed by the Loi de sécurité financière of 2003 did not change this. It is interesting to note that the Commission des Finances, du Contrôle Budgétaire et des Comptes Économiques de la Nation (2003) in its report on the "projet de loi de sécurité financière" proposed an amendment aimed at instituting a legal definition of the audit committee (comité des comptes) and establishing its organization and mission, while preserving its optional character. For the commission, the best practice recommendations were not enough. The objective of the amendment was to create a "label," intended to prevent the constitution of cosmetic committees.

The commission proposal was not adopted by the Senate and hence today the only normative text concerning audit committees is article 90 of the Décret 67-236 du 23 mars 1967, which relates in a general way to the committees that can be created within the board of directors. It stipulates that the board of directors can decide on the establishment of committees charged with studying questions on which the board itself or its president requests an opinion. These committees carry out their activities under board responsibility; their members do not have to be members of the board of directors or to be independent.

While not mandatory, audit committees are common for public companies; 86 percent of the companies on the SBF120 index of the Bourse de Paris have an audit committee, and many have adjusted their operations to the rules recommended by the Rapport Bouton (Altedia 2003).

7 Professional liability

7.1 Liability for disciplinary action

Pursuant to Article 88 of the Décret du 12 août 1969, statutory auditors may become subject to disciplinary action if they are involved in a violation of a law, regulation, or professional rule, gross negligence, or other act lacking in integrity, regardless of whether these acts are committed by an individual auditor or a firm of auditors. Auditing firms may be subject to civil lawsuits, which can result in damage payments if a third party has been injured.

Potential liability extends to acts not directly related to the practice of auditing (e.g. driving while intoxicated). The disciplinary structure is based on regional disciplinary bodies, which are composed of the same members who admit new auditors into the CRCCs (see previous section). The H3C serves as an appellate disciplinary body if there is an appeal from a regional disciplinary body. If a statutory auditor becomes the subject of a disciplinary action, it is the regional body that decides on the action that should be pursued, regardless of where the alleged violation took place (Code de commerce, Art. L822-6). In the regional disciplinary bodies, practicing auditors constitute only a minority of members. The French government appoints the majority of the members of these bodies. Article L822-7 of the Code de commerce specifies that a magistrate from the prosecutor's office must be involved in each regional disciplinary body, as well as in the national disciplinary body. The magistrates are designated by the French Ministry of Justice.

The potential disciplinary penalties include: a warning, a reprimand, a temporary suspension of practice for a period not to exceed five years, or expulsion from the list of CACs (Décret 69-810 du 12 août 1969, Art. 89). Appeal against a decision is possible to the H3C. Disciplinary decisions are not made public and therefore it is not possible to know the extent of the disciplinary actions that have been imposed. The H3C is organized into regional appellate chambers. These bodies both enroll and discipline CACs. This regulatory structure replaces the former Chambre Nationale de Discipline.

7.2 Criminal liability

Legislation and case law establish criminal penalties for statutory auditors for infractions of laws and rules concerning incompatible occupations, issuing false information, non-revelation of illegal acts, and violations of professional confidentiality. The criminal liability of an auditor is established by the Penal Code. Certain incompatible activities are specified by articles L822-10 to 13 of the Code de commerce. Incompatible activities include situations where there is a close familial or marital relationship between the auditor and persons who hold a position of influence at the audit client. The crime of issuing or being connected with the issuing of false information exists if the auditor is complicit in the issuing of fraudulent or misleading financial information. Committing this crime can result in imprisonment for up to two years and a fine of €20,000. The crime of not revealing illegal acts relates to not informing the state prosecutor of acts known to the auditor that have been committed by a client, including embezzlement or fraud.

7.3 Civil liability

The liability of the auditor for civil penalties stems from Article L225-241 of the Code de commerce, which specifies that:

> Commissaires aux Comptes are liable to the commercial enterprise (the client) and to third parties for damages arising from negligent acts committed by them in the exercise of their functions. They are not responsible for

infractions committed by management or directors except in the case where they have knowledge of the infractions and do not reveal this knowledge in their report to the general assembly.

8 Conclusion

In France statutory auditing is performed by Commissaries aux Comptes governed by a legal framework conferring on them the status of a regulated profession and imposing on them a number of constraints relating to their duties and their internal functioning. However, the profession has enjoyed a great deal of latitude regarding the means utilized to realize its objectives of organizing and regulating statutory auditors (Bédard et al. 2002).

France reacted in 2003 to the accounting scandals and the Sarbanes-Oxley legislation with the Loi de sécurité financière. This law reaffirmed the principle of shared regulation whereby the state integrates auditors into its system of regulatory control by conferring certain responsibilities and powers on the profession, while also placing certain constraints on their behavior. The law consolidated the guarantees of the independence of the profession mainly by establishing the Haut Conseil du Commissariat aux Comptes to exercise independent supervision of the profession and adding some rules regarding auditor independence. As indicated by the Commission des Lois Constitutionnelles, de Législation, du Suffrage Universel, du Règlement et d'Administration Générale (Hyest 2003: 14), if the Loi de sécurité financière "focuses on auditing and the auditing profession, it does not have as an aim to stigmatize this profession which, particularly in France, is far from having demerit." It is possible that many of the specificities of regulation pertaining to the Commissariat aux Comptes were precautionary, and that the need for the Loi de sécurité financière was purely preventive, with a concern for reinforcing the credibility of the statutory audit in a context of turbulence in the capital markets.

Notes

1 See Mikol (1993) for a review.
2 There is also an Ordre des Experts Comptables, whose members serve as advisers to companies regarding accounting and tax matters. Legally, the professions of Expert Comptable and Commissaire aux Comptes are distinct, but they are practiced simultaneously by many accountants in France, provided that the auditing function and the accounting advisory function are not carried out at the same time for the same client.`
3 For example, the Rapport Bouton recommends that two-thirds of the directors on the audit committee be independent directors. In addition, it stresses the importance of the presence of members having finance and accounting competence on the audit committee. It also considers the use of external experts' services, but without tackling the question of the financing of such an operation.

References

Altedia (2003). Online. Available at: <http://www.altedia.fr/altedia_fr.nsf/> (accessed 21 February 2007).

Bédard, J.R.C., Baker C.R., and Prat dit Hauret, C. (2002) "La réglementation de l'audit: une comparaison entre le Canada, les États-Unis et la France," *Comptabilité, Contrôle et Audit*, 8 (Numéro Spécial): 139–68.

Code de commerce.

Code monétaire et financier.

Commission des Finances, du Contrôle Budgétaire et des Comptes Économiques de la Nation. Sénat session ordinaire de 2002-2003, rapport fait au nom de la commission des finances, du contrôle budgétaire et des comptes économiques de la nation (1) sur le projet de loi de sécurité financière, par M. Philippe Marini, Sénateur. Tome I: Rapport.

Compagnie Nationale des Commissaires aux Comptes (2004) *Normes professionnelles et code de déontologie*, Paris: CNCC Edition.

Décret du 8 août 1935 modifiant la loi du 24-07-1867 sur les sociétés en ce qui concerne la responsabilité pénale des administrateurs et le choix et les attributions des commissaires, J.O. 9 août 1935, p. 8683.

Décret du 29 juin 1936 sur l'application de l'article 4 du décret du 8 août 1935, J.O. 30 juin 1936, p. 6815.

Décret n° 67-236 du 23 mars 1967 sur les sociétés commerciales, J.O. 12 février 2005.

Décret n° 69-810 du 12 août 1969 relatif à l'organisation et au statut professionnel des commissaires aux comptes, J.O. 27 novembre 2003.

Haut Conseil du Commissariat aux Comptes (H3C) (2004) Avis rendu par le Haut Conseil du Commissariat aux Comptes au titre de la promotion des bonnes pratiques professionnelles (art. L. 821-1, 5ème alinéa du Code de commerce).

Hyest, J.-J. (2003) Avis 207 (2002-2003) – Commission des Lois. Avis présenté au nom de la commission des lois constitutionnelles, de législation, du suffrage universel, du règlement et d'administration générale (1) sur le projet de loi de sécurité financière, par M. Jean-Jacques Hyest, Sénateur.

Loi du 23 Mai 1863 sur les sociétés à responsabilité limitée.

Loi du 24 juillet 1867 sur les sociétés.

Loi no. 66-537 du 24 juillet 1966 sur les sociétés commerciales, J.O. 26 juillet 1966, p. 6402.

Loi no. 2003-706 du 1er août 2003 de sécurité financière, J.O. n° 177 du 2 août 2003, p. 13220.

Mikol, A. (1993) "The Evolution of Auditing and the Independent Auditor in France," *European Accounting Review*, 2(1): 1–16.

Ordonnance n° 2000-912 du 18 septembre 2000 relative à la partie législative du code de commerce.

Rapport Bouton (2002) *Pour un meilleur gouvernement des entreprises cotées* - Rapport du groupe de travail présidé par M. Daniel Bouton, 23 septembre 2002.

Rapport Viénot 1 (1995) *Le conseil d'administration des sociétés cotées* - Rapport du groupe de travail présidé par M. Marc Viénot, Association Française des Entreprises Privées et Conseil National du Patronat Français.

Rapport Viénot 2 (1999) *Rapport du comité sur le gouvernement d'entreprise* presidé par M. Marc Viénot, Association Française des Entreprises Privées et Mouvement des Entreprises de France.

6 Audit regulation in Germany

Improvements driven by internationalization

Annette G. Köhler, Kai-Uwe Marten, Reiner Quick and Klaus Ruhnke

1 Introduction

1.1 Historical background

The origins of auditing in Germany are linked to the Fugger and Welser trading houses and to the government trading companies which were founded in the sixteenth century. These often had many widely dispersed branches in Germany and beyond, whose managers were given considerable independence. This later became the reason for the introduction of internal auditing. The large amount of capital needed by the trading companies mostly came from external investors, which in turn entailed a separation of ownership and management. Senior executives had to write reports to account for their activities, and external auditors, who were independent of the company, were required to review these reports. The amendment of the German company law of 11 June 1870, which for the first time expressed a legal monitoring duty, was decisive for auditing in Germany. In 1870, § 225a, 2 Old German Commercial Code (Allgemeines Deutsches Handelsgesetzbuch, ADHGB), specified that the audit of the financial statements and the suggested distribution of profits were the duty of the supervisory board.

In 1890 the German-American Trust Company (Deutsch-Amerikanische Treuhand-Gesellschaft) was founded (later the company was renamed the Deutsche Treuhand-Gesellschaft, DTG) (Stürmer 1990: 26). It acted as a protective organization for the German owners of American investment securities, performed and supervised investments on their behalf, and represented the interests of German investors (Becker 1928: 221). Due to DTG's experience in auditing and reorganizing mortgage banks, the company was frequently appointed by the Deutsche Bank as an auditor of companies which had encountered financial difficulties and were attempting to overcome the crisis by obtaining external credit (Lansburgh 1908: 853). The first audit of financial statements, which DTG carried out independently of trustee operations, was a review of the balance sheet, income statement, and books of the Siemens&Halske Aktiengesellschaft in 1902 (Pankow 1990: 151). Following the example of the DTG, further auditing and trustee companies soon appeared. Most of them were founded by large banks and banking groups and later also by the government (for further details see Quick 2004). According to § 266 of the Commercial Code (Handelsgesetzbuch, HGB), the general meeting could decide to have a voluntary external audit. However, until the turn of the century this option was only exerted with caution, since it was feared that it signaled financial difficulties. This changed after the business failures between 1900 and 1903. Initially, the bank representatives on the supervisory board pushed for annual audits (Passow 1906: 43).

Finally, the world economic crisis was the crucial reason for the introduction of the statutory audit in Germany (Born 1965). Significant business collapses like those of the Frankfurt General Insurance Stock Corporation (Frankfurter Allgemeine Versicherungs-Aktien-Gesellschaft, FAVAG) in August 1929 and the large North Wool Group (Nordwolle-Konzern) in Bremen in June 1931 revealed supervisory boards' failures and resulted in German banks, in particular the Danat Bank, being drawn into the crisis. The amendment of company law through the president's decree on company law, public surveillance of banking, and a tax amnesty of 19 September 1931 were the means of overcoming the banking crisis.

The amendment of company law in 1931, introducing mandatory financial statement audits, also introduced the profession of German public auditor (Wirtschaftsprüfer, WP). The government decided against granting the right to perform statutory audits to the existing profession of sworn-in auditors (gerichtlich beeidigte Bücherrevisoren), but instead created a new profession. The profession experienced and enforced political conformity during the regime of the National Socialists. After the end of the Second World War, the profession was rebuilt, and in 1961 the Law Regulating the Profession of German Public Auditors (Wirtschaftsprüferordnung, WPO) came into force and the Chamber of Public Accountants (Wirtschaftsprüferkammer, WPK; cf. http://www.wpk.de) was founded.

It is evident that the primary task of the statutory auditor is to assist the supervisory board. Thus, the statutory auditor plays a very specific role in the German corporate governance system.[1]

1.2 Triggering events and initiatives

History has demonstrated that changes in audit regulation have usually been spurred by economic recessions and related business failures uncovering corporate governance deficiencies. As in other countries, there has also been an increasing number of fraudulent financial statements in Germany which have not been revealed by the statutory auditor. Prominent examples are Balsam, Schneider, Holzmann, Flowtex, and Comroad. The last of these is described as an example.

Comroad was a supplier of traffic telematics systems, which from 1999 to 2002 reported extreme increases in sales and profits, always beyond expectations. A large proportion of sales was generated in Asia by a subsidiary in Hong Kong, which later appeared to be fictitious. Despite discrepancies between Comroad's figures on sales and the corresponding figures of its major customer Skynet, Comroad received an unqualified opinion from its statutory auditor, KPMG. After press releases questioning the correctness of Comroad's sales figures, KPMG resigned in February 2002. The succeeding auditor, Rödl&Partner, later found out that in 1998 63 percent, in 1999 86 percent, and in 2000 97 percent of the sales could not be traced. It can be assumed that KPMG audit procedures had been insufficient.

Both national scandals and those abroad influence the standard setting process in Germany, since it is highly dependent on developments at the international and European levels, i.e. the amendment of the Eighth EU Directive and IFAC standards are crucial for national standard setting. In addition, it is due to the audit of US-listed German multinational corporations and German subsidiaries of US-listed firms that US listing requirements have a major impact on audit regulation in Germany.

Relevant recent legislative initiatives were:

*   Law on Control and Transparency in Enterprises (Gesetz zur Kontrolle und Transparenz im Unternehmensbereich, KonTraG) of 1998;
*   Law on Transparency and Publicity (Transparenz- und Publizitätsgesetz, TransPuG) of 2002;
*   Law on Financial Accounting Standards Reform (Bilanzrechtsreformgesetz, BilReG) of 2005;
*   Law on Financial Accounting Controls (Bilanzkontrollgesetz, BilKoG) of 2005;
*   Law on Public Auditor Oversight (Abschlussprüferaufsichtsgesetz, APAG) of 2005;
*   Law on Professional Oversight Reform (Berufsaufsichtsreformgesetz, BARefG) of 2006.

The latter three laws contain amendments which had been announced by the German government in its ten-issues program of 2003. Another initiative is the German Corporate Governance Code (Deutscher Corporate Governance Kodex, DCGK, cf. http://www.corporate-governance-code.de).

The remainder of this chapter is structured as follows. The next section gives an overview of the German corporate governance regime. Section 3 provides an overview of auditors' qualification and continuous training. The current approach to auditing standard setting is described in section 4. Special consideration is given to auditing standards enhancing trust. Since the debate on trust-enhancing ethical measures is focused on auditors' independence issues, section 5 emphasizes current initiatives concerning independence standards. Section 6 deals with various aspects of the supervision of the auditing profession as well as with enforcement issues. In section 7 the liability exposure of German auditors is analyzed. Finally, section 8 summarizes the results and draws conclusions.

2 Corporate governance regime

2.1 The German two-tier system

For limited liability companies, the German corporate governance system is characterized by a clear division between management and supervision. This can be demonstrated particularly with reference to public limited companies. In contrast to the Anglo-Saxon one-tier system, where all members of the board of directors are assumed to represent shareholders' interests, representation in Germany is explicitly manifold and therefore linked to a two-tier system (see Figure 6.1). The executive board (Vorstand) is responsible for the management of the company (§ 76 Stock Corporation Act (Aktiengesetz, AktG)). However, the executive board is appointed (§ 84 AktG) and monitored (§ 111 AktG) by a second institution, the supervisory board (Aufsichtsrat). Supervisory board composition corresponds to the continental understanding of a network-oriented governance which is supposed to ensure effective monitoring by explicitly involving various stakeholders, e.g. banks, parent companies, and particularly employees and trade unions. That is why usually, at least in public limited companies with more than 2,000 employees, half of the twenty supervisory board members are employees' representatives (§ 96 AktG; § 7 Law on Codetermination (Mitbestimmungsgesetz, MitbestG)).

In practice, the continuous monitoring function is exerted by passing a list of items that require the approval of the supervisory board. Also, the executive board

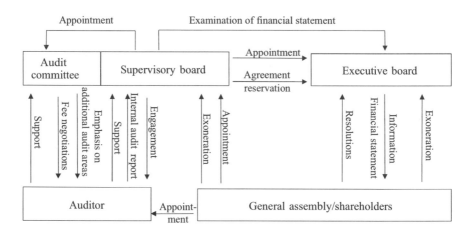

Figure 6.1 Corporate governance setting in Germany

has to inform the supervisory board of all major decisions and plans in advance (irrespective of a potential need for approval). In addition, the supervisory board has to examine the annual financial statement for which the executive board is responsible. This audit is usually based on the findings of the statutory auditor, i.e. the auditor not only contributes to the credibility of financial statements from an external stakeholder perspective but also enhances the monitoring function of supervisory boards. Consequently, auditor selection, auditor engagement (subsequent to auditor election by the general assembly), and the determination of additional emphasis on specific audit areas are the responsibility of the supervisory board. It is also the supervisory board – not the executive board – that is the addressee of the long form audit report (Prüfungsbericht).

Initiated by a recommendation in the DCGK issued in 2002 and enforced by a comply-or-explain principle according to § 161 AktG, most German listed companies have in the meantime established supervisory board committees dealing primarily with financial reporting and auditing issues (German audit committees) even though according to Art.41, para.1, sentence 5 of the Eighth EU Directive (amended 17 May 2006) this is not obligatory for supervisory bodies that perform the functions assigned to the audit committee. However, German audit committees show major differences from audit committees established in a one-tier corporate governance setting.

First, the delegation of decisions to single board members or committees in general is prohibited (plenary reservation according to § 107, 3 AktG). Hence, German audit committees may only take over preparatory work prior to board decisions or communication duties such as audit fee negotiations. This means that the scope of tasks for audit committees in the US is larger than in Germany. Second, unlike in the US, German audit committees do not *constitute* the monitoring institution within corporate governance, but rather strengthen monitoring efficiency by bundling resources and enhancing a division of labor within the supervisory board. In fact, the distinction between German audit committees and audit committees is crucial, since it makes clear that the introduction of audit committees in the Anglo-Saxon corporate governance system has actually moved it considerably nearer the continental two-tier model.

However, the amendment of the Eighth EU Directive and SEC listing requirements with respect to audit committee formation, duties, personal requirements, and accountability as a result of the Sarbanes-Oxley Act of 2002 have spurred discussion of supervisory board member characteristics in Germany. In particular, codetermination via supervisory boards and the shift of former executive board members to the supervisory board are considered to impair necessary member qualification and independence. These concerns are all the more serious the more one considers the link between the monitoring function of the supervisory board on the one hand and of the statutory auditor on the other. The higher the supervisory board member qualification and independence, the more effective the cooperation with the statutory auditor, i.e. the higher audit quality.

2.2 The institutional environment of the audit profession

In order to assure high audit quality, auditors in Germany, as in all Western industrial countries, are organized as a profession embedded in a system that combines public oversight with self-administration (see Figure 6.2). However, in contrast to other countries, with respect to the oversight of auditors the Federal Financial Supervisory Authority (Bundesanstalt für Finanzdienstleistungsaufsicht, BAFin, see http://www.bafin.de, responsible for integrated financial market supervision) plays no major role. Instead, the main responsibility lies with the Federal Ministry of Economics and Technology (Bundesministerium für Wirtschaft und Technologie, BMWi; see http://www.bmwi.de), the WPK, the Auditor Oversight Commission (Abschlussprüferaufsichtskommission, APAK; see http://www.apak-aoc.de), and the Institute of Public Auditors in Germany, an incorporated association (Institut der Wirtschaftsprüfer in Deutschland e.V.; see also sections 6.2 and 6.3 and http://www.idw.de).

It is important to understand that the WPK is not an institution of self-regulation but rather of self-administration, i.e. it is an entity established under public law and carrying specific *fiduciary* duties toward the public, supervised by the BMWi. Consequently, WPKmembership of all auditors and audit firms is mandatory. According to § 57 WPO, the WPK is responsible for the oversight of the profession, the representation of its members' interests, auditor examination, and auditor registration. In addition, the WPK has passed bylaws regulating the rights and duties of German public auditors in exercising their profession in its professional statutes (Berufssatzung für Wirtschaftsprüfer).

In addition, auditors who breach their professional duties are subject to disciplinary court procedures. If indications for material breaches exist, the public prosecutor initiates a court procedure by bringing a charge.

However, since the WPK is dominated by professionals, the effectiveness of its oversight function in particular has come under fierce criticism. This brought about a major change in the institutional setting of auditing in Germany. In 2005

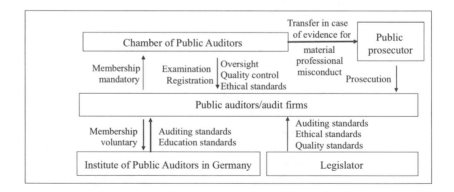

Figure 6.2 Institutional environment of auditors in Germany

a new element of public oversight, the APAK, entered the German public oversight system due to the APAG. This commission has the ultimate responsibility for matters administered by the WPK in connection with the examination, approval and registration of public auditors, adoption of professional and ethical standards, quality assurance, and disciplinary investigations and proceedings. As a consequence, the actual decision-making power in these areas will no longer rest with the WPK but be transferred to the APAK, with the Chamber rather serving as an administrative or executive body.

Finally, the German profession has founded the IDW, a private non-profit organization. IDW membership is voluntary. Apart from the WPK, the IDW is responsible for representing auditors' interests and offering continuing professional education to its members (see section 3). Its main duty, however, is auditing standard setting (see section 4). The institutional environment of auditing in Germany is summarised in Figure 6.2.

3 Education and training

The confidence placed in the profession of public auditor and the associated responsibility presuppose particular personal aptitudes and professional qualifications. For the formulation of corresponding training standards, the International Federation of Accountants (IFAC; http://www.ifac.org) gives recommendations in the International Education Standards (IES 1–6) for standard setting of national member organizations, in which the objective, the preconditions, and the elements of training are discussed in more detail.

The admission procedure for the public auditor examination thus has the task of ensuring both professional selection and fulfillment of personal conditions. The latter are not given if:

• the applicant is not able to hold public office due to a criminal conviction;
• the applicant is guilty of conduct which would justify exclusion from this profession;
• the applicant is incapable, not only temporarily, of correctly practicing the profession of public auditor as a result of physical affliction, weakness of his mental powers, or due to an addiction;
• the applicant is not financially secure (§ 16, 1 WPO).

An application for permission to take the public auditor examination, which is decided on by the examination board for the public auditor examination at the WPK (§ 7 WPO), is to be accompanied by certificates of professional qualification and practical experience. These depend on the path of access chosen. The conventional path (approximately 90 percent of members of the profession engaged as public auditors) involves a course of study at a university or college (Elkart and Schmidt 2002: column 178).

Following this course of study, the graduate must be able to furnish evidence of at least three years' work experience as an employee of an audit firm. During this work experience they should have participated for two years in audits of annual financial statements and assisted in the preparation of long form audit reports (§ 9, 1–3 WPO). If proof of audit experience is furnished during the course of a special (accredited) university program, this can be credited up to a maximum period of one year (§ 9, 6 WPO). The same applies to activities as a tax consultant, as an internal auditor in large companies or at the audit association of German banks, as an auditor in the public sector, or as an employee of the WPK or the IDW (§ 9, 5 WPO). In the last few years a step-by-step reduction in the necessary amount of auditing activity has occurred. This takes into account the fact that German public auditors are often already in their mid-thirties at the time of their appointment and therefore face a massive competitive disadvantage internationally (Willeke 2003: 1058). However, the most important reason for that change was to increase the attractiveness of the audit profession as a whole. Even if the new regulation is in line with the rules of most other European countries, it may not be considered to enhance trust in the audit profession.

Proof of the completion of a course of study at university can be waived in the case of at least ten years of auditing activity at an auditor authorized to carry out statutory audits (§ 8, 2 no. 1 WPO) or five years' practice of the profession of sworn-in auditor or tax consultant (§ 8, 2 no. 2 WPO), if at least two years thereof were spent with a public auditor or an audit firm (§ 9, 2 nos. 1 and 2 as well as section 3 WPO). In the case of tax consultants and sworn-in auditors with over 15 years of professional experience, no proof of auditing activity is required (§ 9, 4 WPO).

After receiving permission to sit the examination, the applicant has to prove his professional expertise in the examination in the following four areas (see § 4 Public Auditor Examination Regulation [Wirtschaftsprüferprüfungs- verordnung, WiPrPrüfV])):

- auditing, company valuation, and professional law (two examinations);
- applied business administration, economics (two examinations);
- commercial law (one examination);
- tax law (two examinations).

The duration of the written examinations is four to six hours. If the applicant attains an overall grade in the examination of at least poor (5.00 = E) and also attains an average grade of at least 5.00 (E) in the subjects of auditing, company valuation, and professional law (§ 13, 2, and 3 WiPrPrüfV), an oral examination follows, which should not exceed two hours (§ 15, 3 WiPrPrüfV). For certain groups of persons, an abridged form of the examination is possible. This concerns:

- tax consultants (examination in tax law not taken);
- sworn-in auditors who are also lawyers (examination in applied business administration, economics, and tax law not taken);
- sworn-in auditors who are also tax consultants (examination in applied business administration, economics, and tax law not taken);
- university graduates who have passed examinations during their course of study whose equivalence with the requirements of the audit examination subjects of applied business administration, economics, and commercial law is recognized by the examination board in the admission process, or who have taken these examinations as part of a university course recognized in accordance with § 8a WPO (§§ 13, 13a, and 13b WPO).

The abridged examination in accordance with § 13a WPO for sworn-in auditors is accompanied by the closing of access to the profession of sworn-in auditor on 31 January 2004. After this, already sworn-in auditors are able to continue practicing their profession while retaining their professional title or to apply for the abridged public auditor examination by 31 December 2007 (§ 13a WPO). The examination requirements commission of the examination board is responsible for selecting the examination requirements. The applicant may repeat the examination twice (§§ 8, 22 and 33 WiPrPrüfV). Candidates who have obtained a degree in a member state of the European Union or another contractual state of the agreement on the European Economic Area which entitles them to perform a statutory audit of annual financial statements can be appointed after taking an aptitude test as a public auditor (§ 131g WPO). The written part of the examination covers the areas of commercial and tax law, and the oral examination the subjects of auditing, professional law, and an optional subject chosen by the applicant (§ 27 WiPrüfV).

The high level of training should also be maintained after swearing in. As the activities of a public auditor take place in a very dynamic environment, continuing professional education of the members of the profession is one of the most important success factors. There therefore exists an obligation for independent continuing professional education (§ 43, 2 clause 4 WPO). This should take globalization and the increasing influence of information technology (IT) into account (Behr 2004: 194–5, Coenenberg *et al.* 1999: 377) just as much as the personal specialization of the individual public auditor. At an international level, IFAC deals in even more detail with the continuing professional education requirements in the area of IT (IEG 11.63-130) and also ethical questions (IEG 10.16-19 and IES 4). In the announcement VO 1/1993, the IDW specifies a total minimum number of hours of continuing professional education of 40 per year, but leaves the type and scope of training to the discretion of the public auditor.

4 Auditing standard setting

4.1 Overview of standard setters and the standard setting process

Auditing standards define the objective of the audit and govern the overall process of generating the auditor's opinion. Thus, auditing standards regulate the audit process from the auditor's acceptance of the appointment, through audit planning, the methods for obtaining audit evidence, the accompanying documentation and communication, to the requirements for reporting. Auditing standards enhance public confidence in the audit if the standards are set in a transparent way and if the application of the standards leads to a high audit quality and therefore to reliable financial statements.

The auditor is bound by *laws and legislative rules*. In Germany, the HGB and the WPO are particularly relevant. Medium-sized and large limited liability companies (Kapitalgesellschaften) are generally subject to audits in accordance with § 316, 1 HGB; consolidated financial statements are also subject to audits in accordance with § 316, 2 HGB. The annual financial statements are normally set up in accordance with the German accounting standards included in the HGB. From 2005, the consolidated financial statements of listed companies have to be set up according to International Financial Reporting Standards (IFRS) (§ 315a, 1 HGB). According to § 319, 2 HGB, audits can be performed by individual auditors as well as audit firms.

The most important auditing standard is § 317, 1 clause 3 HGB. According to this standard, the objective of an audit is to express an opinion as to whether the financial statements have been prepared in all material respects in accordance with the applied accounting standards. However, the German legislator does not define in detail how the audit is to be carried out, but rather places it in the due care of the auditor (see for example § 320, 2 clause 1 HGB; § 43, 1 WPO).

The general legal auditing standards are substantiated by the standards of the IDW. These IDW standards are not laws but, strictly speaking, just opinions of a registered society, which are only binding for its members. Nevertheless, it can be assumed that the auditor is actually bound by these standards due to his duty of professional care in accordance with § 43, 1 clause 1 WPO. If he deviates from these standards, he must be able to justify this deviation in case of a lawsuit (Marten *et al.* 2007: 98–9).

The IDW standards are primarily auditing standards (Prüfungsstandards, IDW PS). It is also recommended that the auditing instructions issued by the IDW be followed (Prüfungshinweise, IDW PH), which mostly interpret existing IDW PS. The IDW standards are categorized. The central categories are: subject matter of an audit and audit engagement (IDW PS 200-249), audit approach (IDW PS 250-299), conduct of an audit (IDW PS 300-399), audit opinion, long form audit report and certificates (IDW PS 400-499), audit of companies of certain industries (IDW PS 500-799), and reviews and other assurance engagements (IDW PS 800-999). The IDW has allocated a total of about 70 auditing standards and instructions to the above categories.

Legal standard setting is subject to the normal legislation process, in which the Federal Parliament (Bundestag*)* and the Federal Council (Bundesrat) are involved. Normally, the Federal Government introduces bills or draft bills which have been elaborated in the ministries; the process also includes regular hearings of the groups involved and of experts. The standard setting process of an IDW standard consists of a due process which is, however, not explicitly standardized. Thus, it could be improved to enhance transparency. Standard drafts are presented to the interested parties with a request for proposals for amendments or supplements. Based on the proposals received, the Auditing and Accounting Board (Hauptfachausschuss) of the IDW then decides on the adoption of the IDW PS or IDW PH.

4.2 Relationship to international auditing standards

IFAC is the central organization responsible for international auditing standard setting. The international auditing standards of IFAC are the International Standards on Auditing (ISA) and the International Auditing Practice Statements (IAPS); the ISA are comparable with the IDW PS and the IAPS with the IDW PH.

From the point of view of reinforcing public confidence in the audit, difficulties with the assessment of the reliability of financial statement information audited according to varying auditing standards can be avoided by the application of worldwide uniform auditing standards. Therefore, the mission of IFAC is the development of harmonized standards. However, national regulations (e.g. national laws) may require the application of IFAC standards not directly but taking national considerations into account. This idea corresponds to the standard setting philosophy of IFAC, according to which the international standards are not to be applied directly but are to be transformed into national standards. Where a national requirement (e.g. national law) leads to a national standard (e.g. IDW PS) which is in conflict with an international standard, the national standard must prevail.

In the meantime, the IDW has almost completed the transformation of the international to national standards. Both standard systems are similarly detailed. Unfortunately, the IDW PS classification deviates from the ISA classification. In terms of content, only a few differences remain, which are mostly caused by the fact that the IDW can only transform the IFAC standards into IDW PS with a time lag. Some significant differences are discussed in more detail below:

- The IFAC standards are based on a framework which classifies the audit of the annual financial statement as a type of assurance engagement and which provides a description of characteristic elements (e.g. assurance level).
- There is no German standard providing guidance on matters relating to the audit of group financial statements comparable to ED ISA 600; here the reason for the difference is that the IDW can only follow the international

standard setting with a delay. Furthermore, there is still no German standard with regard to the audit of segment reporting (ISA 501.42-45).The same is true for the audit of derivative financial instruments covered by IAPS 1012, as well as for the standard "Electronic Commerce – Effect on the Audit of Financial Statements," set forth in IAPS 1013.

- At the same time there exist German auditing standards that lack an international counterpart, e.g. IDW PS 880 on the "Issuance and Use of Software Attestation Reports."

The IFAC followed the notion of developing a more problem- and risk-oriented audit approach. The International Auditing and Assurance Standards Board (IAASB) believes that the new "audit risk standards" (ISA 315, 330, 500, and ISA 200.appendix) will increase audit quality as a result of better risk assessment and an improved linkage of audit procedures and assessed risks. The new standards include a stronger business risk audit approach (Ruhnke 2006). This has been accounted for by the IDW, which has issued two auditing standards addressing these issues (IDW PS 261, 300).

In the context of reinforcing public confidence in statutory audits, the recent developments within the European Union are particularly important. According to article 26 no. 1 of the amended Eighth EU Directive, statutory audits are to be performed in compliance with the international auditing standards (ISA, IAPS). The IDW has already reacted to this requirement by changing its procedures in such a way that the ISAs are no longer transformed into IDW PS, but are rather translated and complemented by additional paragraphs dealing with particular German requirements. It is also noteworthy that the numbering of the IDW PS is to be based on that of the ISAs in future. In addition, there will be particular German IDW PS (e.g. IDW PS 340 for the audit of the early risk detection system; see section 4.3). Since the IAASB is currently revising its standards due to the Clarity-Project, the IDW has suspended its ISA translations and amendments since the beginning of 2006. However, due to the already existing similarity of the IDW PS and the international auditing standards, a major change in audit practice is not to be expected.

4.3 Special issues of German auditing standards to restore public confidence

In addition to the transformation of international standards into German standards, further efforts have been made to boost public confidence which are not directly connected with a specific transformation requirement. The German standards mentioned hereafter are still valid after the implementation of the Eighth EU Directive, as they exclusively cover national particularities. Some of the central requirements are described below.

In Germany, according to § 321 HGB and IDW PS 450, a written Prüfungsbericht (long form audit report) is the crucial instrument of internal reporting (in particular to the supervisory board). The KonTraG had already led to various amendments of reporting standards, aiming at a more problem-oriented reporting. The pursued course of a problem-oriented approach was consistently continued by further changes as part of the TransPuG (Gross and Möller 2004: 317ff.). Important changes involved the obligation to report the consequences of discretionary accounting practices. Internationally, there is no report corresponding to the written long form audit report. ISA 260 is most closely comparable with the German standards. The disadvantage, however, is that ISA 260.15 prescribes both written and verbal reporting as alternatives. Overall, the German regulations appear preferable to the international standards.

Another German requirement concerns the obligation to establish an *early risk detection system* in accordance with § 91, 2 AktG. The auditor has to audit this system (§ 317, 4 HGB in connection with IDW PS 340) and to report on the result of the audit in the long form audit report (§ 321, 4 HGB; Marten *et al.* 2007: 286ff.). In addition, the corporation must carry out risk reporting in the *management report* (§§ 289, 1, 315, 1 HGB; at group level the German accounting standards 5 and 15 [Deutscher Rechnungs- legungsstandard, DRS 5, 15] are also relevant). It is to be noted that German companies applying IFRS also have to publish a *group management report* in accordance with § 315a, 1 HGB which fulfills the requirements of § 315 HGB. Risk reporting is also a subject matter of the audit (§ 317, 2 clause 2 HGB). Corresponding IFAC standards are not available. As *risk reporting* is usually relevant for the decision-making of stakeholders, the German auditing standards are preferable as regards the establishment of public confidence.

In addition, the executive board and the supervisory board of German stock corporations must state annually in a declaration of conformity whether and to what extent they have complied with the recommendations on corporate governance as defined in the DCGK (§ 161 AktG). This declaration is published in the notes (§§ 285 no. 16, 314, 1 no. 8 HGB). The auditor in turn has to audit whether this declaration has been published and made accessible to the shareholders in a continuous manner (§§ 316, 1, 2 in connection with 317, 1 clause 2 HGB, and IDW PS 345). A material audit is not carried out; however, in accordance with § 321, 1 clause 3 HGB the auditor has to report on facts revealed in the course of performing the audit which indicate that the contents of the declaration of conformity are incorrect (Marten *et al.* 2007: 570). As the code is explicitly aimed at making the German corporate governance system transparent and comprehensible and at promoting the confidence of stakeholders in the management and monitoring of German listed stock corporations, the German regulations seem to be ahead of IFAC standards, where no corresponding requirements exist.

5 Independence standards

The statutory auditor evaluates the correctness of financial statements. The long form audit report is only beneficial if it contains reliable information. If addressees do not believe that an auditor is independent of a company, they will have little confidence in the auditor's opinion. The IFAC distinguishes between independence in mind and independence in appearance. Independence in mind is defined as "the state of mind that permits the provision of an opinion without being affected by influences that compromise professional judgment, allowing an individual to act with integrity, and exercise objectivity and professional scepticism." Independence in appearance is defined as "the avoidance of facts and circumstances that are so significant that a reasonable and informed third party … would reasonably conclude a firm's … integrity, objectivity or professional scepticism had been compromised" (IFAC 2001: 32). The requirement that a statutory auditor should be independent addresses both.

New auditors must bear technological start-up costs. Thus, incumbent auditors possess a comparative advantage over competitors. Transaction costs associated with changing auditors provide another advantage for the incumbent auditor (DeAngelo 1981: 118). Consequently, an incumbent auditor can capture future benefits from technological and transaction cost advantages by setting future audit fees above the avoidable costs of producing audits, i.e. the auditor can expect future quasi-rents. As a consequence, the client could use the threat of a termination of the contract and demand a clean audit opinion. Thus, the existence of client-specific quasi-rents may constitute a decrease in independence. Alternatively, the endangering of independence could be explained by agency theory. The auditor is provided with more and better information on audit quality which is not completely observable by the client (hidden action, Arrow 1985). As a consequence, there is the potential for moral hazard (Spremann 1990: 571–2). The auditor could decide to expend less effort in carrying out the audit, i.e. decrease production costs or renounce his independence and accept side-payments from management for not truthfully reporting as the owner expects (Ewert 1990: 140–6). If an auditor accepts such side-payments, he is not independent.

Recently, numerous German initiatives to improve audit quality have been observable. In so far as they refer to ethical rules, they primarily affect auditors' independence. In 1998 the KonTraG came into effect (Böcking and Orth 1999, Forster 1998). It brought three important changes with regard to auditors' independence:

- within a stock corporation (Aktiengesellschaft, AG) it became the duty of the supervisory board to engage the statutory auditor (before 1998 auditors were engaged by the executive board);
- it introduced a mandatory internal auditor rotation for audits of listed clients after seven years;

• it reduced the maximum total fee from one audit client from 50 percent to 30 percent of total revenues.

The DCGK was published in 2002 (Seibt 2002). It presents essential statutory regulations for the management and supervision of German listed companies and contains internationally and nationally recognized standards for good and responsible governance. Two regulations are related to auditors' independence. The supervisory board must set up an audit committee which in particular handles issues of accounting and risk management, the necessary independence of the auditor, auditor engagement, the determination of the emphasis on specific audit areas, and fee negotiation (DCGK 5.3.2). Prior to submitting a proposal for election of the statutory auditor, the supervisory board or the audit committee must obtain a statement from the proposed auditor stating whether and, where applicable, which professional financial and other relationships exist between the auditor and his/her executive bodies and head auditors, on the one hand, and the enterprise and the members of its executive bodies on the other hand that could call his/her independence into question (Pfitzer and Orth 2002). This statement must include the extent to which other services were performed for the enterprise in the past year, especially in the field of consultancy, and which are contracted for the following year (DCGK 7.2.1). The TransPuG of 2002 introduced § 161 into the AktG. According to this article, the management board and the supervisory board pronounce annually either that they have complied with the recommendations of the code or which recommendations have not been applied. In the latter case they should explain the deviations from the recommendations (DCGK 3.10).

On 25 February 2003 the German government announced its ten-issues program to strengthen the protection of investors and the integrity of corporations. The intended catalog of measures included a number of points related to independence:

• prohibition of certain advisory services;
• notification of the supervisory board regarding advisory services;
• approval of the supervisory board for advisory services;
• a further reduction in the maximum total fee from one audit client;
• limitation of advisory fees (in relation to audit fees);
• increased frequency of internal auditor rotation.

Some of these measures have been implemented in German law by the BilReG (Veltins 2004). The maximum total fee from a listed client is now 15 percent (§ 319a, 1 p.1 no. 1 HGB of total revenues. Originally it was planned to reduce the period for internal rotation, which is required only for listed clients, from seven to five years. This plan was abandoned, but a cooling-off period of three years was introduced. The main focus of the amendment relates to the provision of advisory services. In the past, only bookkeeping and the preparation of financial statements were explicitly forbidden. Furthermore, an auditor was obliged to reject an audit engagement if he felt non-independent or if non-independence could be perceived. According to the concept of functional decision competence (funktionale Entscheidungskompetenz) (BGH 1997), consulting services by the auditor were permitted as long as the decision-making authority remained with the client. Now three other services are prohibited:

1   internal audit services;
2   management and financial services;
3   actuarial and valuation services;

provided that these activities are material (§ 319, 3 p.1 no. 3 HGB). Concerning audits of listed clients, the following services are prohibited in addition:

• tax advisory and legal services (as long as their extent is above pure recommendations for tax configurations);
• development, design, and implementation of financial information systems.

A shift from a more principle-based approach to a more rules-based approach is obvious. Furthermore, the new rules are stricter. This development was triggered less by business failures and irregularities not detected and not reported by auditors than by developments in the US. Large German audit firms feared that their audit opinions could not be accepted in the US if the German independence rules were not in compliance with US regulations.

Advisory services are the most important issue of the BilReG. If the statutory auditor provides consulting services to the audit client, the information gained as a consultant can be used to reduce audit costs (knowledge spill-overs). As a result, the economic bond between the auditor and the client is strengthened, since quasi-rents from auditing services increase. Thus, the risk that the auditor's independence may become impaired increases (Beck *et al.* 1988). Moreover, the auditor can use the information gained as an auditor to decrease consulting costs. Thus, the total quasi-rents from auditing and consulting services are higher than the quasi-rents from auditing services. This increases the threat to an auditor's independence (Ostrowski and Söder 1999). In the agency theory approach, consulting services could be used to lend side-payments a legal character (Antle 1984).

Most empirical studies which have investigated the effect of non-audit services on independence in mind did not find a negative impact (Corless and Parker 1987, Dopuch and King 1991, Barkess and Simnett 1994, Davidson and Emby 1996, DeFond *et al.* 2002, Ashbaugh *et al.* 2003, Chung and Kallapur 2003, Raghunandan *et al.* 2003, Geiger and Rama 2003). Nevertheless, the new rules could be beneficial, because prior research quite often revealed a negative effect of advisory services on independence in appearance (e.g. Canning and Gwilliam

1999, Swanger and Chewning 2001, Raghunandan 2003; a complete overview is provided by Quick 2002).

In contrast to international developments, tax advisory services are regarded as critical in Germany. This is a result of the direct link between financial and tax accounts. According to the so-called authoritative principle (Maßgeblichkeitsprinzip), the financial statements build the authoritative basis for the tax accounts. Furthermore, many tax depreciations can only be used if the same valuation method is applied in the financial accounts. This leads to a reversal of the authoritative principle, i.e. tax rules influence financial statements. As a consequence, tax advisory services could have a direct impact on financial accounting and thus on an auditor's independence.

German auditors were always allowed to provide non-audit services. According to §§ 2 and 3 WPO, the tasks of a professional accountant comprise tax advisory services, business advisory services, expert activities, trustee and auditing services. This observation might have a historical explanation. Originally, the primary activity of most German audit and trust companies was the provision of trust and consulting services and not auditing (Quick 2004).

6 Oversight, monitoring, disciplinary observance and enforcement

6.1 Overview

6.1.1 Reasoning

The German professions of public auditor and sworn-in auditor are not subject to a conventional monitoring procedure, but – since 1 January 2005 – to external quality control organized according to the model of modified self-administration. The obligation of quality control is based on a law concerning changes in the Regulations on the Activity of Public Auditors (Wirtschafts-prüferordnungs-Änderungsgesetz, WPOÄG), which came into force on 1 January 2001. The main reasons for the introduction of that system were the need to reduce the expectation gap and increase public confidence in the profession, the desire to maintain professional self-administration, and the need to ensure international acceptance of German auditor services. Due to progressive international developments and the accounting scandals of the past few years, there have been far-reaching amendments to professional oversight in Germany and thus also to the quality control system of 1 January 2005 as a consequence of the APAG. In autumn 2007 the Law on Professional Oversight Reform (Berufsaufsichtsreformgesetz, BARefG) has come into effect. Its aim is to enhance professional oversight independence and power by conveying additional responsibility and authority to the WPK (see Marks and Schmidt 1998, Marten *et al.* 2003, and Sahner *et al.* 2001).

6.1.2   Structure of the system of external quality control in Germany

Generally, all public auditors, audit firms, sworn-in auditors, and sworn-in audit firms are obliged to undergo quality control reviews if they perform mandatory audits of annual financial statements in accordance with §§ 316-324 HGB. A quality control review has to take place at least once every three years. According to the Law on Professional Oversight Reform, this period has been extended to six years for all auditors who do not carry out mandatory audits of publicly traded companies. The review may only be carried out by a quality control auditor (Prüfer für Qualitätskontrolle, PfQK) registered with the WPK. Sworn-in public auditors and sworn-in audit firms may only carry out quality control as a PfQK of other sworn-in auditors and audit firms.

A registered PfQK must refuse to accept an engagement for quality control if capital, financial, or personal relationships to the audit firm to be reviewed exist, or if independence in appearance or independence in fact may generally be impaired or concerns regarding bias exist, i.e. if a so-called reason for exclusion is given. As regards boosting public confidence in the system of external quality control, more demanding registration conditions for the PfQK could be considered.

The commission for quality control (Kommission für Qualitätskontrolle, KfQK) is entrusted with all matters of quality control as an independent body of the WPK. It consists of at least nine members of the profession who are registered as PfQKs and who are elected for a period of office of three years. The KfQK issues certificates of exemption from participation in the system of external quality control, registers the PfQKs, receives the quality control reports, issues and revokes certificates of participation, takes further measures, and settles disputed issues in connection with quality control. The system of external quality control in Germany is one of peer review with monitoring elements (see §§ 57a, 57e and 130 WPO, IDW PS 140, as well as Niehus 2000).

The KfQK may only forward the information obtained in the course of quality control on the failure of a member of the profession to the WPK for the purpose of punishment in the context of disciplinary oversight if a revocation of the engagement as public auditor may be considered. In addition, the facts communicated cannot be used in disciplinary court procedures against the member of the profession. This strict separation of quality control and professional oversight, also referred to as a "firewall," can, however, also be interpreted as a potential weakness in the German system (see § 57e WPO).

6.1.3   Process and implementation of quality control reviews

Until 2004, every audit firm selected and engaged its own PfQK. Since 2005, the audit firm has to submit proposals to the KfQK for up to three PfQKs and then engages a PfQK not rejected by the KfQK. This new regulation is intended to contribute to reinforcing public confidence in the quality control system and therefore in the public auditor's services. If the public auditor possesses the necessary knowledge and experience and if none of the above reasons for exclusion exist, he may accept the engagement offered.

The subject matter of the quality control review is the internal quality assurance system of the audit firm being reviewed, the mandatory establishment of which is also explicitly defined in § 55b WPO. A quality control review is not a second audit of the annual financial statement but a test of the control of the system with the aim of assessing the appropriateness of the internal quality assurance. The quality assurance system is deemed to be appropriate if it fulfills the legal and statutory requirements – in particular those of the HGB, the WPO, and the professional statutes. The effectiveness of the system is to be regarded as given if the basic principles and measures of quality assurance introduced in the reviewed audit firm are known to the management and the employees and are implemented in their daily work.

The results of the audit procedures are to be communicated to the management of the audit firm and to the KfQK in the form of a quality control report including an audit opinion. An unqualified or a qualified opinion or a disclaimer to submit an opinion is possible.

After receiving the quality control report, the KfQK issues a participation certificate (Teilnahmebescheinigung) to the reviewed audit firm as proof of participation in the system of external quality control. In accordance with § 319, 1 clause 3 HGB, a member of the profession may only be engaged as a statutory auditor if he/she or his/her firm possesses such a certificate. If the PfQK has refused to award an audit opinion or the quality control review was carried out by an auditor who does not fulfill the requirements of § 57a, 3 WPO, no certificate of participation is issued. The KfQK has an override right on the certificate of participation (see §§ 57a and 57e WPO, §§ 55b and 57a WPO, IDW PS 140, as well as Heininger and Bertram 2004 and Poll 2003).

6.2 Public oversight in Germany

6.2.1 Auditor Oversight Commission (Abschlussprüferaufsichtskommission)

The new regulations from 2005 led to the creation of the APAK. The APAK is entrusted in indirect public administration with the performance of professional oversight of the activities of the WPK, which is responsible for oversight of members of the profession who perform statutory audits of financial statements. These activities are: audit examination, appointment or recognition, revocation and registration, quality control, professional oversight, basic professional principles, and continuing professional education.

As a new body following the example of the PCAOB in the US, the APAK is therefore positioned above the WPK but below the BMWi. It has a right of final decision, i.e. in addition to ordering a second review of the decisions of the WPK, it can also decide to cancel such decisions and oblige the WPK to implement the decisions of the APAK in its own name. To be able to carry out its tasks, the APAK has a right of information and inspection with regard to the WPK, as well as the right to participate in its meetings in an advisory capacity. Irrespective of this, in the first instance, responsibility for professional oversight remains with the WPK.

The APAK is made up of six to ten members working in an honorary capacity, who are non-practitioners, independent, not subject to instructions, and who are mainly from the fields of accounting, finance, industry, academia, and jurisdiction. They are appointed by the BMWi for a period of office of four years; personal membership of the WPK in the five years prior to appointment to the APAK is not permitted. The costs incurred by the work of the APAK are borne by the WPK and therefore indirectly by the members of the profession as a result of their compulsory membership of the WPK.

Other tasks of the APAK consist in cooperation with foreign organizations responsible for professional oversight of public auditors, oversight of the endorsement of auditing standards, and monitoring of quality control reviews. Establishment of the APAK considerably restricts the self-administration of the profession, as a commission consisting solely of non-practitioners has been granted a right of final decision.

According to the Law on Professional Oversight Reform, the Auditor Oversight Commission has gained additional competencies. In particular, it will be entitled to commission the WPK to carry out inspections. Inspections may be initiated on the basis of evidence of a violation of professional duties, in reaction to inquiries of foreign institutions cooperating with the Auditor Oversight Commission, or randomly (see § 66a WPO, as well as Heininger and Bertram 2004, Lenz 2004, Marten *et al.* 2006 and Schmidt and Kaiser 2004).

6.2.2 Federal Ministry of Economics and Technology (Bundesministerium für Wirtschaft und Technologie)

The BMWi has higher authority than the APAK and is thus the highest instance for professional oversight in Germany. In this connection, the ministry is responsible for the appointment, and in special cases the early recall, of members of the APAK as well as for reviewing the decisions of the APAK, if the WPK considers them to be unlawful (see § 66a WPO).

6.3 Professional oversight

6.3.1 Disciplinary oversight by the WPK

In the context of its oversight function in accordance with § 57 WPO, the WPK takes measures against a member of the profession in the case of professional failures – by name instruction or reprimand. An instruction is issued if a violation of professional duties which has become known to the WPK does not appear sufficiently serious to require a reprimand or the instigation of professional tribunal proceedings. If an instruction is considered to be insufficient to react to a failure, and if, on the other hand, no disciplinary court procedures are to be instigated, the executive board of the WPK issues a reprimand in connection with a possible fine of up to €50,000. In contrast to an instruction, a reprimand can only be issued in writing and after hearing the member of the profession involved. An appeal against the written notification of reprimand by the person reprimanded is also possible within a period of one month (see §§ 57 and 63 WPO as well as Marten *et al*. 2007 and Quick 2001).

The Law on Professional Oversight Reform brings about additional responsibilities for the WPK. The WPK itself has to prosecute light and medium violations of professional duties. Only severe cases are left to professional tribunals. Hence, the WPK's authority is extended. Auditors are obliged to provide information to the WPK and to submit all relevant working papers if necessary. Where the investigation relates to a mandatory audit, the auditor cannot refuse to give evidence. In the event of the auditor's refusal to give evidence, the WPK is entitled to visit the auditor's property during office hours as well as to inspect and copy documents. If the auditor conducts mandatory audits of firms of public interest, the WPK may carry out these investigations even in the absence of any evidence (so-called "inspections"). Based on the investigation or inspection results, the WPK then has to decide whether any of the sanctions described above has to be taken or whether the case has to be transferred to a professional tribunal (see §§ 62 and 62b WPO and Marten *et al*. 2006).

6.3.2 Disciplinary oversight by the chief public prosecutor

In the event of serious violations of professional duties, the executive board of the WPK transfers the responsibility for punishment to the chief public prosecutor's office in Berlin, which, where applicable, instigates professional tribunal proceedings. Professional measures consist of a fine of up to €500,000 , exclusion from certain fields of activity, or professional debarment for a duration of one to five years, as well as complete exclusion from the profession. The different measures can also be taken simultaneously. However, exclusion from the profession is only rarely applied and presupposes extremely serious misconduct of the member of the profession. For example, embezzlement, fraud, disloyalty, or the forgery of documents as well as foreclosure measures against the member of the profession, the submission of an affirmation in lieu of an oath, a warrant for arrest, or being brought before the court by a bailiff inevitably leads to a suspension (see §§ 68 and 84 WPO, as well as Marten *et al*. 2007 and Quick 2001).

6.4 Enforcement

The standards to be observed by members of the professions of public auditor and sworn-in auditor are enforced at different levels. At the level of auditing standards, disciplinary oversight by the WPK should be mentioned, which has been supported by the introduction of the APAK, a body which increases transparency and therefore confidence and public interest. Auditing standards are also enforced by the threat of the punishment of violations of duty by a professional tribunal of the kind described in the previous section.

With the passing of the BilKoG, the enforcement of accounting standards was introduced in Germany for the first time in 2005, according to which the annual financial statement and director's report last recorded or the last approved consolidated statement and consolidated director's report of listed companies are based on an audit by an institution which acts alongside the supervisory board and the statutory auditor. The German enforcement system has a two-level structure (see Figure 6.3): the first level is the civil-law Financial Reporting Enforcement Panel (Deutsche Prüfstelle für Rechnungslegung e.V., DPR), see http://www.frep.info), which can re-audit respective parts of individual financial statements in the event of incriminating factors such as financial statements mistakes (so-called reactive audit) or by random samples (so-called proactive audit). As cooperation with the DPR is voluntary, the company concerned can refuse to cooperate. In such a case, responsibility for auditing is transferred to the BaFin, which can enforce the audit and publication of financial accounting mistakes with sovereign powers.

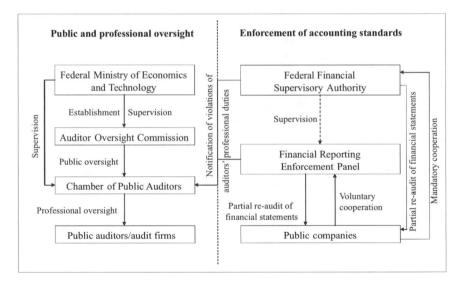

Figure 6.3 Oversight and enforcement bodies in Germany

If violations of professional duties by an auditor are detected by the DPR or the BaFin, the WPK is to be informed. This feedback is intended to contribute to increasing confidence not only in the annual financial statements but also in the services of the auditor. The decision as to whether and how these violations should be punished is the responsibility of the WPK (see Baetge *et al*. 2004, Ernst 2004, Hommelhoff and Mattheus 2004, and Wolf 2004).

7 Liability

When discussing auditor's liability, it is necessary to distinguish between an auditor's liability to the client (section 7.1) and an auditor's liability to third parties (section 7.2).

7.1 Liability to the client

According to § 323, 1 HGB, the auditor, his assistants, and the legal representatives of the auditing firm engaged in the audit are liable to pay damages for any harm caused to the company and also, where applicable, to any affiliated company. Their liability requires that they deliberately or negligently ignored their duties. § 323, 1 HGB does not include liability to third parties (e.g. shareholders or creditors).

The first prerequisite for liability is the violation of a statutory rule dealing with auditing, or the violation of auditing standards or ethical rules of the profession (Hopt 1992: 794). In addition, the auditor is only liable for fault. Fault means negligent and intentional conduct. Furthermore, the violation of an auditor's duties must result in damages to the client. Finally, it is necessary that a causal link between the violation of duties and the damage exists (Quick 1992). If the audit, or part of the audit, is performed by assistants, the auditor is liable for their actions too (§ 278 BGB). He cannot exculpate himself by claiming that he thoroughly selected, trained, and supervised his assistants. If an audit firm is selected as auditor, it is liable for its legal representatives (§ 31 BGB). Several persons are jointly liable (§ 323 HGB).

If the auditor is deemed to have acted in a negligent manner in performing his professional duties, the liability for compensatory damages is limited to €1 million and €4 million in the case of audits of listed companies. The following arguments are used in defending this liability cap:

- Auditing is an activity which implies a very high risk of damages (Schlechtriem 1984: 1182).
- The liability cap is necessary to guarantee the livelihood of an auditor (Nann 1985: 333).
- Usually, the auditor is confronted with opposing interests of the parties involved. Such a situation increases risk.
- It is more difficult to insure against unlimited liability (Mertens 1977: 27).

- The competition within the profession would be endangered if liability was unlimited, since only a few auditors/audit firms could afford the increased insurance premiums.
- The structure of the profession would change if liability was unlimited, since larger audit firms would become more attractive because of a higher resource potential (Forster 1984: 148).
- If liability was unlimited, a risky client would face problems in finding an auditor.
- The limitation of an auditor's liability strengthens his neutrality.
- Unlimited liability would not be appropriate in relation to current audit fees (Zilias 1974: 76).

On the other hand, one might argue that the limitation of an auditor's liability protects the auditor unfairly, and that other free professions (e.g. lawyers or physicians) are not protected in such a way. In addition, it is questionable whether a universal cap is fair, since the relative compensation for the loss suffered increases with the declining extent of damage. Unlimited liability would be an incentive for better audit quality, would deter auditors who are not experienced in special kinds of audit (e.g. of insurance companies) from performing such audits, and could increase public confidence in the audit of financial statements.

The limitation of auditors' liability is also valid in cases of gross negligence. If the auditor acts intentionally, his liability is unlimited. It is impossible to reduce or to eliminate auditors' liability according to § 323 HGB by contract (§ 323, 4 HGB). An agreement which contradicts this rule is illegal and therefore void (§ 134 BGB). A contractual increase in the maximum amount of liability is not excluded by law, but it is suggested that any attempt to negotiate a higher cap could be construed as unethical behaviour. The competition resulting from an increased cap would be unfair (Kaminski 1992).

7.2 Liability to third parties

The prerequisites listed above for defining an auditor's liability to clients are also prerequisites for defining an auditor's liability to third parties. Auditors' liability to third parties in Germany has been addressed both by tort law and contract law. Tort law offers two potential bases for a claim (§ 823, 2 BGB and § 826 BGB).

According to § 823, 2 BGB, the auditor is liable to third parties when he violates a protective law which has as one of its objectives the individual protection of a third party from an explicitly defined kind of damage (Ebke 1983: 45). Protective laws which might be violated during the audit of financial statements are mainly rules for the protection of property interests under criminal law, e.g. fraud (§ 263 Criminal Code (Strafgesetzbuch, StGB)) or falsification of documents (§ 267 StGB). Furthermore, § 332 HGB (violation of the duty to report) and § 333 HGB (violation of the duty to keep clients' business secrets confidential) are considered as protective laws. All of these rules apply to intentional conduct only. The auditor is also liable to third parties if he unethically violates his duties with the intent of damaging a third party (§ 826 BGB). In summary, the applicability of tort law is limited due to restrictive prerequisites, in particular intent. Alternatively, a third party could base a claim on contract law.

In the area of contract law, there are no statutory rules that grant a third party a claim against the auditor. However, German courts have developed two constructs which could give rise to claims on the part of third parties and which are quasi-contractual: contract with a protective effect for third parties (Vertrag mit Schutzwirkung zugunsten Dritter) and implicit contract for information (stillschweigender Auskunftsvertrag). The first one is of particular interest.

For this legal construct to apply, the following prerequisites must be fulfilled (Hagen 1971: 15):

- The third party must be closely connected to the auditor's work, as shareholders and creditors are. They use the audit opinion as one basis for their decisions (Nann 1985: 144–5, Keitel 1987: 126).
- It must be the wish of the parties to the contract to include third parties, although this need not be explicitly defined (BGH 1988). Implicit inclusion is allowed, and it may be argued that one party (e.g. the auditor) that has expertise and monopoly rights of provision granted by the state (on behalf of the society) therefore has an implicit duty to a wider set of parties in society. Since auditors are perceived to be experts, they need to be aware that third parties place trust in their professional assessment. Auditors use the public confidence in their expertise within their profession. Therefore, it can be assumed that the contract implicitly contains the duty to protect third parties.
- The auditor must be aware that third parties are included and that they place trust in the audit and use the information for decision-making. Such awareness may be of a quite general form and does not require that individual names be known, nor that the number of third parties be known, but merely that such a group is clearly distinguishable (BGH 1983, Lang 1989: 8)

The lower relevance of the construct "implicit contract for information" is due to the fact that the Federal Court of Justice (Bundesgerichtshof, BGH) introduced two additional prerequisites for its application. On the one hand, the third party should have asked for the involvement of the auditor, and, on the other hand, the auditor must then have given the information directly to the third party (Lang 1989: 61–2, Schmitz 1989: 1909–11, Hohenlohe-Oehringen 1986). These prerequisites are rarely given and therefore the new ruling of the BGH limits the possibility of applying the "implicit contract of information" principle.

Until recently, a "contract with a protective effect for third parties" could not be applied to statutory audits. The main argument was that the legislator had developed a specific article for auditors' liability (§ 323 HGB). If he had intended to hold third parties liable for negligent misconduct, he would have mentioned it in this article. In 1998 the BGH changed its view and decided that the "contract with a protective effect for third parties" construct is applicable to third party liability (BGH 1998). However, the BGH also decided that the liability cap would still be valid in such a case. So far, the BGH has not explicitly defined what type of third parties should be protected (Quick 2000).

In February 2003 the German government published its ten-issues program (see section 5) for strengthening the protection of investors and the integrity of corporations. Within this agenda, an increased liability (either as a cap or as a multiple of the audit fee) and an extension of protected third parties were announced. Up to now, implementation has not taken place. The amendment of the Eighth EU Directive, enacted at the beginning of 2006, does not regulate the civil liability of the statutory auditor.

Overall it is possible to conclude that the limited liability of German auditors in cases of negligent misconduct is still a German particularity (Gietzmann and Quick 1998). This limited liability exposure could be explained by three factors:

- From a historical point of view, it was the duty of the supervisory board to control financial statements. Due to the fact that the supervisory boards did not correctly exercise this function, the demand for external audits arose. Therefore, the primary addressees of audits in Germany are the supervisory boards and not third parties, which explains the limited liability to third parties.
- German audits firms were mainly founded by banks and the state and hence their clients. Therefore, clients were not interested in an unlimited third party liability, because then they would have had to pay themselves (as an owner) for their damages.
- In the German economy, banks and insurance companies are important providers of debt as well as of equity capital. As a consequence, they have their representatives on the supervisory boards and thus an insight into internal financial information. Therefore, information from audited financial statements is less useful for them and it is less important to protect them through the extended liability exposure of the auditor.

In order to cover liability risks German auditors are obliged to have indemnity insurance covering at least the liability cap mentioned above (§ 54 WPO). Apart from civil liability there is also the criminal liability of statutory auditors. In particular, a statutory auditor can be fined or imprisoned if he or she violates the reporting duties or confidentiality (§§ 332, 333 HGB).

8 Conclusion

Germany has been affected by national as well as international scandals, triggering a whole range of regulatory and institutional changes for auditors. The effect on trust in the audit profession and hence the audit itself, however, is hard to determine. Yet since most of the measures are quite similar to the measures taken abroad, they should serve as a signal for trust enhancing efforts.

For example, in Germany audit committees have entered the corporate governance system. In general, they are perceived to strengthen the monitoring function of the auditor as in the Anglo-Saxon corporate setting they are necessary to assure accounting and auditing quality. Nevertheless, it is questionable whether this is really the case in Germany. Due to the German two-tier system, the audit committee is only a committee of the supervisory board – a body that has rigorous monitoring duties (including those of audit committees) anyway. Thus, an increase in the trust in audits can only be achieved if all the people with monitoring responsibilities meet all the necessary qualification requirements.

Recent legislation might be perceived as supporting trust in the audit profession. However, legal standard setting takes its time and can only shape the institutional framework of audits. Standard setting by the profession is much faster and more flexible in reacting to a changing environment, even if it could be perceived as being biased toward the profession's interests. Overall, it seems to be crucial that national standard setting follows international standards in order to assure a high degree of comparability or even similarity of audit services.

In Germany, trust in the auditing profession is enhanced by national auditing standards that lack an ISA counterpart. However, there also exist International Auditing Standards that have not yet been transformed into German auditing standards. Due to the amendment of the Eighth EU Directive, the international auditing standards referring to statutory audits will have to be applied directly in EU member states in future, so that these differences will vanish. It is also helpful that during the course of the clarity project the ISAs will be improved with respect to their structure, scope, and language. However, these revisions are not expected to be complete until 2011. Hence, during this interim phase the IDW will have to turn back to the transformation instead of the translation of international auditing standards. That, of course, will not contribute to the international comparability of audits.

It is remarkable that in recent years the requirements for becoming an auditor in Germany have been relaxed. For example, admission to the audit exam is now possible after three years of professional practice instead of five years, and parts of the exam can now be waived if the candidates have passed certain university exams in business administration and/or law. *A priori*, this development should not be conducive to enhancing trust. However, the abolition of the second qualification in auditing, so-called "sworn-in auditors," in this respect is favorable. The audits of sworn-in auditors may have been perceived as being of lower quality than the audits of "full" auditors. The public impression that two different types of audits exist will be eliminated.

As revealed by prior research, the problem of the provision of non-audit services has no negative impact on independence in fact but does on independence in appearance. Thus, the new German rules which prohibit certain advisory services could be perceived as an improvement. An unsolved problem is that advisory services that are not explicitly prohibited, such as the acquisition of accounting staff, could be still viewed as rather problematic. Furthermore, the application of the new independence rules leaves considerable room for interpretation. For example, tax consulting services are only forbidden if they have a direct and material effect on financial statements. However, the law does not exemplify when this is the case.

The introduction of external quality controls definitely increases trust in audits. This also holds for the establishment of the German Public Oversight Commission. In the case of the latter, the positive effect is constrained by the fact that all the members act on an honorary basis. Another positive development is the extension of the set of potential disciplinary sanctions. In addition, the possibilities for active controls have been increased and more information rights have been granted to the monitoring bodies. Nevertheless, some deficiencies still remain. On the one hand, certain interest groups (e.g. investors or creditors) are not represented in the disciplinary courts. On the other hand, the disclosure of individual disciplinary cases is far from being complete.

As far as auditor liability is concerned, there has been no significant change made in the system of civil liability. In particular, the limited liability to third parties and the existence of a liability cap are not conducive to fostering trust. Theoretical research has shown that audit quality may be reduced if auditors' liability exposure is capped (Dye 1995, Bigus 2004, Frantz 1999, Thoman 1996, Schildbach 1996, Moore and Scott 1989).

Notes

1   In 2005 there were 12,500 auditors and 2,300 audit firms registered.

References

Antle, R. (1984) "Auditor Independence," *Journal of Accounting Research*, 22 (Spring): 1-20.

Arrow, K.J. (1985) "The Economics of Agency," in J.W. Pratt and R.J. Zeckhauser (eds.) *Principals and Agents: The Structure of Business*, Boston: Harvard Business School, pp. 37–51.

Ashbaugh, H., LaFond, R., and Mayhew, B.W. (2003) "Do Nonaudit Services Compromise Auditor Independence? Further Evidence," *The Accounting Review*, 78(3): 611–39.

Baetge, J., Thiele, S., and Matena, S. (2004) "Mittelbare Sicherung der Prüfungsqualität durch Enforcement geprüfter Jahres- und Konzernabschlüsse – Überlegungen aus ökonomischer Sicht," *Betriebswirtschaftliche Forschung und Praxis*, 56(3): 201–18.

Barkess, L. and Simnett, R. (1994) "The Provision of Other Services by Auditors: Independence and Pricing Issues," *Accounting and Business Research*, 24(94): 99–108.

Beck, P., Frecka, T.J., and Solomon, I. (1988) "A Model of the Market for MAS and Audit Services: Knowledge Spillovers and Auditor–Auditee Bonding," *Journal of Accounting Literature*, (7): 50–64.

Becker, C. (1928) "Treuhandgesellschaften," *Die Wirtschaft und das Recht*, 3: 221–8.

Behr, G. (2004) "Wirtschaftsprüfung – Neue Wege in der Ausbildung," *Der Schweizer Treuhänder*, 3: 193–6.

BGH (1988) "Urteil vom 11.10.1988 – XI ZR 1/88," *Der Betrieb*, 42: 101–2.

BGH (1997) "Urteil vom 21.4.1997 – II ZR 317/95," *Der Betrieb*, 50: 1394–6.

BGH (1998) "Urteil vom 2.4.1998 – III ZR 245/96," *Betriebs-Berater*, 53: 1152–4.

BGH (1983) "Urteil vom 2.11.1983 – IVa ZR 20/82," *Neue Juristische Wochenschrift*, 37: 355–7.

Bigus, J. (2004) "Limited Liability, Bounded Rationality and Auditors' Effort." Online. Available at: <http://www.law.ugent.be/grond/midterm/papers/Bichus%20Jochen.pdf> (accessed 20 April 2005).

Böcking, H.-J. and Orth, C. (1999) "Mehr Kontrolle und Transparenz im Unternehmensbereich durch eine Verbesserung der Qualität der Abschlußprüfung?," *Betriebswirtschaftliche Forschung und Praxis*, 51(4): 418–36.

Born, K.E. (1965) "Die Weltwirtschaftskrise als zeitgeschichtlicher Hintergrund der Einführung der gesetzlichen Pflichtprüfung," in V. Muthesius (ed.), *75 Jahre Deutsche Treuhand-Gesellschaft 1890–1965*, Frankfurt am Main: Deutsche Treuhand-Gesellschaft, pp. 53–97.

Canning, M. and Gwilliam, D. (1999) "Non-Audit Services and Auditor Independence: Some Evidence from Ireland," *The European Accounting Review*, 8(3): 401–19.

Chung, H. and Kallapur, S. (2003) "Client Importance, Nonaudit Services, and Abnormal Accruals," *The Accounting Review*, 78(4): 931–55.

Coenenberg, A.G., Haller, A., and Marten, K.-U. (1999) "Accounting Education for Professionals in Germany – Current State and New Challenges," *Journal of Accounting Education*, 17(4): 367–90.

Corless, J.C. and Parker, L.M. (1987) "The Impact of MAS on Auditor Independence: An Experiment," *Accounting Horizons*, 1: 25–9.

Davidson, R.A. and Emby, C. (1996) "Should Auditors Provide Nonaudit Services to Their Audit Clients?," *Research on Accounting Ethics*, 2: 1–20.

DeAngelo, L.E. (1981) "Auditor Independence, 'Low Balling', and Disclosure Regulation," *Journal of Accounting and Economics*, 3(2): 113–27.

DeFond, M.L., Raghunandan, K., and Subramanyam, K.R. (2002) "Do Non-Audit Service Fees Impair Auditor Independence? Evidence from Going Concern Audit Opinions," *Journal of Accounting Research*, 40(4): 1247–74.

Dopuch, N. and King, R.R. (1991) "The Impact of MAS on Auditors' Independence: An Experimental Markets Study," *Journal of Accounting Research*, 29 (Supplement): 60–98.

Dye, R.A. (1995) "Incorporation and the Audit Market," *Journal of Accounting & Economics*, 19(1): 75–114.

Ebke, W. (1983) *Wirtschaftsprüfer und Dritthaftung*, Bielefeld: Gieseking, Ernst und Werner, GmbH, Verlag.

Elkart, W. and Schmidt, G. (2002) "Aus- und Fortbildung des Prüfers," in W. Ballwieser, A.G. Coenenberg, K. v. Wysocki, (eds) *Handwörterbuch der Rechnungslegung und Prüfung*, 3rd ed., Stuttgart: Schäffer-Poeschel, col. 176–84.

Ernst, C. (2004) "BB-Gesetzgebungsreport: Regierungsentwurf des BilKoG," *Betriebs-Berater*, 59(17): 936–7.

Ewert, R. (1990) *Wirtschaftsprüfung und asymmetrische Information*, Berlin: Springer.

Forster, K.-H. (1984) "Die Jahresabschlussprüfung im Spiegel der Erörterungen der Unternehmensrechtskommission sowie des Regierungsentwurfs eines Bilanzrichtliniengesetzes und des Entwurfs einer 5. EG-Richtlinie," in W. Hadding, U. Immenga, H.-J. Mertens, K. Pleyer, and U.H. Schneider (eds), *Handelsrecht und Wirtschaftsrecht in der Bankpraxis*, Berlin and New York, pp. 131–51.

Forster, K.-H. (1998) "Abschlussprüfung nach dem Regierungsentwurf des KonTraG," *Die Wirtschaftsprüfung*, 51(2): 41–56.

Frantz, P. (1999) "Auditor's Skill, Auditing Standards, Litigation, and Audit Quality," *British Accounting Review*, 31(2): 151–83.

Geiger, M.A. and Rama, D.V. (2003) "Audit Fees, Nonaudit Fees, and Auditor Reporting on Stressed Companies," *Auditing: A Journal of Practice & Theory*, 22(2): 53–69.

Gietzmann, M.B. and Quick, R. (1998) "Capping Auditor Liability: The German Experience," *Accounting, Organizations and Society*, 23(1): 81–103.

Gross, G. and Möller, M. (2004) "Auf dem Weg zu einem problemorientierten Prüfungsbericht," *Die Wirtschaftsprüfung*, 57(7): 317–24.

Hagen, H. (1971) *Die Drittschadensliquidation im Wandel der Rechtsdogmatik. Ein Beitrag zur Koordinierung von Rechtsfortbildungen*, Frankfurt am Main: Athenaeum.

Heininger, K. and Bertram, K. (2004) "Neue Anforderungen an Berufsaufsicht und Qualitätskontrolle durch das Abschlussprüferaufsichtsgesetz (APAG)," *Der Betrieb*, 57(33): 1737–41.

Hohenlohe-Oehringen, P. (1986) "Die Rechtsprechung zur Auskunftshaftung," *Betriebs-Berater*, 41(14): 894–5.

Hommelhoff, P. and Mattheus, D. (2004) "BB-Gesetzgebungsreport: Verlässliche Rechnungslegung – Enforcement nach dem geplanten Bilanzkontrollgesetz," *Betriebs-Berater*, 59(2): 93–100.

Hopt, K.J. (1992) "Haftung des externen Prüfers," in A.G. Coenenberg and K. Wysocki (eds.), *Handwörterbuch der Revision*, 2nd ed., Stuttgart: Schäffer-Poeschel, col. 791–802.

Kaminski, H. (1992) "Der Beruf des Wirtschaftsprüfers," in IDW (ed.), *Wirtschaftsprüfer-Handbuch 1992*. 10th ed., Düsseldorf: IDW, pp. 1–84.

Keitel, H.-J. (1987) "Rechtsgrundlage und systematische Stellung des Vertrages mit Schutzwirkung für Dritte," PhD dissertation, University of Bielefeld.

Lang, A. (1989) "Zur Dritthaftung der Wirtschaftsprüfer," *Die Wirtschaftsprüfung*, 42(3): 57–64.

Lansburgh, A. (1908) "Revisions-Gesellschaften," *Die Bank*, 853–64.

Lenz, H. (2004) "Referentenentwurf eines Abschlussprüferaufsichtsgesetzes: noch unzureichende Kontrolle des Berufsstandes!," *Betriebs-Berater*, 59(36): 1951–6.

Marks, P. and Schmidt, S. (1998) "Einführung einer externen Qualitätskontrolle im Berufsstand der deutschen Wirtschaftsprüfer," *Die Wirtschaftsprüfung*, 51(22): 975–87.

Marten, K.-U., Köhler, A.G. and Meyer, S. (2003) "Umbruch im Peer-Review-System – Deutscher Status quo und der Sarbanes-Oxley Act of 2002," *Die Wirtschaftsprüfung*, 56(1–2): 10–17.

Marten, K.-U., Quick, R., and Ruhnke, K. (2007) *Wirtschaftsprüfung – Grundlagen des betriebswirtschaftlichen Prüfungswesens nach nationalen und internationalen Normen*, 2nd ed., Stuttgart: Schäffer-Poeschel.

Marten, K.-U., Köhler, A.G., and Paulitschek, P. (2006) "Enforcement der Abschlussprüfung in Deutschland – Kontext und Ansatzpunkte des Referentenentwurfs eines Berufsaufsichtsreformgesetzes," *Betriebs Berater*, 17 (BB-Special 4/2006): 23–30.

Mertens, H.J. (1977) "Erwartung und Wirklichkeit der aktienrechtlichen Pflichtprüfung," in W. Busse von Colbe and M. Lutter (eds), *Wirtschaftsprüfung heute. Entwicklung oder Reform?*, Wiesbaden, pp. 15–28.

Moore, G. and Scott, W.R. (1989) "Auditors' Legal Liability, Collusion with Management, and Investors' Loss," *Contemporary Accounting Research*, 5: 754–74.

Nann, W. (1985) *Wirtschaftsprüferhaftung. Geltendes Recht und Reformüberlegungen*, Frankfurt am Main, Bern and New York: Peter Lang.

Niehus, R.J. (2000) "Peer Review in der deutschen Abschlussprüfung – ein Berufsstand kontrolliert sich," *Der Betrieb*, 53(23): 1133–42.

Ostrowski, M. and Söder, B.H. (1999) "Der Einfluss von Beratungsaufträgen auf die Unabhängigkeit des Jahresabschlussprüfers," *Betriebswirtschaftliche Forschung und Praxis*, 51(5): 554–64.

Pankow, M. (1990) "100 Jahre Dienstleistungen," in Vorstand der KPMG Deutsche Treuhand-Gesellschaft, Berlin und Frankfurt am Main (ed.), *100 Jahre Dienstleistungen – Zur Geschichte der Deutschen Treuhand-Gesellschaft*, Berlin/Frankfurt am Main: KPMG Deutsche Treuhand-Gesellschaft, pp. 145–73.

Passow, R. (1906) *Die Bedeutung des Aufsichtsrats für die AG*, Frankfurt am Main: Thünen-Archiv.

Pfitzer, N. and Orth, C. (2002) "Die Unabhängigkeitserklärung des Abschlussprüfers gegenüber dem Aufsichtsrat im Sinn des Deutschen Corporate Governance Kodex," *Der Betrieb*, 55(15): 753–5.

Poll, J. (2003) "Externe Qualitätskontrolle in der Praxis – Erfahrungen mit dem Peer Review in Deutschland, Grenzen und Chancen," *Die Wirtschaftsprüfung*, 56(4): 151–7.

Quick, R. (1992) "Die Haftung des handelsrechtlichen Abschlußprüfers," *Betriebs-Berater*, 47(24): 1675–85.

Quick, R. (2000) "Nationale und internationale Haftungsrisiken deutscher Abschlußprüfer," *Die Betriebswirtschaft*, 60 (Sonderdruck 1): 60–77.

Quick, R. (2001) "Externe Qualitätskontrolle im deutschen Prüfungswesen – Zur Einführung eines Peer Review-Systems in Deutschland," *Der Schweizer Treuhänder* (1–2): 25–31.

Quick, R. (2002) "Abschlussprüfung und Beratung – Zur Vereinbarkeit mit der Forderung nach Urteilsfreiheit," *Die Betriebswirtschaft*, 62(6): 622–43.

Quick, R. (2004) "Gründung und frühe Entwicklung deutscher Wirtschaftsprüfungsgesellschaften," *Vierteljahrschrift für Sozial- und Wirtschaftsgeschichte*, 91: 281–309.

Raghunandan, K. (2003) "Nonaudit Services and Shareholder Ratification of Auditors," *Auditing: A Journal of Practice & Theory*, 22(1): 155–63.

Raghunandan, K., Read, W.J., and Whisenant, J.S. (2003) "Initial Evidence on the Association between Nonaudit Fees and Restated Financial Statements," *Accounting Horizons*, 17(3): 223–34.

Ruhnke, K. (2006) "Business Risk Audits: State of the Art und Entwichlungsperspektiven," *Journal für Betriebswirtschaft*, 56(4): 189–218.

Sahner, F., Schulte-Groß, H., and Clauß, C. (2001) "Das System der Qualitätskontrolle im Berufsstand der Wirtschaftsprüfer und vereidigten Buchprüfer," *Wirtschaftsprüferkammer-Mitteilungen*, Sonderheft April: 5–17.

Schlechtriem, P. (1984) "Summenmäßige Haftungsbeschränkungen in Allgemeinen Geschäftsbedingungen," *Betriebs-Berater*, 39(19): 1177–87.

Schildbach, T. (1996) "Die Glaubwürdigkeitskrise der Wirtschaftsprüfer - zu Intensität und Charakter der Jahresabschlußprüfung aus wirtschaftlicher Sicht," *Betriebswirtschaftliche Forschung und Praxis*, 48(5): 1–30.

Schmidt, M. and Kaiser, S. (2004) "Öffentliche Aufsicht über Abschlußprüfer – Schwerpunkt der Reform des Berufsrechts der Wirtschaftsprüfer 2004," *WPK Magazin*, 3: 38–41.

Schmitz, B. (1989) "Die Vertragshaftung des Wirtschaftsprüfers und Steuerberaters gegenüber Dritten. Eine Auseinandersetzung mit den Haftungsausdehnungstendenzen der Rechtsprechung des BGH," *Der Betrieb*, 42(38): 1909–15.

Seibt, C. (2002) "Deutscher Corporate Governance Kodex und Entsprechenserklärung (§ 161 AktG-E)," *Die Aktiengesellschaft*, 47(5): 249–58.

Spremann, K. (1990) "Asymmetrische Information," *Zeitschrift für Betriebswirtschaft*, 60(5–6): 561–86.

Stürmer, M. (1990) "Zur Bilanz des 20. Jahrhunderts," in Vorstand der KPMG Deutsche Treuhand-Gesellschaft, Berlin und Frankfurt am Main (ed.), *100 Jahre Dienstleistungen – Zur Geschichte der Deutschen Treuhand-Gesellschaft*, Berlin/Frankfurt am Main, pp. 21–36.

Swanger, S.L. and Chewning Jr., E.G. (2001) "The Effect of Internal Audit Outsourcing on Financial Analysts' Perceptions of External Auditor Independence," *Auditing: A Journal of Practice & Theory*, 20(2): 115–29.

Thoman, L. (1996) "Legal Damages and Auditor Efforts," *Contemporary Accounting Research*, 13: 275–306.

Veltins, M.A. (2004) "Verschärfte Unabhängigkeitsanforderungen an Abschlussprüfer," *Der Betrieb*, 57(9): 445–52.

Willeke, C. (2003) "Zum Gesetz zur Reform des Zulassungs- und Prüfungsverfahrens des Wirtschaftsprüfungsexamen," *Steuern und Bilanzen*, 23: 1058–62.

Wolf, K. (2004) "Entwicklungen im Enforcement unter Berücksichtigung des Referentenentwurfs für ein Bilanzkontrollgesetz (BilKoG)," *Deutsches Steuerrecht* (6): 244–8.

Zilias, M. (1974) "Die Harmonisierung der Haftungsvorschriften für Abschlussprüfer in den Mitgliedstaaten der Eg. Künftig unbeschränkte Haftung und Haftung gegenüber Aktionären und Dritten?," *Die Wirtschaftsprüfung*, 27(3): 69–78.

7 Auditing in Italy

The development of a highly-regulated setting before and after the Parmalat case

Mara Cameran

1 Introduction

Auditing in Italy underwent significant development toward the middle of the 1950s (although the first audit firms, both national and international, appeared from 1910 through to the 1920s) due to the desire on the part of foreign audit firms to have offices *in situ* which could audit the Italian subsidiaries of large multinational groups. Nevertheless at that time full audits were barely known by local players in Italy and almost ignored by public opinion. The concept of financial auditing began to spread, albeit slowly, in the late 1960s and early 1970s. The profession, which had developed exclusively by supporting the activities of foreign groups, began to find clients directly in the domestic market, which was undergoing a phase of intense development. National firms, desiring to compete in international markets and becoming increasingly aware of the fact that these markets rewarded credibility and transparency in external communications, began to overcome their traditional reluctance to subject themselves to an audit of their financial statements.

National legislation intervened in various ways. Presidential Decree No. 136/75, which regulated the auditing activity carried out by audit firms and indeed made it compulsory for the most important firms (e.g. listed companies), was especially important. This law introduced double statutory control over the accounting documents of some companies in Italy. In particular, as described in greater depth below, two statutory "auditors" were provided for in Italy. The first, named Collegio Sindacale, does not carry out a full audit, but monitors the proper administration of the entity and its compliance with laws and regulations. The second type of auditor is a full auditor (an individual or an audit firm). Before the issuing of the Decree No. 136/75, a full audit was not mandatory for any Italian firms, even though a law issued in 1939 regulated audit firms operating in Italy which carried out voluntary audit activity (see section 4).

The spread of auditing in Italy was further accelerated by the difficult financial situation of the times, characterized by the oil shocks from 1974 to 1983, which led external financiers to demand the provision of agreed figures and the implementation of adequate controls.

From the second half of the 1970s, audit firms operating in Italy focused increasingly on local clients and employed almost exclusively Italian professionals, even if they maintained relationships at an international level and kept the name of the foreign parent firm. At the same time, the audit firms of Italian origin realized that they needed structures which crossed national boundaries and sought to merge at an international level, partly in order to share the methodologies which they could use in their professional activities. During the 1990s, following the outcry created by the "Clean Hands" investigation and by some more recent financial scandals, including Enron and Parmalat, which has been described as "Europe's Enron," clear differences have emerged between the public's expectations and the real aim of the financial audit (a so-called expectation gap). In April 2002 a Commission (Galgano Commission) was set up with the aim of studying a possible solution in order to enhance the quality of the financial information of listed companies. In the final report, issued in September 2002, the Commission cited the Enron scandal as the reason for its creation. In April 2003 a bill was proposed concerning new rules guaranteeing auditor independence. In December 2003 Parmalat's financial problems became known publicly, because this, the world's largest dairy firm with 36,000 employees, ranked as the eighth largest company in Italy, had difficulty making a €150 million bond payment. The company was supposed to have been sitting on €3.95 billion in cash, so Italian bankers were puzzled by its predicament. Parmalat's problems quickly worsened after the admission that the €3.95 billion, supposed to be in a Bank of America account held by Bonlat, a subsidiary based in the Cayman Islands, did not exist. Parmalat's primary auditor was one of the Big Audit Firms (by which I mean the top-tier international audit firms), but the Milan branch of Grant Thornton dealt with some of the company's subsidiaries, including Bonlat. Grant Thornton checked Parmalat's Bank of America cash accounts, receiving a letter of confirmation of the existence of the funds. However, Bank of America said the letter was forged. Two partners of the Italian affiliate of Grant Thornton were the first individuals to be prosecuted in the scandal. The company sought protection from its creditors after the Italian government rushed through an emergency decree allowing companies to apply to the Ministry of Industry to appoint an administrator with immediate powers. When Parmalat filed for bankruptcy protection, it revealed that its net debt was more than €14 billion – eight times more than it had claimed. Enrico Bondi was appointed special administrator of the company in December 2003. He launched a series of lawsuits against the banks in an attempt to recover some money for the company and its investors.

The trial started on 28 September 2005, nearly two years after the collapse of Parmalat. Parmalat's former head (Callisto Tanzi) and 15 others were accused of market-rigging, providing false accounting information, and misleading Italy's stock market regulator over the scandal. Prosecutors had sought to bring 27 people to trial. Eleven of those, including three of Parmalat's former chief financial officers, were sentenced to up to two and a half years in prison under plea bargains in June 2005, while the separate trial began in January 2005 of two accountants who worked at Grant Thornton. Prosecutors also asked for the indictment of several global banks and security companies, including Citigroup, Morgan Stanley, Deutsche Bank, and UBS, for security law violations. Prosecutors alleged that the banks had provided false information about Parmalat's finances to investors and encouraged them to buy Parmalat stocks and bonds in the run-up to the crash. In the meantime, the April 2003 bill continued its examination by the Senate Committee of the Italian Parliament. In October 2005 the bill was included in a wider bill regarding the "Dispositions for savings protection and for financial markets regulation" proposed in March 2005, which dealt with other auditing related issues (e.g. the length of the audit engagement and the determination of audit fees). This was approved by Parliament on 23 December 2005 and partly modified by Legislative Decree No. 303/06 of 29 December 2006.

2 Corporate governance

In Italy statutory audits on accounting documents are carried out in different ways, depending on the system of corporate governance that the firm has implemented. In the past there were two types of statutory "auditors." The first type, named Collegio Sindacale, did not carry out a full audit, but monitored the proper administration of the entity and its compliance with laws and regulations. The result of this monitoring activity was then summarized in a report enclosed with the financial statements. The second type was a full auditor authorized to carry out full audits. By law, the first law having been issued in 1975 (the previously cited Presidential Decree No. 136/75), companies that were subject to mandatory full audits had to engage both a Collegio Sindacale and a full auditor. The Collegio Sindacale carried out audits limited to particular account balances, e.g. cash and research and development expenses. So, in part, the duties of the Collegio Sindacale and those of full auditors overlapped. In 1998 Legislative Decree No. 58/98 (the *Legge Draghi)* changed this situation for some companies (notably the listed ones). The Collegio Sindacale of some of the companies subject to Legislative Decree No. 58/98 had no duties regarding auditing. The audit responsibilities were entirely transferred to external accountancy firms (Zambon 2001). The Collegio Sindacale of listed companies had to declare in the annual report to the stakeholders that it had "checked the adequacy of the company's organizational structure for those matters within the scope of its authority, the internal control system and the administrative and accounting system as well as the reliability of the latter in correctly representing the company's transactions." However, for most companies operating in Italy, the situation did not change after Legislative Decree No. 58/98. The Collegio Sindacale continued to carry out limited audits on the same account balances as the full auditors appointed, either voluntarily or compulsorily, to audit and issue their opinions. A further change was determined by the reform of the Italian

Commercial Law in 2003. This reform came into effect on 1 January 2004 and, in some cases, offered the possibility of appointing a full auditor (individual or audit firm) instead of the Collegio Sindacale for auditing activity. Individual companies could choose whether or not to engage an individual auditor or an audit firm instead of the Collegio Sindacale. Nowadays, for the control of the accounting documents there are three alternative corporate governance models for stock corporations (*società per azioni*). They are summarized in Table 7.1. The choice of the corporate governance model determines the way the control of accounting documents must be carried out.

More precisely, for a stock corporation the following alternatives exist:

- in firms which borrow from the equity markets, the audit must be carried out by an audit firm listed in the Register of Revisori Contabili, which, limited to these duties, is subject to the discipline of audit firms registered with Consob (the Regulatory Body for the Italian Stock Exchange) (see below section 4);
- in firms which do not borrow from the equity markets and which have to prepare consolidated financial statements, control of the financial statement can be exercised by an individual auditor or an audit firm enrolled in the Register of Revisori Contabili;
- in firms which do not borrow from the equity markets and which do not have to prepare consolidated financial statements, control of the financial statement can also be exercised by the Collegio Sindacale. In this case the Collegio Sindacale is made up of individual auditors enrolled in the Register of Revisori Contabili. More precisely, companies may choose to engage one of the following for the control of the accounting documents: Collegio Sindacale, individual auditor, or audit firm enrolled in the Register of Revisori Contabili.

Table 7.1 Corporate governance models for stock corporations (*Società per azioni*)

	Traditional system	*Unitary system*	*Two-tier system*
Country of origin	Italy	United Kingdom	Germany
Management administration	Board of directors	Board of directors	Management board
Monitoring activity of management administration	Collegio Sindacale	Audit Committee[a]	Supervisory board[a]
Auditing activity	Individual auditor, audit firm, or Collegio Sindacale[b]	Individual auditor or audit firm	Individual auditor or audit firm

Notes: a One or more of its members must be listed in the Register of Revisori Contabili.
 b All the members must be listed in the Register of Revisori Contabili.

Moreover, a corporate governance code (the *Codice Preda*), revised in March 2006, was set out for listed companies in 1999. The code regulates the relationship between directors, Collegio Sindacale, and full auditors.

The Code states that listed companies are governed by a board of directors, made up of executive directors (those directors who perform management functions within the company) and non-executive directors. Non-executive directors bring their specific expertise to board discussions and contribute to the taking of decisions that are consistent with the shareholders' interests. An adequate number of non-executive directors must be independent, in the sense that they:

1   do not entertain, directly or indirectly or on behalf of third parties, nor have recently entertained business relationships with the company, its subsidiaries, the executive directors, or a shareholder or group of shareholders who controls the company to the extent that it is able to influence their autonomous judgement;
2   neither own, directly or indirectly or on behalf of third parties, a quantity of shares enabling them to control the company or exercise a considerable influence over it nor participate in shareholders' agreements to control the company;
3   are not immediate family members of executive directors of the company or of persons in the situations referred to in points 1 and 2.

The board of directors is responsible for the internal control system; it must lay down the guidelines for the system, periodically check that it is adequate and working properly, and verify that the main risks facing the company are identified and managed appropriately. The board of directors must establish an internal control committee, charged with the task of giving advice and making proposals and made up of non-executive directors, of whom the majority must be independent. The chairman of the Collegio Sindacale or another auditor appointed by the same must participate in the committee's meetings. Moreover, it should be specified that Law 262/05, following what was stated by the Sarbanes Oxley Act, introduced in Italy the 'Dirigente Preposto', who must issue a report which certifies to third parties the correctness of the financial statement. He is also responsible for the adequacy and effective application of the company's internal control procedures.

In particular, the internal control committee must:

1   assist the board in performing the tasks related to the internal control system;
2   assess the audit program prepared by the persons responsible for internal control and receive their periodic reports;
3   assess, together with the heads of administration and the external auditors (of an audit firm), the appropriateness of the accounting standards adopted and, in the case of groups, their uniformity with a view to the preparation of the consolidated accounts;

4   assess the proposals put forward by audit firms to obtain the audit engagement, the audit program for carrying out the audit, and the results thereof as set out in the auditors' report and their management letter;

5   report to the board of directors on its activity and on the adequacy of the internal control system at least once every six months, at the time the annual and half-year accounts are approved;

6   perform the other duties entrusted to it by the board of directors, particularly as regards relations with the auditing firm.

In general terms, the Collegio Sindacale of a listed company is required to oversee the following:

- the company's compliance with the law and with the articles of association;
- the company's compliance with principles of good administration and management;
- the adequacy of the corporate structure for matters falling within its scope of responsibilities, such as the systems of internal control, the accounting system, and the reliability of these systems to properly record and reflect transactions in the accounting system;
- the adequacy of management supervision and the flow of information between the company and companies controlled by the company.

In addition, the Collegio Sindacale has responsibilities with respect to the independent audit firm engaged to perform the statutory audit of the financial statements. While the shareholders make the selection of the independent audit firm and set the audit fees at the shareholders' meeting, the Collegio Sindacale must express its opinion on the appointment itself and on the audit fees. The opinion issued by the Collegio Sindacale must contain assessments of the independence and technical expertise of the independent audit firm, with special regard to the adequacy and soundness of the audit plan in relation to the scope and complexity of the business operations being audited. Also, the independent auditing firm must report the results of the audit to the Collegio Sindacale and the two bodies must meet at least quarterly for the mutual exchange of relevant data and information in order to perform their respective responsibilities and duties. The Collegio Sindacale will communicate any misconduct and irregularities of the assigned audit firm to the Italian regulator for the stock exchange (Consob).

If the company chooses the unitary or the two-tier system, the Code states that all the rules set out above apply to the bodies provided for by the new systems of corporate governance. As these systems were introduced only in 2003 with the reform of the Italian Commercial Law, which became effective in 2004, and few companies have decided to adopt one of the two alternative systems of corporate governance to date, there was no reference to practice on which the Code could have based its statements; some years will have to pass before the effects of this reform become clear.

3 The profession

The regulation of the accounting profession is governed by law. Chartered auditors in Italy must be enrolled in the Register of Revisori Contabili (chartered auditors). The characteristics of Revisore Contabile were stated in a 1992 Law (Legislative Decree No. 88/1992) which enforced the Eighth EU Directive on the approval of people responsible for carrying out the statutory audits of accounting documents. To be a Revisore Contabile one is required to be in possession of a three-year university degree in Business Administration or the equivalent and to have completed three years' training followed by a state examination. More precisely, the candidate is required to have three years of practical experience working with a Revisore Contabile or an audit firm registered with Consob (see below). The exam is held annually and consists of three written tests and an oral test. Its purpose is to ascertain the theoretical knowledge of the candidates and their ability to put this theory into practice (within the limits of being able to exercise control over accounting and financial reports). Once the state exam has been passed, the audit candidate has the right to forward his/her application for listing on the Register of Revisori Contabili. According to the law, this is a public register held by the Ministry of Justice, in which all Italian chartered auditors are listed. In January 2006 the management of the Register was transferred to the Register of Dottori Conmercialisti ed Esperti Contabili by Legislative Decree No. 28/2006 (see section 8). There are, therefore, also audit firms in the Register. To be enrolled they are obliged to have as their business purpose either auditing or accounting organization, and all the members of the board of directors and the majority of partners have to be enrolled in the Register as well. Table 7.2 shows the members listed in the Register at the end of the 1990s. Most of the individuals enrolled as Revisore Contabile are Italian certified public accountants (Dottori Commercialisti and Ragionieri), who perform activities such as helping the vast number of small to medium-sized firms which characterize the Italian market, carrying out their accounting actions and tax obligations. Traditionally, the Italian

Table 7.2 Members listed in the Register of Revisori Contabili

Categories	Number	Percentage
Dottori Commercialisti	25,549	35.74
Ragionieri	18,559	25.96
Lawyers	1,826	2.55
Employment consultants	1,812	2.53
Members listed on other professional registers (e.g. engineers)	2,094	2.93
State functionaries	5,537	7.75
Other	15,885	22.22
Audit firms	225	0.31
Total	71,487	100.00

Source: *The Accountant*, April 1999

accounting profession is organised into the two categories of Dottori Commercialisti and Ragionieri (the latter now renamed by law Esperti Contabili). This division is the result of a historical heritage: the duties of the two types of professionals are more or less the same. The vast majority are also Revisori Contabili, so they meet the requirements of the EU Eighth Directive, although in Italy belonging to one of these two categories does not necessarily mean being a chartered auditor in the sense of the cited directive. Table 7.2 illustrates the subdivision of those registered as Revisori Contabili; 25,549 Dottori Commercialisti and 18,559 Ragionieri are registered, whereas on 31 December 1996 there were 37,697 Dottori Commercialisti and in July 1997 35,033 Ragionieri. Even taking the time difference into account when interpreting these figures, there are at least 12,000 Dottori Commercialisti and 16,000 Ragionieri who are not members of the Register of Revisori Contabili. A law issued at the end of June 2005 (Legislative Decree No.139/2005) unified the two categories of the Italian accounting profession in a single register with two separate sections. This new register will become effective on 1 January 2008. In order to be accepted and listed on this register, a candidate needs to have the required level of both education (different for the two sections) and practical experience. It is necessary to have at least a three year university degree, with specific course requirements covering economics, corporate, and legal subjects. In addition, the candidate is required to have three years' practical experience working with a professional who has been on the register for more than five years. Finally, to be listed on the register candidates must pass a state exam.

4 The regulatory environment for the audit firm

Regarding audit firms, under Italian law there are three different categories of "legal actors" who can issue an audit opinion:

1   Audit firms authorized by law 1966/39 (235 on 31 December 2001): these firms are authorized and supervised by the Ministry of Industry.
2   Audit firms registered with Consob (the Stock Exchange Regulatory Body) (24 on 31 December 2001): these firms are registered in a special list kept by Consob, which undertakes supervisory activities.
3   Revisori Contabili (275 of which were audit firms in 2001) in accordance with Italian legislative decree 88/92, which enforced the EU Eighth Directive: in the case of audit firms, they must have auditing and accounting organization of client companies as their business purpose and must be listed on the register of auditors held at the Ministry of Justice, which undertakes appropriate supervisory activities.

Even if the membership of the three categories partially overlaps (e.g. on 31 December 2001, 168 of the 235 audit firms authorized by law 1966/39 were also enrolled on the Register of Revisori Contabili), these three categories are characterized by different professional qualifications and are subject to different regimes of control. In particular, audit firms registered with Consob are the only ones authorized to audit the financial statements of listed companies. Their business purpose must respect the limits set out for audit firms listed on the Register of Revisori Contabili.

In terms of demand, the Italian audit market can be divided into two parts:

1   demand for audit reports due to legal requirements (mandatory audit client segment);
2   demand for audit reports due to reasons other than legal obligations (voluntary audit client segment).

Until 2004, when the reform of the Italian Commercial Law became effective, the first kind of demand (mandatory audits) could be sub-divided further (Antitrust 2000) into:

a   *Revisione legale* (legal audits): the most relevant entities subject to this kind of auditing are companies listed in Italy or in other EU countries, Italian companies controlled by listed companies and insurance companies. This type of audit can only be supplied by Consob audit firms.
b   *Revisione obbligatoria* (obligatory audits): e.g. companies that obtain grants from the Italian state for more than €516,456, broadcasting networks (TV or radio) and cooperatives. This kind of audit can be supplied only by the types of auditor indicated in the particular laws that oblige them to be audited.
c   Other compulsory audits required by particular laws other than national ones: e.g. by regional laws or by some controlling bodies such as the Italian Football League. Entities that are authorized to supply this type of audit are identified by specific laws.

For mandatory engagements other than *revisione legale*, Consob audit firms are in competition with other auditors. This is true for voluntary audits as well.

Most of the available data concern Consob-registered audit firms and only permit a distinction between revisione legale engagements and other types of engagement (mandatory and voluntary).[1] In the 1990s more than 90 percent of Consob audit firm engagements were obtained outside the revisione legale. This means that the survival of Consob audit firms, whose revenues in 1997 represented 90 percent of the total revenues of the leading audit firms on the Italian market (*International Accounting Bulletin*, 30 September 1998), depends on engagements for which they compete with audit firms not registered with Consob. Furthermore, the Big Audit Firms generated more than 90 percent of the revenues (1989–99) of all Consob audit firms (source: Consob annual reports). Finally, most of the audit revenues of the Big Six/Five/now Four were obtained through voluntary audits (68.72 percent in 2002, 69.57 percent in 2003).[2] It is clear, therefore, that the voluntary audit service segment is the most competitive, as all three categories of full auditors can supply such audits. Revenues from this segment are estimated by the Antitrust to be 420 billion Italian lire (€217 million), while the revenues of the mandatory audit segment were estimated at 138 billion Italian lire (€71 million) in 1997/8 (Antitrust 2000). This trend continued until the end of 2003. The reform of the Italian Commercial Law came into force on 1 January 2004. The space for the voluntary audit demand was restricted due to the enlargement of the number of legal subjects that should/could engage an individual auditor or an audit firm for the control of the accounting documents (see section 2). Data for 2004, show that, with regard to the Big Audit Firms, the percentage of voluntary audit revenues over mandatory ones is about 70.69 percent, almost in line with previous years. The effect that reform on the audit market structure becomes clear from 2005. In this year the situation changed significantly (as shown in Table 7.6). In fact, the percentage of voluntary audit revenues, with regard to the Big Firms only, fell to 55.37 percent, thus showing that the reform of the Italian Commercial Law actually introduced some significant changes within the audit market structure.

4.1 The audit firms operating in Italy

As in many other European countries, in Italy the Big Audit Firms are the undisputed market leaders in terms of revenues (89 percent of the total), as can be seen from Table 7.3.

In December 1999 Coopers & Lybrand and Price Waterhouse merged, more than a year after the merger in the UK. Market shares for 1999–2000 calculated on the total turnover of the Big Audit Firms, as reported in their financial statements, showed that Arthur Andersen was the market leader (see Table 7.4). However, 1999 data are not significant for PwC because that was the year in which PW merged with C&L. Data available from Antitrust investigations showed that in the previous years (1997–8) PW and C&L combined market shares were not very different from the AA market share. Starting from 2001 PwC became the Italian market leader. Deloitte & Touche was fifth among the Big Five throughout all the years from 1999 to 2003, with a significantly different market share in comparison with the others.

The situation changed after the merger with AA which became effective from July 2003 when Arthur Andersen ceased to operate on the Italian market, and the AA employees and partners were taken over by Deloitte. In 2004, in fact, Deloitte & Touche is ranked second among the Big Four, and the market shares of the other Big Audit Firms are similar with the exception of the market leader (PwC). In 2005 the percentages changed significantly with respect to two audit firms, with PwC gaining market share (from 32 percent in 2004 to 35 percent in 2005) and Deloitte losing its quota (from 24 percent to 19 percent), ranking it last among the Big Four.

Table 7.3 Revenues of the most important audit firms in Italy in 2005

Audit firm	Member of Consob list	Revenues 2005 (€m)	% growth
PriceWaterhouseCoopers	yes	217.9	30.0
Reconta Ernst & Young (e)	yes	155.9	18.0
KPMG	yes	151.0	18.0
Deloitte (e)	yes	133.1	18.0
HLB International	no	28.9	12.0
Mazars	yes	23.4	52.0
PKF Italia	yes	11.5	8.0
BDO Sala Scelsi Farina	yes	10.3	29.0
Moore Stephens Italia	no	10.1	-4.0
Bompani Audit/MRI	yes	9.0	8.0
Baker Tilly Consulaudit	yes	9.0	6.0
IGAF Worldwide	no	8.5	47.0
DFK Italy	no	8.4	5.0
DITRAG/BKR International	no	6.1	7.0
CT&P/Horwath International	no	5.4	6.0
Rodl&Partner	no	4.4	40.0
Nexia International	no	4.0	–
Kreston International	no	3.6	-15.0
Polaris International	no	2.6	-7.0
SC International	no	2.4	4.0
Morison International	no	1.7	-11.0
MGI Midgley Snelling Chartered Accountants	no	1.4	83.0
Moore Stephens Auditing Firm Axis	yes	1.2	20.0
Studio Maviglia/GMN Enterprise	no	0.7	-15.0
Total	–	810.5	21.0

Note: (e) IAB Estimate

Source: IAB data (March 2006) processing

Table 7.4 Market shares among the Big Auditors in Italy (percentages calculated on total turnover)

	1999	2000	2001	2002	2003	2004	2005
AA	30.88	26.71	21.73	19.90	16.41	–	–
Deloitte	8.47	8.17	5.47	5.75	8.12	23.61	19.25
KPMG	23.27	19.51	20.88	22.72	23.62	22.56	22.99
PwC	14.72	25.05	31.34	37.47	32.07	31.52	35.38
R&Y	22.66	20.56	20.58	14.16	19.78	22.31	22.38
Total	100.00	100.00	100.00	100.00	100.00	100.00	100.00

Note: AA and R&Y market shares relating to 2002 are calculated on the basis of, respectively, a nine and a sixth month financial statement period.

As mentioned in the previous section, Big Audit Firms, under national law, may provide services limited to the accounting organization of the firms, as well as auditing services. As shown in Table 7.5, auditing activities account for about 90 percent of total revenues for the Big Firms, even if the percentages for the various firms can differ significantly from this average in different years.

With reference to the Big Audit Firms, we can also distinguish between revenues generated from voluntary audits and total audit revenues (the sum of the fees obtained from both voluntary and mandatory audit clients) by using the data provided by these companies in their financial statements (see Table 7.6). In the case of the Big Audit Firms, from 1999 to 2003 the revenues from voluntary audits accounted for an average of about 69 percent of the total audit revenues. For all the firms belonging to the group of Big Audit Firms, revenues from voluntary audits accounted for more than half of the total audit revenues, with significantly different trends between firms (on average more than 80 percent for KPMG, more than 75 percent for PwC, and more than 65 percent for Deloitte, while the shares were smaller for Andersen and Reconta, who all show significant variations over the period).

It is clear therefore that, as mentioned in section 4, a typical feature of the Italian audit market is the relevance of the voluntary audit demand compared with the mandatory one. This demand, on the basis of available data, is not evenly distributed among the Big Audit Firms. The situation changed with the reform of the Italian Commercial Law.

Although we have only "preliminary" data concerning the first two years of the application of that reform, which came into force in 2004, a substantial restriction of the voluntary audit market from 2005 can clearly be observed. The share of voluntary audit revenues earned by the Big Audit Firms in fact dropped from 71 percent in 2004, almost in line with previous years, to 55 percent in 2005. This could be the effect of the enlargement as a result of the reform of the number of legal subjects that should/could engage an individual auditor or an audit firm for the control of the accounting documents.

5 Approach to setting auditing standards

The reference sources for carrying out an audit are the rules and auditing standards set out by the national councils of Dottori Commercialisti and Ragionieri (see section 3), organizations which also dealt with setting Italian accounting standards. In 2001 another organization, OIC (Organismo Italiano di Contabilità), was founded, replacing the national councils of Dottori Commercialisti and Ragionieri in carrying out the task of setting out accounting standards.

Auditing standards are endorsed by Consob and they must be applied in all legal audit (revisione legale) engagements (see section 3). Moreover, the same principles must be used in all other engagements, including voluntary ones.

The Italian auditing standards have recently been completely revised in order to accommodate the recommendation of the European Commission regarding the

Table 7.5 The Big Audit Firms: split of revenues (€000)

	AA		D&T		KPMG		PwC		R&Y		Total	
1999												
Auditing fees	77,976	87.37%	22,029	89.96%	61,725	91.78%	38,509	90.51%	63,576	97.06%	263,814	91.27%
Other revenues	11,270	12.63%	2,458	10.04%	5,527	8.22%	4,038	9.49%	1,927	2.94%	25,220	8.73%
Total	89,246	100.00%	24,487	100.00%	67,251	100.00%	42,547	100.00%	65,503	100.00%	289,035	100.00%
2000												
Auditing fees	87,913	91.96%	25,549	87.37%	60,357	86.46%	83,079	92.68%	68,704	93.38%	325,602	90.98%
Other revenues	7,686	8.04%	3,692	12.63%	9,451	13.54%	6,565	7.32%	4,872	6.62%	32,267	9.02%
Total	95,599	100.00%	29,241	100.00%	69,808	100.00%	89,645	100.00%	73,576	100.00%	357,868	100.00%
2001												
Auditing fees	85,648	89.08%	22,878	94.58%	72,790	78.75%	110,927	80.00%	82,408	90.49%	374,651	84.67%
Other revenues	10,498	10.92%	1,311	5.42%	19,642	21.25%	27,730	20.00%	8,665	9.51%	67,846	15.33%
Total	96,146	100.00%	24,189	100.00%	92,432	100.00%	138,657	100.00%	91,073	100.00%	442,497	100.00%
2002												
Auditing fees	65,882[a]	84.86%	21,790	97.12%	73,950	83.45%	126,648	86.62%	53,062[b]	96.06%	341,332	87.49%
Other revenues	11,758	15.14%	647	2.88%	14,669	16.55%	19,555	13.38%	2,175	3.94%	48,804	12.51%
Total	77,640	100.00%	22,437	100.00%	88,619	100.00%	146,203	100.00%	55,237	100.00%	390,136	100.00%
2003												
Auditing fees	65,808	83.60%	38,400	98.54%	96,155	84.84%	140,514	91.34%	91,785	96.74%	432,662	90.19%
Other revenues	12,913	16.40%	569	1.46%	17,183	15.16%	13,321	8.66%	3,096	3.26%	47,082	9.81%
Total	78,721	100.00%	38,969	100.00%	113,338	100.00%	153,835	100.00%	94,881	100.00%	479,744	100.00%
2004												
Auditing fees			93,948[c]	82.87%	88,543	81.75%	137,931	91.13%	98,601	92.09%	419,023	87.28%
Other revenue			19,424	17.13%	19,768	18.25%	13,420	8.87%	8,464	7.91%	61,076	12.72%
Total			113,372	100.00%	108,311	100.00%	151,351	100.00%	107,065	100.00%	480,099	100.00%
2005												
Auditing fees			95,756[c]	88.28%	108,533	83.78%	185,719	93.15%	120,146	95.24%	510,154	90.52%
Other revenues			12,713	11.72%	21,017	16.22%	13,667	6.85%	6,003	4.76%	53,400	9.48%
Total			108,469	100.00%	129,550	100.00%	199,386	100.00%	126,149	100.00%	563,554	100.00%

a Data referring to nine month period;
b Data referring to six month period;
c Data referring to "Deloitte & Touche SpA", created by the integration of activities between "Deloitte& Touche Italia SpA"(ex Andersen) and "Deloitte & Touche SpA".

Table 7.6 The Big Audit Firms: audit revenues (€000)

	AA	D&T	KPMG	PWC	R&Y	Total
1999						
Voluntary audit fees	48,649	14,667	51,319	30,497	38,082	183,215
Total audit revenues	77,976	22,029	61,725	38,509	63,576	263,814
% voluntary audit	62.39	66.58	83.14	79.20	59.90	69.45
2000						
Voluntary audit fees	51,609	15,707	49,965	65,196	38,081	220,558
Total audit revenues	87,913	25,549	60,357	83,079	68,704	325,602
% voluntary audit	58.70	61.48	82.78	78.47	55.43	67.74
2001						
Voluntary audit fees	51,275	14,531	58,113	79,522	49,677	253,118
Total audit revenues	85,648	22,878	72,790	110,927	82,407	374,650
% voluntary audit	59.87	63.51	79.84	71.69	60.28	67.56
2002						
Voluntary audit fees	39,335[a]	14,044	61,923	94,335	24,919[b]	234,556
Total audit revenues	65,882	21,790	73,950	126,648	53,062	341,332
% voluntary audit	59.71	64.45	83.74	74.49	46.96	68.72
2003						
Voluntary audit fees	35,793	26,481	82,671	109,403	46,668	301,016
Total audit revenues	65,808	38,400	96,155	140,514	91,784	432,661
% voluntary audit	54.39	68.96	85.98	77.86	50.85	69.57
2004						
Voluntary audit fees	60,034[c]		73,775	107,920	54,475	296,204
Total audit revenues	93,948		88,543	137,931	98,601	419,023
% voluntary audit	63.90		83.32	78.24	55.25	70.69
2005						
Voluntary audit fees	51,966[c]		70,816	113,790	45,923	282,495
Total audit revenues	95,756		108,533	185,719	120,146	510,154
% voluntary audit	54.27		65.25	61.27	38.22	55.37

a Data referring to nine month period
b Data referring to six month period
c Data referring to "Deloitte & Touche SpA," created by the integration of activities between "Deloitte & Touche Italia SpA" (ex Andersen) and "Deloitte & Touche SpA"

adoption of common auditing standards at an international level; as far as possible and within the limits of compatibility with local legislation, the standards were borrowed from international auditing standards (ISAs).

At present, the auditing standards that must be followed are those set since 2002 by the joint commission for auditing standards established within the National Council of Dottori Commercialisti and Ragionieri, recommended by Consob. These auditing standards comply with the ISAs recommended by IFAC, from which they are taken; they follow them so closely that they even use the same numbering system. The joint commission, having verified the applicability of the ISAs to Italian procedure, quickly adopted the new standards with a view to bringing international practices of auditing into line with those of accounting.

6 Ethical standards

The major scandals in Italy have shown that a lack of ethical awareness and independence on the part of the actors involved, including the auditors, is a serious threat to the system of governance of firms and groups.

According to current legislation, there are situations, expressly defined by law, in which there is an absolute presumption of lack of independence. The primary reference is Legislative Decree No. 58/98, which was modified the first time by Parliament on 23 December 2005 and finally on 29 December 2006. This Legislative Decree governs, among other things, the accounting control of firms listed on the stock exchange. Article 160 defines the following situations as incompatible with the independence of the audit firm and of the auditor: contractual or shareholding relationships between the audit firm and the auditee; blood or work relationships; the undertaking of auditee company duties by stockholders, directors, Collegio Sindacale members, or general managers of the audit firm. In particular, the engagement cannot be granted to an audit firm which finds itself in an incompatible situation deriving from contractual or shareholding relationships or whose stakeholders, directors, Collegio Sindacale auditors, or general managers:

- are relatives or in-laws to the fourth degree of the directors, Collegio Sindacale members, or general managers of the auditee or other firms or entities which control it;
- are linked to the auditee or to other firms or entities which control it through a professional relationship (whether autonomous or subordinate), or where there have been such relationships in the three years preceding the appointment;
- are directors or Collegio Sindacale members of the auditee or of the firms or entities which control it, or have been such during the three years which precede the appointment;
- find themselves in any other situation which compromises their independence with regard to the auditee.

Article 160, as modified by Parliament on 23 December 2005 and successively on 25 December 2006, also affirms that specific criteria are laid down by Consob in order to establish whether a specific entity does or does not belong to an audit firm network, by which it means the broader structure to which the audit firm belongs (including holding, controlled and associated companies, and companies subject to common control) and which uses a common trading name. Consob also states the criteria which must be considered in order to establish whether an engagement or a relationship could compromise independence, and how an audit firm must publish the amount of fees received by the auditee firm and by other entities belonging to the same network, specifying the amount of fees deriving from audit activity and from other services. Consob, furthermore, may set down instructions and recommendations aimed at preventing shareholders of the audit firm or of other entities belonging to the same network, and other subjects who carry out administrative, managing, and auditing functions, from interfering in audit activity and thus compromising the independence and objectivity of the people carrying out auditing. It must be pointed out that many regulations concerning these matters are still to be issued by Consob.

Article 160, finally, limits the kinds of activity which can be carried out by an audit firm. In particular, audit firms may not provide the following services to auditee companies:

- keeping of accounting books and other services relating to data – booking and financial-statement reports;
- designing and producing information systems;
- services concerning evaluation and estimate activities and the issuing of *pro-veritate* opinions;
- actuarial services;
- external managing of internal-control services;
- consulting activity concerning personnel selection, training, and management or legal consulting;
- security brokerage, investment consulting, or other services concerning bank investments;
- services of legal defense;
- other services not strictly linked to audit activities.

Furthermore, stockholders, directors, Collegio Sindacale members, or employees of the audit firm cannot undertake the duties of director or Collegio Sindacale member of the auditee, nor can they undertake work (either as employees or otherwise) for the auditee, until three years have passed since the end of the appointment or since they ceased to be stockholders, directors, Collegio Sindacale members, or employees of the audit firm.

In the Civil Code there are some regulations that define the incompatibility of subjects engaged to control the accounting documents of stock corporations. These are similar to those illustrated with regard to listed companies.

Consob in resolution No. 15185 of 5 October 2005 recommended to audit firms subject to its control the adoption of a document concerning "principles related to auditor independence" issued by the joint commission of Dottori Commercialisti and Ragionieri at the end of 2004. This document put into practice what the appendix to Italian Auditing Principle 200 (that is, the equivalent of ISA 200 "Objective and General Principles Governing an Audit of Financial Statements") established. This standard discussed the general principles with which auditors must comply (independence, integrity, objectivity, competence and diligence, confidentiality, professional behavior, respect for technical principles), and in the appendix it recalled the ethical norms which auditors are required to observe when undertaking their activities (as well as the legal responsibility outlined above, relationships between auditors, auditors' compensation, and the use of the professional services of other auditors who are appointed). These are essentially the audit principles which outline the conditions necessary for ethical conduct in carrying out a professional audit. The cited standard must be applied by all auditors enrolled on the Register of Revisori Contabili and, given the fact that Consob recommended it, by all audit firms subject to its control.

Moreover, since 1974 a law requiring mandatory auditing for listed companies and the mandatory rotation of audit firms has been in force in Italy.[3] More precisely, the duration of a single audit appointment is fixed at nine years and the same audit firm cannot be reappointed to do the same task if at least three years have not passed since the previous engagement. Furthermore, a partner cannot be the person responsible for the audit with reference to the same auditee company for more than six years, and neither can he be reappointed before three years have passed since the previous engagement expired. As mentioned above, the mandatory rotation rule was modified by the reform of Legislative Decree No. 58/1998, approved by Parliament on 23 December 2005 and then modified again on 25 December 2006. Before this reform, mandatory rotation was compulsory every nine years. More precisely, the duration of a single audit appointment was three years, and the same audit firm could be reappointed only twice. Moreover, the mandatory rotation of the partner responsible was introduced in Italy only after that reform.

The mandatory rotation rule was introduced in Italy in order to increase the independence of audit firms, but the real impact is doubtful. From a theoretical point of view, the mandatory rotation rule has an impact on the costs sustained by the auditee. In fact, empirical research has highlighted how, during the first year of a new engagement, "getting to know" the economics of the auditee can even lead to an increase in the costs sustained by the audit firms undertaking the task. In particular, "European Accounting firms estimate that their costs would be around 15 percent higher for long-term levels for a new client in a familiar industry, and around 25 percent higher for those in unfamiliar industrial sectors" (Ridyard and de Bolle 1992). It is also evident that the auditee incurs an increase in the weight of its burden, caused by the greater amount of time devoted to interaction with the new audit firm by managers, personnel, and internal auditors, if any, who supply the necessary information to the audit firm on aspects concerning corporate governance, internal control systems, organizational structure, market relations, and so on. Opinions on the audit fee paid by the auditee in Italy are, however, divided. In an unpublished Italian work prepared by the staff of Bocconi University, based on interviews conducted with a group of partners of Big Italian Audit Firms in 2002, showed unanimous agreement that, when changing the audit firm at the end of its nine-year period, the fees for services were similar to or lower than those paid to the former auditor (Cameran *et al.* 2003). These partners underlined the fact that, because of mandatory audit rotation, fierce competition arises concerning the fees for services. Audit partners' opinions are consistent with the evidence obtained in the Anglo-Saxon countries. Simon and Francis carried out a study in the US from 1979 to 1984. Results pointed to a significant fee reduction in the initial engagement year

(Simon and Francis 1988). The evidence obtained for the UK market is also compatible with "low-balling" behavior on the part of the new auditor (Gregory and Collier 1996, Pong and Whittington 1994).

In terms of the effective impact of the mandatory rotation rule on an auditor's independence, the Bocconi study assumes that a certain relationship exists between quality and independence; particularly when an audit service has been considered of high quality, it is automatically assumed that the auditor had a high degree of independence. Contrarily, the low quality of an audit service could be due to a variety of reasons, including a low degree of independence. In this study the number of suspensions of partners brought about by Consob (regarding the partners of audit firms registered on its special list) is used as a possible measure of the quality of audit services (in the sense of the ability to detect errors). Generally, in fact, suspensions arise in situations in which material misstatements were not pinpointed by auditors. The number of partner suspensions in Italy carried out during the 1992–2001 period, amounted to 40. It was possible to analyze 31 of these cases in depth. It was found that the suspensions were mainly concentrated in the very first year of an appointment, in which – it was assumed – the auditor had not yet acquired detailed knowledge of the audited company. By analyzing the distribution of suspensions over engagement length, it can be deduced that mandatory rotation seems to have a negative impact on the quality of the work carried out by the audit firm during the first year of an appointment. The number of suspensions carried out over the following years, however, dropped dramatically, presumably because, as the years pass, the audit firm acquires greater knowledge of the audited company.

Different results are obtained by analyzing the impact of the mandatory rotation rule on perceived independence. The Bocconi study points out that the majority of the managers who participated in the survey (by filling in a questionnaire) regarded the prohibition, set by the mandatory rotation rule, on reconfirming an audit engagement after the end of the nine-year term positively. The main reason that emerged for the managers' support of mandatory audit rotation was that they believed that over the years audit firms tended to concentrate on routine activities and to pay less attention to making suggestions/improvements. The recent reform of Legislative Decree No. 59/1998 also introduced mandatory rotation for the responsible partner. As mentioned above, an audit firm must now change the person responsible for the engagement regarding a specific company at least every six years and the partner cannot be reappointed before three years have passed since the previous engagement expired.

7 Liability

The Italian auditor liability regime is traditionally less litigious than that in the US or the UK; it is more similar to those of other continental European countries. In Italy, since the beginning of the 1990s, audit firms have been sued increasingly often when the auditee is insolvent. The auditor gives an opinion on whether the audited financial statements comply with the prevailing legislation and Italy's generally accepted accounting principles, and on whether these statements give a true and fair view of the company's performance and financial position. Audits are carried out as required by the generally accepted auditing standards in Italy. The extension of the auditor's liability to client and third parties (e.g. creditors) depends on the type of engagement. The regime is more severe when an auditee is obliged by law to appoint an auditor. In a voluntary audit, when the auditor's opinion is used to raise funds among investors, the auditor's liability to third parties is similar to the liability stipulated for a mandatory engagement. In all cases the auditor is not held liable to the injured parties unless negligence is involved.

The civil responsibility of the auditor, which is regulated by Legislative Decree No. 58/1998 and by the Civil Code, originates from a harmful or negligent act by the auditor (professional negligence), whose breaches or errors are so serious as to have a significant bearing on the judgment expressed and consequently cause damage to others. The responsibility of the auditor in civil actions is covered by sentencing for the payment of damages. In summary, the breaches or errors in the auditing activities must be considered as such if the auditor has not applied – or has mistakenly applied – the auditing principles, or, in general, if he/she has operated without a sufficient level of professional diligence. However, the auditor is not held responsible when he/she has not discovered errors or inaccuracies in the financial statements despite a diligent application of the auditing principles.

The auditing firm – and, with it, those who have undertaken the audit – must recompense the client firm, its stockholders, and third parties for damage arising from breaches according to the law. When ascertaining the civil responsibility of the auditor, the concept of the materiality of the error must be taken into consideration, that is the scale of an omission or error in the accounting information due to which, given the circumstances, it is likely that the judgment of a reasonable person who trusts this information would be changed or influenced by the omission or error.

As far as the criminal responsibility of the auditor is concerned, this involves charges of false communication (article 174, Legislative Decree No. 58/98; article 2624, Civil Code), auditor corruption (article 174, Legislative Decree No. 58/98), illegal financial relationships with auditees (article 177, Legislative Decree No. 58/98), illegal earning of fees other than those legally agreed with the client company (article 178, Legislative Decree No. 58/98), obstruction to Consob's or the Ministry of Justice's oversight functions (article 2638, Civil Code), as well as any other act which could be seen as a crime and was committed while carrying out his/her duty. Specific laws govern the criminal responsibility of auditors.

Furthermore, an independent auditor is subject to the responsibilities laid down by law and he/she is also subject to disciplinary measures issued by the professional bodies and associations to which he/she belongs (see section 4). The responsibility of the auditor therefore involves the civil sphere, the criminal sphere, and the professional sphere.

8 Oversight system

As mentioned above, auditors are subject to the disciplinary measures of the professional bodies to which they belong (see section 4) under the terms set out in the relevant regulations. The accounting profession has established a series of clear ethical norms – for example relating to diligence and advertising – which, if not observed, lead to appropriate sanctions on the part of the bodies to whom the auditor is professionally answerable.

Nor should the professional sanctions issued by Consob be forgotten. In particular, article 162 of Legislative Decree No. 58/98, which was modified by the reform approved by Parliament on 29 December 2006, states that Consob must supervise the activities carried out by audit firms registered on its special list, in order to control their independence and technical qualifications. Consob periodically, and in any event every three years, verifies the independence and the existence of the technical qualifications both of the audit firm and of the people responsible for audit activity and summarizes its conclusions in a specific report.

Consob, furthermore, in the performance of its duties:

- states, after having asked the Italian accounting profession for an opinion, the standards and the criteria to be adopted while carrying out audit activity;
- requires, periodically, the communication of information and the transmission of acts and documents;
- carries out inspections and gathers information and explanations from partners, directors, members of audit committees, and general managers of audit firms.

Article 162 of Legislative Decree No. 58/98 also states that all audit firms registered on Consob's special list must communicate, within thirty days, any substitutions among directors, partners, and general managers, and any transfer of shares or any other variations occurring within the partners' structure.

Whenever Consob ascertains serious irregularities in the undertaking of auditing functions, it may impose a pecuniary sanction of from €10,000 to €500,000. Consob may also order the auditing firm not to use for up to five years the person to whom it has ascribed the irregularities. For example, on 25 March 2004 Consob told one of the Big Audit Firms not to use the partner responsible for the audit of the Cirio group for two years.

Consob can furthermore forbid audit firms from accepting new assignments for a period of up to three[4] years, or, in the case of particularly serious matters, it can remove the firm from the special list. On 28 July 2004, following the events linked to the Parmalat scandal, Consob removed Italaudit S.p.A. (previously Grant Thornton S.p.A.) from the list. The company had been undertaking the audit of the financial statements of Bonlat Financing Corporation, a firm in the Parmalat group, on 31 December 2002 (see section 1).

Consob may also remove from its special list any audit firms that have not carried out audit activity for a continuous period of five years. All these measures are communicated to all those concerned and to the Ministry of Justice.

The above paragraphs concern audit firms registered on Consob's special list.

With regard to the Revisori Contabili, oversight activity is carried out by the Ministry of Justice. More precisely, according to Legislative Decree No. 88/1992 and to Presidential Decree No. 99/1998, the Ministry supervises, through its Central Commission, all individual auditors and audit firms on the Register of Revisori Contabili. The Central Commission, a professional body made up of members appointed by the government who remain in post for a period of four years, renewable for another four years, must check the existence of all the qualifications required in order to be registered as a Revisore Contabile (see section 3). When the Commission finds a lack of qualifications, it informs the registered auditor/audit firm, giving him/it a maximum term of six months to rectify all the deficiencies. If the individual auditor or the audit firm does not remedy his/its omissions within the assigned term, the Ministry, after having heard the concerned party, orders his/its removal from the Register. The Ministry, furthermore, whenever it ascertains the existence of facts which could seriously compromise the professional qualifications necessary to properly undertake audit activity, such as serious technical incapability, lack of moral integrity, serious professional negligence, or non-observance of the independence requirements, may order the interruption of audit activity for a period of up to a year. The removal from the Register of Revisori Contabili can also be ordered if the registered person/firm continues to carry out audit activity within the suspension period, or if he/she/it has been suspended more than twice.

In January 2006 Legislative Decree No. 28/2006 was passed by the government. This attributes the oversight of the Register of Revisori Contabili to the unified accounting profession set up by Legislative Decree No. 139/2005 (see section 3). More precisely, the bill states that the Register will be managed by the unified Italian accounting profession (Dottori Commercialisti and Ragionieri, the latter now renamed by law Esperti Contabili) through a different information system, which will be locally accessible; a certain degree of autonomy and independence for Revisori Contabili, however, will still be guaranteed. In summary, the administrative functions will pass to the unified accounting profession, whereas the competence of deliberating on registrations, suspensions, and cancellations will remain under the Central Commission's jurisdiction. This shift of competences became effective on 1 October 2006.

9 Summary and conclusions

Regulation of auditing in Italy has a complex history, and it is not directly comparable to regulation in English-speaking countries. In fact various bodies have responsibility for controlling company activity in Italy.

In 1882 a governance system for stock corporations was created, which included a control board, usually referred to as the Board of Auditors (Collegio Sindacale). This has the duty of monitoring the proper administration of the entity and its compliance with laws and regulations, and of summarizing its activity in a report enclosed with the financial statements. It does not carry out full audits. A law of 1939, which is still in force, regulates both fiduciary companies and audit firms, and, after the Second World War, the branches of the major international accounting firms operating in Italy had to carry out their services according to this law.

In Italy mandatory full auditing for some companies was introduced in the mid-1970s. They had to engage both the Collegio Sindacale and full auditors; this applied to listed companies from 1975 until 1998. The situation was changed by Legislative Decree No. 58/98 (for listed companies) and, for all other companies, by the reform of the Italian Commercial Law. This reform came into effect on 1 January 2004 and, in some cases, required or offered the possibility of the appointment of a full auditor (individual or audit firm) instead of the Collegio Sindacale.

With regard to full auditors, and in particular audit firms, the Italian setting is characterized by certain special features. First of all, there are different categories of "legal actors" who can issue an audit opinion and who have different professional qualifications and are subject to different regimes of control. Second, the major part of audit revenues derives from voluntary audits (demand for audit reports for reasons other than legal obligations). This situation partially changed in 2005 due to the reform of the Italian Commercial Law, which restricted the market for voluntary audits (see section 4). It will be some years, however, before the long-term effects of this reform on the audit market structure become clear. There are, moreover, other special features such as, from a legislative point of view, the mandatory rotation rule and the prohibition on supplying management advisory services. Furthermore, Italian law defines some situations as incompatible with the independence of an audit firm.

In recent years many laws aiming at reinforcing investors' confidence in Italian markets have modified the Italian corporate governance system. The recent reform of Legislative Decree No. 58/98, approved by Parliament at the end of December 2005 and revised in December 2006, which reinforced Consob's vigilance powers over audit firms, specified stricter sanctions, and introduced mandatory partner rotation, could also be seen as an important step toward greater credibility in audit activity.

Commentators, however, note that this bill may be considered only as a first step in this direction, because many issues remain outside its scope and many regulations to which the bill makes reference are still to be issued. Moreover, the adoption of the modified Eighth EU Directive in Italy does not seem to have greatly changed current Italian company law, and in particular the law relating to auditing. In fact, for example, mandatory rotation (of audit firms) and the almost total prohibition on auditor provision of non-auditing services have been effective in Italy for many years. Moreover, a list of incompatibilities is stated by law for directors, Collegio Sindacale, and audit firms. Unfortunately Europe's Enron – the Parmalat scandal – took place in one of the EU countries with the most restrictive norms regarding auditor independence.

An important role in rebuilding public confidence in audit activity could be played by more effective regulatory oversight. Traditionally the Italian oversight system for auditor professional responsibility was characterized by a low number of disciplinary measures from the professional bodies. In recent years this situation has changed but within this framework the reform of Legislative Decree No. 58/98 of 23 December 2005 and of 29 December 2006, the modified Eighth EU Directive, and the Commission decision of 14 December 2005 ("setting up a group of experts to advise the Commission and to facilitate cooperation between public oversight systems for statutory auditors and audit firms") may be an important chance to strengthen the system and improve the public's perception of the effectiveness of the oversight system for auditors. The same might be said of the system of quality assurance, which could be made more effective by the adoption of the modified Eighth EU Directive.

Notes

1 Data regarding 17 of the 24 Consob audit firms in 1997–8, including the Big Six, show that revenues from compulsory engagements other than revisione legale amount to 68 percent of the revenues of the revisione legale. Revenues from voluntary audits represent over 70 percent of total audit fees.
2 Data obtained by processing the financial statements of the Big Audit Firms.
3 The obligation of audit firm rotation, originally imposed upon listed companies, has been extended over the last 30 years to other companies (e.g. insurance companies).
4 Before the reform of Legislative Decree No. 59/1998, approved on 23 December 2005, the maximum period of time for which a partner could be banned from carrying out audit activity was two years, whereas one year was the maximum period for which Consob could forbid an audit firm from carrying out audit activity.

References

Autorità garante della concorrenza e del mercato (Antitrust) (2002), *Provvedimento n. 7979 (1266) del 28/01/2000*, Assirevi/Società di Revisione.
Cameran, M., Livatino, M., Pecchiari, N., and Viganò, A. (2003) "A Survey of the Impact of Mandatory Rotation Rule on Audit Quality and Audit Pricing in Italy," Paper presented at the Second European Auditing Research Network Symposium, 31 October–1 November 2003, Manchester.
Cndc. Online. Available at: <http://www.cndc.it> (accessed 21 February 2007).
Comitato per la Corporate Governance, Codice di autodisciplina, March 2006.
Consob, Resolution No. 13809, October 2002.
Consob, Resolution No. 15185, October 2005.
Consob, Deliberation No. 14488, March 2004.
Consrag. Online. Available at: <http://www.consrag.it > (accessed 21 February 2007).

FEE (Fédération des Experts Comptables Européens), "Discussion Paper on the Financial Reporting and Auditing Aspects of Corporate Governance," July 2003.

Gregory, A. and Collier, P. (1996) "Audit Fees and Auditor Change: An Investigation of the Persistence of Fee Reduction by Type of Change," *Journal of Business Finance & Accounting*, 23(1): 13–28.

Guardian (newspaper). Online. Available at: <http://www.guardian.co.uk> (accessed 21 February 2007).

Pecchiari, N., Pogliani, G., and Livatino, M. (2005), *Auditing*, Milan: Egea.

Pong, C.M. and Whittington, G. (1994) "The Determinants of Audit Fees: Some Empirical Models," *Journal of Business Finance and Accounting*, 21(8): 1071–95.

Ridyard, D. and de Bolle, J. (1992) *Competition in European Accounting*, Dublin: Lafferty.

Senato. Online. Available at: <http://www.senato.it> (accessed 21 February 2007).

Simon, D.T. and Francis, J.R. (1988) "The Effects of Auditor Change on Audit Fees: Test of Price Cutting and Price Recovery," *The Accounting Review*, 63(2): 255–69.

Zambon, S. (2001) "Italy," in D. Alexander and S. Archer (eds), *European Accounting Guide*, 3rd ed., London, New York: Harcourt Brace.

8 The auditing profession in the Netherlands

From Limperg's principles to detailed rules

Roger Meuwissen and Philip Wallage

1 History and development of the Dutch auditing profession

The auditing profession in the Netherlands started up at the end of the nineteenth century, with the appearance of the modern company and the separation between ownership and control. Resulting agency problems led to a major bookkeeping scandal in 1876. The management of a Rotterdam-based company called Pincoffs had forced two bookkeepers to falsify the company accounts. Instead of a loss of eight million Dutch guilders, Pincoffs reported a profit of two million guilders. However, when the company was not able to finance its current operations, the fraud was discovered. This created a need for an independent financial expert to verify the financial reports of management on behalf of the shareholders. Accordingly, in 1879 the first independent external accountant was appointed by the Nieuwe Afrikaansche Handelsvennootschap. The birth of the accounting profession was a fact. As such, the origin of the audit profession can be seen as consistent with the ideas of agency theory. In the years that followed, accountants tried to organize the profession and in 1895 established the first professional body of accountants, called Nederlands Instituut Van Accountants (NIVA). Thereafter, several other professional bodies of accountants were established, but most of them disappeared after mergers.[1] This process eventually led to a situation (from 1938 on) where there were four professional bodies of accountants in the Netherlands: NIVA, Vereniging van Academisch Gevormde Accountants (VAGA), Nederlandse Unie van Accountants, and Nederlandse Broederschap van Accountants. In 1967, these four professional bodies merged into the Dutch Institute of Registered Auditors (Nederlands Instituut van Registeraccountants, or NIVRA).[2] In this year the accounting profession was regulated by the 1962 Act on Registered Auditors, and the statutory auditor was officially created.[3] According to this act, only members of NIVRA, called Registered Auditors, were granted the right to conduct statutory audits. Furthermore, the professional body NIVRA was charged with regulating the auditing profession. They became responsible for the education and licensing of statutory auditors and the issuance of auditing standards as authorative guidance for their members. In 1993, after the implementation of the Eighth EU Directive, members of the Dutch Association of

Certified Accountants (Nederlandse Orde van Accountants-Administratie-consulenten) were also empowered to conduct statutory audits according to the 1993 Act on Certified Accountants.[4] Before 1993 certified accountants were not allowed to render auditing services and mainly provided bookkeeping, tax, and consultancy services for smaller companies. After this change in the law, both *registeraccountants* (registered auditors) and *accountants-administratie-consulenten* (certified accountants) were permitted to perform statutory audits, and the two professional bodies were charged with regulating the auditing profession.

Currently, there are approximately 13,000 registered auditors and 6,000 certified accountants. Of these 19,000 professionals, about 5,500 are in public practice. The other members work in business or government as internal auditors, controllers, etc., or only engage in non-audit services. Figure 8.1 provides an overview of the development of the number of auditors in the Dutch market for audit services from 1879 until now. Figure 8.1 shows that the Dutch market for audit services, measured in terms of the number of auditors, grew steadily until 1970. Thereafter the market rapidly expanded, with a massive increase in the number of auditors in the 1990s because, as of 1993, licensed certified accountants were also allowed to conduct statutory audits.

The increase in the number of auditors from 1970 on is mainly the result of demand-side regulation. Before 1970 there was no statutory audit requirement in the Netherlands. All the audits conducted were voluntary audits of, for example, companies listed on the Amsterdam Stock Exchange or companies that were subject to private loan agreements. The first legal audit requirement was introduced in 1970 with the 1970 Act on Annual Accounts of Enterprises.[5]

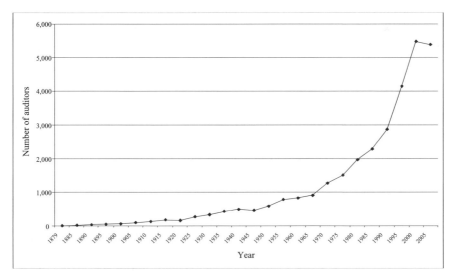

Figure 8.1 The Dutch market for audit services, 1879–2005

According to this act, all listed public limited liability companies (open naamloze vennootschappen), large private limited liability companies (besloten vennootschappen), and large co-operative associations (coöperaties) and large mutual guarantee companies (onderlinge waarborgmaatschappijen) were required to have their financial statements audited.[6] Then, in 1983, medium-sized and large non-listed public limited liability companies (besloten naamloze vennootschappen), medium-sized private limited liability companies (besloten vennootschappen), and medium-sized co-operative associations (coöperaties) and medium-sized mutual guarantee companies (onderlinge waarborgmaatschappijen) were also required to publish audited financial statements.[7] With this change, Dutch law was adapted to the EC 4th Company Law Directive,[8] leading to a situation where all medium-sized and large public limited liability companies, private limited liability companies, co-operative associations, and mutual guarantee companies were required to have their annual accounts audited. Furthermore, financial institutions (banks, insurance companies, and credit institutions) were also required to have their financial statements audited.[9] This demand-side regulation has remained unchanged since then.

The next major regulatory change in the Netherlands was the Dutch reaction to the US and European accounting scandals and the subsequent regulatory changes by the Securities and Exchange Commission and the European Commission. In 2006 the Supervision of Auditors' Organizations Act (Wet Toezicht Accountants) was implemented, creating an independent oversight board (Netherlands Authority for the Financial Markets – Autoriteit Financiële Markten) for the audit profession. Furthermore, the law specifies standards on, for example, the expertise, independence, and integrity of auditors and audit firms. This implies that the self-regulatory nature of the Dutch audit profession has to a large extent been replaced by government regulation as the Supervision of Auditors' Organizations Act has taken away some of the regulatory responsibilities of the professional bodies. The consequences of this act will be discussed in more detail in section 5.

When we focus on the audit market itself, we see that the global Big Four firms dominate the Dutch market with a market share of about 65 percent. In 2006 the audit fees of the Big Four firms amounted to about €2.5 billion out of a total estimated market for audit services of about €3.8 billion. Table 8.1 shows the audit fees of the ten largest audit firms in the Netherlands. Deloitte is the largest audit firm in the Netherlands with a fee income of €665 million, followed by PricewaterhouseCoopers, Ernst & Young, and KPMG.

2   Education and training

According to EU legislation, there are two routes to qualification as an auditor. Candidates can either follow the experience route or the educational route. To follow the educational route candidates must attain university entrance level, complete a course of theoretical instruction, undertake practical training for at

Table 8.1 Top 10 audit firms in the Netherlands in 2006

	Audit firm	Fee income (in million €)
1	Deloitte	665
2	PricewaterhouseCoopers	626
3	Ernst & Young	606
4	KPMG	604
5	BDO	180
6	Baker Tilly Netherlands (Berk)	72
7	Mazars & MRI	66
8	PKF Wallast	26
9	Foederer DFK Accountants	20
10	RSM Niehe Lancee	13

Source: *International Accounting Bulletin (2006)*

least three years, and pass an examination of professional competence which includes both a test of theoretical knowledge and a test of its practical application. In the experience route, the person may omit the first two or three of these requirements (but must still pass the examination of professional competence), and instead demonstrate that they have either seven or fifteen years respectively of experience of engaging in professional activity. These latter periods may be reduced by undertaking periods of theoretical instruction.

In the Netherlands candidates can only qualify as an auditor via the educational route, but within this route there are two alternatives: the practical avenue organized by the professional body, the Royal NIVRA, and the university avenue organized by the universities.

The practical route is only available for registered auditors and extends over eight years of part-time study. Candidates follow the program while already being employed by an audit firm or elsewhere. The typical way to enter the program is after completing secondary school. Candidates can also enrol on the practical program after finishing a four-year bachelor degree course in accountancy or business administration. The remaining part of the practical program will then take four years of part-time study. Although the nominal period of study for the practical route is eight years, in practice it appears that – due to the combination of work and studies – the average time taken to qualify as an auditor via this route is about 11 years.

Candidates can also follow the university route, which is available for both registered auditors and certified accountants. Registered auditors follow a three-year Bachelor of Science course offered by universities, or a four-year bachelor degree program offered by professional university-colleges, a one-year Master of Science program in accounting, and a two-year postgraduate course. Certified accountants follow a four-year bachelor program, a one-year master program, and a two-year post-master program. The bachelor and master programs are offered by Dutch universities as full-time courses. After completion of the master program, candidates start working at an audit firm or elsewhere and follow the postgraduate or post-master program on a part-time basis. When candidates finish the educational program of the university route, they have completed the theoretical part of the educational program. In order to qualify as a registered auditor or certified accountant, candidates in addition need to have at least three years of practical training in auditing. As they have already gained two years of practical experience during the postgraduate or post-master program, they need another year before taking the final examination to qualify as an auditor.

The courses of the auditor education program are in the following fields: general economics, business economics (management accounting, finance, management control), law, mathematics, statistics, bookkeeping, general organization, tax law, external reporting, administrative organization, and auditing. Furthermore, candidates have to write a graduation thesis and defend it in the final examination. After passing either the practical program or the university program, candidates can apply for inscription on the professional register of Royal NIVRA or NOvAA.

The educational requirements are specified by law. The 2006 Supervision of Auditors' Organizations Act stipulates that the Committee on the Auditor Education Examination Requirements (Commissie Eindtermen Accountantsopleiding) is responsible for issuing the educational requirements and monitoring the practical training.[10] Further requirements for registered auditors are specified in the Act on Registered Auditors[11] and for certified accountants in the Act on Certified Accountants.[12] These acts stipulate, for example, that both professional bodies are responsible for their educational programs. The undergraduate, graduate, and postgraduate examinations, organized by the universities, are under the responsibility of the individual universities and monitored by the Dutch Ministry of Education. The Committee on the Auditor Education Examination Requirements is responsible for monitoring the final educational requirements.

3 Approach to audit standard setting

In the 1890s the profession of independent auditor in the Netherlands originated from the need to verify the accounting of the funds entrusted to the management of an entity on behalf of those who had a direct financial interest in the results of the entity. In these early days, however, the auditing profession had no auditing standards; it took until the 1970s for the first auditing standards to develop. These standards are inspired by the ideas of Theodore Limperg (1879-1961), one of the most prominent members of the Dutch auditing profession. Around 1930 Limperg developed a set of basic audit concepts, which became known as the "theory of inspired confidence." This theory greatly influenced the Dutch audit approach and is still influential in the education of Dutch auditors. The theory of inspired confidence connects the societal needs for reliable financial statements with the technical possibilities of auditing to meet these needs; it also takes into account the changes in needs over time (Blokdijk *et al.* 1995: 23).

The theory of inspired confidence requires auditors to perform their task in such a way that they do not betray expectations (general auditing norm), while on the other hand they should not arouse greater expectations than their audit justifies. According to Limperg, society expects that an unqualified opinion means that the relevant facts have been taken into account correctly and completely and that the presentation of these facts is not misleading (true and fair view).

Because of Limperg's normative theory there was no need for specific auditing standards for almost 80 years! The general auditing norm directly determines the nature and amount of the work to be performed, given users' expectations. In order to satisfy the general auditing norm, the auditor should prepare a specific audit program for each engagement (Blokdijk *et al.* 1995: 24). As a consequence, auditing education in the Netherlands was strongly based on "Limperg's principle."

In 1977 Royal NIVRA decided to adopt international auditing standards. This was done wherever practical under local circumstances and in so far as there was no Dutch equivalent. Among others, the following specific Dutch rules existed (Blokdijk *et al.* 1995):

*   non-acceptance of client-imposed scope limitations;
*   the concept of axiomatic reservations (inherent limitations on the audit);
*   indispensable internal controls could lead to a disclaimer of opinion.

Because of the globalization of the profession (driven by the mergers of several large audit firms in the 1980s and 1990s) specific Dutch elements of auditing theory disappeared (Wallage 1991: 226).

The first auditing standards were issued by Royal NIVRA in 1986. Since then, the number of standards has grown considerably. In 1992 the NIVRA Board decided to adopt the International Auditing Guidelines (IAGs), referring to its obligation as a member of IFAC. In 1996 Royal NIVRA decided to adopt the first set of revised International Standards on Auditing (ISAs). The ISAs have been translated into Dutch as closely as possible. Sometimes a specific paragraph (called an A Paragraph) is added. On behalf of Royal NIVRA, the Auditing Practices and Standards Committee is charged with the development of approved standards on auditing that are related to the ISAs as closely as possible. This committee consists of Royal NIVRA members and covers all the sectors in which auditors can be active (public, internal, government).

The working procedure is as follows. The IAASB-ISA exposure drafts are translated by the committee. Subsequently, a review of the contents will take place, taking into account existing standards on auditing, and if necessary the ISAs are adapted for the situation in the Netherlands. Where the Auditing Practices and Standards Committee deems it necessary, additional standards are developed on matters of relevance in the Netherlands not covered by ISAs:

- Standard 205 "Submitting tenders and accepting engagements";
- Standard 621 "Cooperation between auditors and actuaries in the auditing of insurance companies";
- Standard 705 "Publication of auditor's report";
- Standard 780 "The auditor's role in the annual general meeting of shareholders";
- Standard 790 "Governmental, internal and industry auditors";
- Standard 850 "Auditor's involvement with prospectuses";
- Standard 860 "Auditor's involvement with contribution in kind";
- Standard 2410 "Reviewing interim financial reports."

The formal status of the auditing standards highlights their function as a source of guidance. The standards are to be applied in the audit of financial statements. In exceptional circumstances, an auditor may judge it necessary to depart from a standard in order to more effectively achieve the objective of an audit. When such a situation arises, the auditor should be prepared to justify the departure (NIVRA 2002: 23).

Because of the introduction of the law on oversight of audit firms[13] on 1 October 2006, Royal NIVRA is restructuring its bylaws and regulations, including the Standards on Auditing. Of central importance is the distinction between the bylaws and regulations applying to audit firms and those applying to individual auditors. One of the articles in the new law requires statutory audits to be performed in accordance with ISAs as adopted by the European Union. According to the notes,[14] it is expected that the European Commission will adopt the ISAs.

4 Ethical standards and specific independence regulation

Dutch auditors have to comply with the ethical standards (Verordening Gedragscode) of the Dutch professional bodies of auditors.[15] In addition to the ethical standards, the Dutch professional bodies have issued an Independence Guideline (Nadere voorschriften inzake onafhankelijkheid) that further explains the ethical standards.[16] The ethical standards and the Independence Guideline are in line with the Code of Ethics of IFAC (IFAC 2004) and with the recommendation of the European Commission on "Statutory Auditors' Independence in the EU: A Set of Fundamental Principles" (EU 2002).

The ethical standards consist of four parts. The first part relates to all auditors, the second part relates to auditors who are working in public practice, the third part relates to internal auditors and government auditors, and the fourth part relates to auditors in business.

The rules for all auditors relate to the fundamental principles each auditor should adhere to, such as integrity, objectivity, professional competence and due care, confidentiality, and professional behavior. A specific rule with respect to, for example, the fundamental principle that each auditor should acquire and maintain sufficient professional competence is a continuing professional education requirement.

The rules for auditors in public practice relate to the acceptance and continuation of engagements, conflicts of interest, second opinions, fees and other types of remuneration, advertising, kickbacks, custody of client assets, objectivity, and independence. According to these rules, public auditors should refuse to accept an engagement if they: (a) have a personal relationship with the client; (b) have a commercial relationship with the client; (c) have a financial interest in the client; and/or (d) become dependent, with regard to fee income, on particular clients. Regarding the monitoring of audit fees, there are no explicit regulations on the calculation of these fees. However, there is a general requirement that the fees should reflect the amount of work performed on the audit. Audit fees do not have to be published, although for public interest entities it is recommended to do so.[17] Furthermore, auditors in public practice are not allowed to quote a contingent fee for an audit engagement. With respect to advertising, audit firms are allowed to advertise, but it is limited to factual and objective information and needs to comply with professional ethics. All forms of unsolicited offerings are forbidden. The rules on auditor independence relate to, among other things, the provision of nonaudit services, auditor rotation, and peer review. With respect to nonaudit services, audit firms are allowed to provide any services to an audit client within the same legal entity, except in certain situations where independence is at stake. Bookkeeping services are allowed, except if the audit concerns a public interest entity. Auditors are allowed to provide IT services if the client declares that it is ultimately responsible for the IT system. Valuation services and legal advice are allowed, except if they relate to material items in the annual accounts. Internal control consulting is allowed when the client retains ultimate responsibility for the internal control system, and corporate finance consulting is allowed, except in the case of seasoned offerings. Interim management and human resource consulting are allowed, except for executive positions and critical financial positions. For each engagement, however, the Independence Guideline explicitly states that the auditor should always evaluate whether or not the provision of a nonaudit service will impair his independence. For public interest entities, there is also the requirement to rotate each key audit partner on the engagement every seven years. Each key audit partner has a cooling-off period of at least two years. There is no requirement on audit firm rotation. Furthermore, audit firms are required to undergo peer review.

The rules for internal auditors and government auditors relate to the acceptance and continuation of engagements, conflicts of interest, second opinions, kickbacks, objectivity, and independence. The specific requirements here are similar to those for auditors in public practice. One particularity is that auditors do not lose their license when they become employed outside the public auditing profession.

The rules for auditors in business relate to potential conflicts of interest, the compilation and publication of financial information, professional competence, financial interests and kickbacks. These rules relate to the ethical behavior of auditors in business and how they need to create an adequate control environment.

5 Oversight, monitoring, disciplinary observance and enforcement

The auditing profession in the Netherlands was already institutionalized in 1895, but only since 1962 it has been protected by law (1962 Act on Registered Auditors). In this act, the professional body, Royal NIVRA, was assigned the regulation of the auditing profession. In that era of self-regulation, quality inspections were conducted by the CTK (College Toetsing Kwaliteit). Inspections by the CTK focused on testing compliance with professional and ethical standards and were performed by auditors who were independent of the firm being monitored. Hence, there was, until recently, no independent external oversight of the Dutch auditing profession. However, because of the amended Eighth EU Directive, national and international bookkeeping scandals, and the incorporation of the US PCAOB, a law was issued with respect to the oversight and supervision of audit firms (Wet Toezicht Accountantsorganisaties, WTA.)[18] As of 1 October 2006 the independent oversight body has been the Netherlands Authority for the Financial Markets (Autoriteit Financiële Markten, AFM).

According to the 2006 Supervision of Auditors' Organizations Act, the AFM is responsible for independent oversight of the profession and will have the following tasks:

• independent oversight of audit firms and individual auditors in public practice;
• registering audit firms and individual auditors in public practice;
• the issuing of sanctions against audit firms and/or starting a disciplinary court procedure.

The AFM focuses its oversight on the audits of public interest entities as these audits bear a relatively high risk because of the impact on the capital markets and trust in the audit profession. According to the 2006 act, public interest entities are listed companies, banks, insurance companies, and public bodies such as government organizations. The most important oversight instruments are reviews of the internal control system of the registered audit firm and file reviews. The AFM will use the existing inspections by the professional bodies especially to monitor firm-wide procedures and for reviewing the files of non-public interest entities. Figure 8.2 describes the system of independent oversight in the Netherlands. The AFM is responsible for the independent oversight of statutory auditors, i.e. registered auditors and registered audit firms. All other auditors and audit firms – i.e. those conducting non-statutory audits – are subject to inspections by the professional bodies. When irregularities are discovered by the

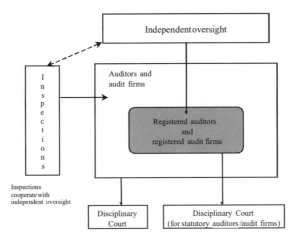

Figure 8.2 The system of independent oversight in the Netherlands

AFM or the professional bodies, the case is transferred to the appropriate disciplinary court.

Audit firms and their auditors will be registered by the AFM as statutory auditors after receiving proof that they comply with the legal requirements set forth in the 2006 Supervision of Auditors' Organizations Act. Only registered firms (and their registered auditors) are allowed to perform statutory audits. The act contains detailed requirements for registered audit firms with respect to:

- the systems of quality control of auditors' organizations;
- the integrity of the business operations of auditors' organizations;
- the independence of auditors' organizations;
- the reliability and professional competence of the day-to-day management of auditors' organizations;
- the professional competence, independence, and integrity of auditors;
- the transparency of auditors' reports.

Additional requirements for audits of public interest entities are (additional elements of) internal control and independence, as well as rotation of key persons in the audit team.

The Supervision of Auditors' Organizations Act further specifies that the issuance of auditing standards will be the responsibility of the professional bodies. However, in the event that the Ministry of Finance concludes the profession is failing, this task will be transferred to the AFM.

If an audit firm does not comply with the act, the AFM can issue several sanctions against that firm. The AFM can give an instruction to the firm, it can fine the firm up to €900,000, or it can revoke the license of the firm. Where the

AFM concludes that the audit firm has violated the law, it can transfer the case to the general prosecutor.

Apart from the sanctions available to the AFM, auditors can also face disciplinary actions. Before the 2006 Supervision of Auditors' Organizations Act, the acts on Registered Auditors and on Certified Accountants contained the disciplinary regulations. All interested parties can file a complaint against an auditor at the Disciplinary Court (Raad van Tucht). The Disciplinary Court consists of a chairman, six registered auditors, six certified accountants, and six others having expert knowledge. It is an independent body as the professional bodies have no influence on the appointment of its members. The Disciplinary Court may impose the following measures: (a) a written warning, (b) a written reprimand, (c) suspension as a registered auditor or certified accountant, or (d) exclusion from the profession. Table 8.2 presents an overview of the decisions of the Disciplinary Court in the period 1998-2005.

It is expected that in 2007 a new disciplinary system will be introduced in the Netherlands, according to the Act on Disciplinary Regulation for Auditors (Wet Tuchtrecht Accountants).

6 Liability of auditors

Besides disciplinary sanctions, legal action can be undertaken against auditors in the Netherlands. There is no specific legislation on the liability of statutory auditors. Hence, the general rules of civil liability apply to auditors. Legal actions against an auditor can be undertaken by the auditee, its shareholders, and any involved third party. The auditor is liable toward the auditee for any breach of contract. Third parties have to prove that there has been a breach of the duty of care toward the third party. However, it is not clear which third parties may bring liability actions against an auditor, as the Supreme Court has not taken a position on which parties the auditor owes a duty of care to. Furthermore, under current

Table 8.2 Disciplinary sanctions against auditors in the period 1998–2005

Year	Total number of sanctions against auditors	Type of sanction	
		Warning or reprimand	Suspension or exclusion
1998	19	16	3
1999	21	19	2
2000	16	15	1
2001	20	19	1
2002	31	31	0
2003	41	39	2
2004	31	27	4
2005	25	24	1

Source: Adapted from the publications of disciplinary sanctions of the Disciplinary Court, 1998–2005

law, class actions against auditors are not allowed. In cases of bankruptcy, the receiver (administrator of the company in bankruptcy) is allowed to take action against the auditor on behalf of the auditee. The receiver may also bring an action on behalf of third parties.

There are several events that lead to liability. Auditors are liable if they issue an irregular or misleading audit opinion (erroneous audit opinion), or if they do not disclose, or disclose too late, fraud or irregularities leading to damages that could have been avoided or to an erroneous audit opinion. Furthermore, the auditor is liable in cases of the breach of other duties, such as the duty of confidentiality or the (non)disclosure of matters that compromise the solvency of the auditee.

A further issue with respect to liability is the limitation of liability. In the Netherlands there are legal as well as contractual limitations to liability. These limitations relate to the time limit of liability, the corporate structure that audit firms may take, the possibility of arranging a contractual liability cap, and the suppression of certain obligations of auditors by contract. With respect to the time limitation of liability, actions against the auditor must be brought within five years after discovery of the damage. After five years, the right to undertake action expires. Dutch audit firms are also allowed to take the structure of a private or public limited liability company to shield them from liability.[19] In this form, partners that do not participate in a specific audit are protected from any possible civil liability arising from that audit. The appointed or signing auditor of the engagement (either an individual auditor or the firm) of course remains liable for damages caused by the audit. Furthermore, although there is no legal liability cap in the Netherlands, it is possible to arrange a contractual liability cap. This limitation of liability, however, does not shield the auditor in cases of wilful misconduct or gross negligence. Other opportunities to limit liability by contract include reducing the statute of limitation (shortening the legal period) and suppressing certain obligations. This contractual suppression, nevertheless, does not hold against third parties.

A final item in Dutch liability legislation is professional indemnity insurance. Auditors are not required to obtain insurance to cover their civil liability. However, it is recommended by the professional bodies that insurance coverage be maintained, and it is therefore common practice in the Dutch auditing profession.

7 Corporate governance

On 9 December 2003 the Dutch Corporate Governance Committee, chaired by Morris Tabaksblat, issued the Dutch Corporate Governance Code, called the Tabaksblat Code (Dutch Corporate Governance Committee 2003). The Code is applicable to all listed companies with registered offices in the Netherlands. The Code contains principles which are to be applied without exception, and best practice provisions which can be deviated from if it is explained why in the annual report (apply or explain principle). The "apply or explain" principle has received a basis in company law (in the Law on Financial Reporting). With respect to the role of non-executive directors, the Dutch civil code imposes two main duties: (1) advising the management board, and (2) supervising the management board.

In the Netherlands, where most large companies have two-tier boards – a supervisory board and a management board – the audit committee is composed of members of the supervisory, or non-management, board and forms a subcommittee of the supervisory board. According to the Tabaksblat Code, the audit committee must in any event focus on supervising the activities of the management board with respect to:

- the operation of the internal risk management and control systems, including supervision of the enforcement of the relevant legislation and regulations, and supervising the operation of codes of conduct;
- the provision of financial information by the company (choice of accounting policies, application and assessment of the effects of new rules, information about the handling of estimated items in the annual accounts, forecasts, work of internal and external auditors, etc.);
- compliance with recommendations and observations of internal and external auditors;
- the role and functioning of the internal audit department;
- the policy of the company on tax planning;
- relations with the external auditor, including, in particular, his independence, remuneration, and any non-audit services undertaken for the company;
- the financing of the company;
- the application of information and communication technology (ICT).

With respect to the audit committee the Code requires that the chairman is not the chairman of the (supervisory) board, nor a former executive director of the company, nor an executive director of another listed company. Furthermore, the audit committee should have at least one financial expert.

Both the executive and the supervisory boards have a responsibility for the financial reporting of the company. The executive board is responsible for the quality and completeness of the financial statements, and the supervisory board must see to it that the executive board is fulfilling its duties. Members of both boards can be held personally liable for damages suffered by shareholders and creditors when financial statements are misleading. There is only limited case law on both civil and criminal sanctions, but it is expected that more cases will occur in future as the AFM starts to supervise the annual accounts of listed companies during 2005. If the AFM considers the financial statements to be incorrect, it can ask the company to revise the statements. If the company refuses to do so, AFM can file a suit with the Enterprise Chamber of the Court of Appeal in Amsterdam to request an order to revise the statements.

The Code contains a number of provisions relating to the audit of financial statements, in particular on the role of the audit committee and the external auditor. Some important elements are:

1   The audit committee is responsible for the relationship with the external auditor, in particular his/her independence and remuneration.
2   The audit committee is the first point of contact for the external auditor when he/she finds irregularities in the financial statements.
3   At least once a year the audit committee meets with the external auditor without members of the executive board.
4   The external auditor is appointed by the general meeting, upon the nomination of the supervisory board. The audit committee and the executive board advise the supervisory board on the appointment.
5   The executive board and the audit committee report annually on the relationship with the external auditor, in particular on his/her independence. At least once every four years the services of the external auditor are reviewed in full and reported to the shareholders' meeting.

New for the external auditor is the Code's requirement for him/her to be present at the general meeting where he/she can be asked questions by shareholders about his/her audit and auditor's opinion. To provide guidance on the participation of the auditor at the general meeting, Royal NIVRA issued auditing standard 780 describing the responsibilities of the board and auditor and the way the auditor should prepare himself/herself for the meeting. Last but not least, the auditor's responsibilities in responding to questions about the audit and audit opinion are set out. It is of course the board that is responsible for the financial statements. Despite the fact that initial experiences show that shareholders are interested in the view of the auditor, it is the board who should answer questions about the financial statements.

According to the Tabaksblat Code, the report of the external auditor must contain the matters which the external auditor wishes to bring to the attention of the management board and the supervisory board in relation to the audit of the annual accounts and the related audits. Examples of matters of interest are:

*   with regard to the audit:

    -   information about matters of importance to the assessment of the independence of the external auditor;
    -   information about the course of events during the audit and cooperation with internal auditors and/or any other external auditors, matters for discussion with the management board, a list of corrections that have not been made, etc.
*   with regard to the financial figures:

- analyses of changes in shareholders' equity and results which do not appear in the information to be published, and which, in the view of the external auditor, contribute to an understanding of the financial position and results of the company;
- comments regarding the processing of one-off items, the effects of estimates and the manner in which they have been arrived at, the choice of accounting policies, when other choices were possible, and the special effects of such policies;
- comments on the quality of forecasts and budgets.

• with regard to the operation of the internal risk management and control systems (including the reliability and continuity of automated data processing) and the quality of the internal provision of information:

- points for improvement, gaps, and quality assessments;
- comments about threats and risks to the company and the manner in which they should be reported in the particulars to be published.

There are no current plans to include any of the above in legislation, but this may follow from the adoption of the EU Directive on Statutory Audits (Eighth Directive) (Winter 2004: 45).

8 Summary

This chapter has offered an overview of the regulation of the Dutch auditing profession. The Dutch audit profession started in 1879, when the first independent external accountant was appointed by the Nieuwe Afrikaansche Handelsvennootschap. In those days there were no auditing standards. It was not until the 1970s that the first auditing standards were developed. These standards were inspired by the ideas of Theodore Limperg (1879–1961). Around 1930 Limperg developed a set of basic audit concepts, which became known as the "theory of inspired confidence." This theory requires auditors to perform their tasks in such a way that they do not betray expectations (general auditing norm), while on the other hand they should not create greater expectations than the audit justifies. Due to Limperg's normative theory, there was no need for specific auditing standards for almost 80 years; Royal NIVRA decided to adopt international auditing standards only in the 1970s and Dutch auditing standards in the 1980s. This situation, with the professional bodies of auditors acting as regulators of the auditing profession, existed until 2006. As a reaction to the accounting scandals in the US and Europe, the regulatory power was transferred from the professional bodies to an oversight body called the Authority for the Financial Markets (AFM). The AFM is responsible for independent oversight of audit firms and individual auditors in public practice, registering auditors and audit firms that conduct statutory audits and issuing sanctions against audit firms and auditors that violate the 2006 act.

While the AFM is responsible for the oversight of statutory audits and the basic regulation of the statutory audit profession, the professional bodies are responsible for education and training, and the ethical standards. With respect to education and training, the two avenues to qualify as an auditor have been described: the practical avenue organized by the professional body, Royal NIVRA, and the university avenue organized by the universities. The profession currently numbers about 19,000 auditors, of whom 5,500 are in public practice. The two types of auditor that are eligible to conduct statutory audits are registered auditors (registeraccountants) and certified accountants (Accountants-Administratieconsulenten). They are allowed to audit any company that requires a statutory audit: listed companies, financial institutions, medium-sized and large public limited liability companies, private limited liability companies, co-operative associations, and mutual guarantee companies.

Registered auditors and certified accountants have to comply with the ethical standards of the Dutch professional bodies of auditors. In addition to the ethical standards, the Dutch professional bodies have issued an Independence Guideline that further explains the ethical standards. The ethical standards and the Independence Guideline are in line with the Code of Ethics of IFAC and the EU recommendation on the independence of statutory auditors. When auditors violate the ethical standards, disciplinary sanctions can be taken against them.

Besides disciplinary sanctions, legal action can be undertaken against auditors. There is no specific legislation on the liability of statutory auditors. Hence, the general rules of civil liability apply to auditors. Legal actions against an auditor can be undertaken by the auditee, its shareholders, or any involved third party. Auditors cannot shield themselves from liability by means of a legal liability cap, but they can choose an organizational form that – under certain circumstances – shields them from liability.

A final piece of regulation discussed in this chapter is the regulation on corporate governance, called the Code Tabaksblat. The Code is applicable to all listed companies with registered offices in the Netherlands. The Code contains principles which are to be applied without exception, and best practice provisions which can be deviated from if it is explained why in the annual report (the apply or explain principle).

The regulatory developments described in this chapter have led to a change from self-regulation to government regulation. However, the Dutch audit market regulation can still be considered liberal.

Notes

1 For example, in 1899 a second professional body of accountants called Nederlandse Bond van Accountants, was founded, and in 1902 another body called Nederlandsche Academie van Accountants was created.
2 "Royal" NIVRA since 1995.

3 28 June 1962: Wet op de registeraccountants.
4 6 August 1993: Wet op de Accountants-Administratieconsulenten. According to this law, the right to perform audits is only applicable to those certified accountants who have completed the new education program for certified accountants or to certified accountants who have enrolled on a transitional program.
5 10 September 1970, Wet op de Jaarrekening van Ondernemingen, Wetboek van Koophandel.
6 The act was enforced in stages: public limited liability companies and large co-operative associations and mutual guarantee companies were required to publish audited annual accounts in 1971 and private limited liability companies in 1973.
7 Title 8 of Book 2 of the Dutch Civil Code. This act was also enforced in stages: public limited liability companies and large co-operative associations and mutual guarantee companies were required to publish audited annual accounts in 1984 and private limited liability companies in 1990.
8 78/660/EEC: Fourth Council Directive of 25 July 1978 (Fourth Directive).
9 Wet Toezicht Kredietwezen, 1992; 86/635/EEC: Council Directive of 8 December 1986 (Bank Accounts Directive); 91/674/EEC: Council Directive of 19 December 1991 (Insurance Accounts Directive).
10 The Committee on the Auditor Education Examination Requirements is a semi-governmental body consisting of an independent chair, two registered auditors, and two licensed auditors.
11 28 June 1962: Wet op de registeraccountants, amended on 6 August 1993 when the new Act on Certified Accountants was implemented.
12 6 August 1993: Wet op de Accountants-Administratieconsulenten.
13 On 1 October 2006 the Supervision of Auditors' Organizations Act came into force. This law (Wet Toezicht Accountantsorganisaties) complies with the Eighth EU Directive.
14 Nota van Toelichting Ontwerp Besluit Toezicht Accountantsorganisaties, paragraph 3.1.
15 1 January 2007: Verordening Gedragscode. This replaced the old ethical standards called Gedrags en Beroepsregels Registeraccountants and Gedrags en Beroepsregels Accountants-Administratieconsulenten.
16 1 January 2007: Nadere voorschriften inzake onafhankelijkheid van de openbaar accountant, Royal NIVRA.
17 An entity qualifies as a public interest entity if it is (a) a listed company, (b) a bank, (c) an insurance company, or (d) a public body such as a government organization.
18 1 October 2006: Wet Toezicht Accountantsorganisaties (Supervision of Auditors' Organizations Act)
19 A common organizational form that audit firms choose, but which does not protect against liability, is a general partnership.

References

Blokdijk, H., Drieënhuizen, F., and Wallage, P. (1995) "Reflections on Auditing Theory: A Contribution from the Netherlands," Kluwer Bedrijfsweten-schappen, Limperg Institute, 1995.
Carmichael, D.R. (2004) "The PCAOB and the Social Responsibility of the Independent Auditor," *Accounting Horizons*, 18(2, June): 127–34.
Dutch Corporate Governance Committee, Tabaksblat Code, December 2003. Online. Available at: <http://www.commissiecorporategovernance.nl> (accessed 21 February 2007).

EU (European Union) (2002) "Statutory Auditors' Independence in the EU: A Set of Fundamental Principles," Brussels: European Commission.

Fraser, I., Henry, W., and Wallage, P. (2000) *The Future of Corporate Governance: Insights from the Netherlands*, Edinburgh: The Institute of Chartered Accountants of Scotland.

IFAC (International Federation of Accountants) (2004) *Code of Ethics for Professional Accountants*, IFAC: New York, 2004.

International Accounting Bulletin (2006) "Country Survey: Netherlands," July 2006.

Limperg, T. (1926) "The Accountant's Certificate in Connection with the Accountant's Responsibility," the International Congress of Accountants, Amsterdam.

NIVRA (2005) *Netherlands Standards on Auditing, Edition 2005*, Royal NIVRA: Amsterdam.

NIVRA (2007) *Nadere voorschriften inzake onafhankelijkheid van de openbaar accountant*, Royal NIVRA: Amsterdam.

Vergoossen, R.G.A. and Wallage, P. (2004) "Toezicht op het accountantsberoep. Ontwikkelingen in de VS, het VK, Nederland en Duitsland," *Maandblad voor Accountancy en Bedrijfseconomie*, December: 542–53.

Wallage, P. (1991) "Methodology and Degree of Structure: A Dissertation on the Audit Process," University of Amsterdam.

Winter, J. (2004) "Corporate Governance in the Netherlands Company Law and Corporate Governance Code," in *European Corporate Governance in Company Law and Codes*, draft of 14 October 2004 prepared for the European Corporate Governance Conference, The Hague, Netherlands.

9 The development of the auditing profession in Spain

Fast evolution in a highly regulated environment

Maria Antonia García-Benau,
Cristina de Fuentes Barberá and
Antonio Vico Martinez

1 A short history

The auditing profession developed late in Spain compared to neighboring countries. It was, in fact, only when Spain joined the European Union in 1986 that legislation was enacted to adapt to EU Directives, transforming not only Spanish company law but also the regulatory framework governing accountancy, not least through the requirement for mandatory audits.

Before the legislative reform, auditing was carried out by the international audit firms established in the country, whose main customers were the Spanish affiliates of the multinational corporations that had begun to arrive in the early 1960s. The audit market increased after the stock exchange reform of 1964, since the annual accounts of the listed companies had to be certified by an expert accountant registered with the one and only professional corporation, then named Instituto de Censores Jurados de Cuentas. The financial statements of credit institutions and government companies were also supervised by independent and expert accountants, but the practice of the audit service was scarcely used until the approval of the Audit Law in 1988, which implemented mandatory auditing for companies over a certain size.

At present, companies meeting two out of three basic parameters for two consecutive years are required to arrange for the audit of their financial statements. These parameters are assets of €2,374,000, revenues of €4,748,000, and an average headcount of 50 employees.

Annual audits were well received by users, who saw the practice as improving the quality and transparency of accounting information (see García-Benau and Humphrey 1992, García-Benau *et al.* 1993, and Ruiz Barbadillo 1996). The climate changed sharply in the mid-1990s, however. Various large audit firms were heavily fined by the Spanish accounting regulator (Instituto de Contabilidad y Auditoría de Cuentas or ICAC) for poor quality work, and the term *audit expectation gap* appeared with increasing frequency in the local accounting literature, particularly after the scandal at Banco Español de Crédito, better known as Banesto (García-Benau *et al*. 1999).

In line with the Spanish legislative tradition, the rules governing auditing in Spain are issued by government agencies and are basically enshrined in the Audit Act of 1988 (Law 19/ 12 July 1988) and the secondary regulations established by Royal Decree 1636/ 20 December 1990. Meanwhile, specific issues are dealt with in the Technical Standards issued by the ICAC, which is an agency of the Ministry of Economy and Finance.

The legislation has recently been amended, as Spain could not stand aloof from the wave of changes in audit regulation at the international level, the impact of recent financial scandals, and the increasing importance of codes of good governance aimed at improving the conduct of corporate affairs by company boards. The Financial System Reform Act 2002 and the Listed Companies Transparency Act 2003 established a number of rules regarding audit independence, including, for instance, mandatory disclosure of fees for audit and non-audit services, the rotation of audit firms, and the compulsory implementation of an audit committee.

1.1 Auditing: A non-self-regulated profession

Before the Audit Act, auditing was regulated, although only partially, by the former Instituto de Auditores Censores Jurados de Cuentas de España, the oldest professional association in Spain. Thus, the Companies Act 1951 and the Stock Market Regulations of 1967 provided for the examination and control of annual financial statements by members of the Institute in certain circumstances.

Far from bolstering the self-regulation of the profession, however, the Audit Act assigned almost all powers to the ICAC, which is a government agency. These powers include oversight and control, as well as the authority to impose sanctions. The early legislation thus allowed auditors scarcely any room to regulate their profession, partly because of the Spanish tradition of regulation by the state.

In the course of the 1990s, however, the rising numbers of practicing auditors and the growing influence of the three professional corporations (Instituto de Auditores Censores Jurados de Cuentas de España, Registro de Economistas Auditores, and Registro General de Auditores) elicited intense debate on the advantages of self-regulation along the lines of other countries, such as the United Kingdom. This recognized the need for the professional associations in Spain to have a greater say in both the standards issued and the sanctions imposed, a point also made by some scholars (see Vico 1997 and Larriba and Serrano 1999). Moreover, lobbying by the profession contributed to the removal of the mandatory rotation of audit appointments.

The professional associations' calls for a reform of the Audit Act gained increasing ground in the second half of the 1990s, following the retirement as president of the ICAC of Ricardo Bolufer, during whose term of office audit professionals and firms had been fined a total of €3,576,000 (*Expansión* 9 Oct.

1996: 36). Most of these fines were the consequence of a lack of evidence to support the opinion included in the audit report. Thus, a study commissioned by the Instituto de Auditores Censores Jurados de Cuentas showed that a large majority of accounting professionals favored a self-regulatory audit system (*Expansión* 3 July 1997: 43).

However, delays in drafting the new Audit Act, disunity and a lack of consensus in the profession itself, and the impact of recent financial scandals both in Spain and internationally have set back the goal of self-regulation. The new legislative provisions have rather strengthened the role of the public regulator than empowered the professional associations (Sánchez Fernández de Valderrama 2003: 39).

1.2 The recent disclosure of audit and non-audit fees

Until recently, companies were not required to disclose fees for audit and non-audit services. Therefore, the only publicly available information was the ICAC data for the average hourly rates charged by both audit firms and independent auditors.

As shown in Figure 9.1, billings per hour are slightly higher in the case of firms, amounting on average to the equivalent of €39 in 1990 and rising to approximately €62 in 2005. We may also note here that audit prices increased only gradually between 1990 and 2003, and even dipped slightly in 1996 and 2004.

One of the key provisions of the Financial System Reform Act 2002, however, is the disclosure of audit fees, a measure that will greatly facilitate studies of the market. The companies audited must disclose the fees paid to their auditors in the

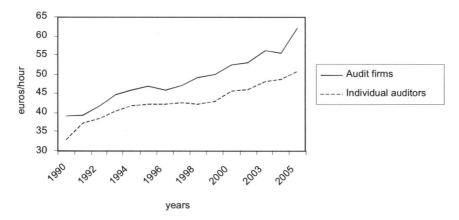

Figure 9.1 Evolution of hourly audit prices in Spain

Source: *Official Bulletin of the ICAC*, nos. 9, 13, 18, 21, 25, 30, 37, 41, 46, 50, 54, 58, 62 and 66

notes to the financial statements, as well as amounts paid to any company forming part of the same group as the auditor, or any company related to the auditor by common ownership, management, or control. Although the act does not set any limit on the fees billed in respect of audit and/or *additional services*, public disclosure of both types of fees will allow some assessment of auditors' commitments to their clients.

1.3 The audit market in Spain and Big Firms' dominance

The audit market received a major boost from the mandatory audit requirement established by the Audit Act, but by the mid-1990s the market had become increasingly mature and competition to win clients had intensified, particularly between the smaller audit firms (García-Benau *et al.* 1999).

As Table 9.1 shows, growth rates were high in the early 1990s both on the supply side (the number of audit firms increased by 10.5 percent) and on the demand side (one-off 20 percent growth in the number of mandatory audits carried out in the first year the Act came into force, and growth of 10 and 19 percent in voluntary audits in 1992 and 1993). Growth rates in the number of audits differ depending on whether demand for the service is voluntary or

Table 9.1 Evolution of the audit market in Spain

Year	Audit firms	% growth	No. of statutory audits and other services (a)	% growth	No. of voluntary audits and other services (b)	% growth	Total no. of audits (a+b)	% growth	% of voluntary audits (b)/(a+b)
1991	645		18,008		6,638		24,646		26.9
1992	713	10.5	21,686	20.4	7,328	10.4	29,014	17.7	25.3
1993	735	3.1	22,542	3.9	8,718	19.0	31,260	7.7	27.9
1994	744	1.2	22,613	0.3	8,484	-2.7	31,097	-0.5	27.3
1995	757	1.7	23,581	4.3	9,659	13.8	33,240	6.9	29.1
1996	802	5.9	24,287	3.0	10,204	5.6	34,491	3.8	29.6
1997	850	6.0	25,258	4.0	9,761	-4.3	35,019	1.5	27.9
1998	876	3.1	26,070	3.2	11,500	17.8	37,570	7.3	30.6
1999	930	6.2	26,665	2.3	12,271	6.7	38,936	3.6	31.5
2000	962	3.4	29,003	8.8	13,127	7.0	42,130	8.2	31.2
2001	997	3.6	33,818	16.6	15,019	14.4	48,837	15.9	30.8
2002	1,070	7.3	35,252	4.2	16,360	8.9	51,612	5.7	31.7
2003	1,115	4.2	37,006	5.0	14,524	-11.2	51,530	-0.2	28.2
2004	1,155	3.6	39,783	7.5	14,930	2.8	54,713	6.2	27.3
2005	1,187	2.8	42,805	7.6	15,509	3.9	58,314	6.6	26.6

Source: *Official Bulletin of the ICAC*, nos. 9, 13, 18, 21, 25, 30, 37, 41, 46, 50, 54, 58, 62 and 66

Note: Statutory services include those required by the Companies Registries and the courts, as well as bankruptcy proceedings.

mandatory. While the rate for mandatory audits is positive, due to the growth of companies, the demand for voluntary services is much more volatile, fluctuating between negative growth in 1994 or 1997 and expansion as high as 18 percent in 1998. As may be observed from the last column in Table 9.1, the voluntary audit component of demand represents approximately 26 percent of total services. This implies that voluntary audit services must have a considerable influence on the configuration of total demand for reports. The main reason for submitting the annual accounts to external supervision is to guarantee transparency and to satisfy the financial institutions' requirements.

In more recent years, we find sharp increases in demand in 2000 and 2001, followed by a steep fall in voluntary audit services, impacting the total hours billed in 2003. This may have been a consequence of the loss of confidence in the reliability and credibility of reports that occurred internationally as a result of the Enron and Parmalat scandals in the United States and Italy.

On the supply side, the dominance of the big audit firms in Spain can be explained as follows. In an initial period ending in the 1970s, the supervision of financial statements was principally limited to the Spanish affiliates of multinational corporations, in response to the requirements of their foreign headquarters. Due to the absence of an audit tradition in Spain at that time, and therefore of national audit firms, these annual accounts were examined exclusively by the international audit firms. As a result of the experience and prestige gained by their professionals in an activity for which there was no national expertise, the Big Firms were in a strong position to obtain a large slice of the Spanish audit market after the passing of the Audit Act 1988, by which it was made mandatory for all large and medium-sized companies to audit their financial statements.

Empirical studies carried out in Spain (e.g. García-Benau *et al.* 1998, García-Ayuso and Sánchez 1999, Carrera *et al.* 2005) show that the market for audit services does not differ significantly from that in neighboring countries in terms of structure and is highly concentrated. As shown in Table 9.2, concentration indices for the six leading firms are around 80 percent with some slight variations depending on the year and the sample considered. Based on the empirical evidence obtained to date, the former Arthur Andersen clearly dominated the market with a share of 43 percent by volume of clients' revenues in 1994. This firm was followed at some distance by Price Waterhouse with 12 percent, and Coopers & Lybrand and Ernst & Young (both with 10 percent). Peat Marwick was in fifth place with 9 percent of the market and in last place was Deloitte & Touche with a 2 percent share (García-Benau *et al.* 1998).

This structure was altered by the mergers between Price Waterhouse and Coopers & Lybrand, and Arthur Andersen and Deloitte & Touche. In general, these mergers have further increased the market share of the Big Four to the detriment of other audit firms. According to a recent study of listed companies (De Fuentes Barbera 2005), the major international firms audited 98.66 percent of the total volume of business generated by client companies in 2003, while the merged firm of Deloitte España, S.L. accounted for 67 percent.

Table 9.2 Most relevant studies of the concentration of the audit market in Spain

Author (year published)	Years studied	Sample size/ audit surrogate	CR4[a]	CR6[a]	CR8[a]
García-Benau *et al.* (1998)	1992 1994	314 companies of differing sizes/ no. of audits	72	85	n/a
		293 companies of differing sizes/ no. of audits	76	86	n/a
García-Ayuso and Segura (1999)	1991–1995	1,100 regulated by the Spanish Securities Market Commission/ no. of audits	79	88	n/a
Carrera *et al.*(2005)	1990–2000	5,510 regulated by the Spanish Securities Market Commission/ no. of audits	75	80	83

Notes: CRn: nth order concentration index
    a Data for the last year analysed.

2 Education and training

Mandatory audits in Spain may only be carried out by a member of the Official Register of Auditors (Registro Oficial de Auditores de Cuentas or ROAC) kept by the ICAC. The process by which auditors qualify to practice is established in articles 6 and 7 of the Audit Act, implemented by articles 22ff. of the Audit Regulations, and in the ICAC Technical Standards amended in accordance with the Eighth EU Directive.

As in other European Union member states, candidates must show both wide professional experience and appropriate technical training in order to qualify as auditors. These requirements may be met either via the academic or via the professional route (see Figure 9.2).

Candidates taking the academic route to ROAC qualification must hold a BA degree, but this need not be related to economics or business studies. However, the holders of BA and MA degrees in these subjects are not required to study some theoretical courses. The basic content of theoretical training is shown in Table 9.3. These theoretical courses are normally organized by the professional associations and universities and must be approved by the ICAC in order to guarantee quality and content.

Recognition can be obtained for university studies in other European countries in accordance with Royal Decree 1665/ 25 October 1991 and the Ministerial Order issued on 19 May 1995, which govern the general system for the

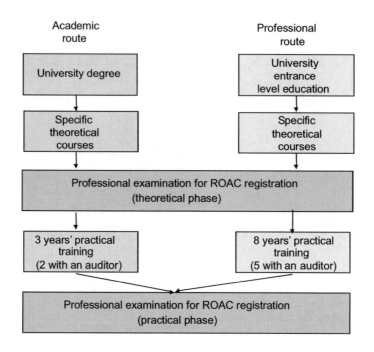

Figure 9.2 Routes to registration on the Official Register of Auditors

Table 9.3 Content and duration of theoretical training

Auditing	180 hours
Financial accounting	120 hours
Advanced accounting (cost accounting, financial statement analysis, consolidated accounts, etc.)	120 hours
Law (civil, company and labor law, etc.)	120 hours
Other subjects (mathematics, statistics, financial management, etc.)	100 hours
Total	640 hours

recognition of higher education qualifications requiring a minimum of three years' study obtained in other EU member states.

As mentioned above, the recent reform of audit legislation has shorn the professional associations of some of their power, at the same time as reinforcing the position of the official regulators. In the field of training, the associations no longer devise their own tests for qualifying for ROAC registration; all three are now required to set the same examination, which must be approved by the ICAC.

Both the academic and the professional route require considerable practical experience, lasting for eight years in the case of the latter. This experience must be related to the preparation and examination of annual accounts and consolidated or analogous financial statements, and it is controlled and certified by the ICAC via the forms submitted by the practicing auditors and audit firms responsible for trainee personnel.

Candidates can only be registered on the ROAC, qualifying them to sign off audit reports, after they have demonstrated the minimum professional experience and passed the requisite practical examination.

The recent Financial System Reform Act 2002 also allows civil servants to become qualified auditors and be registered on the ROAC list, if they are able to accredit a minimum of three years' experience in the supervision of the financial statements of public sector entities, financial institutions, or insurance companies.

One indicator of the current situation of auditing in Spain is that no ROAC examinations have been held for over four years, partly because of regulatory change, but also in order to restrain the growth in the number of auditors since 1990 and the saturation of the market, especially in the small firms segment.

Prior to the audit reform, it was common practice for practicing auditors to attend courses and seminars in order to widen and update their knowledge and skill. Such continuous training has now become obligatory in accordance with paragraph 4, article 6, of the Audit Act introduced by the Financial System Reform Act, which requires auditors to follow continuous training courses. Nevertheless, the regulatory conditions and duration of these courses have yet to be approved.

In our opinion, the theoretical and practical training currently required in Spain is sufficient to guarantee a standard level of audit quality, although specific training and qualifications should perhaps be required to audit certain clearly differentiated sectors, such as financial services and insurance.

3 Audit standard setting

Until 1998 auditors and expert accountants followed the practical guidelines issued by the Instituto de Censores Jurados de Cuentas. In the absence of an audit tradition in Spain, this corporation issued a set of rules and standards inspired by the Anglo-Saxon practice. Since the Audit Law of 1988, the regulation of technical and procedural matters in Spain has been contained in the Technical Auditing Standards issued by the ICAC. In accordance with article 13 of the Audit Regulations, the Technical Standards constitute the principles and requirements that must be observed by auditors in the course of their activities, and on which all actions necessary to express a responsible technical opinion must be based.

Technical Standards are prepared, amended, and revised to ensure that they are in line with the general principles and common practice in the member states of the European Union, as well as the ISAs issued by IFAC and by the representative public law associations of the audit profession. These standards are valid only if published in the *Official Bulletin of the Institute of Accounting and Auditing* (ICAC). They have the same legal status as official resolutions and are therefore of a lower order than the Audit Act and the Audit Regulations.

The mechanism by which standards are prepared is as follows. Where deemed necessary, the ICAC may require the auditors' professional associations to draft, amend, or revise the Technical Standards, and if they fail to do so within a period of two months the ICAC proceeds accordingly.

The Technical Auditing Standards relate to the following issues:

- general standards concerning the qualifications and experience of the auditor, and conduct in the course of audit activities;
- standards concerning the preparation and performance of the work carried out by the auditor. These regulate the examination and inspection techniques applicable to the items in the accounts and relevant events for the books audited, on the basis of which the auditor forms a responsible and independent opinion;
- standards concerning reports regulate the principles that must be observed in the preparation and presentation of the audit report, establishing the length and content of the different types of report and the basic criteria underlying the model report to be used in each case.

The earliest Technical Auditing Standards issued by the ICAC date from January 1991, and there are currently 23 in effect. The ISAs prepared by IFAC are not directly applicable in Spain, but it is nevertheless clear that Spanish standards draw some inspiration from them.

4 Independence standards

In Spain, as in other countries, auditor independence has been a hotly debated issue both within the profession and within the academic community. The origins of this debate may be found in the financial scandals of the mid-1990s, particularly Banesto, the Torras Group, and PSV (see Vico 1997).

In accordance with article 8 of the Audit Act, auditors must be, and be seen to be, independent of the companies and organizations audited, and they are required to take action when their objectivity in connection with the verification of accounting documents could be compromised. The measures established to preserve auditor independence are contained basically in the Audit Act and the Audit Regulations. These provisions may be classified into two groups:

1 incompatibilities and prohibitions;
2 rotation system.

4.1 Incompatibilities and prohibitions

The regime governing incompatibilities is established in article 8 of the Audit Act and article 37 of the Audit Regulations.

Aside from the incompatibilities established in other legislative instruments, the Audit Act defines the circumstances in which the auditor is deemed not to have sufficient independence from the company or organization audited as follows:

a   Where the auditor holds executive or management office, is an employee, or is responsible for internal oversight in the organization audited or in any other organization directly or indirectly related therewith in the manner and under the conditions defined in the regulations. In any event, such cases shall include any office held in an organization that directly or indirectly owns more than 20 percent of voting rights in the organization audited, or in which the organization audited directly or indirectly owns over 20 percent of voting rights.

b   Where the auditor has a direct financial interest in the organization audited, or there is a significant indirect interest for either party.

c   Where the auditor is related by blood or marriage to the second degree with the owners, managers, or financial officers of the companies or organizations audited.

d   Where the auditor keeps the books or prepares accounts or financial statements for the organization audited.

e   Where the auditor provides the audit client with other services involving the design and implementation of the financial information technology systems used to generate data included in the client's financial statements, unless the client takes overall responsibility for the internal control system or the services, is provided in accordance with specifications established by the client, who is also required to take responsibility for the design, implementation, assessment, and functioning of the system.

f   Where the auditor provides the audit client with appraisal services leading to the valuation of significant amounts in the client's financial statements, if such valuation work involves a significant degree of subjectivity.

g   Where the auditor provides internal audit services to the customer, unless the management of the company or organization audited is responsible for the overall internal control system, for the definition of the scope, risk parameters, and frequency of internal audit procedures, for the analysis of internal audit findings, and for the implementation of recommendations.

i   Where the auditor maintains business relations with the audit client, unless such relations are compatible with normal business activity and are not significant to the auditor or to any person with the capacity to influence the results of the audit, or to the organization audited.

i   Where the auditor simultaneously provides legal services to the same client or to any organization that may have been a client within the preceding three years, unless such services are provided by distinct juridical persons with different boards of directors.

j   Where the auditor is involved in contracting senior officers or key personnel for the audit client, where the same is an organization subject to official supervision or has issued securities listed on an official stock market.

k   Where the audit partner responsible for signing the audit report provides services other than audit to the organization concerned.

l   Where the auditor earns fees for the provision of audit and non-audit services to a single client wherever such fees constitute an improperly high percentage of the auditor's total annual revenues based on the average for the last five years.

The period in which the incompatibilities described above apply runs from the year in which the audit work is actually carried out to the third year prior to the date of the financial statements audited. However, the incompatibilities described in point (b) must be resolved prior to acceptance of the audit engagement.

Auditors may not form part of the governing bodies or executive of any organization audited for a period of three years after they cease to perform the audit function, nor may they hold any post or direct financial interest in such organization, or any indirect interest that is significant for either party.

4.2 Rotation system

Article 8.4 of the original Audit Act, drawn up in 1988, established that auditors could not be engaged by the same company or organization for a period of less than three and more than nine years. The auditor could not be contracted again until a period of three years had elapsed from the termination of the prior engagement. This rule was clearly intended to preserve auditors' independence, but it aroused considerable opposition from the outset.

The major international firms basically favored abolition. The profession's arguments for ending rotation were basically in line with those advanced in other countries, namely that maintaining the engagement over long periods generates economies, while changing the auditor results in transaction costs. In this case, the laws of the market should prevail. Furthermore, maintaining the engagement need not necessarily compromise the independence of the auditor, since the issue is one of personal integrity and professional ethics. The root of the problem was that numerous undertakings would find themselves obliged to change auditors at the end of nine years.

The argument was finally won by the profession, when the Private Limited Companies Act (Law 2/ 1995) amended article 8.4 of the Audit Act, which was reworded as follows: "Auditors may be engaged for a specified initial period of time, which may not be less than three years or more than nine as from the commencement of the first year audited. Thereafter they may be contracted on an annual basis." The result was to abolish mandatory rotation at nine years on the sole condition that subsequent engagements be for annual periods.

In the case of organizations subject to official supervision, companies whose securities are listed on official stock markets, and companies generating net annual revenues of over €30,000,000, rotation of the lead audit partner is mandatory after seven years from the initial engagement, together with all members of the audit team. These professionals may not audit the organization concerned again until at least three years have elapsed.

5 Oversight, monitoring and disciplinary observance

5.1 Supervisory agencies

Among the different tasks attributed to the ICAC (i.e. issuance of financial accounting standards or control of access and registration of certified auditors) in accordance with article 22, paragraph 1, of the Audit Act, the ICAC is the body responsible for oversight of the auditing profession. Accordingly, the ICAC may take action ex officio in the form of reviews and inspections in the public interest. It also has disciplinary power over individual auditors and audit firms, which can be penalized with financial sanctions or removed from the auditors' registration list (ROAC).

In accordance with article 22, paragraph 2, of the Audit Act, the ICAC may require any information from individual auditors and audit firms deemed necessary for the performance of its duties. The ICAC may also carry out inspections to obtain such information or confirm the veracity thereof.

Auditors are consequently under an obligation to provide the ICAC with access to any books, records, or documents in any format that the Institute may require, including computer software and magnetic, optical, and other files. The wording of this paragraph has aroused considerable opposition within the audit profession, because it allows the ICAC to access any information it may wish, which could in some cases result in breaches of professional secrecy.

It is also a matter of no small concern that article 14, paragraph 3.c), of the Audit Act allows the Bank of Spain, the National Securities Market Commission, and the Directorate General of Insurance and Pension Funds access to auditors' working papers by virtue of their powers of oversight and control in particularly serious cases where it may have proved impossible to obtain the specific documentation to which they seek access from the organizations concerned.

Article 22, paragraph 3, of the Audit Act assigns additional supervisory powers to auditors' professional associations, without prejudice to the powers of the ICAC, to oversee the quality of their members' work and to report the individual results of the controls carried out to the Institute of Accounting and Auditing at the year end. There would thus seem to be some duplication of control functions, an issue that has caused some unease on the part of professional associations, not only because their supervisory powers are ill defined but also because only the ICAC has been assigned any specific source of funds, the charge levied on audit reports, to cover the costs incurred in control functions.

5.2 Infractions

Technical controls may reveal the existence of infractions in audit work. Such infractions are classified as very serious, serious, or minor in accordance with article 16, paragraph 1, of the Audit Act. Here we shall consider only the first two grades, which give rise to the most significant sanctions in the Spanish system.

Very serious infractions comprise:

- the issuance of audit reports in which the auditor's opinion is not based on the evidence obtained in the course of the audit, as a consequence either of willful misconduct or gross negligence;
- non-compliance with the auditor's duty of independence;
- defiance of or resistance to the supervisory and disciplinary powers of the Institute of Accounting and Auditing, or refusal to submit to the said agency all such information and documents as it may require in the exercise of its legally established supervisory and disciplinary powers over the audit profession;
- non-compliance with the duty of confidentiality;.
- utilization by auditors of information obtained in the course of their duties to benefit either themselves or third parties.

Serious infractions comprise:

- non-compliance with the obligation to perform a mandatory audit in a firm engagement;
- non-compliance with auditing standards that could have a significant effect on the results of the auditor's work and, accordingly, on the audit report;
- non-compliance with the matters provided in articles 8.3b) and 8.4 of the Audit Act;
- failure to report the periodic or eventual information required by law or by the regulations to the Institute of Accounting and Auditing when enjoined so to do;
- acceptance of audit work in excess of the auditor's annual capacity in hours, as established in the Technical Auditing Standards;
- non-compliance with the final provision of the Audit Act;
- participation as an auditor in engagements other than those regulated by article 1 of the Audit Act, or other than those non-audit engagements assigned by law to auditors;
- performing audit work without being registered as a practicing auditor on the Official Register of Auditors.

5.3 *Sanctions*

The regime for sanctions is set forth in article 17 of the Audit Act and is based on the seriousness of the infraction committed, distinguishing between those committed by individual auditors and those by audit firms (in the latter case including infractions that might be attributable to the partner responsible for the same). The sanctions applicable to very serious infractions which have the greatest impact on the profession, are listed below.

Sanctions for very serious infractions committed by individual auditors include the following.

- The auditor may be temporarily struck off the Official Register of Auditors for a period of between two years and one day and five years.
- The auditor may be permanently struck off the Official Register of Auditors.
- Fines may be imposed between a minimum of €12,001 and €24,000.

Sanctions for very serious infractions committed by audit firms include the following.

- Firms may be fined between 10.1 percent and 20 percent of the fees billed in respect of audit work undertaken in the year immediately prior to that in which the fine is imposed. The minimum fine applicable in any event is the lower of €300,000 or six times the amount billed in respect of the audit engagement in the course of which the infraction was committed.
- If the infraction was not committed in connection with a specific audit engagement, the applicable fine is between 10.1 percent and 20 percent of the fees billed by the firm in respect of audit work undertaken in the year prior to the sanction. The resulting fine may not be less that €18,001.
- The audit firm may be permanently struck off the Official Register of Auditors.

The following sanctions are applicable to the partner responsible for any very serious infraction committed by an audit firm.

- Fines may be imposed between a minimum of €12,001 and €24,000.
- The audit partner may be temporarily struck off the Official Register of Auditors for a period of between two years and one day and five years.
- The audit partner may be permanently struck off the Official Register of Auditors.

Where sanctions are imposed in connection with very serious or serious infractions committed in the course of an audit engagement with a specific company or organization, the individual auditor or audit firm concerned is also banned from auditing the annual financial statements of such company or organization for the three years commencing subsequent to the date of the sanction.

The sanctions imposed on auditors for very serious and serious infractions in Spain are made public; they are published in the *Official Bulletin of the ICAC*, in accordance with article 18.1 of the Audit Act. The details published refer only to the nature and amount of the sanctions but do not include a description of the grounds for the imposition thereof.

6 The professional liability of auditors

The professional liability of auditors is clearly defined in Spain, but it is nevertheless an issue that has given rise to considerable conflict between regulators and the profession. In the original wording of article 11 of the Audit Act 1988, auditors were directly and jointly liable to the companies or organizations audited and to third parties for any damages incurred as a result of non-compliance by auditors with their obligations. Meanwhile, if the audit in question was performed by an auditor forming part of an audit firm, both the auditor and the firm were held jointly and severally liable. In addition, the remaining partners of the firm who had not signed the audit report had subsidiary joint and several liabilities for damages. This regime was sharply criticized by professionals and especially by audit firms, because it meant that any partner could be held liable for any damages resulting from litigation, whether or not they had signed off the audit report (see Gonzalo Angulo 1995). It was finally eliminated through the new wording given to article 11 of the Audit Act by the Financial System Reform Act 2002.

The Audit Act also requires auditors to provide guarantees. Thus, in accordance with article 12 of the Audit Act, individual auditors and audit firms "shall be obliged to make deposits in cash or public debt securities, or to provide bank warranties or civil liability insurance by way of guarantees. In any event, the amount of such guarantees shall be proportional to the auditor's or audit firm's volume of business."

Additionally, in legal terms auditors may have civil or criminal liability. Regarding civil and criminal matters, Spanish company law does not establish the consequences of actions giving rise to civil or criminal liability on the part of auditors. As a consequence, in each case liabilities must be established by analogy with similar conduct defined in the Civil and Criminal Codes, respectively (see Carbajal 1994).

7 Implementation of codes of good governance

The corporate good governance framework considers relations between company management, the board of directors, shareholders, and other stakeholders, providing the structure for the organization to establish its objectives and the resources available to attain them, and to supervise and control compliance therewith. Corporate governance is supposed to ensure that accurate and regular information is disclosed with regard to all significant issues affecting the company, including the results of the operational and financial situation, ownership, and the conduct of affairs (Cañibano 2004).

There is no tradition of codes of good governance in Spain such as that existing, for example, in the United Kingdom and United States. However, the economic changes in the 1990s and the need to protect the interests of minority shareholders and improve the transparency and effectiveness of management have stimulated increasing interest in corporate governance practices in recent years. As Ruiz Barbadillo (1996) has argued, the physical gap and differences of interest between managers and owners in today's large companies has encouraged shareholders to demand an ever expanding range of external controls to mitigate the uncertainties and risks inherent in the actions of management.

The first initiatives taken in Spain to address the functioning of boards of directors, especially in listed companies, date from the end of the 1990s. The main objective was to strengthen the role of the stock markets in the financial system as a whole. In 1998 the Spanish government appointed a special commission to make recommendations concerning the structure, composition, and functions of the board of directors. The resulting code of best practice, known as the Olivencia Code (CEECECAS 1998), recommended the creation of various delegate committees, including an audit committee, appointments committee, and remuneration committee.

The audit committee thus emerged as a delegate committee with the mission of assisting the board of directors with one of the key functions vested in it by law, namely the preparation of the company's financial statements to present a true and fair image of its net equity, financial situation, and results of operations (Cañibano 2004).

In 2003, meanwhile, the Aldama Commission prepared a report stressing the need to implement good governance practices and assigning a key role to the audit committee, which became mandatory for all listed companies with the enactment of the Financial System Reform Act 2002 and the Securities Market Act 2003 (Law 26/ 17 July 2003).

As a consequence, listed companies are now required to follow the recommendations enshrined in the Olivencia and Aldama reports and the Securities Market Commission's circulars.

Despite the Olivencia Code recommendation that all of the members of the audit committee should be non-executive independent directors or shareholder representatives, the new legislation is more lax, and article 47 of the Financial System Reform Act requires only that the majority of members be non-executive directors. Consequently, executive members of the board of directors may sit on the audit committee.

The Financial System Reform Act 2002 establishes the minimum duties of the Audit Committee as follows:

- to report to the annual general meeting on relevant issues raised by shareholders;
- to propose the appointment of external auditors to the board of directors for ratification at the annual general meeting;
- to supervise internal audit services where the company structure includes an office of this nature;
- to examine the financial reporting process and the company's internal control systems;
- to maintain relations with the external auditors for the purpose of receiving information on such issues as might compromise their independence and any other issues connected with the audit process, as well as providing a channel for the communications required in legislation governing auditing and the Technical Audit Standards.

Given that the reliability and transparency of the financial information companies report is one of the key issues of corporate governance, the mission of the audit committee is basically to assess the accounting verification system, ensure the independence of the external auditor, and review the internal control system.

The Olivencia Code and the Aldama report have been recently merged and updated in the Unified Code of Good Governance (also known as the Conthe Code) approved on 22 May 2006, which also takes account of recent OCDE and European Commission documents approved in December 2004 and February 2005. Although the implementation of the Code from 2008 will be voluntary, listed companies will have to explain and justify to the CNMV (Stock Exchange Commission in Spain) the recommendations that are not applied, if any.

Among its novelties, the president and members of the audit committee need to have an accounting, auditing, or financial background that would allow them to forestall potential problems. In this regard, the audit committee should establish proper mechanisms that facilitate the anonymous reporting by employees of any irregularity (*whistleblowing*).

8 Conclusion

Although mandatory audits are a comparatively recent development in Spain, the main areas of debate that have emerged since their introduction, such as the drive for greater self-regulation by the profession, the question of auditors' liability, and the regulation of independence, are similar to those in other countries with a longer tradition, and the development of the audit market is now comparable. Spain has also had its share of financial scandals (for instance Banesto, Grupo Torras, PSV, Gescartera) in which the role of the auditors has at times been controversial and resulted in court action. Combined with the recent high-impact affairs in the European Union (i.e. Parmalat) and the United States (the so-called Enron affair), these scandals paved the way for amendments to the regulatory framework in Spain, which not only provided greater scope for the involvement of the profession in regulation but also strengthened the role of official regulators and stiffened the regime governing incompatibilities.

From the institutional point of view, auditing in Spain can be characterized as an activity highly regulated by the government authorities, since most of the key issues (i.e. access to the profession and the supervisory and sanctioning functions) are under the control of the ICAC, despite the opposition of the professional corporations.

Regarding the regulation of auditing in Spain, although several amendments have recently been made, more changes in legislation remain on hold at present due to the recent approval of the new Eighth EU Directive and the adoption of International Standards on Auditing.

Finally, the audit market is clearly dominated by the major international firms, led by the former Arthur Andersen, the majority of whose partners opted to join Deloitte in the wake of the Enron disaster to create Deloitte España, S.L.

References

American Institute of Certified Public Accountants (AICPA) (1978) *The Commission on Auditors' Responsibilities: Reports, Conclusions and Recommendations*, the Cohen Commission.

Arthur Andersen (1998) *Global Best Practices for Audit Committees*, Chicago, IL: Arthur Andersen.

Beasley, M.Y. and Salterio, S. (2001) "The Relationship between Board Characteristics and Voluntary Improvements in Audit Committee Composition and Experience," *Contemporary Accounting Research*, 18(4): 539–70.

Cañibano, L. (2001) Curso de Auditoría Contable, Madrid: Pirámide.

Cañibano, L. (2004) "Información Financiera y Gobierno Corporativo," Real Academia de Doctores, Discurso de ingreso como Académico Numerario, Madrid, 21 Jan. 2004.

Carbajal, J. (1994) "La Responsabilidad de los Auditores de Cuentas," *Revista Técnica del Instituto de Auditores Censores Jurados de Cuentas*, 5: 11–31.

Carrera, N., Gutierrez, I., and Carmona, S. (2005) "Concentración en el mercado de auditoría en España: análisis empírico del período 1990–2000," *Revista Española de Financiación y Contabilidad*, 34(125, April–June): 423–57.

Código unificado de buen Gobierno para las Sociedades cotizadas (2006) *Informe de la Comisión Conthe del 19 de Junio de 2006*.

Comité Especial para el Estudio de un Código Etico de los Consejos de Administración de las Sociedades (CEECECAS) (1998) *El Gobierno de las Sociedades Cotizadas*, Comité Olivencia, CEECECAS, Madrid.

De Fuentes Barbera, C. (2005) "Factores determinantes de la evolución del mercado de auditoria en España," Doctoral thesis, University of Valencia.

Directive 2006/43/CE on Statutory audits of Annual Accounts and Consolidated Accounts, 17 May 2006. *Official Journal of the European Union*, L157, 49 (9 June 2006).

García-Ayuso, M. and Sánchez, A. (1999) "Un análisis descriptivo del mercado de la auditoría y de los informes recibidos por las grandes empresas españolas," *Actualidad Financiera*, Segunda Epoca, Número monográfico, 3: 41–52.

García-Benau, M.A. and Humphrey, C.H. (1992) "Beyond the Audit Expectations Gap: Learning from the Experiences of Britain and Spain," *European Accounting Review* 1(2): 303–31.

García-Benau, M.A., Humphrey, C.H., Moizer, P., and Turley, S. (1993) "Auditing Expectations and Performance in Spain and Britain: a Comparative Analysis," *International Journal of Accounting*, 28: 281–307.

García-Benau, M.A., Pucheta Martínez, M.C., and Zorio Grima, A. (2003) "Los comités de auditoría, ¿útiles y necesarios," *Revista de Contabilidad*, 6(11): 87-122.

García-Benau, M.A., Ruiz Barbadillo, E., Humphrey C.H., and Husaini, W. (1999) "Success in Failure? Reflections on the Changing Spanish Audit Environment," *European Accounting Review*, 8(4): 701–30.

García-Benau, M.A., Ruiz-Barbadillo, E., and Vico, A. (1998) *Análisis de la Estructura del Mercado de Servicios de Auditoria en España*, Madrid: ICAC, Ministerio de Economía y Hacienda.

Gonzalo Angulo, J.A. (1995) "La auditoría, una profesión en la encrucijada de los noventa," *Revista Española de Financiación y Contabilidad*, April–June: 595–629.

Gonzalo Angulo, J.A. (2003) "Influencias recíprocas entre la información financiera y gobernanza empresarial (a propósito del Libro Blanco sobre la Contabilidad en España)," in E. Bueno (ed.) *El gobierno de la empresa*, Barcelona: Ed Ariel.

Guerra Martin, G. (2005) "El Comité de Auditoría: balance crítico y perspectivas de reforma ante la Recomendación de la Comisión Europea de febrero de 2005," Ponencia presentada en la V Jornada de Trabajo de Auditoría de ASEPUC, La auditoría ante las NIIF.

Informe de la Comision Especial para el Fomento de la Transparencia y la Seguridad en los Mercados Financieros y las Sociedades Cotizadas (CEFTSMFSC) (2003), Comisión Aldama, Madrid.

Larriba, A. and Serrano, Y.F. (1999) "La ley de auditoría española, su significación y bases para una posible reforma," *Revista de Contabilidad*, 2(4): 49-107.

Ley 19/1988, de 12 de julio, sobre Auditoría de Cuentas (BOE de 15 de julio de 1988).

Ley 44/2002, de 22 de noviembre, de medidas de reforma del sistema financiero (BOE no. 281 de 23 de Noviembre de 2002).

Ley 26/2003, de 17 de julio, de transparencia de las sociedades anonimas cotizadas.

Real Decreto 1636/1990, de 20 de diciembre (BOE, de 25 de 12 de 1990) por el que se aprueba el Reglamento que desarrolla la Ley 19/1988 de Auditoría de Cuentas.

Ruiz Barbadillo, E. (1996) "La crisis de los fallos de auditoría: un análisis de las fases del conflicto en el entorno de la auditoría en España," *Revista Española de Financiación y Contabilidad*, 25(89): 785-820.

Sánchez Fernández de Valderrama, J.L. (2003) *Teoría y práctica de la auditoría, I. Concepto y metodología*, 3rd ed., Madrid: Ed Pirámide.

Vico, A. (1997) "Expectativas ante la auditoría: La independencia del auditor," Doctoral thesis, Universidad Jaume I, Castellón.

10 Developments in the framework of auditing regulation in the United Kingdom

Stuart Turley

1 Introduction

The United Kingdom (UK) financial reporting system has conventionally been classified as one that relies primarily on professional self-regulation, where professionalism and flexibility are preferred to statutory control and uniformity (Gray 1988) and non-governmental rules are supported by professional enforcement (Nobes 1992). While this characterization does convey important points about the traditions and conventions of the UK system, the full picture on auditing regulation in any environment is normally much more complex than is implied by a simple classification between professional and governmental regulation (Puxty *et al*. 1987). A mixture of mechanisms contributes to regulation and it is the balance between complementary elements that creates the actual regulatory environment. That balance can also change significantly over time. This chapter discusses how recent changes in the regulatory framework in the UK have emphasized a transition to more independent regulation and resulted in an approach that no longer relies on professional self-regulation as the primary means of promoting reliable auditing.

The chapter looks at important developments that have changed the regulatory landscape for auditing in the UK within recent years. Although the process of change was given added impetus by reactions to the events associated with corporate scandals in 2001–3, this is not the entire explanation for the developments that have taken place. Regulatory change was already under way or under advanced consideration, and this chapter refers to that context as well as the actual reforms that have been introduced. The discussion is organized into sections reviewing in turn several significant areas where regulation has changed: the overall framework of regulation and standard setting (section 2); the impact of internationalization (section 3); ethical standards (section 4); and auditor liability (section 5). Reforms in auditing need to be seen in the context of the broader regime of corporate governance and some significant developments in corporate governance relevant to the role and position of auditing are also presented (section 6). The final section draws together some overall comments about the character and direction of change.

2 The framework of auditor regulation and standard setting

For approximately a quarter of a century between 1976 and 2002, regulatory responsibility for the development of practice standards for auditing rested with, first, the Auditing Practices Committee (APC) and, from 1991, the Auditing Practices Board (APB).[1] When first established, the APC was constituted as a committee of the joint professional bodies of the accountancy profession.[2] The standards it developed were effectively recommendations which only became standards when adopted by the professional bodies as applicable to their members. From 1991 the APB had authority to issue standards itself, and its membership changed to include non-practitioners, but it remained under the authority of the profession's structures. Compliance was only loosely monitored and disciplinary action for non-compliance was the responsibility of the bodies themselves and was rare. Ethical standards were also controlled by the individual professional institutes through ethical guides (for example, ICAEW 2001). This position was consistent with the model of professional self-regulation often taken to be characteristic of the UK approach, albeit one that over time was modified to fit within the supervisory framework of the Eighth EU Directive. In the recent past that position has changed in several significant ways. Currently the setting of practice standards, monitoring of compliance, the development of ethical standards for auditors and the discipline of accountants in public interest cases are all within a structure of independent regulation established under the Financial Reporting Council. The evolution of the present system is best understood as a two-stage process of change – a structure introduced in 2002 and a subsequent revision effective from 2004.

2.1 The regulatory structure 2002–4

Major changes in the framework of regulation for auditing were introduced in 2002 as a result of reviews of the self-regulatory structure undertaken through the professional bodies. Under the banner of 'Independent Regulation for the Accountancy Profession' (Accountancy Foundation 2002), a new Accountancy Foundation was established together with a number of boards with responsibility for different aspects of oversight and regulation. With the exception of the APB, the elements of this structure, which is illustrated in Figure 10.1, all involved newly created boards. The APB was newly constituted, involving significant changes in its constitution and membership structure, though in practical terms there was considerable continuity with the pre-existing board in matters such as the technical secretariat and work programme.

The responsibilities of the different constituent bodies in the structure were as follows:

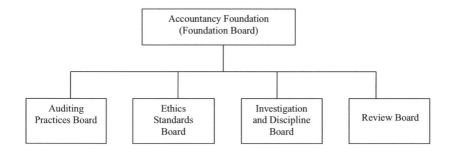

Figure 10.1 The structure of audit regulation 2002–4

- The *Accountancy Foundation Board* was responsible for overall management of the Foundation's activities and making appointments to the subsidiary boards.
- The *Auditing Practices Board* was to continue to establish standards applying to audit practice.
- The *Ethics Standards Board* (ESB) had oversight of ethical standards as established by the professional bodies.
- The *Investigation and Discipline Board* (IDB) was expected to investigate relevant matters arising from major accounting and auditing scandals.
- The *Review Board* had responsibilities for oversight of certain aspects of the educational and disciplinary actions of the accountancy bodies, although those bodies retained the primary responsibility for education and discipline themselves. In addition the Review Board was responsible for scrutiny of the activities of the other boards (APB, ESB and IDB).

This structure essentially followed a principle of review and external scrutiny of the profession's activities. For example, the professional bodies retained responsibility for setting ethical standards, but their activities in this regard were made subject to independent review and oversight. The APB was an exception to this pattern. Its role was already well established, the pre-existing APB having been the primary source of practice standards for almost thirty years. Within the new framework it retained responsibility for establishing the standards to apply to audits in the UK, but it was no longer owned by the accountancy professional bodies (via CCAB) and instead was to be subject to internal oversight through the Review Board. In addition, the constitution of the board was changed to specify that at least 60 per cent of the members should be from outside public practice auditing and should represent the public interest in standard setting.

The framework introduced in 2001 is of interest for a number of reasons. First, it demonstrates that a process to establish 'independence' in the regulation of auditors and to move away from a model of self-regulation was underway well before the corporate scandals of 2001 and 2002 became public. Second, the degree of reliance on models of review reflects the position that the professional bodies did retain active responsibility over certain areas of regulation. The fact that the professional bodies were responsible for financing the Accountancy Foundation may also have been relevant to the design of the structure. Third, this framework proved to be only a temporary arrangement. As the bodies within the structure were themselves becoming established and commencing operation, the scandals of 2001–2 broke and government action led to a further significant round of reform and another new framework.

2.2 The regulatory structure from 2004

In early 2002 the UK government established a number of reviews relating to accounting and auditing, 'looking at the consequences of US corporate failures to ensure that the UK regime provided effective protections against anything similar happening here' (DTI 2003, paragraph 1.4). The nature of these reviews as explicit reactions to the scandals occurring in the United States is evident within the terms of reference. Specifically, the Co-ordinating Group on Accounting and Auditing Issues (CGAA) was set up to 'ensure that there is a co-ordinated and comprehensive work programme by individual regulators to review the UK's current regulatory arrangements for statutory audit and financial reporting in the light of the collapse of Enron' (CGAA 2003: 7). An associated Review of the Regulatory Arrangements for the Accountancy Profession followed. Interim reports or consultative papers were issued within 2002 (CGAA 2002, DTI 2002) and by 2003 final reports and recommendations had been published (CGAA 2003, DTI 2003).

Notwithstanding a generally favourable conclusion that: 'The UK's existing regulatory system is widely acknowledged to be amongst the best in the world … we found no evidence that the system was seriously flawed', recommendations were made 'to further strengthen the independence of the system of regulation of audit and to achieve a clearer, more authoritative and more transparent regulatory structure' (DTI 2003, paragraph 1.8). These recommendations involved terminating the Accountancy Foundation, transferring its responsibilities to the Financial Reporting Council (FRC), the structure that already existed to oversee accounting standard setting and enforcement, and effectively creating a new merged body as 'the independent regulator' for accounting and auditing. The professional bodies' responsibilities for ethical standards relating to audit were transferred to the APB and as a consequence the ESB was dissolved (Fearnley and Beattie 2004). Other boards and units were recommended, continuing, extending or replacing the roles of monitoring, inspection, discipline and general oversight from the Accountancy Foundation regime. The resulting framework finally introduced in 2004 is illustrated in Figure 10.2. Five operating boards were established to make decisions in different areas of regulatory responsibility.[3] The

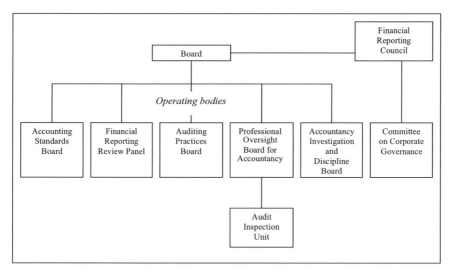

Figure 10.2 The structure of audit regulation from 2004

costs of the new structure are shared between the government, business and the professional bodies.

A summary of the responsibilities of the component parts of the structure is as follows:

*   The *Financial Reporting Council* (FRC) is the independent regulator for corporate reporting and governance. Its responsibilities include setting, monitoring and enforcing accounting and auditing standards, oversight and regulation of auditors and oversight of the regulatory responsibilities of professional accountancy bodies. Members of the FRC Board are appointed by the Secretary of State for Trade and Industry. The *Board* determines general strategy and priorities, appoints the overall 30-person *Council* (which includes the chairs of the operating bodies and representation from the business, investment and professional communities) and members of the operating bodies, and is responsible for the transparency and accountability of the structure. The five operating bodies make regulatory decisions in their areas of responsibility.
*   The *Auditing Practices Board* is charged with responsibility for establishing high standards of auditing. This responsibility now includes both practice standards and ethical standards relating to auditing and assurance services. Ethical standards on other matters remain with the profession. The APB's objectives also include meeting the developing needs of users of financial information and acting to ensure public confidence in the audit process.
*   The *Accountancy Investigation and Discipline Board* (AIDB) replaces the IDB, which had been delayed being established, and acts as an independent, investigative and disciplinary body for accountants. The AIDB is concerned

with public interest cases; other matters will still be dealt with by individual accountancy bodies. Normally the AIDB will act on referral of a case by a professional body but it can also initiate action without such referral.

- A new *Audit Inspection Unit* was created to monitor the audits of public interest entities.
- The *Professional Oversight Board for Accountancy* (POBA) provides oversight of the regulation of accounting and auditing by the supervisory and qualifying professional bodies and monitors the quality of auditing for public interest entities. The Secretary of State also delegates to POBA responsibility for the recognition of supervisory bodies and qualifications within the Eighth EU Directive framework introduced in the Companies Act 1989.
- The *Accounting Standards Board* and *Financial Reporting Review Panel* are essentially concerned with the financial accounting aspects of reporting and their remit is not discussed further in this chapter.
- The *Committee on Corporate Governance* reflects the FRC's responsibilities with respect to corporate governance. It is expected to review developments in corporate governance generally, and to monitor the operation of the Combined Code on Corporate Governance for listed companies and to suggest action by FRC where appropriate.

A number of points are worth highlighting about the revised regulatory structure. First, under the new FRC, the structure reunites audit regulation with the accounting standards regime. Auditing has thus eventually followed the path to independent regulation which had applied to accounting since 1990. Second, the structure continues to place reliance on the model of monitoring and oversight, alongside standard setting activities, as the principal means of independent regulation rather than direct control by government. The mechanisms of oversight have been strengthened, however, with more active inspection and with greater responsibilities for POBA. Third, the assignment to the APB of responsibility for establishing the ethical standards applying to auditing and assurance services represents a major shift in regulatory responsibilities and perhaps reflects particular concerns about how to establish confidence in auditors (see later discussion of ethics).

The developments described above indicate that the UK has moved from a position of self-regulation *by* the profession to independent oversight and regulation *of* the profession. Major aspects of this change include the move to establish independent standard setting, giving responsibility for ethical standards for auditors to the APB and the introduction of independent investigation, discipline and oversight of professional bodies and professional activities. While not governmental in the sense of direct regulation by a government department, the structure is government mandated and was introduced through reviews sponsored by the government. The current structure reflects a two-stage evolution. The first stage was a product of the profession's own reviews and attempted to establish greater credibility for its regulatory processes. The second stage resulted from reactions to the crises around major corporate scandals and consequent concerns about a possible loss of confidence in auditing.

3 Internationalization

Although this chapter focuses on the development of the regulatory framework in a single country, the increasing importance of the international context of audit regulation must be recognized. The European Union has developed significantly its activities with respect to auditing (see, for example, EC 2002 and 2003), establishing a European Committee on Auditing and bringing forward a new auditing directive (EC 2006), and organizations such as the International Organization of Securities Commissions (IOSCO) have shown an interest in auditing, publishing principles for the kind of regulation they are willing to endorse (IOSCO 2002). The development of national frameworks must therefore be seen in the broader international context. One significant development in the UK towards internationalization is the move to recognize International Standards on Auditing (ISAs) published by the International Auditing and Assurance Standards Board (IAASB) as the definitive standards for audit practice.

In May 2004 the APB announced its intention to adopt ISAs for application in the UK and Ireland, and by December 2004 a complete new set of practice standards was issued – *International Standards on Auditing (UK and Ireland)* (APB 2004c). The APB had for some time voiced its support for the principle of harmonized international standards but the timing of such a move had been unresolved. The justification for the UK, a country with a long tradition of setting national standards for auditing, moving to adopt ISAs at this point in time rested partly on issues of practicality and partly on views regarding the future of standard setting.

For a number of years the IAASB had been developing new standards in the areas of audit risk, fraud and quality control. This process, which had been undertaken in partnership with American standard setters, resulted in new standards being issued in 2004 (Curtis and Turley 2005). Given the development of these standards, and a view that they represented a strengthening of standards in relation to the issues of fraudulent financial reporting and aggressive earnings management, the APB had to choose either to develop its own separate equivalent standards or to adopt the new ISAs. As there would be a need for conforming changes to be made to a large number of other standards, there was a further choice over whether to revise the existing body of UK Statements of Auditing Standards (SASs) or to take advantage of the fact that IAASB had already made conforming changes to the existing ISAs. The APB considered that the most efficient way both to recognize the improvements present in the new risk and fraud ISAs and to make other standards consistent with these new developments was simply through immediate adoption of ISAs (APB 2004a).

An important area of debate concerned whether the ISAs should be adopted in their extant form or whether areas of difference between the existing SASs and the ISAs should be acknowledged – the debate between 'pure ISA' adoption and 'ISA plus'. Differences existed because of some specific regulatory conditions that applied in UK legislation (for example legal requirements affecting auditors' reporting responsibilities) but also because equivalent SASs/ISAs had been developed at different times and so reflected different stages of development in audit practice. To overcome concerns about the potential loss of certain higher standards in SASs, the ISA plus route has been followed and ISAs (UK and Ireland) include some additional material from the pre-existing SASs. This material is clearly distinguished in the presentation of the standards and the stated aspiration is that, as ISAs continue to develop and be revised, the need for any such additions, other than those related to specific national legal conditions, will be removed. The intention is therefore that in due course ISAs will apply without variation, except where necessary to recognize UK legislation, rather than be adapted to the standards for the UK by routinely adding or removing elements to reflect national preferences.

A further consideration in the timing of the UK adoption of ISAs was a judgement regarding the strategy that would best position the APB to influence the future development of standards. Given an expectation that the EC would follow its recognition of international accounting standards with a similar policy for auditing, as reflected in the then draft and now final directive on auditing (EC 2004 and 2006), it could be anticipated that ISAs would become required standards at least for the audit of listed enterprises in the EU. By incorporating ISAs as the basis of standards applicable in the UK, the APB could be seen as an 'early adopter', signalling a commitment to harmonization, and could seek a cooperative position with IAASB through which to influence future standards setting.

4 Ethics

As discussed in section 2, a notable change in the structure of regulation for auditors has been that the responsibility for standards concerning the integrity, independence and objectivity of auditors has been transferred from the professional bodies to the APB. This only applies to those ethical matters in the context of auditing and assurance services; guidance or rules relating to ethics in other areas of professional activity remain with the bodies. As a consequence of the change, a series of new Ethical Standards (ESs) have been introduced (APB 2004b), which apply to audits for financial years commencing from 1 January 2005 onwards. These standards have been developed in the post-Enron period and reflect perceptions of the kind of restrictions needed in order to establish confidence in the behaviour of auditors and to respond to some of the areas of concern following the scandals. While the contents of the standards cannot be discussed in detail, the position adopted can be illustrated by reference to the provisions in a number of key areas.

4.1 The ethics partner

An innovation in the new Ethical Standards is the requirement for all firms with more than three partners to designate one partner as the 'ethics partner', with responsibility for the firm's policies in relation to objectivity and independence, compliance with relevant standards and communication of policies and procedures to staff (ES1, paragraph 21). The requirement to nominate a specific ethics partner is an attempt to link a general principle of reliance on firms having adequate policies and leadership with a more specific identifiable assigned responsibility to ensure this principle is valid.

4.2 Management threat

The standards are also unusual in comparison with other ethical codes, which follow a threats and safeguards approach, in identifying specifically a 'management threat', separate from the more commonly recognized threats of self-review and familiarity.[4] The management threat arises where the audit firm 'undertakes work that involves making judgements and taking decisions which are the responsibility of management' (ES1, paragraph 28) because such activities can erode the distinction between firm and client and result in the firm becoming too closely aligned with company management.

4.3 Economic dependence

Two aspects of the economic relationship between an audit firm and a client company are generally considered for regulation – the scale of the firm's fees from a client relative to the size of the firm's business and the relative proportions of fees from audit and non-audit services. The position adopted by the APB is to focus on the *total* fees from the relationship with the client as the source of any possible economic dependence. No specific limits have been introduced regarding a ratio of fees from audit and non-audit services that would be seen as threatening the objectivity of the audit. However, more stringent limits have been set on the levels of fees that could jeopardize auditor independence, and those limits are applied with reference to total fees, not audit fees alone. For listed clients, an audit firm is deemed to be economically dependent if total fees are expected to amount to 10 per cent of relevant firm fee income (15 per cent for non-listed) and should not continue with the appointment on that basis (ES4, paragraphs 23–4). There are also requirements for explicit consideration and action when the level of total fees is between 5 and 10 per cent of firm income (10 and 15 per cent for non-listed). The per centage levels are specified with reference to the income of that part of a firm on which the engagement partner's remuneration is based; otherwise in large audit firms levels based on firm-wide fees would make economic dependence virtually impossible.

4.4 Auditor tenure and rotation

The threat to the auditor's independence from long tenure is sometimes used to justify suggestions for rotation of audit appointments. The ESs apply this logic to the individuals with primary responsibility for the audit engagement but not the tenure of the audit firm. For listed companies there is a prohibition on acting as engagement partner or independent partner for more than five years (combined service in either role) and a limit of a further five years before returning to either role subsequent to having served for that period (ES3, paragraph 12). These limits are more restrictive than previously applied but reflect the view signalled by the government that a five year limit is appropriate and that rotation of firm appointments is not necessary (CGAA 2003, paragraphs 1.51–2).

4.5 Non-audit services – areas of effective prohibition

Finally, the ESs also address some issues concerning the provision of particular non-audit services to audit clients. The approach here is to require auditors to follow a general principle that non-audit services should not be provided where 'it is probable that a reasonable and informed third party would regard the objectives of the non-audit service as being inconsistent with the objectives of the audit of the financial statements' (ES5, paragraph 14). Thus, auditors are required to apply a standard based on the perceptions of third parties to the engagement.

For certain specific types of non-audit services the standards impose conditions which effectively prohibit the provision of those services to audit clients (ES5). For example:

- internal audit services should not be provided where the auditor would also place significant reliance on the internal audit work;
- information technology services should not be provided where the systems are significant to producing the financial statements and would be relied on in the audit;
- valuation services should not be provided where the valuation both involves significant judgement and is material to the financial statements;
- taxation services that involve acting as an advocate for an audit client on an issue that is material to the financial statements or depends on an audit judgement should not be undertaken.

Restrictive conditions are also imposed with respect to non-audit services in relation to recruitment and remuneration, corporate finance, litigation support etc., and there is a general prohibition on undertaking services that would involve the audit firm undertaking part of the role of management. Firms are also required to establish their remuneration policies for partners in a way which does not incentivize or reward audit staff for selling non-audit services to an audit client (ES4, paragraph 36).

Alongside the development of ethical standards relating to non-audit services, the UK government has also implemented plans for extending the requirement for disclosure of aggregate non-audit fees to disclosure of fees by category of non-audit service (DTI 2005).[5]

5 Auditor liability

As a common law legal system applies in the UK, many of the issues in relation to auditor liability are based on case law resulting from court decisions, which are outside the scope of consideration in this chapter (see Gwilliam 1997). In addition, it continues to be the case that a large proportion of claims against auditors are settled out of court and the extent of actual liability in practice is therefore difficult to estimate. However, the conditions surrounding auditor liability have been the subject of regular debate and review. A government-sponsored review of liability in the mid-1990s concluded against the introduction of possible limits on auditor liability through a statutory cap on the amount of liability or the introduction of proportionate liability. Following the election of a new government in 1997, a major review of UK company law was announced, including possible reform in respect of auditor liability. Although consideration was given to extending the duty of care of auditors, no change was ultimately recommended (DTI 2001) and the general position remains that an auditor's duty of care is restricted to actual shareholders in the company at the time of the audit. That duty relates to shareholders only in respect of their governance rights and so excludes even existing shareholders who rely on the audit report when buying or selling shares. Two developments are relevant to comment on further in relation to auditor liability in the UK in the future – the creation of limited liability partnerships (LLPs) and the introduction of proportional liability.

5.1 Limited liability partnerships

From the mid-1990s, following developments establishing LLPs in the US, some of the major audit firms sought to promote the introduction of similar business structures in the UK. They brought pressure on the UK government by promoting the enactment of legislation in Jersey and threatened to move their audit businesses 'off shore' (Cousins *et al.* 1999). In response the government announced an intention to introduce the LLP vehicle (DTI 1997) and legislation to create the new type of entity was introduced in the Limited Liability Partnership Act 2000. This became effective from April 2001 and subsequently several firms have adopted this form of structure. While an LLP does offer some protection to individual partners, it does so only in the last resort. Any settled claim is met first from the assets of the firm and it is only should those assets be insufficient, that is that the firm ceases to exist, that the protection of a partner's personal assets would become effective. Thus the LLP does not provide a solution to the claimed threat of liability to the audit business – it only becomes effective when that threat is realized.

5.2 Proportionate liability by contract

In December 2003 the UK government published a consultation on directors' and auditors' liability. As a result, in 2004[6] changes were introduced concerning directors' liability but, in the absence of any clear consensus about the position for auditors, the government concluded that it would be inappropriate to permit capping of auditor liability to a predetermined amount and no change in the position of auditors was legislated for at that time. Discussions of possible change continued and more recently the government has been persuaded of the benefits of change. A new Companies Act (CA) completed its passage through Parliament in autumn 2006 and includes legislation to permit shareholders to agree limitations to auditors' liability – proportionate liability by contract (DTI 2006).

The new approach allows shareholders to agree to limit the auditor's liability for damages incurred by a company to a level that is determined by the courts to be fair and reasonable in relation to the extent of the auditor's responsibility for the damage incurred (CA Sections 553–8). This limitation only applies to the extent the court determines is fair and reasonable in the circumstances, and the provisions state that 'it is immaterial how a liability limitation agreement is framed' and need not include a predetermined limit at a specific maximum monetary amount or a quantifiable formula such as a multiple of the audit fee (Section 535(4)). Where proportionate liability applies to the auditor, it is expected that the company would seek to recover separately the loss attributed to any other parties. The auditor continues to be fully liable in situations where he or she is party to any fraud.

In negotiating the terms of the audit contract, the directors are not able to set specific limits on the amount of liability but can propose to shareholders that, in the situation where there has been damage to which the auditor's conduct has contributed, the auditor's liability be limited to that proportion of the damage that the court determines is just and reasonable. The company can thus agree that proportionate liability will apply, as opposed to the long-standing principle of joint and several liability,[7] but it is the court that will determine the consequence in terms of the amount of liability an auditor subsequently faces. Shareholders must give explicit agreement for the directors to negotiate the audit contract to include this limitation of liability and that agreement must be repeated each year. In addition the financial statements should include a disclosure of the existence of the liability limitation agreement (Section 538).

It is interesting to note the contrast between the approach taken in the new legislation and the conclusion on proportional liability reached in the Company Law Review:

> we reject, as contrary to principle, the 'proportionality' solution, which would cap auditors' liability absolutely at the share attributable to them of the blame for the events, as compared with that attributable to others, normally the company and its officers and employees. In this we follow the conclusions of a report on behalf of the Law Commission. The effect of the

proportionality approach would be to impose on a plaintiff who is wholly innocent the risk that a party in the wrong may be unable to satisfy a claim, rather than imposing a burden on another party (the auditor) whose fault has caused the loss.

(DTI 2001, paragraph. 8.138)

While this development in the liability regime appears beneficial from the point of view of the auditor, it has been linked to other considerations which impose some additional burdens on auditors. It has become a criminal offence to knowingly or recklessly give an incorrect audit opinion (increasing the potential penalty for misreporting) and other requirements linked to the idea of promoting audit quality have also been introduced (see section 6). It is also important to note that limiting liability has been approached partly as an economic issue, as part of promoting a competitive audit market. Eventually it would seem the UK government has been persuaded of the claimed potential inequity in the deep-pocket argument that auditors could be held liable for 100 per cent of damages even though they only share the blame with other parties. Following the loss of Andersen in the aftermath of Enron, concern over the potential consequences for the audit market of the demise of another large audit firm has strengthened the remaining firms' argument for liability reform. Indeed the announcement of the proposed package of changes was described in the press as the result of agreement between the government and the major audit *firms*, rather than the professional institutes,[8] as representatives of the profession.

6 Auditing and corporate governance

The specific changes described above with respect to auditing regulation must also be seen in a broader context of general development in the framework of corporate governance in the UK. For a period of over 15 years the structures of corporate governance have been the subject of repeated scrutiny and review with the objective of making directors and chief executive officers more accountable to shareholders (see, for example, Cadbury 1992, Hampel 1998). The resulting recommendations have been captured in the Combined Code on Corporate Governance (FRC 2003). In this section a number of developments that have specific relevance to or implications for auditing are briefly discussed.

6.1 Independent directors and audit committees

Independent or non-executive directors are expected to represent the interests of shareholders and to be able to take an independent view of the actions of the executive board. In relation to financial reporting, the position of the auditor is affected by the role of the 'audit committee', a majority of whose members should be non-executive directors.

Specifically in the UK, the role and significance of the audit committee as a governance structure have developed substantially during the last decade (Smith Committee 2003). The audit committee has been given additional responsibilities with respect to making recommendations for the appointment, reappointment and removal of the auditor and for approval of the auditor's remuneration. It has also been given a more explicit guardianship role with respect to auditor independence. The audit committee must monitor independence and establish policy regarding the use of the auditor to provide non-audit services and, if non-audit services are provided, report how independence is protected (FRC 2003: paragraphs C.3.2 and C.3.7). The changed importance of the audit committee is also reflected in the increased emphasis placed in auditing guidance on the communication between auditors and the audit committee. The relevant standard on communication contains a significant amount of additional UK guidance beyond the requirements of the IAASB standard (APB 2004c, ISA(UK&I) 260).

6.2 Corporate governance disclosures

One consequence of the reviews of corporate governance and company law has been the extension of the reporting and disclosure requirements for companies. Managements of listed companies are required to make a statement (on a 'comply or explain' basis) concerning the application of and compliance with the Combined Code. With respect to internal control, management is expected to review the effectiveness of internal control at least annually and to report to shareholders that this has been done. Although during 2005 the UK government abandoned its intention to make an Operating and Financing Review (in some countries Management Discussion and Analysis) an additional mandatory legal component of the statutory report and accounts for listed companies, narrative disclosure of this nature has in practice become a common feature of corporate reports. As such reporting requirements change, there are inevitable questions concerning the related responsibilities of auditors with respect to new disclosures, for example, whether auditors should express an opinion on the disclosures or simply confirm the process on which disclosure is based and what the consequences are for liability if auditors' responsibilities are extended.

The approach adopted in the UK has been a mixture of retaining the existing approach that the requirement to 'audit' is restricted to the financial statements and adding requirements to 'review' certain statements, and 'read' reports for consistency with the financial statements. For example, auditors are expected to review the management statement regarding compliance with the Combined Code on Corporate Governance, but only with reference to nine (out of a total of forty-eight) Code provisions. Indeed, with respect to internal control, the recommended format for the auditor's report includes an explicit statement that: 'We are not required to consider whether the board's statements on internal control cover all risks and controls, or form an opinion on the effectiveness of the group's corporate governance procedures or its risk and control procedures' (APB

2006: paragraph 37). If the auditor believes that there has not been proper disclosure of a departure from a Code provision, this must be included in the audit report, but it would not lead to a qualified opinion on the financial statements. The developments in company reporting have thus had some impact on auditors' reporting responsibilities but not on the underlying scope of what is subject to audit.

6.3 Shareholder engagement with the audit process

As part of the package of proposed reforms that includes changes to auditor liability, the government has also introduced additional changes which it believes will enhance the quality of the audit process. These changes have been justified with the objective of 'enhancing shareholder engagement' with companies, reflecting a wider corporate governance agenda to promote more active involvement of shareholders with the companies they invest in as part of a long-term investment culture, and seek to make the audit process more transparent. Specifically, provisions have been included in the Companies Act (DTI 2006) which involve developments in the following areas:

- *Disclosure of the terms of the audit contract* – disclosure of the terms of the audit is seen as one way of increasing transparency and third parties' understanding of the audit; the Secretary of State has the power to establish the basis for such disclosure (CA, Section 493).
- *Shareholders' rights to question auditors* – Shareholders are able to publish on the company's website statements concerning the audit or auditor that they intend to ask questions about at the next meeting of the company that considers audited accounts (CA, Section 527).
- *Disclosures when an audit appointment ceases* – An auditor ceasing to hold office should deposit a statement with the company, even if there are no circumstances the auditor considers should be brought to the attention of shareholders. The provisions also impose obligations on the auditor to disclose the statement to the audit authority, as designated by the Secretary of State (CA, Sections 519–25).
- *Audit lead partner to sign the audit report in their own name* – As a means of encouraging personal responsibility for the audit the name of the senior statutory audit partner, as well as that of the audit firm, should be on the audit report (CA, Section 505).

7 Concluding comments

Taken together, the developments reviewed in this chapter indicate that the overall regulatory position for auditors in the UK in 2005 is markedly different from the position at the beginning of the 1990s, or even that at the turn of the century. Changes have affected the regulatory structures, the scope of regulation, the liability regime and the contribution of auditors to the corporate governance framework. The amount of change introduced in the last few years may suggest that much has been initiated as a result of the scandals that affected major corporations and hit the headlines in 2001–3. To that extent, recent history has repeated the pattern of earlier years, where regulatory change followed various corporate crises and alleged failures. However, one of the main points evident from the discussion in this chapter is that recent changes have to a considerable extent simply continued and strengthened trends that have been in process over a longer period of time.

In summary, the following major trends in regulation are evident both in the recent changes and in the pattern of earlier developments in the UK:

- Significant aspects of regulation have been taken away from the control of auditing professionals and a structure of independent regulation has been established, affecting standard setting, inspection of audit practice and discipline of auditors.
- Within that structure there is reliance on principles of monitoring and oversight alongside more direct regulation through standard setting activities.
- There is a commitment to internationalization as a major component in the regulatory approach.
- The scope of independent standard setting has been extended, particularly to include ethical matters relating to auditing.
- Reforms have been introduced that have some effect on auditor liability, and the introduction of a form of proportional liability may reflect concerns about maintaining a competitive audit market.
- Attempts are being made to refine aspects of the auditor's role in relation to changes in corporate governance more generally and to improve the transparency of audit through improved communication with audit committees and shareholders.

Notes

1 In 2006 the Board for Actuarial Standards was added to this structure and has responsibility for establishing standards for the actuarial profession.
2 See Chandler (1997) for a discussion of the history of the standard setting regime in the UK and the change from the APC to APB.
3 Several institutes offer professional accountancy qualifications in the UK, including three Institutes of Chartered Accountants (England and Wales, Scotland, and Ireland respectively), the Association of Chartered Certified Accountants, the Chartered Institute of Management Accountants, and the Chartered Institute of Public Finance and Accountancy. These bodies collaborate on certain activities through the Coordinating Committee for Accountancy Bodies (CCAB) and this organization was the legal parent of the Auditing Practices Committee.
4 The IFAC Code of Ethics, for example, identifies self-interest, self-review, advocacy, familiarity, and intimidation as possible threats (IFAC 2005).
5 The categories of non-audit service are: services pursuant to legislation; services relating to taxation; services relating to information technology; valuation and actuarial services; internal audit services; services relating to litigation; recruitment

and remuneration services; services relating to corporate finance transactions; all other services.
6   Audit Investigations and Community Enterprise Act 2004. Provisions are effective from April 2005.
7   Under joint and several liability any individual defendant found guilty can be held liable for the entire amount of damages determined by the court, irrespective of the potential contribution of other parties to the circumstances giving rise to those damages.
8   The *Financial Times*, 15 December 2004, announced the news of a possible agreement between the government and the audit firms under the headline and sub-heads: 'Auditors to face jail threat; False advice from accountants may prompt criminal charges; Boost for firms with government agreeing in return to a limit on liability' (page 1).

References

Accountancy Foundation (2002) *Independent Regulation of the Accountancy Profession*, London: Accountancy Foundation.

APB (2004a) 'APB Announces Its Intention to Adopt International Standards on Auditing for 2005', *Press Release*, London, Auditing Practices Board, 6 May 2004.

APB (2004b) *Ethical Standards 1–5*, London: Auditing Practices Board.

APB (2004c) *International Standards on Auditing (UK and Ireland)*, London: Auditing Practices Board.

APB (2006) *The Combined Code on Corporate Governance: Requirements of Auditors under the Listing Rules of the Financial Services Authority and the Irish Stock Exchange*, Bulletin 2006/5, London: Auditing Practices Board, September.

Cadbury (1992) *Report of the Committee on Financial Aspects of Corporate Governance*, London: Gee and Co.

CGAA (2002) *Interim Report to the Secretary of State for Trade and Industry and the Chancellor of the Exchequer*, URN 02/1092, Co-ordinating Group on Audit and Accounting Issues, London, Department of Trade and Industry, July.

CGAA (2003) *Final Report to the Secretary of State for Trade and Industry and the Chancellor of the Exchequer*, URN 03/567, Co-ordinating Group on Audit and Accounting Issues, London, Department of Trade and Industry, January.

Chandler, R. (1997) 'The Auditing Practices Board and Auditing Standards in the UK', in M. Sherer and S. Turley, *Current Issues in Auditing*, 3rd edn, London: Paul Chapman Publishing.

Cousins, J., Mitchell, A. and Sikka, P. (1999) 'Auditor Liability: The Other Side of the Debate', *Critical Perspectives on Accounting*, 10(3): 283–311.

Curtis, E. and Turley, S. (2005) 'From Business Risk Audits to Audit Risk Standards', Paper presented at the European Accounting Association Congress, Gothenburg, May 2005.

DTI (1997) *Limited Liability Partnership – A New Form of Business Association for Professions*, Consultation Paper, London, Department of Trade and Industry.

DTI (2001) *Modern Company Law for a Competitive Economy Final Report*, Vol. 1, London, Department of Trade and Industry, July.

DTI (2002) *Review of the Regulatory Regime of the Accountancy Profession: A Consultation Document*, London, Department of Trade and Industry, October.

DTI (2003) *Review of the Regulatory Regime of the Accountancy Profession: Report to the Secretary of State for Trade and Industry*, London, Department of Trade and Industry, January.

DTI (2005) *The Companies (Disclosure of Auditor Remuneration) Regulations 2005, Statutory Instrument no. 2417*, London: HMSO.

DTI (2006) *Companies Act 2006*, London: HMSO. Online. Available at: <http://www.berr.gov.uk/bbf/co-act-2006/index.html> (accessed July 2007).

EC (2002) *Statutory Auditors' Independence in the EU: A Set of Fundamental Principles*, Commission Recommendation 2002/590/EC of 16 May 2002.

EC (2003) *Reinforcing the Statutory Audit in the European Union*, Commission Communication COM/2003/286 May 2003.

EC (2004) *Proposal for a Directive of the European Parliament and of the Council on Statutory Audit of Annual Accounts and Consolidated Accounts and Amending Council Directives 78/660/EEC and 83/349/EEC*, COM/2004/0177 final – COD 2004/0065, European Commission, November.

EC (2006) Directive 2006/43/EC on statutory audits of annual accounts and consolidated accounts, published in the *Official Journal of the European Union*, 9 June 2006. Online. Available at <http://ec.europa.eu/international_market/auditing/directives/index_eu.htm> (accessed July 2007).

Fearnley, S. and Beattie, V. (2004) 'The Reform of the UK's Auditor Independence Framework after the Enron Collapse: An Example of Evidence-based Policy Making', *International Journal of Auditing*, 8(2, July): 117–38.

FRC (2003) *The Combined Code on Corporate Governance*, London, Financial Reporting Council.

Gray (1988) 'Towards a Theory of Cultural Influences on the Development of Accounting Systems Internationally', *Abacus*, 24(1): 12–13.

Gwilliam, D. (1997) 'Changes in the Legal Environment', in M. Sherer and S. Turley (eds) *Current Issues in Auditing*, 3rd edn, London: Paul Chapman Publishing.

Hampel (1998) *Committee on Corporate Governance – Final Report*, London: Gee and Co.

ICAEW (2001) 'Introduction and Fundamental Principles', *Institute of Chartered Accountants in England and Wales Members' Handbook, Section 1.2 Guide to Professional Ethics*, London: ICAEW.

IFAC (2005) *Code of Ethics for Professional Accountants*, International Federation of Accountants, June.

IOSCO (2002) 'Principles for Auditor Oversight', Statement of the Technical Committee of the International Organisation of Security Commissions, IOSCO, October. Online. Available at: <www.iosco.org/library/pubdocs/pdf/IOSCOPD134.pdf> (accessed 21 February 2007)

Nobes, C.W. (1992) *International Classification of Financial Reporting*, 2nd edn, London: Routledge.

Puxty, A.G, Willmott, H.C., Cooper, D.J. and Lowe, A. (1987) 'Modes of Regulation in Advanced Capitalism: Locating Accountancy in Four Countries', *Accounting, Organizations and Society*, 12(3): 273–91.

Smith Committee (2003) *Audit Committee Combined Code Guidance*, London: Financial Reporting Council.

11 Regulation and trust in auditing in Russia

Anna Samsonova

1 Introduction

The accountancy profession plays a vital role in the functioning of society, and therefore public trust in the work of an auditor has an important social meaning. The main objective of this chapter is to provide a comparative view on the ways in which trust is being established in auditing in the Russian economic environment which developed as a result of the transformation of the Soviet command economy into the market economy. In Russia the introduction of auditing has been envisaged as an appropriate way of accelerating the ongoing transition processes and establishing confidence in the operation of business. Recent years have seen a gradual change in the perceived roles of auditing, with an increased emphasis on its quality and a resultant questioning of auditors' technical expertise and ethical conduct. The chapter will therefore provide an overview of the regulators' endeavors aimed at enhancing the stature and functionality of the auditing profession in Russia.

The chapter is structured as follows. The next section describes the system of revision as the major means of state financial control in the former USSR, portrays the beginnings of auditing in Russia, draws a comparison between revision and auditing, and examines the legislative framework for auditing that has been introduced. The third section describes the present state of audit developments, portrays a visible shift toward a greater concern with public trust in the quality of auditing, and analyzes the various attempts that have been made to restore trust. The last section offers some concluding remarks.

2 The emergence and development of auditing

This section will provide a brief historical account of the emergence of auditing in Russia from the late 1980s, when it was first introduced. It is argued that auditing first emerged as an alternative to the old Soviet system of revision and, later, came to be seen as a legitimizing tool for enhancing trust in companies' operations and improving capital-raising opportunities.

2.1 From revision to auditing: introduction of a financial statement audit in Russia

In Tsarist Russia financial control was always concentrated in the hands of the state. The tradition of state control first emerged as a result of the establishment of a Department for Accounting Affairs in 1655. The post-revolutionary (after 1917) reorganization of state control appeared to be structural rather than methodological (Enthoven *et al.* 1998 and 2001). In the USSR, up to the late 1980s, the system of state financial control – revision – was an integral part of the national economy. Control checks were exercised by the local offices of the Revision and Control Department of the Ministry of Finance and aimed at ensuring the fulfillment of state production plans and preventing the misappropriation of assets (Enthoven *et al.* 1998). Revision checks, as defined by Sokolov and Terekhov, were periodic, annual or every second year: "the activities of enterprises, organizations or individuals were checked with the purpose of identifying the legitimacy of operations by means of a thorough examination of relevant documentation and accounting records" (Sokolov and Terekhov 2004: 187). At the core of the Soviet revision system was the aspiration of the state to exert total control over economic entities, which resulted in a great number of checks and comprehensive inspections that enterprises had to undergo on a regular basis. In 1986 a single enterprise, depending on its size, could be subjected to revision as many as sixteen times, each with the involvement of dozens of inspectors (Danilevsky 1987).

Revision was regulated by a Decree of the Supreme Soviet of the USSR and the Soviet Republics, which required revision to be undertaken by nationwide and special controlling agencies (*interdepartmental revision*); within ministries, departments, and other institutions (*departmental revision*); or by enterprises themselves (*internal revision*). The Revision and Control Department of the USSR Finance Ministry had an extensive apparatus of inspectors across the country who undertook inspections of the local budgets, monitored the activities of lower-level revision departments, and, most importantly, carried out revision checks of all forms of enterprise. Some control functions were also delegated to the Central Bank, State Statistics Committee, and State Tariff Committee. The major outcome of revision was not an audit report, but a *statement of revision* supplemented with various tables, copies and originals of supporting documents, and certificates. This statement was a sort of message communicated to the authorities, the public, and the enterprise management that contained very detailed information on the state of enterprise accounting and recommendations for its improvement. Understandably, an indication of an inspector's proficiency was the number of accounting failures uncovered in the course of revision. Heads of the revision departments and even regular inspectors could, in fact, decide on what and how to check; this resulted in a high degree of corruption among them. Revision checks, for instance, might be "ordered" and the revision data used with the sole purpose of gathering information aimed at compromising the enterprise's management (Sokolov and Terekhov 2004).

Soviet revision appeared fully pertinent to the needs of a centralized economy which rejected any sort of private ownership (Podolsky *et al.* 2003, Sokolov and Terekhov 2004). However, as economic conditions changed, triggered by the reforms of the 1980s, so did the system of revision, and as private forms of business appeared, debates arose about the ineffectiveness of revision with respect to private sector enterprises and the need for new forms of professional practice more befitting the new economic realities. By analyzing the accounting literature of the period, it is possible to gather ample evidence of a lively debate around auditing as a new self-financed, as opposed to state-subsidized, form of practice widespread in the Western world (for a discussion, see, for example, Danilevsky 1987).

Today, revision appears to have been virtually replaced by auditing and is only undertaken by local tax authorities or on the specific orders of various state services. However, in some countries, such as Sweden, Norway, and Denmark, "*revision*" is a translation of the word "auditing." Hence, in order to avoid possible misinterpretations, it is useful to draw a comparison between auditing and revision and to explain the differences between the ways in which these two notions are understood in Russia (see Table 11.1).

Table 11.1 exemplifies the ways in which auditing differs from revision, namely in terms of the rationales, the relations with a client, or the principles of reporting. Auditing appears to be a broader notion, as besides verification of the financial statements of economic entities auditors are also concerned with their clients' overall financial position.

Western-style auditing appeared in modern Russia during the perestroika (restructuring) period of the late 1980s, marking two important developments that may be regarded as the starting points of Russian auditing, namely the formation of new – private – forms of business and the opening up of the Soviet economy (Enthoven *et al.* 1998, Sokolov and Terekhov 2004). The appearance of new types of business structures – first cooperatives and then corporations, unions, commercial banks, public organizations, and others – triggered by the adoption of the Law "on Cooperatives" issued in 1988 and privatization of the state-owned enterprises, resulted in a demand for independent verification of the financial information presented by enterprise management (Danilevsky 1991). Another impetus for the development of auditing was the endorsement of the legislation regulating the activities of joint ventures, which legitimized the opening up of the Russian market to foreign direct investment. The term "auditing" was initially mentioned in three government decrees of 1987 regulating the activities of joint ventures.[1] The same year a group of accounting professionals established the first audit firm – "Inaudit" with share capital amounting to eight hundred thousand roubles and shares distributed between government ministries, commercial banks, and large enterprises. A few years later the company was privatized and the government sold its shares to the employees. Despite the fact that in 1992 "Inaudit" discontinued its operations and split up into several independent audit

Table 11.1 A comparative overview of auditing and revision

Issues to be compared	Auditing	Revision
Objective	To authenticate information presented in the financial statements	To determine the legitimacy of operations or find possible thefts or embezzlements
Legal basis	Civil law	Administrative law: administrative regulations, guidelines, orders, instructions
Methods	The methods are often identical though used in different ways due to the differences in objectives	
What is being checked	Everything that weakens client's financial position	Everything that contradicts the existing legislation or enterprise's accounting policy
Organizational model	Decentralized organizational model	Centralized organizational model
Service fee	Clients pay for the services provided	Upper-level or government organizations bear all the expenses
Outcomes	Audit report	Statement of revision specifying accounting failures and providing recommendations

Source: Terekhov 2003: 126–127

firms, its role in the development of audit reform cannot be understated (Terekhov 2003).

The vast majority of Russian audit firms started out by helping potential businessmen officially register their enterprises under the privatization framework, followed by the provision of audit services to the newly registered companies on the basis of government regulations (Enthoven *et al.* 1998). By 1991 the number of audit firms in Russia had reached eight hundred. As the number of businesses grew, the roles of auditors were becoming more explicit. Also, in 1990 Ernst & Young became the first international audit firm to enter the Russian market, soon followed by other big auditors.

In Russia, especially in the early stages of audit development, the conceptual and technical contextualization of the audit function appeared a challenge, as it took place in a setting lacking a fundamental understanding and knowledge of business, including that of auditing. In consequence, alongside the national accounting system, Russian auditing has remained predominantly tax-oriented, contextualized by companies limiting the role of auditors to tax assistants rectifying accounting errors in order to minimize potential penalties due to the tax authorities. Some managers believed that auditing was only necessary if they needed to replace a chief accountant or dismiss a certain staff member who was suspected of fraud or theft. Additionally, company managers often could not adequately distinguish between audit and revision. Thinking of the audit as if it was some new form of revision with payment by the enterprise, managers perceived auditors as inspectors and often appeared reluctant to let auditors access company documentation (Terekhov 2001). This simplistic understanding of the intrinsic meaning of auditing was also quite common among state servants, many of whom envisaged auditing as merely an additional instrument for restraining and controlling private sector companies.

2.2 The development of the auditing legislative framework[2]

The program of audit reform has been developed in Russia, as in many economies in transition, in the light of the experiences of the world's market economies. Many of the reform agendas, namely the creation of the necessary legal infrastructure, the establishment of the mechanisms for audit regulation, and the adoption of a system of compliance, have been formulated, to a large extent, under the influence of a Western account of audit practice.

It is common in today's Russia for speedy social, economic, and political transformations to race ahead of the related changes in legislation. The development of regulations on auditing has also followed this pattern. A considerable period elapsed between the importance of auditing being acknowledged in practice and the actual steps being taken to introduce a comprehensive system of audit legislation. The work on the legislative framework for auditing commenced when two different drafts of the Law on Auditing were submitted to Parliament – the State Duma – in 1993. The first, "presidential," draft was prepared by government officials and the second, "parliamentary," version was developed with the participation of Russian and foreign audit practitioners. These drafts reflected a conflict between two large professional groupings. One group of practitioners, in order to justify a state-oriented model of regulation, claimed the auditing profession was weak and therefore incapable of regulating itself, whereas another group opposed the idea of strong state involvement in audit regulation. The presidential draft was developed on the basis that the leading role in audit regulation should be given to the government, whereas in the parliamentary draft this role was assigned primarily to the professional auditing organization(s).

After a series of heated debates, subsequently referred to as the "war of the laws" (Sokolov and Terekhov 2004: 259), the second draft passed two readings in Parliament but did not receive approval from the President. As a result, instead of the law, the State Duma adopted the Temporary Rules on Auditing (Vremenniye Pravila) prepared on the basis of the first, presidential, draft of the law. Although the Rules were intended as a temporary solution, in practice it took significantly more time before they were replaced by the Law on Auditing. The work on the new draft of the law resumed in 1995 but progressed slowly. It was only in 1999 that the new text was submitted to the Duma. In April 2000 it was accepted on its first reading. This resulted in active discussion among members of the profession. In order to represent the views of audit professionals, a council of experts was set up consisting of 200 members whose function was to collect and review all comments on and amendments to the text of the draft by the professional auditing organizations, practitioners, and other interested groups. Finally, after having been approved by the President, the Law on Auditing came into force in August 2001.

Several writers (Remizov and Podlesnyh 2001, Terekhov 2003, Dolotenkova 2001) have identified the law as an important breakthrough. The law defines what a financial statement audit is and tackles such issues as auditors' rights and responsibilities, certification and licensing, ethics, professional education, and the regulation of auditing. The law highlights the responsibilities of the government and the professional auditing organizations with respect to the regulation of auditing. The state, particularly the Russian Federation Finance Ministry's Department for the Organization of State Financial Control, Auditing, Accounting, and Reporting, has primary responsibility for audit regulation, including: drafting auditing rules (standards) and other regulations and submitting them to the Russian government for approval; organizing certification, professional training, and audit licensing; supervising the compliance of audit firms and individual auditors with the licensing requirements; enforcing the compliance of audit firms and individual auditors with federal auditing rules (standards); maintaining registers of authorized auditors; and granting accreditation to the professional auditing organizations.

Another pivotal element of audit legislation relates to auditing standards. The work on the development of the standards commenced in 1993, when the research institute of the Ministry of Finance drafted the first group of standards. Later, responsibility for developing the standards was delegated to the Presidential Audit Commission. The Commission prepared thirty-seven standards based on the International Standards on Auditing (ISAs). The main difference between the Russian standards and ISAs was the degree of prescriptiveness. Since auditing remained a novel professional practice for both the public and practitioners themselves, the first Russian standards needed to be more explanatory and often functioned as detailed manuals for practitioners (Terekhov 2001). Such an approach to standard setting soon attracted criticism for being far too intricate and leaving no room for the exercise of professional judgement. This necessitated the development of a new set of standards that better fitted the evolving economic realities.

Drafting of the new standards[3] began in 2001 within the framework of the TACIS (Technical Aid for the Commonwealth of Independent States) project "Audit Reform in Russia". As a Russian coordinator of the project commented:

The project was launched at the time when the Russian government identified audit reform and the adoption of ISAs as its priorities; this was to contribute to the increased credibility of financial statements prepared by Russian companies. Being almost an exact translation of ISAs, the new auditing standards give clearer definitions and are fairly brief.[4]

Over the two years of the project's implementation (2001–3), collaboratively with the Finance Ministry and local practitioners, the first group of new auditing standards (in total 31 standards) was adopted. Work on the next group of new standards is expected to be resumed within the next few years.

During the period 1993–2001, the number of audit firms in Russia tripled, indicating that the audit market was becoming increasingly competitive. A growing proportion of audit firms were also becoming members of the professional auditing organizations (PAOs) that now have branches in almost every large province in the country. There are now nearly 3,000[5] audit firms operating in the Russian audit market, most of which are members of one of the seven[6] professional auditing organizations. Over the years of audit reforms, there has been a continuous evolution of the nature and scope of the actual responsibilities of the professional auditing organizations with respect to professional self-regulation. As stated in the economic literature of the 1990s, the range of roles performed by PAOs remained circumscribed to those of abstract intermediaries between the state and the professionals (Danilevsky 1995). In much later statements made by those involved in the regulation of auditing, one may see a gradual shift in the discretionary tasks of PAOs. Specifically, Krikunov (2003: 23) – a former head of the Department for the Organization of Auditing (a government agency solely in charge of the statutory regulation of auditing which, in 2004, was re-formed into the Department for the Organization of State Financial Control, Auditing, Accounting, and Reporting) – regarded PAOs as "groups of interested professionals":

> Accredited professional auditing organizations, in my opinion, should play the role of *interested groups* whose major role should be in systematizing, balancing, and bringing together the interests of their members in order to further communicate these interests to the federal body responsible for the [state] regulation of auditing [the Finance Ministry's Department for the Organization of State Financial Control, Auditing, Accounting, and Reporting].

There was a considerable time lag between the first professional auditing bodies being established in Russia and their jurisdiction being officially defined by legislators. A comprehensive definition of the term "accredited professional auditing organization"[7] first appeared in the Law on Auditing (adopted in 2001). The law also established the basic requirements as to the responsibilities of the professional structures, the key ones being the introduction of a uniform set of professional standards on the basis of the federal ones and binding quality control procedures. According to the law, the major functions of the professional auditing organizations also include:

- developing training programs and teaching plans for the professional training of audit practitioners;
- conducting audit quality control inspections among members and giving advice and recommendations based on the results of such inspections;
- representing members' interests when dealing with international professional accountancy bodies as well as government agencies, courts, and other institutions;
- publishing educational materials, journals, and periodicals in the field of accounting and auditing.

Furthermore, the law provided for the formation of the Audit Council, a representative body attached to the Ministry of Finance that is to foster collaboration between audit professionals, the government, and the users of financial reports. The law requires that more than half of the Council be composed of members of the professional auditing organizations. The Council has been delegated the following functions:

1 taking part in drafting audit regulations;
2 developing and revising auditing standards;
3 collecting comments and amendments received from professional auditing organizations and submitting them to the Federal Department for the Organization of State Financial Control, Auditing, Accounting and Reporting.

In fact, the Council has become a major channel for the members of the auditing profession to influence and take part in the process of developing auditing legislation and regulatory procedures. One of the latest legislative endeavors of the Council was the adoption, in 2003, of the Ethics Code for Auditors, a recommendatory regulation specifying ethical principles and norms for auditing. The text of the Code is merely a word-for-word translation of the Code of Ethics issued by IFAC. Overall, the introduction of the Ethics Code appears to mark an important stage in the development of auditing, where ethical constructs are acknowledged as being just as vital as technical ones.

3 The present state of audit development

The remainder of this chapter will analyze the present state of auditing in Russia, as well as a number of contextual factors that slow down/impede audit development, will outline the rationale behind the apparent shift toward a greater concern with audit quality and public trust in auditors' work, and will examine some recent regulatory measures intended to enhance trust in auditing that have been adopted by government officials and the professional bodies.

3.1 Russian auditing today: major obstacles to effectiveness

Unraveling the manner in which various regulatory endeavors become realized in practice is impracticable without consideration of the contextual setting in which they occur. This subsection, therefore, presents an overview of a number of factors that have characterized the environment in which audit developments have taken place in Russia.

Limited economic imperatives for a voluntary audit

In accordance with the Anglo-Saxon view of the audit function, auditors should provide both current and potential financiers with independently verified information about the company's performance. The significance of coherent accounting and auditing systems becomes even more apparent in the context of a diversified shareholder structure and widespread ownership (Watts and Zimmerman 1983). In Russia the weakness of the national capital market and the lack of professional investors hinder the extensive use of accounting and auditing information for the purpose of investment decision-making (Sokolov and Terekhov 2004). It may be argued that companies' "pay-offs" from demonstrating the reliability of their financial reporting have been low because of the restricted external fund-raising opportunities available to them through either participating in the capital market or applying for bank loans. When the "pay-offs" from ensuring the quality of their financial reports are limited and the costs of doing so remain high, most companies appear to lack the motivation to commission a voluntary audit. The exception, perhaps, is the large business dependent on foreign capital. While the number of such companies is limited in Russia and the general level of demand for voluntary audits remains low, the vast majority of audits will be undertaken on a mandatory basis (statutory audits)[8] or for tax purposes, where the role of auditing is normally limited to a formal check of accounting records prior to the submission of the company's financial statements to the tax authorities. This is essential in order to understand the role that auditing plays in Russia and the level of importance that society places on the quality of audits.

Absence of an adequate system of auditor liability

One of the principal impediments to Russian audit reforms has been the absence of an adequate system of auditor liability. In Russia, auditor liability is specified in the contract between auditors and their clients. Forms and types of liability are also discussed in the Civil and Criminal Codes and audit-specific regulations. None of these documents refers specifically to auditors' liability to company shareholders (owners), and all leave auditors' responsibilities limited to those stipulated in the agreement between the auditor and a client. Since the client of the auditor is most often the management of the audited entity in Russia, managers are in a better position, compared to other stakeholders, to protect their interests in court in the event of litigation. As a result, cases in which auditors suspected of providing poor quality services become involved in litigation initiated by, for example, a company's shareholders, are quite exceptional.

On the one hand, the fact that an auditor's liability to the owners is not adequately specified by existing legislation is an additional illustration of the current economic realities in Russia, where the capital market is often just a diminutive "consumer" of audit services. On the other hand, the absence of an audit liability system becomes an obstacle hindering the development of the capital market itself. In Russia, in situations where auditor liability is questioned, conflicting parties usually appear doubtful about seeking justice in the courts. This, in turn, deprives interested users of a company's financial reports from exercising their right to sanction an auditor whose proficiency they question and, as a result, reduces the motivation of some auditors to raise the standard of their work.

3.2 A changing emphasis on public trust in audit quality

The previous section portrayed the emergence and subsequent development of regulatory frameworks to enable the jurisdictional capacity of the newly introduced auditing profession. It may be argued that, especially during the years following the inception of auditing, tackling short-term problems regarding the basic functioning of the profession was given priority over the strategic concern with the degree of actual efficiency of the profession's performance, and quality was often neglected in favor of quantity. In other words, the primary goal was to ensure a sufficient inflow of practitioners to support the new profession's development, while the quality aspect of auditors' work was virtually rendered secondary and left to future consideration (Terekhov 2001). It may be further suggested that an adequate concern with quality occurs only with the emergence of interested parties for whom quality is an important issue. Moreover, audit quality may mean different things to different groups of users, and the conception of what audit quality constitutes is highly affected by the perceived roles and objectives of auditing. What an auditor is expected to accomplish has a direct impact on the perceived quality of his/her services. Given the weakness of the Russian capital market and the initial stage of development of the banking system and, at the same time, the tax orientation of Russian accounting, it would not be wrong to suggest that the major user of financial reports verified by an auditor in the early 1990s was the State Tax Agency. This had a direct impact on the nature of public expectations with respect to the contents and scope of auditors' responsibilities. In particular, auditors were expected, normally prior to the submission of the client's financial report to the tax authorities, to detect errors and *at the same time* to provide consulting and technical assistance to the company's management regarding various aspects of the company's internal accounting and reporting systems.

The rationale behind the steadily growing emphasis on public trust in auditing has been twofold. First, public demands for reliable audits have increased as a consequence of the use of audited accounting information becoming more explicit. This has been due to Russian companies' increasing participation in foreign stock exchanges[9] and, in part, to the development of the national capital market. Since the perceived roles of auditing have started gradually to move from a mere precondition for tax inspections towards an instrument for enhancing a company's accountability and transparency for current/potential stakeholders, the value of auditing has begun to be associated with the degree of assurance that an auditor is believed by the public to provide.

> We need to look at the [quality] problem from the user's point of view. A user is interested in having an auditor as a respected professional, with an impeccable reputation, and necessary professional knowledge and skills. Society becomes gradually aware of the fact that auditing is not simply a form of business, not just a type of professional activity; its major role is in protecting the public interest.
>
> (Excerpt from an interview with Leonid Shneidman, Head of the Finance Ministry's Department for the Organization of Financial Control, Auditing, Accounting, and Reporting)[10]

Additionally, the last few years have seen a number of illustrations of the growing demands from interested users as to the reliability of financial reports prepared by companies and verified by auditors. Among recent cases has been that of the world's largest gas producer, Gazprom. In 2001 the company's auditor – PricewaterhouseCoopers – was accused by Gazprom's minority shareholders of approving several deals that allegedly resulted in asset losses worth billions of US dollars. The accusation provoked audit regulators to investigate the ways in which Gazprom and other large companies had been audited. As a result, in February 2002 the Big Five auditors and managers from some of Russia's largest companies gathered to discuss ways to prevent a corporate scandal in Russia.[11] The very fact that a case like this occurred in Russia signals the public's growing awareness of auditors' stewardship on behalf of company stakeholders (as opposed to the management) and an increased emphasis on the users' expectations and perceptions of auditing.

The second rationale underlying the increasing concern with public trust in auditing has been the generally low perceived quality of auditors' work in Russia. In particular, a number of scholars have pointed to auditors' perceived ethical conduct and technical expertise as having been increasingly questioned by the users of accounting reports (see, for example, relevant discussions by Kapustin 2001, Dolotenkova 2001, Sokolov and Terekhov 2004). Kapustin (2001), for instance, provides a multi-layered portrayal of the Russian auditing profession by referring to a group of "image-" or "ethics-conscious" practitioners and their opposites, i.e. those whose primary interest is in retaining a client even though it may entail compromised independence. Many writers recognized that the origin of the problem lay in the low entry barriers to the profession in the early 1990s, when a large number of today's practitioners received their certificates, and, also, the lack of quality control measures that need to be adopted by both the government and professional auditing organizations.

In response to the problem of diminishing trust acknowledged by audit consumers and academics, a set of quality-enhancing measures has been progressively incorporated by audit regulators into their legislative and enforcement endeavors.

3.3 Enhancing trust in auditing: some developments since 2002

Recognizing the need for effective trust-enhancing measures, the government has revisited its enforcement and oversight policies with respect to the quality of the services provided by auditors. In particular, audit legislation adopted by the government is intended to provide for a three-level system of audit quality control comprising the *federal* level – control exercised by government institutions (i.e. the Finance Ministry, the Central Bank, and others); the level of *professional auditing organizations* – control carried out by professional auditing organizations; and the *firm* level – quality control procedures introduced within an audit firm.

In the early 1990s, when auditing was in its initial stages in Russia, the auditor certification system was aimed at attracting as many specialists as possible to the newly established audit market. It didn't take much effort to get a certificate once an applicant met some basic criteria – a university or college degree and a minimum of three years of professional experience, not necessarily as an auditor. As a result, many practitioners with generally low qualifications flooded the market. In some large audit companies, for example, only one in fifteen candidates was able to successfully pass the selection procedure in order to be offered a position (Kapustin 2001: 339). Important changes in the system of certification took place after the adoption in 2002 of a government order reinforcing certification criteria regarding the amount of professional training (not less than 40 hours per year) and education (a university degree became an obligatory requirement). Also, the system of audit firm licensing was tightened in 2003, when the government Decree "On Audit Licensing" was issued. In Russia, both certification and licensing are carried out by a government institution – the Federal Department for the Organization of State Financial Control, Auditing, Accounting, and Reporting. Besides licensing, the department is also empowered to control inspections of the audit firms to which licenses have been granted. Such inspections are aimed at ensuring that the activities of audit firms comply with the respective criteria set by the normative documents, and may be initiated either by the licensing body itself or at the request of the client or public prosecutors.

In addition, the Law on Auditing required that the personnel of the audit firm should include a minimum of five certified auditors, which subsequently resulted in mergers between small companies and the larger ones and the disappearance of individual audit units (those owned and run by one person), which, before the adoption of the law, represented a large segment of the market. The rationale behind this measure was a concern with the ethical conduct of small audit firms, particularly their ability and willingness to resist management pressure, and, more importantly, an aspiration to restrain and limit the numbers of "uncontrollable" small firms. Overall, the enlarged audit firms were intended to force out, completely or substantially, unprofessional auditors.

Despite the large number of professional auditing organizations operating in Russia, their self-regulatory capacity remains limited because of the traditional dominance of the government in matters of regulation, including that of the auditing profession. One of the major areas where the activities of the PAOs vis-à-vis quality control are most noticeable is the peer review program. Based on the experience of their overseas "colleagues," some of the organizations have begun to introduce binding peer review procedures for their members. The Institute of Professional Auditors of Russia (IPAR) was among the first PAOs to introduce a project named "Implementing and Disseminating Quality Control Procedures for Audit Work in the Russian Federation," aimed at creating a system of peer reviews similar to that developed by professional bodies in the West. The peer review program introduced by IPAR generated an incentive for other PAOs to develop similar programs. It may be that peer review practices have become a way for PAOs to claim professional status and a distinguishing feature that helps to contrast their activities with those of other PAOs.

In general, the very fact that peer review programs have been launched indicates the increased emphasis that the profession places on the underlying problem of trust in auditing and a recognition of the need for some regulatory policies to enhance this trust. However, the effect of the measures adopted by some of the professional auditing organizations on the perceived audit quality is sometimes questioned by the public, who argue that some professional organizations are reluctant to set high entrance requirements that may discourage potential members (Terekhov 2003). Besides, auditors themselves often seem to object to the idea of being peer-reviewed by their colleagues/competitors (Dolotenkova 2001).

The third, and final, element of the system of audit quality control established by the government is the firm's internal policies and procedures for monitoring the ways in which an auditor's responsibilities are executed through the different stages of the audit process. Issues of internal quality control are addressed in the new auditing standard No. 7 (Internal Quality Control for the Audit). In particular, the standard (Article 6) develops a set of rules, adherence to which is crucial for the delivery of a quality audit product. Among these rules are the following:

- individual auditors are required to follow major principles of auditor professional behavior (independence, integrity, objectivity, due care, and others);
- individual auditors need to possess a sufficient degree of technical competence to be able to perform their duties;
- members of the audit team for a particular audit engagement need to be carefully selected and the area of their professional expertise should correspond to the specifics of this audit engagement;
- audit team members need to be directed and monitored by their senior colleagues in order to provide a reasonable assurance of a sufficient level of quality of their work;
- if necessary, auditors should consult external specialists regarding an audit engagement to provide a reasonable assurance that their work is of a sufficient quality;
- auditors should consider all circumstances pertinent to a particular client that may give rise to situations where auditor independence or the ability to conduct an audit of sufficient quality may be questioned;
- audit firms should undertake a regular examination of the internal quality control measures adopted by the firm.

The formative influence of the standard consists in the fact that it has obliged audit firms to introduce or revisit internal quality control policies and ensure their proper functioning. Personnel recruitment and training policies, the introduction of quality control committees, and the careful selection of future clients, which were previously implemented by a small number of progressively thinking auditors, were made compulsory elements of audit practice for the remaining majority of audit firms through adopting the standard.

4 Conclusion

This chapter has presented an analysis of the system of auditing in a country outside the European concept of auditing by providing an overview of the major developments in the audit professional field in Russia from its inception (in the late 1980s) to the present. It has been demonstrated that, *de facto*, a primary role in the regulation of auditing has been played by the government and, in particular, the Finance Ministry. In addition to issuing audit legislation, the government has initiated the creation of the necessary structural frameworks to enable the proper implementation and enforcement of audit legislation with the purpose of restraining, framing, and motivating professional behavior.

Regulation, including occupational regulation, may be seen as the web of bounds that society imposes on the choices available to a professional – i.e.

implicit regulation – or the constraining measures developed by various regulatory structures – i.e. *explicit* regulation (Kling 1988). Implicit regulation is usually undertaken by the professional bodies, whereas explicit regulation is often the prerogative of the state. In a situation where societal rules have yet to be consistently formulated and thoroughly understood by all practitioners, explicit instruments are given priority over implicit ones. The chapter has illustrated the disposition of the controlling functions with respect to the regulation of auditing among the government and the professional auditing organizations and documented a visible shift toward the dominant role of the former. Heavy intervention by the government agencies in matters of audit regulation may be seen as an attempt to claim regulatory primacy and, perhaps more vividly, to take control over a body of professionals that has yet to reveal sufficient ability and a readiness to regulate itself. Moreover, it may be argued that the regulatory dominance of the government was presaged by the economic, social, and political imperatives that constituted the contextual setting for audit developments. Indeed, it would be problematic to assume the possibility of the instant emergence of a fully self-regulated profession in a country, such as Russia, that not long ago cast off the Soviet past with its state supremacy and restricted civil powers of individual citizens. A further factor contributing to the relative apathy of the Russian auditing profession has been the novelty of auditing, on the one hand, and the confusing effects of the deep-rooted traditions of Soviet revision, on the other. Meanwhile, one would expect the diminishing trust in the profession's functionality, which may potentially undermine its stature and even its prospects for survival to eventually become a strong incentive for the professional bodies to step up their regulatory processes and claim their exclusive jurisdiction.

Notes

1   The three Decrees are: (1) Decree of the USSR Supreme Soviet No. 6362-XI "*On the formation and activities of joint ventures, international organizations and associations with the participation of Soviet and foreign companies, organizations and state institutions*," (2) Decree of the Council of Ministers of the USSR No. 48 "*On the formation and activities of joint ventures, international associations and organizations of the USSR and other countries which are members of the Council for Mutual Economic Aid*," (3) Decree of the Council of Ministers of the USSR No. 49 "*On the formation and activities of joint ventures with the participation of Soviet organizations and companies from the capitalist and developing countries*," The latter two documents contained identical articles stating that "checks of financial and commercial activities of joint ventures on the correctness of tax calculations are to be carried out by a Soviet self-financing audit organization for pay."
2   See Appendix 1 for a detailed overview of auditing legislation.
3   For a full list of the standards that have already been adopted, see Appendix 2.
4   Excerpt from an internal report of the "Audit Reform in Russia" project. Source: http://www.fbk.ru
5   Excerpt from a report of the Moscow Audit Chamber. Source: http://www.m-auditchamber.ru
6   The seven professional structures are the Audit Chamber of Russia, the Moscow Audit Chamber, the Association of Accountants and Auditors – "Sodruzhestvo"

(Commonwealth), the Institute of Professional Auditors of Russia, the Russian Collegium of Auditors, the National Federation of Consultants, and the Institute of Professional Accountants of Russia.

7 As stated in the law a certified professional auditing organization is "a self-regulated association of auditors, individual auditors, and audit firms that has been established in accordance with the RF legislation for the purpose of fostering favorable conditions for the activities of its members and protecting their interests that operates on a non-commercial basis, establishes internal audit and professional ethical rules (standards) binding upon its members, monitors their activities on a regular basis, and has obtained accreditation from the authorised Federal body [the Finance Ministry's Department for the Organisation of State Financial Control, Auditing, Accounting, and Reporting]."

8 As stated in the audit law: "Statutory audit is annual audit checks of accounting and financial reporting of a company or an individual entrepreneur undertaken on a mandatory basis." According to the law, the following organizations are subject to statutory audits in Russia: open corporations, banks and other lending institutions, insurance companies, stock and commodity exchanges, investment institutions, non-budgetary funds, charity funds and other non-investment funds, state unitary enterprises, and companies with a large total annual turnover.

9 Among the Russian companies that have their shares traded on foreign stock exchanges (including those of New York and London) are such giants as Gazprom (gas producer), Lukoil (a large oil company), and Norilsk Nickel (the country's leading producer of valuable metals).

10 See "Leonid Shneidman: the tougher the admission to the profession, the better the audit quality," GAAP report of 9 Feb. 2005. Source: http://www.gaap.ru

11 See also "Big Five Discuss Auditing Problems," *Moscow Times*, 28 February 2002.

References on p. 242

Appendix 1: A review of the system of audit legislation

Law on Auditing

The law was issued in August 2001. The law

- defines a financial statement audit;
- specifies who may be an auditor and what are an auditor's duties and rights;
- specifies the responsibilities and rights of auditees;
- discusses the legal status and use of the auditing standards;
- defines the audit report;
- specifies the requirement for an auditor to be independent;
- discusses matters of audit quality control and administrative sanctions applied to unprofessional auditors;
- specifies certification and licensing criteria;
- specifies mechanisms of accreditation, responsibilities, and control over the activities of professional auditing organisations, etc.

Auditing standards

A total of 31 standards has already been developed on the basis of ISAs. Russian auditing standards provide guidance on auditors' professional conduct and specify the principles of auditors' work, audit techniques, and methodologies that auditors are required to follow in order to provide services of appropriate quality. See Appendix 2 for an overview of the auditing standards.

Auditor

Ethics code for auditors

(Prepared on the basis of IFAC's Code of Ethics for Professional Auditors; it is a recommendatory regulation)

This provides guidance on auditors' ethical conduct. The Code defines the ethical principles that auditors should adhere to in order to ensure a high quality of audits. Among those principles are independence, integrity, objectivity, professional competence and due care, confidentiality, professional behavior, adherence to technical standards.

Audit-specific and other regulations

- The Civil Code (specifies an auditor's duties and rights which may derive from a contract between auditors and their clients).
- Other laws and regulations requiring a financial statement audit (e.g. Law "On Corporations" specifies that open corporations need to undergo regular audits of financial statements prepared by the management). – Art. 87.
- Decrees and orders issued by various government structures addressing matters of audit regulation (e.g. Government Decree No. 80 of 6 February 2002 "About the Statutory Regulation of Auditing in the Russian Federation," etc.)

Appendix 2: A list of Russian auditing standards and corresponding ISAs

No.	Russian auditing standard	No.	ISAs
1	Objectives and general principles of an audit or financial statements	200	Objectives and general principles governing an audit of financial statements
2	Audit documentation	230	Documentation
3	Audit planning	300	Planning
4	Materiality in auditing	320	Audit materiality
5	Audit evidence	500	Audit evidence
6	The auditor's report on financial statements	700	The auditor's report on financial statements
7	Internal quality control for the audit	220	Quality control for audit work
8	Assessment of the audit risks and internal control maintained by the audited entity	400	Risk assessments and internal control
9	Affiliated bodies	550	Related parties
10	Post balance sheet events	560	Subsequent events
11	Applicability of the going concern assumption by the audited entity	570	Going concern
12	Terms of auditing	210	Terms of audit engagements
13	The auditor's responsibility to consider errors and improper actions in an audit	240	The auditor's responsibility to consider fraud and error in an audit of financial statements
14	Consideration of legal acts in an audit	250	Consideration of laws and regulations in an audit of financial statements
15	Understanding the activities of the audited entity	310	Knowledge of the business
16	Audit sampling	530	Audit sampling and other selective testing procedures
17	Obtaining audit evidence under particular circumstances	501	Audit evidence – additional consideration for specific items

No.	Russian auditing standard	No.	ISAs
18	Obtaining by an auditor of confirming information from external sources	505	External confirmations
19	Peculiarities of the first audit of a particular audited entity	510	Initial engagements – opening balances
20	Analytical procedures	520	Analytical procedures
21	Peculiarities of the audit of accounting estimates	540	Audit of accounting estimates
22	Communication of the information received as a result of the audit to management and owners of the audited entity	260	Communications of audit matters with those charged with governance
23	Official representations and clarifications of the audited entity management	580	Management representation
24	Major principles of the federal auditing standards related to the services provided by audit firms and individual auditors	120	Framework of international standards on auditing
25	Audit of financial statements prepared by a specialised entity	402	Audit considerations relating to entities using services organizations
26	Comparative information in financial statements	710	Comparatives
27	Other information in documents containing audited financial statements	720	Other information in documents containing audited financial statements
28	Using the work of another auditor	600	Using the work of another auditor
29	Considering the work of internal auditing	610	Considering the work of internal auditing
30	Performing agreed-upon procedures regarding financial information	920	Engagements on agreed-upon procedures regarding financial information
31	Engagements to compile financial information	930	Engagements to compile financial information

References

Danilevsky, Y.A. (1987) "Finansoviy Kontrol i Ekonomika," *Bukhgalterskiy Uchet*, 51(11): 10–15.

Danilevsky, Y.A. (1991) "Finansoviy Kontrol i Audit – Problemy Stanovleniya," *Bukhgalterskiy Uchet*, 55(3): 3–9.

Danilevsky, Y.A. (1995) "Stanovleniye Audita v Rossii," *Bukhgaltersky Uchet*, Part 1, 58(5): 39–42 and Part 2, 58(6): 54–9.

Danilevsky, Y.A., Ostrovsky, O.M., and Guttseit, E.M. (2001) "Russian Audit Standards: Past, Present and Future," *ICAR International Center for Accounting Reform (Russia) Report*, 4(1): 11–13.

Dolotenkova, D. (2001) "Professional Audit Market Development Following the Adoption of the Federal Audit Law," *ICAR Newsletter*.

Enthoven, J.H., Sokolov, Y.V., and Bychkova, S.M. (1998) *Accounting, Auditing and Taxation in the Russian Federation*, Dallas: University of Texas Press.

Enthoven, J.H., Sokolov, Y.V., Kovalev, V.V., Bychkova, S.M., Smirnova, I.M., and Semenova, M.V. (2001) *Accounting, Auditing and Taxation in the Russian Federation: An Update*, Dallas: University of Texas Press.

Guttseit, E.M. (2003) *Audit: Contseptsiya, Problemy, Effectivnost', Standarty*, Moscow: Uniti Elit-2000.

Kapustin, A.A. (2001) "Zreliy Audit Protiv Chernogo," *Russkaya Gazeta*, No. 50: 339.

Kling, R.W. (1988) "Building an Institutional Theory of Regulation," *Journal of Economic Issues*, 22(1): 197–209.

Krikunov, A. (2003) *Auditorskaya Deyatel'nost: Attestatsiya, Litsenzirovaniye, Otchetnost' i Kontrol Kachestva*, Moscow: Finansovaya Gazeta.

Law on Auditing of the Russian Federation No. 119-FZ of 7 August 2001.

Podolsky, V.I., Savin, A.A., Sotnikova, L.V., Savin, I.A., Makarova, N.S., and Scherbakova, N.S. (2003) *Audit: Uchebnoye Posobiye*, 3rd edition, Moscow: Uniti-Dana.

Remizov, N.A. (2001a) "Federal Auditing Law: Comments," *ICAR newsletter*.

Remizov, N.A. (2001b) "International Accounting Standards and International Standards on Auditing," TACIS project materials, Moscow (see http://auditreform.ru/materials-e07.html)

Remizov, N.A. (2001c) "About Implementation of ISAs in Russia," *ICAR Newsletter*.

Remizov, N.A. and Podlesnyh, V.O. (2001) *Rossiyskiye Standarty Audita: Istoriya Sozdaniya i Neobhodimost*, Moscow: FBK Press.

Sokolov, Y. and Terekhov, A. (2004) *Ocherki Razvitiya Audita*, Moscow: FBK-Press.

Terekhov, A.A. (2001) *Audit: Perspectivy Razvitiya*, Moscow: Finansy i Statistika.

Terekhov, A.A. (2003) *Audit: Zakonodatel'niye Resheniya*, Moscow: Finansy i Statistika.

Watts, R.L. and Zimmerman, J. (1983) "Agency Problems, Auditing, and the Theory of the Firm: Some Evidence," *Journal of Law and Economics*, 26: 613–33.

12 Auditing in the United States

From *laissez faire* to government control in 70 years

Jere R. Francis

1 Introduction

As recently as the 1930s auditing was a *laissez faire* practice in the United States. Today US auditors are arguably the most regulated in the world due to the passage of the Sarbanes-Oxley Act of 2002 (Pubic Law No. 107-204) and the creation of the Public Company Accounting Oversight Board (PCAOB). With this legislation, the United States went from self-regulation by the accounting profession, with government oversight by the Securities and Exchange Commission (SEC), to direct government control via the PCAOB, which has statutory authority to set auditing and ethics standards, and to verify compliance with these standards through the inspection of accounting firms. While the profession retains authority over the national examination to license certified public accountants, virtually every other significant aspect of auditing is now controlled by the PCAOB, at least with respect to publicly listed companies and SEC registrants.[1]

This chapter examines how auditing is currently regulated in the United States and reviews the transformation from *laissez faire* to government control over the past 70 years.[2] A current snapshot of the US audit market is presented in Table 12.1 which summarizes market share data for the 100 largest accounting firms. The US audit market is dominated by the Big Four accounting firms to a greater extent than occurs in many other developed countries. The Big Four firms earn 75 percent of the total fees of the 100 largest accounting firms and audit 84 percent of SEC registrants. The Big Four along with three other large firms with national networks (Grant Thornton, RSM McGladrey, and BDO Seidman) collectively audit 89 percent of SEC registrants and earn 81 percent of the total fees of the 100 largest firms. The remaining 93 accounting firms have small networks and are regional in scope, with aggregate fees of less than $400 million for the next 24 firms, and less than $50 million for the smallest 69 firms in Table 12.1.

Global fees are also reported in Table 12.1 for each of the Big Four firms in 2004 and 2005 as disclosed on their websites. Global Big Four fees were $61.9 billion in 2004 and $71.0 billion in 2005, and the US practices represented 35 percent of global fees in 2005. As recently as the 1980s, US fees represented

Table 12.1 Survey of the 100 largest US public accounting firms

Firm	2004 US fees ($million)	Number of SEC clients	Global fees $bn 2004 (2005)
Deloitte	6,876	3,597	16.4 (18.2)
Ernst & Young	5,511	2,856	14.5 (16.9)
PricewaterhouseCoopers	5,180	3,303	17.6 (20.3)
KPMG	3,808	1,893	13.4 (15.6)
Big Four subtotal	21,375 (75%)	11,649 (84%)	61.9 (71.0)
Grant Thornton	718	367	
RSM McGladrey	661	106	
BDO Seidman	444	358	
Big Seven subtotal	23,194 (81%)	12,210 (89%)	
Next largest 24 firms	3,239	725	
Smallest 69 firms	2,052	855	
Total	28,485 (100%)	13,790 (100%)	

Source: *Public Accounting Report* (2005). Note that the fiscal year-end is 2004 for most firms surveyed, including the Big Four firms. Revenues for the next 24 firms (after the seven largest firms) range from $52 million to $373 million, and revenues for the smallest 69 firms range from $20 million to $49.9 million.

well over 50 percent of global Big Four fees. There are two reasons why the US percentage has declined. First, the spin-off of US consulting operations by all of the large firms (except Deloitte), combined with new restrictions on the scope of consulting services, has significantly reduced US fees from non-audit sources. Second, there has been strong growth internationally in Big Four fees due to the globalization of business operations and the development of capital markets around the world. Thus while the US is still a major source of revenues, the Big Four accounting firms have become truly international businesses.

2 Regulation in the United States

Regulation in the United States occurs at each of three distinct levels of government: the national or federal level, the state level via each of the 50 individual states, and the local level through hundreds of thousands of local government entities within each state, such as cities and counties. The most important distinction for the purpose of accounting regulation revolves around the respective roles of federal and state jurisdictions. The US constitution limits the authority of the federal government and throughout US history there has been tension between the rights of individual states and the authority of the federal government. For example, scholars have argued that the civil war (1861–5), while ostensibly fought over the issue of slavery, was also a political struggle over "states' rights" and who had the ultimate authority to decide the slavery question, each of the individual states or the federal government for the nation as a whole.

The state–federal tension has also affected the way that accounting has evolved in the United States. The earliest professional accounting societies were organized in New York state, where the first certified public accountant (CPA) license was issued in 1896. The modern era of national-level accounting societies began in 1916, when the American Institute of Accountants was formed, and 1921, when the rival American Society of Certified Public Accountants was founded. These two bodies merged in 1936 to become the modern day American Institute of Certified Public Accountants (Carey 1969).

Despite the presence and importance of national-level accounting societies, it is the individual states that have the legal authority to license professional occupations such as accounting, law, and medicine. In other words, there is no national-level licensing in the United States. As noted above, the first CPA was licensed by the state of New York in 1896, and similar licensing laws were quickly adopted by other states. Today each of the 50 states has its own "board of accountancy" that issues licenses and renews the licenses of residents in each state who wish to practice as a CPA. If a person is licensed in one state and moves to another state, it is necessary to apply for reciprocity in order to gain recognition of professional credentials and to practice as a CPA in the person's new home state.[3] Each state's board of accountancy also has an ethics committee which investigates allegations that auditors may have performed incompetently or violated the state's ethics rules which are part of the state's legal code. These committees have the ultimate authority to revoke licenses or to punish licensees in other ways, such as requiring continuing education to remediate competency deficiencies. There has been some harmonization among the states in recent years through the work of the National Association of State Boards of Accountancy and its advocacy of national standardization through the Uniform Accountancy Act and Rules.

There is one aspect of the licensing process that is standardized across the states and is conducted at the national level, and that is the uniform licensing examination, which is prepared and graded nationally by the national-level professional accounting body, the American Institute of Certified Public Accountants (AICPA). However, the exam itself is still administered by each state board of accountancy to ensure those taking the exam are eligible to do so in accordance with the specific education requirements of each state's rules.[4]

Given that accountants are licensed and directly regulated by the laws of individual states, what is the role of the national accounting body, the AICPA, beyond preparing and grading the uniform CPA examination? It may not be very well known outside the United States, but accountants are not required to be members of the AICPA in order to practice as a CPA. The reason is that CPA licenses are administered by state boards of accountancy. So membership of the AICPA is entirely voluntary. Historically, the AICPA has functioned as a professional association and lobbying body on behalf of individual CPAs and accounting firms. Despite the fact that membership is voluntary, the AICPA has been historically an important and powerful organization. In addition to speaking for the accounting profession on matters of public policy, it has developed auditing standards and the code of professional conduct, both of which were subsequently adopted by individual states and incorporated into state legal codes for the purpose of state-level CPA licensure and licensing renewals. In the United States, the term "generally accepted auditing standards" is understood to refer to the body of standards promulgated by the AICPA. So, even though membership is strictly voluntary, the AICPA was clearly the most influential accounting organization in the US until the passage of Sarbanes-Oxley.

The regulation of accountants in the US has historically focused primarily on individuals rather than accounting firms, probably due to the fact that it is individuals who are licensed as CPAs. As noted above, the AICPA has a code of conduct and one can be removed from the AICPA for violating these rules, although this has no direct consequence on licensing since the power to revoke a license is controlled by state boards of accountancy. However, it turns out that most states have copied the AICPA code of conduct in drawing up their own ethics rules and so a violation of the AICPA code of conduct is also likely to result in the violation of each state's code of conduct as well. As a practical matter, the AICPA and state boards of accountancy cooperate and share information when an individual is investigated for the alleged violation of auditing or ethics standards.

State licensing laws permit accounting firms to hold themselves out as CPAs when organized as partnerships, and states also regulate the circumstances under which this can occur. That is, there are additional licensing requirements with respect to accounting firms. The most important of these requirements is the stipulation of how many partners in the partnership must be CPAs. At one time the requirement was that all partners of an accounting firm must be CPAs. This has changed over the past thirty years with the growth of non-audit consulting services, and most states now require that only a majority of a firm's partners be licensed CPAs.

The Securities and Exchange Commission also requires the national registration of accounting firms that audit SEC registrants, and the main requirement is that a firm be in good standing with the state board of accountancy where the partnership is registered. Accounting firms *per se* were not subject to more explicit regulations until 1977, when the AICPA created the SEC Practice Division and the Private Company Practice Division. Firms belonging to these two practice divisions were required to meet a number of quality control standards, including peer reviews and continuing education for employees. The impetus for this new self-regulation was the result of a Congressional inquiry into the accounting profession in the mid-1970s following a series of publicized accounting scandals (United States Senate 1976). The profession was on the defensive and created the Commission on Auditors' Responsibilities in 1974 in order to deter the threat of more direct regulation by the government. The final report issued in 1978 was critical of the profession and proposed a number of changes that were quickly adopted by the AICPA, including the creation of the division of firms and new standards on quality control for accounting firms. Of course since membership in the AICPA is voluntary, it was not necessary for accounting firms to be members of these practice divisions, and many firms, especially smaller firms, declined to participate. The larger accounting firms with national practices voluntarily joined the new practice divisions. This arrangement changed in 1987 when all accounting firms that were members of the AICPA were required to be members of the AICPA's practice divisions and to comply with quality control and other standards (AICPA 1987). Some smaller firms elected to withdraw from the AICPA rather than comply with these new member rules. Around this time the SEC also considered imposing its own quality control requirements, including an SEC-administered peer review program, but in the end self-regulation by the profession was sufficient to stave off direct regulation. However, the SEC added an additional requirement that auditors of SEC registrants must have peer reviews, and thus it became a *de facto* requirement that all auditors registered with the SEC must also belong to the AICPA's SEC Practice Division.

Where exactly does the SEC fit into the US regulatory landscape in terms of the state–federal jurisdiction tensions? One important clause of the United States constitution gives the federal government the authority to regulate "interstate" commerce, and this was the legal basis for the enactment by Congress of the Securities Act of 1933, which regulates public offerings of securities on an interstate basis, and the Securities and Exchange Act of 1934, which created the Securities and Exchange Commission to administer the newly created federal securities laws. The 1934 act also required annual financial reporting and independent audits for entities that are required to register with the SEC. An interesting aside is that the audit requirement was an afterthought in the legislative process and was inserted in the final legislation as a consequence of successful lobbying by the accounting profession.

Through the 1933 and 1934 acts, Congress gave the SEC the direct authority to set both accounting and auditing standards, and to define who is an independent auditor and therefore who is eligible to conduct audits of SEC registrants. In addition, the SEC has the legal authority to punish auditors who are involved in misreporting or who violate other SEC rules such as auditor independence requirements. The SEC generally punishes individual auditors through monetary fines or disqualification from auditing SEC registrants, but occasionally it turns over cases to the Justice Department for the criminal prosecution of the violation of federal securities laws. The SEC has also from time to time punished an entire accounting firm with a fine or prohibition on accepting new clients, and in a few extreme cases has disqualified an entire firm from auditing SEC registrants. The SEC approach has been to police the conduct of SEC registrants, and selectively to pursue individual cases in order to send a general message to the constituency of the kind of behavior that is deemed unacceptable. Generally this takes the form of an administrative action and consent decree in which the SEC issues an Accounting and Auditing Enforcement Release (AAER) that details alleged deficiencies in financial statements or the conduct of auditors (Wilson and Grimlund 1990, Feroz *et al*. 1991, Dechow *et al*. 1996). The company and/or auditor named in the action does not admit to guilt but agrees to refrain in the future from the kind of misconduct described in the AAER. There may also be monetary fines and other restrictions placed on auditors including, in the extreme, deregistration from practicing before the SEC. Recent AAERs issued by the Securities and Exchange Commission are available on the SEC's website at http://www.sec.gov/divisions/enforce/friactions.shtml.

To sum up, auditors are licensed and regulated by state boards of accountancy in the specific states where auditors reside and work, and auditors must meet state-specific requirements (including compliance with state ethics rules) to maintain and renew their licenses. The AICPA is a national-level professional body but membership is voluntary and therefore one need not belong in order to be a CPA. This effectively changed in the late 1980s, at least for auditors of public companies, when the SEC mandated peer reviews which *de facto* required accounting firms that audit SEC registrants to belong to the AICPA SEC Practice Division and to comply with AICPA quality control standards. At the federal level, the SEC through the 1934 act has the authority to define who is eligible to audit SEC registrants, and to punish an individual auditor or an entire accounting firm if an individual auditor and/or firm violates SEC rules. However, the scope of the SEC's authority is limited to public companies and their auditors. Thus private entities in the US are not subject to federal-level regulation by the Securities and Exchange Commission.[5]

3 From *laissez faire* to government control

Three periods are relevant to understanding the transformation of auditing in the United States: the period immediately prior to the 1933 Securities Act, the period from 1933 to 2002, and the post-2002 period. The pre-1933 period was a period of *corporate opacity*, in which accounting was a *laissez faire* practice with little regulation of either financial reporting or auditing. As Carey (1969) notes, the first formal accounting standards in the US were not adopted until 1917 when, at the urging of the Federal Trade Commission, the American Institute of Accountants (now the American Institute of Certified Public Accountants) issued the first authoritative accounting pronouncement with the curious title of "Balance-sheet Audits." An updated version was issued in 1929 under the title "Verification of Balance-Sheet Audits." Despite the existence of nominal financial reporting standards, corporations at this time were not required to submit annual reports to anyone (not even stockholders) and nor was there a requirement to have an independent audit, although by 1926 most companies listed on the New York Stock Exchange were voluntarily having audits (Chow 1982).

After the stock market crash of 1929, there were widespread calls for the reform of many Wall Street business practices blamed for the speculative bubble and crash of the stock market. Among the many reforms enacted in the first 100 days following the inauguration of Franklin D. Roosevelt as President of the United States was legislation to regulate the issuance of public securities. With the passage of the Securities Act of 1933 and the Securities Exchange Act of 1934, the age of opacity gave way to what could be termed the age of *corporate transparency*, in which accounting practices (including audits) were now subject to federal government oversight, at least for public companies. The securities legislation of 1933 and 1934 required annual audits and more transparent financial reporting, and empowered the SEC to prescribe both accounting and auditing standards as well as to determine who was eligible to conduct independent audits of SEC registrants. From its very beginnings, the SEC viewed disclosure and transparency as the best means of regulating financial markets (Merino and Neimark 1982, Seligman 1985). To achieve this goal, the SEC informally allowed the accounting profession to set accounting and auditing standards, and also endorsed the accounting profession's monopoly right to audit public companies. For nearly 70 years, until 2002, the SEC fulfilled its statutory mandate by exercising oversight of the accounting profession's activities rather than pursuing a more direct approach to regulatory standard setting and enforcement.

This is not to say it was an easy relationship between the SEC and the accounting profession, or without complications and periodic crises. For example, over this 70-year period accounting standard setting evolved from a part-time committee within the AICPA to a full-time and financially independent standard setting board, the Financial Accounting Standards Board. On the auditing side, the *laissez faire* approach of no standards gradually gave way to self-regulation through standards developed by the accounting profession, usually at the nudging of the SEC or in response to public crises of confidence. For example, the very first US auditing standards were not issued until 1939 in response to an accounting scandal in the mid-1930s involving the drug company McKesson & Robbins (Carey 1970). A key aspect of the scandal involved non-existent inventory, and the newly drafted auditing standards required auditors physically to observe inventories as well as to confirm the balances of accounts receivable with customers. The auditing standard setting process evolved over the years, and another crisis of confidence in the 1970s led to the creation of the Auditing Standards Board in 1978 as an autonomous senior technical committee of the AICPA with the authority to make public statements without prior clearance from the AICPA Council of Board of Directors. As mentioned earlier, this period also saw the creation of the AICPA practice divisions as a way of improving the quality control of accounting firms. Among other things, accounting firms belonging to the practice divisions were required to have continuing education for their members, a peer review of the firm every three years, and for members of the SEC Practice Division a concurring partner review on engagements and the mandatory rotation of the engagement partner every seven years. Importantly, a new quasi-independent body within the AIPCA, the Public Oversight Board, was created to oversee the new practice divisions and to administer quality control assessments, punishments, and remedies when firms did not meet required standards.

The era of professional self-regulation came to an end in 2002 with the passage of Sarbanes-Oxley (SOX) and the creation of the PCAOB. The PCAOB is empowered by the United States Congress to set auditing standards and ethics rules, to register accounting firms and determine their eligibility to audit SEC registrants, and to inspect accounting firms in order to assess compliance with standards and rules set by the PCAOB. Other provisions that directly affect auditors include new responsibilities to attest to management reports on internal controls under section 404 of SOX, increased auditor rotation through a new requirement to rotate both the lead audit partner and review partner every five years (the former requirement in AICPA rules was seven-year rotation only for the engagement partner), and restrictions on the so-called revolving door policy by prohibiting auditors from auditing a public company if one of that company's top officials, such as the CEO, CFO, or Controller, was employed by the auditor and worked on the company's audit during the previous year.

With the passage of SOX and the creation of the PCAOB, the era has ended in which the accounting profession, primarily the AICPA, controlled auditing practices through a process of professional self-regulation with oversight by the SEC.[6] The AICPA still exists but it is no longer the important or influential organization it once was. The Private Company Practice Division still exists, and the AICPA still provides guidance and sets standards for private sector entities that are not explicitly regulated by the PCAOB. However, in a pragmatic move, the AICPA decided to allow its members to voluntarily elect to audit non-SEC registrants in accordance with either PCAOB standards or AICPA standards. It is difficult to imagine how this two-tier regulatory system can coexist in which one set of standards exists for public companies and another set exists for private companies.[7] With these developments SOX has effectively ended the accounting profession's private sector leadership of accounting in the United States.

4 Auditor independence standards

The development of auditor independence standards parallels the three periods just discussed. Prior to the federal securities acts there was no official requirement in the professional literature with respect to auditor independence. Zeff (2003a) notes that the first ethics standards were adopted by the American Institute of Accountants in 1922, but they were concerned with limiting "self-promotion" and banned advertising and client solicitation, and contained no mention of auditor independence. A few years later, in 1931, the Institute actually upheld the legitimacy of auditors performing dual roles as auditor and as a member of the client's board of directors, a common practice at that time (Berryman 1978).

Following the adoption of the Securities Act of 1933 and the Securities and Exchange Act of 1934, the SEC established auditor independence rules which banned auditors from serving on a client's board of directors and restricted direct financial interests in clients. With these new independence requirements, the presumption was that an auditor was "factually" independent of a client, and the professional standards subsequently focused on appearance-related issues and developed into what has become an elaborate set of rules prohibiting actions or relations with clients that might create the appearance of impropriety. Still, the profession's rules have often lagged behind SEC requirements. For example, Berryman (1978) notes that it was not until the 1962 revision of the profession's code of conduct that the profession banned the most obvious financial relationships with clients which were likely to raise doubts about the independence of auditors and which had been prohibited by the SEC since the 1930s.

In 1994 the SEC questioned whether auditors were being truly independent in standing up to their clients in matters of accounting policy choices (Zeff 2003b). In response to the SEC's criticism, the Public Oversight Board (of the AICPA) appointed an Advisory Panel on Auditor Independence (1994) whose report was highly critical of the accounting profession and its advocacy of client interests, as well as the growing scope of non-audit consulting work, all of which echoed an earlier report by the Public Oversight Board (1993). Eventually these controversies led the AICPA and the SEC in 1998 to jointly create the Independence Standards Board as a new autonomous body to set auditor independence rules. Despite this development the AICPA (1997) had already begun to undermine the new board by advocating a *laissez faire* market approach in which consulting was viewed as doing no harm and in which auditors and their clients were deemed to be in the best position to determine the appropriate scope of the services provided by the auditor. It is easy to see why the SEC was disappointed with the accounting profession and began to push its own agenda to more radically limit the scope of the consulting services that auditors can provide (SEC 2000). The new board was short-lived and was terminated in 2001. Today independence standards are the province of the PCAOB for work involving public companies, and the AICPA has resumed responsibility for independence rules involving audits of non-public companies.

5 How did Sarbanes-Oxley happen?

The political dynamics that led to Sarbanes-Oxley have been well documented (Zeff 2003b, DeFond and Francis 2005, Romano 2005). SOX was passed by Congress in the summer of 2002 in an environment where the stock market was plunging and nearly every day seemed to bring the announcement of another accounting scandal. These events came to a head with revelations first about

Enron and then Worldcom, just a few months prior to mid-term Congressional elections, giving politicians an added incentive to act quickly. In many respects what ensued could be described as "the perfect storm," in which a unique set of accounting circumstances combined with a volatile political situation to create the speedy passage of SOX.

Enron's rapid collapse and bankruptcy in December 2001 was followed by the accounting scandals at Worldcom in June 2002, both of which were Arthur Andersen clients. Another critical event occurred when Deloitte & Touche issued a "clean" peer review report on Arthur Andersen in December 2001, just weeks before Andersen publicly announced its employees had shredded some documents related to the Enron audit. The credibility of the accounting profession was immediately in jeopardy, along with the integrity of the profession's self-regulation program. In short the image of the accounting profession had itself been shredded by January 2002. One must also remember that the profession had lobbied aggressively against the SEC initiative in 2000 to ban most non-audit services. So, even though Arthur Andersen appeared to be the main villain in the Enron and Worldcom scandals, the SEC under Arthur Levitt's chairmanship had been more or less at war with the Big Five accounting firms throughout the 1990s (Levitt 2002).

Given the history of acrimony between the profession and the SEC, it came as little surprise that the profession was punished following Enron's failure and Worldcom's accounting scandal. SOX was drafted with significant input from SEC personnel and it must be presumed that much of the legislation's harshness toward the auditing profession, including the removal of professional self-regulation, was payback for the profession's earlier and highly successful lobbying campaigns against the SEC. Ironically, the accounting profession's success in 2000 in defeating the SEC's proposal to curtail non-audit services probably sowed the seeds for the subsequent retribution it received in 2002.

6 The PCAOB

The PCAOB is structured as a private non-profit corporation with federal statutory authority under Sarbanes-Oxley to regulate auditing practices for SEC registrants. It is not technically part of the federal government, and the PCOAB is self-financing. Fees are set to cover budgeted operating costs ($130.9 million in 2006) and are shared between accounting firms and SEC registrants, all of whom are required to register with the PCAOB or face deregistration by the SEC. This unusual organizational structure was adopted to allow it to operate outside the government's civil service rules and pay-scale limits and to create a more "corporate" type of entity with the ability to pay competitive salaries relative to the private sector. However, the Securities and Exchange Commission retains official oversight over the PCAOB and appoints all of its board members. Regardless of its legal form, the PCAOB is effectively an arm of the federal government, and control of auditing now resides with a *de facto* government agency.

The PCAOB website lists in detail its activities, rules, and current regulatory initiatives (http://www.pcaobus.org). The mission of the PCAOB is "to oversee the auditors of public companies in order to protect the interests of investors and further the public interest in the preparation of informative, fair and independent audit reports." To this end Congress, in enacting Sarbanes-Oxley, specifically empowered the PCAOB to undertake four activities:

1 register public accounting firms that audit public companies;
2 establish standards with respect to auditing, quality control, ethics, independence, and other standards relating to the preparation of audit reports for public companies;
3 conduct inspections of accounting firms to determine compliance with PCAOB standards; and
4 investigate and discipline registered accounting firms and persons associated with those firms.

It is clear from the above list that the regulation of both auditing and auditors, as well as the broader governance process, are now controlled by the PCAOB, superseding all aspects of the profession's self-regulation program, at least with respect to public companies. As a practical measure, on 16 April 2003, the PCAOB adopted pre-existing standards of the AICPA as its interim standards to be used on an initial transitional basis. These include auditing and attestation standards, quality control standards, ethics standards, and independence rules. As of early 2006 the PCAOB has issued new auditing standards and ethics rules, and de-registered accounting firms. In 2003 the first accounting firm inspections were undertaken with a limited review of the Big Four accounting firms. These inspections were critical of all four accounting firms for their failure to apply certain technical requirements correctly with respect to accounting standards. All of the Big Four firms received their first full-scale inspections in 2005 and edited versions of these reports are available on the PCAOB website.

One of the early controversies at the PCAOB, which is still unresolved, is its proposal to register "foreign" accounting firms that audit non-US companies that cross-list in the US and which are thus subject to SEC rules. The reason this is controversial is that the PCAOB is an American regulatory agency that claims to have jurisdiction over virtually any accounting firm in the world if that firm audits an SEC registrant. At issue are fundamental questions of national sovereignty and whether a US agency like the PCAOB can supersede the governance structures that exist in other countries and regulate the accounting profession in these countries.[8] Formal objections to the global reach of the PCAOB have been lodged by professional accounting bodies around the world, including the European Federation of Accountants (Fédération des Experts Comptables Européens, known as FEE).[9] As of March 2005 foreign accounting firms that audit SEC registrants were required to register with the PCAOB. However, the more controversial issue of inspections and compliance with PCAOB rules and regulations has not yet been resolved.

7 Legal liability

The auditor's legal liability in the United States is also affected by state and federal jurisdictions. The US has a common law legal system derived from the British legal tradition rather than the more explicitly codified civil law systems that are typical in European countries. An auditor is directly liable to clients for breach of contract, and contract law is part of common law legal tradition and is adjudicated in state-level courts. Breach of contract would include the explicit failure to meet contractual terms of the audit such as the failure to complete an audit in a timely manner. It would also include the failure to perform the audit in a competent manner in accordance with generally accepted auditing standards. Since auditors are hired by clients, it is the client who is in privity of contract and who has the legal standing to sue the auditor for breach of contract.

For much of the twentieth century the question that has vexed the courts and the accounting profession is whether auditors have a broader duty of care to third-party users of audited financial statements, beyond the narrow duty of care to clients under contract law. The relevant domain here is tort law, which is another aspect of common law that is adjudicated by state-level courts. The landmark US case is the 1931 *Ultramares v. Touche* decision which disallowed third-party liability due to the lack of contract privity. However, in a retrial of the *Ultramares* case, the court pointed out that there would be third-party legal liability if the auditor were fraudulent or grossly negligent, and most state jurisdictions have since followed this precedent. If an auditor commited a fraud or was grossly negligent, then under tort law any third parties who can prove they were damaged by reliance on the auditor's misconduct would have a basis for civil litigation against the auditor for monetary damages.

Since auditors have rarely been found to have commited fraud, or even gross negligence, the more interesting legal question has focused instead on whether an auditor also has a third-party liability for the lesser tort of negligence, which is much easier for a plaintiff to prove. The latter half of the twentieth century saw an ebb and flow in the scope of auditor liability to third parties for negligence. Initially there was expansion of liability to "specifically foreseen" users that an auditor knew would rely on his or her work (such as a client's bank). Later the auditor's third-party liability expanded to an ever broader class of "foreseeable" users of audited financial statements. Of course since these cases were adjudicated in state courts, there were conflicting decisions, and individual courts in different states could choose different legal precedents on which to base their decisions. Since large publicly listed companies (and their auditors) operate nationally, it became a strategic decision by plaintiffs' attorneys with respect to where lawsuits were filed since some state courts embraced an expansive view of auditor liability, while others followed a narrower view.

Liability for the tort of negligence was standardized to some extent after the 1977 Second Restatement of Torts was enacted in state legal codes by most states. Under this reform, the auditor faces third-party liability for negligence to foreseen users that are a reasonably defined and limited group, even though such users might not have been specifically known to auditors. However, a few state courts still follow the more expansive "foreseeable" user doctrine, which effectively opens the door to any potential user of financial statements. At the same time, there have also been some recent cases that have reaffirmed the narrower Ultramares doctrine or limited the auditor's duty of care only to specifically foreseen users of their work.

Auditors also have a duty of care to third parties under federal securities law and such cases are tried in US federal courts. The Securities Act of 1933 regulates the public issuance of securities and imposes third-party liability for auditor negligence. In an unusual aspect of American law, the burden of proof is placed on the defendant (auditor) to prove his or her innocence rather than on the plaintiff, who need only claim to have relied on audited information that was misleading. It turns out that very few cases have been tried under the 1933 act, perhaps due in part to a three-year statute of limitations on the information contained in a prospectus. However, one very important exception is the *McKesson and Robbins* case. The circumstances surrounding the case were well known by the late 1930s, and it led the SEC to conclude in 1939 that the audit practices of the day were deficient and unacceptable. As a result of direct SEC pressure, there was near-immediate development of auditing standards by the AICPA, including requirements to observe inventory and confirm accounts receivable balances.[10]

Auditors also have a liability under rule 10b-5 of section 10 of the Securities and Exchange Act of 1934, whereby it is unlawful to defraud, to make an untrue statement of material fact, or to omit to state a necessary material fact in SEC filings, which include audited financial statements. Relatively little legal action took place under rule 10b-5 in federal courts compared to common law tort actions in state courts. However, in a landmark 1976 Supreme Court case, *Hochfelder v. Ernst & Ernst*, rule 10b-5 was interpreted to require intent to deceive on the auditor's part (termed scienter). Although the court left open the possibility that "reckless behavior" may suffice for third-party liability, the *Hochfelder* case has largely closed the door on 10b-5 litigation under federal securities law.

Even though auditors were rarely sued under federal laws, litigation relief was provided to auditors through the Private Securities Litigation Reform Act of 1995. After significant litigation in the savings and loan and banking industries in the late 1980s and early 1990s, mainly for the tort of negligence, the large international accounting firms lobbied aggressively for broad-based litigation relief in the United States and elsewhere (Andersen *et al.* 1992, International

Federation of Accountants 1995). The lobbying payoff came when the conservative Republican Party gained control of Congress in 1994 and passed litigation relief for auditors under federal securities law by requiring "proportionate liability" whereby auditors would only be liable for their proportionate share of the blame. The extent of legal liability exposure does affect an auditor's incentive, and there is evidence that auditors became less strict after the law was passed and may have turned a blind eye to more aggressive accounting by clients and issued fewer going concern audit reports after 1995 (Francis and Krishnan 2002, Lee and Mande 2003).

In addition to civil liability for monetary damages under both common law and federal securities law, auditors are also subject to prosecution under criminal law for violation of federal securities law. There have been relatively few criminal cases, but occasionally auditors are prosecuted and go to jail for fraudulent misconduct. Sarbanes-Oxley also contains criminal misconduct provisions, although it does not appear these provisions impose any new criminal liabilities for auditors (Romano 2005). However, since auditing standards, ethics, quality control, and independence standards established by the PCOB are now federal law, an auditor's failure to comply with these rules constitutes a violation of federal law. Thus it is possible that ordinary negligence now has the potential to result in both criminal charges and expanded civil litigation against auditors by any third-party user of audited financial statements, although this conjecture is untested.

8 Other corporate governance issues

Sarbanes-Oxley has changed other aspects of corporate governance in addition to displacing the accounting profession's control of auditing. Romano (2005) analyzes several aspects of Sarbanes-Oxley and is critical of its provisions with respect to the requirement for fully independent audit committees, restricting the purchase of non-audit services, the prohibition on corporate loans to officers, and executive certification of financial statements. Her argument is that these mandates were unnecessary, duplicated existing requirements, or did not follow the traditional manner of regulating corporate governance at the federal level through disclosure remedies. By mandating rules to govern the actual behavior of SEC registrants, she argues that SOX also usurps the traditional role of states in regulating corporate governance. Her general thesis is that SOX was "emergency" legislation that occurred in the context of a media frenzy and a charged political atmosphere, all of which contributed to the creation of a very bad law. She further finds no body of research to support the logic of any of these mandates, and she points out that none of the 50 states had previously enacted any of the new mandates imposed by SOX, which suggests that the benefits may be limited since not a single state-level jurisdiction had previously thought such regulations were important enough to be adopted.

One corporate governance change in SOX does directly affect auditing practice. Auditors are now required to report directly to the audit committee of the board of directors rather than the client management, and the audit committee must oversee the auditor's work and must pre-approve all services provided by the auditor, both audit and non-audit services. This requirement is intended to increase an auditor's independence by reducing the power of the client's managers to intimidate an auditor with the threat of dismissal. The new requirement assumes of course that boards of directors in general and audit committees in particular are capable of exercising independent oversight of managers; however, research on the quality of corporate governance by boards is mixed and inconclusive with respect to the effectiveness of boards in controlling managers. The requirement for audit committees to pre-approve non-audit services is intended to regulate the scope of services and to limit those services that might compromise auditor independence or the perception of auditor independence. Assuming that audit committees are competent and independent of management, it is hard to object to these changes since the contracting process is a particularly vulnerable area for auditors in terms of maintaining independence from the influence of a client's management.

The most controversial and most costly aspect of Sarbanes-Oxley is the section 404 requirement for a management report on internal control effectiveness over financial reporting, along with an attestation of the report's accuracy by the auditor. For the auditor this is a new requirement over and above the normal review of internal control undertaken as part of the annual financial statement audit, and is governed by PCAOB Auditing Standard No. 2 issued in 2004. The compliance costs associated with SOX 404 have proved to be far greater than first anticipated. According to the Financial Executives International (FEI), a survey of 217 large companies with average revenue above $5 billion shows the cost of compliance in 2004 averaged $4.36 million (FEI 2004). While these companies also believe that SOX has improved investor confidence in corporate governance, concerns are expressed that the compliance costs exceed the real benefits, especially with respect to section 404.[11] As a result, there has been extensive lobbying to repeal the section 404 requirement altogether, or at least to make it optional for smaller registrants due to its allegedly burdensome cost.

9 The future

The United States has embarked on a regulatory path and control over auditing unlike any other country in the world. In addition to the cost of section 404 internal reports, audit fees have approximately doubled from 2001 to 2004.[12] Does this mean that auditing is twice as good as it was in 2001 or that audit failures will be cut in half? Probably not, as it is doubtful that the direct benefits of SOX from improved audit quality and corporate governance exceed the costs of compliance. Of course, it is possible that the broader (indirect) benefits of SOX are positive if improved investor confidence is also taken into account, although this is very hard to measure and quantify.[13]

How did this all happen? Zeff (2003b) suggests that beginning in the late 1970s the leadership of the accounting profession, and the large firms in particular, became focused on the commercial aspects of their business in terms of growth and global expansion, and that these "business values" displaced traditional "professional values" such as auditor independence and serving the public interest. It is sad that greed seemingly caused the US accounting profession to forget why independent audits exist in the first place. That said, the US experience can still serve as a positive example to the rest of the world in terms of what can happen if the accounting profession loses credibility by appearing to act more in its own self-interest rather than in the public interest which is at the heart of public accounting. As for the United States, perhaps the best that can be said about the changes imposed by Sarbanes-Oxley is that accounting firms seem to be focused again on performing high quality audits, and this is certainly a good thing, although it has come at a very high price to the profession.

Notes

1   The accounting profession retains control over auditing standards for private companies, and the Auditing Standards Board of the American Institute of Certified Public Accountants still exists. This is discussed later in the chapter.
2   For additional background, see Carey (1969, 1970) for official histories of the US accounting profession up to the 1960s, and Zeff (2003a, 2003b) for a more critical assessment of the profession and events leading up to the passage of Sarbanes-Oxley in 2002.
3   Reciprocity is not an automatic process because each state has its own specific rules on the level of education required to sit the uniform licensing examination and the number of years of experience required to become a CPA after passing the licensing exam, and on the code of ethical conduct and other regulations including continuing education requirements.
4   Eligibility rules differ from state to state in terms of whether individuals must have completed a university degree at the time of the exam. In the past, grading was also done on a state-by-state basis and there was evidence of differential grading and "pass rates" across states being dependent on the condition of a particular state's accounting labor market and whether there were deemed to be too few or too many accountants (Young 1988).
5   Even for SEC registrants, specific incorporation and corporate charter requirements and many other aspects of corporate law and governance are traditionally the exclusive province of the state where a company is incorporated. This is why many US companies are incorporated in the state of Delaware, a state which has more lenient corporate governance rules that give boards of directors more flexibility to act without direct shareholder approval.
6   Given the creation of the PCAOB, in 2003 the AIPCA replaced the SEC Practice Division with a new unit called the Center for Public Company Audit Firms. Information is available on the AICPA website at http://cpcaf.aicpa.org. Membership of the new unit is voluntary and its purpose is unclear given the PCAOB regulatory mandate with respect to SEC registrants.

7 The state-level regulation of auditor licensing has also changed as states have revised their laws and have dual requirements for CPAs to comply with new PCAOB rules when auditing public companies, and the existing standards when auditing other (private) entities.

8 A related point is the reach of the PCAOB over non-US operations of the Big Four accounting firms. Since Big Four firms are organized as country-specific partnerships, each country-specific partnership has to register separately if it audits SEC registrants, and presumably each national practice will be required to comply with registration rules including PCAOB inspections.

9 The letter from FEE is available on its website at: http://www.fee.be/publications/default.asp?library_ref=4&content_ref=130

10 The Committee on Auditing Procedure of the AICPA issued the first "Statement on Auditing Procedures" in 1939, which provided guidance on ten general areas of auditing. This standard created a broad framework for auditing, and subsequent standards issued by the AIPCA were primarily an elaboration and further development of the original ten standards.

11 In the first round of section 404 reports, approximately 16 percent of 3,386 companies had one or more material internal control weaknesses, as reported in *Public Accounting Report*, 15 December 2005: 4.

12 Using data from Audit Analytics for 5,994 companies for 2001 and 2004, the median increase in audit fees over this three-year period was 93 percent. The first quartile fee increase was 23 percent from 2001 to 2004, and the 75th quartile increase in fees was 236 percent.

13 The cost of perceived poor corporate governance may be quite large, and for this reason the SEC argued in 2000 that firms should not be able to hire their auditors for non-audit services because it lowers the public's confidence in audit quality. Evidence of this is reported by Krishnan *et al.* (2005) and Francis and Ke (2006), who find that the stock market valuation of earnings surprises is smaller for firms that hire their auditors for non-audit services. Francis and Ke (2006) calculate a "discount" in securities prices of approximately 30 percent for firms with large levels of non-audit fees.

References

Advisory Panel on Auditor Independence (1994) *Strengthening the Professionalism of the Independent Auditor*, Stamford, CT: Public Oversight Board.

American Institute of Certified Public Accountants (1987) *Plan to Restructure Professional Standards*, New York City: American Institute of Certified Public Accountants.

American Institute of Certified Public Accountants (1993) *In the Public Interest: a Special Report by the Public Oversight Board of the SEC Practice Section*, New York City: American Institute of Certified Public Accountants.

American Institute of Certified Public Accountants (1997) *Serving the Public Interest: a New Conceptual Framework for Auditor Independence*, New York City: American Institute of Certified Public Accountants.

Arthur Andersen, Coopers & Lybrand, Deloitte Touche, Ernst & Young, KPMG Peat Marwick, and Price Waterhouse (1992) "The Liability Crisis in the United States. Joint Letter Signed by the Big Six Accounting Firms," *Journal of Accountancy*, 174(5, November): 19-23.

Berryman, R.G. (1978) "Auditor Independence: Its Historical Development and Some Proposals for Research," in S.B. Loeb (ed.) *Ethics in the Accounting Profession*, New York City: John Wiley & Sons.

Carey, J.L. (1969) *The Rise of the Accounting Profession: From Technicians to Professionals, 1896–1936*, New York City: American Institute of Certified Public Accountants.

Carey, J.L. (1970) *The Rise of the Accounting Profession: To Responsibility and Authority, 1937–1969*, New York City: American Institute of Certified Public Accountants.

Chow, C. (1982) "The Demand for External Auditing: Size, Debt and Ownership Influences," *The Accounting Review*, 57(2): 272–91.

Commission on Auditors' Responsibilities (1978) "Report, Conclusions, and Recommendations," Commission on Auditors' Responsibilities: An Independent Commission Established by the American Institute of Certified Public Accountants, New York.

Dechow, P., Sloan, R., and Sweeney, A. (1996) "Causes and Consequences of Earnings Manipulation: An Analysis of Firms Subject to Enforcement Actions by the SEC," *Contemporary Accounting Research*, 13(2): 1–36.

DeFond, M. and Francis, J. (2005) "Audit Research after Sarbanes-Oxley?" *Auditing: A Journal of Practice and Theory*, 24 (Supplement): 5–30.

Feroz, E., Park, K., and Pastena, V. (1991) "The Financial and Market Effects of the SEC's Accounting and Auditing Enforcement Releases," *Journal of Accounting Research*, 29 (Supplement): 107–42.

Financial Executives International (2004) "FEI Special Survey on Sarbanes-Oxley Section 404 Implementation," Florham Park, NJ: Financial Executives International (FEI).

Francis, J.R. and Ke, B. (2006) "Disclosure of Fees Paid to Auditors and the Market Valuation of Earnings Surprises," *Review of Accounting Studies*, 11(4): 495–523.

Francis, J. and Krishnan, J. (2002) "Evidence on Auditor Risk-Management Strategies Before and After the Private Securities Litigation Reform Act of 1995," *Asia-Pacific Journal of Accounting and Economics*, 9(2): 135–57.

International Federation of Accountants (1995) *Auditors' Legal Liability in the Global Marketplace: A Case for Limitation*, New York City: International Federation of Accountants.

Krishnan, J., Heibatollah, S., and Zhang, Y. (2005) "Does the Provision of Nonaudit Services Affect Investor Perceptions of Auditor Independence?" *Auditing: A Journal of Practice and Theory*, 24(2): 111–35.

Lee, H. and Mande, V. (2003) "The Effect of the Private Litigation Reform Act of 1995 on Accounting Discretion of Client Managers of Big 6 and Non-Big 6 Auditors," *Auditing: A Journal of Practice and Theory*, 22(1): 93–108.

Levitt, A. (with P. Dwyer) (2002) *Take on the Street*, New York City: Pantheon Books.

Merino, B. and Neimark, M. (1982) "Disclosure Regulation and Public Policy: A Sociohistorical Reappraisal," *Journal of Accounting and Public Policy*, 1(1): 33–57.

National Commission on Fraudulent Reporting (1987), Report of the Committee of Sponsoring Organizations of the Treadway Commission (COSO). Available at: http://www.coso.org/publications.htm

Panel on Audit Effectiveness (2000) "The Panel on Audit Effectiveness: Report and Recommendations," Public Oversight Board of the American Institute of Certified Public Accountants, New York.

Public Accounting Report (2005) "Top 100 for 2005," Public Accounting Report Extra Report, 31 August 2005.

Romano, R. (2005) "The Sarbanes-Oxley Act and the Making of Quack Corporate Governance," *The Yale Law Journal*, 114: 1523–611.

Securities and Exchange Commission (2000) *Proposed Rule: Revision of the Commission's Auditor Independence Requirements*, Washington, DC: United States Securities and Exchange Commission.

Seligman, J. (1985) *The SEC and the Future of Finance*, New York City: Praeger Publishers.

United States Senate (1976) "The Accounting Establishment, Report of the Subcommittee on Reports, Accounting, and Management of the Committee on Governmental Affairs," Washington, DC: United States Government Printing Office.

Wilson, T. and Grimlund, R. (1990) "An Examination of the Importance of an Auditor's Reputation," *Auditing: A Journal of Practice and Theory*, 9: 43–59.

Young, S.D. (1988) "The Economic Theory of Regulation: Evidence from the Uniform CPA Examination," *The Accounting Review*, 63(2): 283–91.

Zeff, S. (2003a) "How the U.S. Accounting Profession Got Where It Is Today: Part I," *Accounting Horizons*, 17(3): 189–205.

Zeff, S. (2003b) "How the U.S. Accounting Profession Got Where It Is Today: Part II," *Accounting Horizons*, 17(4): 267–86.

13 Understanding regulation in its global context

Christopher Humphrey and Peter Moizer

1 Introduction

Each of the chapters in this book has set out the way in which the statutory audit of companies is conducted and regulated. It can be seen that there is considerable diversity in the ways in which European countries have responded to the issues of education and training, auditing standard setting, oversight and auditors' liability. The year 2007 has been an interesting one in which to review all these issues, as many of the individual country characteristics are likely to be significantly reduced in the future, with the Europeans potentially moving towards the approach to regulation adopted in the US. In this respect, the US chapter forms an interesting point of comparison, demonstrating both the historical autonomy that individual states have had within the federal structure and the trend towards reducing the extent of this autonomy in favour of a more general, overarching system. The passage of the Sarbanes-Oxley legislation in 2002 has speeded up this trend and increased the powers of independent federal auditing regulators. In Europe it can be seen that similar trends and tensions are also at work, with the extent of national differences arguably declining as Europe pushes towards greater integration within its financial reporting system. Europe's equivalent regulatory vehicle to Sarbanes-Oxley is the Revised Eighth Directive, which aims to harmonize auditing within the member states of the European Union. It is too early to say whether Europe will inexorably follow the US federalist approach, but that is certainly the trend, with the emphasis on the use of International Financial Reporting Standards and the adoption of International Standards on Auditing instead of nationally based standards. Only time will tell if the world described in the chapters in this book is one that has a *fin de siècle* feel about it.

2 The revised Eighth Directive

As the chapters have indicated, one of the main forces for change, both historically and contemporarily, in the statutory audit of European countries has been the response to accounting scandals – typified in the UK in the late 1980s/early 1990s by major scandals such as BCCI, Maxwell and Polly Peck and subsequent regulatory initiatives committed to enhancing general standards of corporate governance. The initial reaction of most European auditors to the Enron and WorldCom scandals, however, was that they could not have happened in Europe because of the European emphasis on substance over form, in contrast to the claimed more legalistic, rule-bound traditions in US financial reporting. The British accountancy profession was particularly prominent in arguing that the US scandals were aberrations – products of a US system that did not reflect the realities of UK business in 2002. The then president of the Institute of Chartered Accountants in England and Wales argued forcefully that advances in corporate governance practice and UK financial regulation made the UK something of 'an island of calm, proficient and virtuous practice' (see Evers 2002). However, the advent of scandals in the Netherlands (Ahold), Italy (Parmalat) and Denmark (Nordisk Fjer) pointed to the need for serious reflection on the state of auditing and auditing regulation in Europe. Indeed, it soon became clear that European legislators were seeking revisions to the existing Eighth Directive (Directive 84/253/EEC) to strengthen the provisions relating to the work of the statutory auditor – and, in so doing, to provide a European response to the US Sarbanes-Oxley legislation. Without such legislative reform, European audit firms undertaking audits of US companies could well have been left substantially at the mercy of the US PCAOB, given that existing EU legislation was seen by US regulators as being too weak.

On 25 April 2006 the Council of the European Union adopted a new directive on the audit of company accounts. This Revised Eighth Company Law Directive on Statutory Audit broadened the scope of the application of existing EU legislation (Directive 84/253/EEC). It specified the duties of statutory auditors, their independence and ethics (Downes 2005), introducing requirements for external quality assurance by ensuring better public oversight over the audit profession and improved co-operation between oversight bodies in the EU. The final approved document followed amendments, by the European Parliament on 28 September 2005, to the Commission's proposal for a directive issued in 2004. The amendments put forward by the European Parliament included: granting member states the discretion to exempt certain public interest entities from the obligation to have an audit committee, and requiring the key audit partner to rotate from the audit engagement within seven years (rather than within five as the Commission had proposed).

The main changes that the new directive introduces are as follows:

- *Public oversight over statutory auditors.* Member states are required to establish audit oversight boards, which will be responsible for the approval and registration of audit firms. This will involve: (1) the adoption of national standards on audit ethics, (2) quality control of audit firms and auditors, (3) continuous education of auditors and (4) investigative and, if necessary, disciplinary actions against audit firms. All audit firms and auditors involved in statutory audits will be required to obtain approval from the oversight board and will be registered in the publicly available national register of statutory auditors.

- *Audit quality assurance.* Audit firms involved in statutory audits will be required to have an internal system of quality assurance that is subject to public oversight. This includes conducting reviews that assess and report on an audit firm's internal quality control system. Each firm that audits public interest entities must be reviewed every three years. Member states are required to provide sanctions, including civil, administrative and criminal penalties, for inadequate execution of the statutory audit.
- *Confidentiality of client information.* Information and documents accessed during an audit must be protected by confidentiality rules. Confidentiality, however, will not impede investigations by an oversight board.
- *Audit committees.* Public interest entities, such as banks and companies listed on stock exchanges, are required to establish an audit committee, which is responsible for appointing and/or dismissing the audit firm for statutory audits. Initially the European Commission had proposed that all publicly listed companies should have a separate audit committee. This proposal, however, has been somewhat diluted such that in member states where companies have a two-tier board structure (an operational or administrative board and a supervisory board), the member state will be able to decide whether to make audit committees mandatory or whether an existing supervisory board can perform the functions of the audit committee. An audit committee will be composed of non-executive members of the board, with at least one financial expert. The committee will need to ensure that the company's financial statements are consistent with international accounting standards and that the fee paid to the audit firm is 'fair'. To do this, audit committees and management will need to understand key aspects of an audit firm's corporate governance, quality control and education processes, as well as fees and compensation structures. They will also need to understand international auditing standards and how they apply to the company in question. Auditors are required to report to the audit committee on key matters arising from the statutory audit, particularly on material weaknesses in internal controls related to the financial reporting process.
- *Disclosure of audit fees.* To improve transparency of the audit process, public interest entities are required to disclose fees paid to the audit firm. This includes fees for audit services as well as fees for non-audit services. Member states are required to ensure that statutory audit fees are adequate to allow a proper audit, and that they are not influenced by fees for additional services.
- *Audit firm transparency.* Audit firms will be required to publish an annual transparency report. This report will disclose: (1) the legal structure and ownership of the firm, (2) its internal quality control system, (3) the date of the last quality assurance review, (4) a list of the public interest entities for which statutory audits were conducted in the past year, (5) a breakdown of

the fees charged by the firm and (6) the compensation scheme for audit partners.

- *Auditor independence and objectivity.* The directive includes a number of measures to ensure independence of statutory auditors from their clients. Similar to Sarbanes-Oxley, the new EU directive is likely to prevent auditors from doing non-audit work for their audit clients. The proposal for the new directive requires that 'a statutory auditor or an audit firm shall not carry out a statutory audit if there is any financial, business, employment or other relationship, including the provision of additional services, with the audited entity that might compromise the statutory auditor's or audit firm's independence'. The new directive will require audit firms annually to disclose threats to their independence and to confirm their independence in writing. The new directive will also require rotation of audit partners every seven years.

- *Adherence to international auditing standards.* To improve the quality of audits, audit professionals will be required to meet certain educational requirements and to follow specified international auditing standards. Audit firms will be required to maintain professional ethics and to adopt a common standard audit report consistent with international standards.

- *Group auditor responsibility.* An audit firm performing an audit for a group of companies will be required to take full responsibility for the audit report in relation to the consolidated accounts. This group auditor responsibility extends to the work of other audit firms, possibly in another jurisdiction, including the retention of copies of the other firms' audit working papers for that group audit.

The new directive has led to the creation of three new EU bodies:

1 *Audit Regulatory Committee (AuRC)* – this is composed of the national ministries charged with audit regulatory responsibilities. The AuRC held its first meeting on 22 November 2005 and has delegated authority with regard to implementing the requisite measures identified in the directive. These are likely to relate to questions of auditing standards and 'third country' auditors.

2 *European Group of Auditors' Oversight Bodies (EGAOB)* – this was established on 14 December 2005 and is composed of high-level representatives from the entities responsible for the public oversight of statutory auditors in member states or, in their absence, of representatives from the competent national ministries. Only non-practitioners can be designated as members of EGAOB. The first aim of the Group is to ensure the effective coordination of new public oversight systems of statutory auditors within the EU. It will also provide technical input to the Commission on implementing measures as required in the directive, beginning with the adoption of auditing standards and the assessment of 'third country' auditors. EGAOB has established two sub-groups to deal with these issues.

3   *European Forum on Auditors' Liability* – this was established on 15 November 2005 to assist the Commission in meeting the obligation set by the directive to produce a report on auditor liability by the end of 2006. The Forum will gather market players' views on limiting financial burdens for auditors and will consider market-led solutions to mitigate litigation risks. The Forum comprises twenty market experts from various professional backgrounds (such as auditors, bankers, investors, company directors, insurers and academics) with particular experience and knowledge of the subject. Their report will examine the impact of liability rules on statutory auditors and insurance conditions. If appropriate, the European Commission will then issue recommendations to member states. As part of this process, the Commission has launched a study on the economic impact of alternative liability regimes, competition in the audit market and the availability of insurance. It is envisaged that the Commission, working in conjunction with the Forum and drawing on the findings of the study, will undertake public consultation on the issue as part of the preparation for completing its report. EGAOB and AuRC will also provide input on this important issue.

Perhaps the most controversial provision of the Revised Eighth Directive comes under the 'International' heading, where a new requirement is being introduced for auditors and/or audit firms from 'third countries' that issue audit reports in relation to securities traded in the EU. Such auditors/audit firms will now have to register in the EU and be subject to member state systems of oversight, quality assurance and investigations and sanctions. In what could be classified as the European post-Sarbanes-Oxley regulatory retaliation, US auditors/audit firms are left in the position of seeking an authorization mechanism to allow them to carry out statutory audits in member states.

3 Theorising the international commitment to audit regulation and public oversight

In seeking to understand what is happening in today's increasingly international regulatory arena and the implications for national regulatory systems, it is worth reviewing some of the theories that have evolved in attempts to explain both the origins and the practice of regulation – namely, the public interest theory of regulation, the economic theory of regulation and the public choice theory of regulation.

Public interest theory (or market failure theory) is based on the normative view that government intervention may be appropriate in cases where markets 'fail' in some way. A market failure occurs when the unregulated market outcomes are suboptimal relative to some social welfare objective function, such as in the 'efficient' allocation of resources. However, market failure is not a sufficient reason to generate government regulation, as regulation is not necessarily the only solution available to government (e.g., it could use taxes or subsidies to change behaviour). Therefore, public interest theory requires not only a market failure but also that regulation is deemed to be the most efficient way of bridging the gap between price and marginal (social) cost. The implicit assumption is that some activities will function best in the public interest given a sufficient level of supervision and control, which will be partly determined by the amount of coercive power that the state can bring to bear on the issue. Public interest theory hypothesizes that regulation will occur when it delivers a net social gain. This view is reinforced by the way that much regulation, particularly in the financial reporting area, is introduced following some form of crisis or public dissent, usually caused by a major corporate scandal involving fraud and the suffering of the innocent. The main problem with this theoretical perspective is that it does not explain the mechanisms by which regulatory change will occur and the processes by which politicians, civil servants, etc. generate a regulatory outcome that is claimed (and demonstrated subsequently) as best serving the public interest. The image of the government as a costless and reliable instrument for altering market behaviour has been extensively questioned (Uche 2001), with significant costs being incurred in the provision of data and information to regulators, not to mention the dysfunctional (unintended) consequences that regulatory action can engender. For instance, regulation can serve to reduce the reactivity and flexibility of organizations in the face of changing environments. Regulation can also affect management style, as managers become more oriented towards satisfying the regulators than meeting their normal objectives, in turn raising questions about the extent to which government intervention is beneficial to the public.

Stigler's theory of economic regulation (Stigler 1971), or what is probably better referred to as an economic theory of regulation, has been used to explain the presence of regulation in different industries and has helped to create an awareness of the incentives and wealth-redistribution consequences of economic regulation. Three basic premises of his theory were that:

1   The basic resource of government is the power to coerce.
2   An interest group that can convince the government to use its coercive power to its benefit can improve its well-being at the expense of others.
3   Individual actors in the process (companies, politicians, civil servants, interest groups, etc.) are rational and try to maximize their own utility.

From these premises, regulation is supplied in response to the demands of interest groups acting to maximize their own well-being. Stigler observed that the legislators were driven by their desire to stay in office, which normally involved maximizing their political support. In the US, regulation has become one way of redistributing wealth, and interest groups compete for that wealth redistribution by offering political support in exchange for favourable legislation. The implication of this theory is that regulation is likely to be biased towards benefiting interest groups that are better organized and have more to gain from the wealth redistribution. As there are often competing interests on a particular issue, the economic theory of regulation suggests that regulation will reflect a balance of political forces.

Public choice theories have sought to take such analysis further by analysing explicitly the behaviour of the different actors involved in the regulatory decision-making process (whether they be politicians, bureaucrats and/or other interest groups) and the impact of this interaction on regulatory developments. It is generally claimed that politicians and bureaucrats will attempt to improve their own well-being, which means pursuing regulatory policies that help to keep their voter-determined jobs while maximizing their expected life-time earnings.

The above three theories can help to explain some of the processes that brought about Sarbanes-Oxley and the European Eighth Directive. A normative public interest theory would suggest that politicians believed that the state of financial accounting and auditing that existed at the turn of the millennium was failing. The only remedy was a regulatory one and so politicians sought to introduce regulations that would have the effect of remedying the market failure that they identified. In terms of auditing, the market failure that seemed most important to politicians was that the management of Enron and Parmalat knowingly prepared false financial reports and that the auditors did not comment on them. Sarbanes-Oxley and the Eighth Directive contain a number of regulatory strands. The first is to increase the penalties for allowing misleading audited financial statements to be published. The second is to increase the number of checks in the process, by expanding the role of the audit committees and creating new regulatory oversight boards. A third strand is the provision of more information, which is particularly true of Sarbanes-Oxley and the now notorious Section 404, which requires that management include an internal control report in the company's annual report. A fourth strand involves taking measures to strengthen auditor independence by such means as restricting the services that auditors can provide that are not directly connected with the audit and rotating the lead audit partner. The effect of these measures has been to increase costs dramatically. The group that bears the brunt of the costs comprises the shareholders, who suffer reduced profits because of the direct costs on the companies. The effect on the profitability of audit firms is less clear – with much depending on the extent to which they have been able to increase audit fees to cover the increased costs of audit work under the new regulatory regimes. Recent performance data released by the Big Four firms does suggest that they have substantially benefited financially from the imposition of the new regulatory rules. Further, within the audit services market, there are suspicions of a greater divergence between those accounting firms able and prepared to undertake the statutory audit of large scale, public interest entities and those (smaller audit firms) that are not.

One effect of the regulatory initiatives, therefore, has been to strengthen the market dominance of the Big Four firms and to increase the effective concentration of the audit services market. In the UK, the effect has become so marked that a report in April 2006 by Oxera Consulting Ltd contained the following conclusions:

> Oxera has found evidence that higher concentration has led to higher audit fees (in line with economic theory and with several other recent empirical studies). While there is a degree of price sensitivity among companies, and some bargaining on fees takes place during the annual audit firm reappointment process, in general the focus of audit committee chairs is more on quality (and reputation) than on price. Separately from the impact of concentration, audit fees seem to have risen in recent years as a result of cost increases, caused by factors such as changes in regulation.
>
> On the question of choice, Oxera has found that a limited number of UK-listed companies, primarily in the financial services sector of the FTSE 100, have no effective choice of auditor in the short run. This elimination of choice is driven by high market concentration, auditor independence rules, supply-side constraints, and the need for sector expertise.

An economic theory of regulation would suggest that the larger audit firms would not be unhappy at the turn of events, even though they cannot be said to have lobbied overtly for the introduction of Sarbanes-Oxley or the Eighth Directive. It could also be that concerns over market concentration and auditor capacity will prove beneficial for mid-tier firms if they serve to generate more institutional pressure for the Big Four divide to be closed. A public interest theory would suggest that politicians (particularly US ones) have seen that it is in their interest to bring in such legislative regulatory provisions and that the compliance costs were a minor consideration. It would also suggest that the regulatory 'bureaucrats' staffing public oversight boards in the audit arena will have a primary desire to continue in business and, if possible, to grow larger and extend their influence and impact, usually without any reference to the costs involved. Increasing regulation has been a boon for the bureaucrats and it will take some considerable time before any deregulation can be envisaged. The difficulty faced by anyone proposing a reduction in regulation in this area is that any subsequent scandal is highly likely to be attributed to any such act of deregulation, leaving somebody to pay a high political price for the resulting perceived 'regulatory failure'.

4 The question(ing) of audit regulation

What is potentially most striking about today's international regulatory arena is the very fact that we are increasingly prepared not only to talk and conceive of regulatory initiatives and systems in global terms but also to believe in them and see them as achievable. Many an international accounting or auditing conference is rooted these days in notions of opportunity – a once-in-a-lifetime chance to break with long histories of national difference and to secure harmonization, consistency and equivalence in accounting and auditing practices. Such a set of beliefs is something that auditing academics have to treat with a degree of analytical scepticism, especially given the scale of differences in the regulatory arrangements and traditions revealed in this book. Indeed, rather than being a golden opportunity to break with the traditions and obstacles of past regulatory diversity and hindrances, the pursuit of global harmonization might also be regarded as something of a naïve dream – misplaced wishes destined to fall foul of the day-to-day complexities and differences in accounting and auditing practices and traditions that will inevitably confront regulators with (or even without) extra-territorial reach.

Whatever perspective is taken on the prospects for global regulatory harmonization in auditing, acknowledgement has to be given to the growing array of international standard setting and associated regulatory bodies that comprise today's global financial infrastructure. Likewise, it can be seen that there is evident pressure on national regulatory bodies to gain a foothold or recognition as key players in such an arena – whether in terms of securing enhanced powers of jurisdictional reach, playing a direct role in global standard setting processes or developing more indirect roles as thought leaders. A global regulatory system is certainly in the process of being established, although there are still competing views as to whether it is yet capable of being regarded as a Taj Mahal or Versailles-like structure (polished, complete and awe-inspiring) or is still very much a building site, in which different groups and representative interests battle and negotiate for recognition and significance (see Giovanoli 2000).

In this context, auditing regulation becomes a subject that needs to be studied from both national and international perspectives, particularly in terms of the changing interface between national and global regulatory systems. This was the conclusion of a speech given by Charlie McCreevy, the European Commissioner for Internal Market and Services:

> Regulatory frameworks for auditing might differ across the world. There are different traditions; we have different types of institutions and different rules on our statute books. But, in an increasingly global auditing market where big international networks cater for clients who are active around the world, there is a growing need for co-operation between regulators and supervisors. Industry is right to ask us for rules that are devised for a global industry and not only on the basis of national borders that have long been transcended in real life.
>
> (McCreevy 2006)

There is a difficulty with this vision, which can be put in its bluntest terms by noting that we have no global government from which global regulators take their orders, or to whom global regulators are directly accountable (see Loft *et al.* 2006). The authority of 'global' regulators accordingly derives from other sources, such as the demands and dictates of global capital markets, the extraterritorial privileges gained by being the creation of a particularly powerful individual nation or group of nations, or well-publicized (and acknowledged) claims to serve generic notions of 'public interest'. As such, the legitimacy of regulatory organizations on the global stage should not be taken for granted – but has to be kept under regular review and analysis, so that it is clear what is being done and what is being privileged (or ignored) in the name of global governance.

Such a commitment is particularly important at the present time. The failings attributed, post-Enron, to self-regulated systems required, and continue to require, an independent regulatory response. Enron and associated scandals arguably have come to symbolize the passing of a threshold beyond which self-regulation by diverse national professional bodies can never be trusted. Or, put another way, the idiosyncrasies of different national regulatory systems and traditions can no longer be allowed to get in the way of international capital movements. The vision of global harmonization and the-post Enron challenge to (if not demise of) self-regulated professional regimes mean that those 'independent' oversight institutions endowed with regulatory authority currently operate from a very strong position. It could be said that we are living in a period of 'regulatory heaven' in which certain regulators can do little wrong, as they hold the upper ground, through being either independent of the auditing profession or committed to public-interest global agendas, rather than private-interest or nationally oriented goals.

5 A case for thinking differently

A primary responsibility of auditing researchers (and others with an interest in the operation of global capital markets) is not to take regulation and regulatory bodies for granted – nor to overly presume the effectiveness of the working of regulators or those (auditors) that they are regulating. It is essential to retain a degree of scepticism or inquisitiveness as to the ability of regulators to cast light on, and improve, audit practice. How efficient and effective are contemporary regulatory practices? Are regulations working? Are they pitched at the right level? Are they delivering improved audit quality? Are regulators engendering concrete developments in audit practice? Or are achievements more about giving out the right signals – delivering changes that are more symbolic than real? Where is the revised Eighth Directive having an impact? Will Europe be able to operate a regulatory system that is distinctive in practical implementation from the US Sarbanes-Oxley regime, or is the latter destined to dominate as global capital markets drive ever more for the harmonization and convergence of accounting and auditing practices? Are regulatory methodologies and the findings of regulatory investigations sufficiently transparent? Do we know enough about what is being done in the name not just of auditing, but also of auditing regulation?

The fact that such questions (and many more questions) can be asked of regulators is very telling. We simply do not know enough about the practical operation of regulatory systems. This book has sought to make a substantive start to what is a compelling research agenda by bringing together a collection of commentaries on different regulatory systems and the issues confronting national regulators. The sheer range of regulatory practices and traditions described in the book firmly establishes the importance of a 'thinking', contextually sensitive, approach to auditing regulation – an approach that relies on in-depth understanding of the development of regulatory systems rather than a loosely bound collection of myths and generalizations about the origins and development of particular practices. Critical here is the need to caution against a regulatory response which automatically delivers yet more regulations in the aftermath of major corporate scandals and presumed cases of audit failure. Regulation does fail. Regulations can struggle to reach the areas and activities that they are supposed to reach. They routinely can have unintended consequences, encouraging game-playing on the part of those being regulated rather than stimulating innovation in (audit) practice. Furthermore, it is always more difficult to remove regulations than it is to introduce new ones.

A typical problem for regulators is getting stuck in regulatory routines which fail to address the limits of existing systems or recognize the potential benefits of alternative approaches. As an illustration, just think how many regulations there are, and have been over time, concerning auditor independence – and yet auditor independence remains a persistent problem. Audit failures may well be the consequence of a lack of competence of auditors and shortcomings in their audit methodologies and testing regimes, yet somehow regulatory concern, as it has post-Enron, routinely ends up concentrating much more on issues of auditor independence and over-presuming levels of auditor competence (for more discussion see Humphrey *et al.* 2006). In many respects, we need regulators that are capable of thinking maybe not the unthinkable, but at least of routinely challenging the regulatory status quo. For instance, are more dependent auditors (e.g. those working more closely with client management) more likely to be effective in detecting material fraud and error? Have we got too many regulations? Are there ones that could easily be removed without there being any effect on audit practice? Which regulations have a positive impact on auditor performance? Is today's checklist-compliant, post-Sarbanes-Oxley auditor a more effective auditor? Have audit technologies kept pace with the sophistication of and technological advancement in corporate information and data processing systems?

Putting the case for thinking differently in terms of auditing regulation is not to signal any privileging of the recommendations and preferences of any particular school of auditing thought. It is probably better seen as a call for a more sensitized and knowledge-based approach to auditing regulation. It should also be one that is willing to engage in regulatory experimentation. Too much regulation can take the form of knee-jerk reactions to corporate scandals and the associated political pressures for action that such scandals can bring – a case of symbolic (but potentially ineffective) action ruling over considered, evidence-based deliberation and development. There has in this respect been much debate over whether Sarbanes-Oxley was a regulatory over-reaction, prompting competing responses from regulators that the operational problems are ones of interpretation failings on the part of auditors rather than inherent faults with regulatory provisions.

A less visible but equally fascinating indication of the political nature of the regulatory arena is the case of mandatory audit firm rotation. As a regulatory initiative, it is potentially the one that gets closest to the heart of the independence issue by setting a very clear limit (in terms of the number of years of tenure) on the auditor's economic interests in their audit client. Yet, it is the one that an independence-oriented international regulatory era has certainly shied away from. The grounds for such inaction rest primarily on the asserted failings of such a regulation in Italy and Spain, although the cited empirical evidence, on closer analysis, has been shown to be very weak, especially given that Spain never in practice forced companies to rotate their chosen audit firm (for more discussion see Carrera *et al.* 2006). Rumours and myths, albeit ones propounded by powerful international accounting organizations, are not the basis on which a sound, global regulatory system should be built. Unfortunately, too often in regulatory circles this is what happens.

Lobby groups can be seen to use all sorts of mechanisms and arguments for securing the regulations with which they feel most happy. This can have negative consequences in that regulatory development comes to be seen as partial and self-interested or self-serving, which in turn restricts fundamentally the degree of experimentation that is allowed. The result can be damaging in that it leads to initiatives never being given the chance to operate or to different camps in the regulatory debate taking very entrenched views from which it is difficult to secure progress, and making any resulting regulatory action an uncomfortable and, ultimately, ineffective political compromise. It can also encourage regulatory posturing in which all sides are desperately keen to avoid being tarred in the future with the blame for any major corporate failures (which potentially could be held to be endemic to any capitalist system and probabilistic, risk-based systems of auditing and regulation). The real regulatory intent then becomes not one of collectively working to deliver improved audit practices but one of ensuring compliance with the form (but not necessarily the substance) of regulatory requirements so that when things go wrong, different interest groups or organizations can emerge unscathed and free to develop alternative regulatory approaches.

A striking feature of regulatory systems is that existing regulations can tend to be more willingly accepted than proposed new regulations – the latter being seen to be too controversial, risky, one-sided, applicable only in certain circumstances or just generally unproven. It is forgotten that this was just how the regulations in place today were probably once viewed (when initially proposed) and yet they somehow managed to make it on to the statute book or the official regulatory code. If there is one overriding message to come out of this book, it is that no one regulation is ever likely to be all embracing and all conquering. Regulatory impact is going to depend significantly on a range of contextual factors. This is an important message in the sense that rather than inviting a conclusion that 'nothing works', it is a signal for innovation and experimentation. Regulatory solutions do not necessarily have to be comprehensive, nor do they have to be set in stone and deemed unalterable. Thus, if the auditing profession is genuine in its belief that changes in (or even clarifications of the ruling principles of) the auditor liability regime will deliver significant improvements in audit practice, maybe the most constructive way forward is to undertake an experiment. This could be limited in terms of the participating organizations or by the period of application, but with an explicit commitment that its effect and impact will be closely monitored and evaluated, particularly in terms of the significance of cultural or contextual variables, before any general or permanent change is made to the regulatory system. The opportunities for such experimentation may well be greater in Europe than in the US in that, despite similarities with Sarbanes-Oxley, the revised Eighth Directive contains far fewer provisions and detailed prescription, giving the impression that it is more intent on establishing an overarching regulatory framework than a complete A–Z manual of regulatory action.

There is always a danger that notions of experimentation and flexibility will, in today's global regulatory arena, be perceived as too piecemeal or microscopic. However, in closing it is worth reflecting on two critical dimensions of this regulatory arena. The first is the importance of recognizing the distinction between the roles of standard setting and compliance. It is one thing to set international or global standards – it is another to enforce them. Indeed, by far the most attractive dimension of global regulation is the capacity to set standards. This can easily be characterized as a creative, forward looking, dynamic role – taking practice to levels where it has never been before, removing petty national differences and putting in their place a more uniform and consistent regime and one better placed to encourage innovation and entrepreneurial activity. It stands in rather stark contrast to the all together more messy, complex, frustrating, difficult, if not dull world of compliance and enforcement – of ensuring that the advocated global standards are implemented in places where global regulatory regimes have never been, or only recently been, officially accepted. Some may talk of the sheer scale of the resources being pumped into global standard setting initiatives, but this pales into insignificance in terms of the level of investment, both economically and culturally, that will be required to ensure global compliance with such standards. It is not surprising to find that international standard setters want to set shorter, more principle-based standards – as this inevitably passes the buck of interpretation and detailed application down the regulatory line.

If anything else is needed to convince people of the imbalance or mismatch between standard setters and compliance units, just consider how much more difficult it is to find bodies claiming to be global enforcers rather than global standard setters. Or just look at how many compliance units, in comparison to standard setting bodies, are understaffed and struggling to recruit. It is clear where the power and prestige lie, although for how long any such imbalance can be allowed to exist is a critical question. Standard setters that cannot demonstrate effective compliance may well have a short shelf life, although such a conclusion does assume that the measurement of compliance is relatively unambiguous when, in reality, it is anything but. Indeed, it is arguable whether more resources are being devoted to designing (short-cut) compliance metrics than studying compliance at the grass-root levels of practice.

A second significant dimension of today's regulatory arena is that global standard setting bodies not only have few recruitment difficulties, but also, ironically, in today's global world, appear to draw their members/staff from a relatively restrictive band of people – as some may argue, they comprise the usual regulatory suspects taken from the more powerful and influential institutions in the fields of accounting and finance. It is not unusual to see today's global standard setting bodies being referred to as a global regulatory club – with concerns being expressed about the consequences of replacing former commitments to global representation with the belief that standard setters have to be experts, particularly in terms of the Anglo-American predominance that this can establish on standard setting bodies. A missionary zeal to educate the world and bring it into line with Anglo-American standards of corporate governance is one that could well benefit from being tempered by a greater desire for experimentation and an emphasis on contextual understanding and learning. It also has to be asked what can be expected from a club-like arena where there is a relatively close interaction between different participant groups. Regulators will often be ex-auditors. Public oversight board members are often individuals well known to the auditing profession. Is it a system in which people can really think differently or are they all destined to be looking over their shoulders, fearful or concerned about what others are recommending or what others think of their recommendations?

As the contents of this book make clear, it is important to know more about what exactly audit regulation comprises in different nations – before committing all to the normative power thrust of global regulation. Likewise, as this chapter has emphasized, it is important to subject the global regulatory arena to a similar focus and not to presume that it is being constructed in a fashion consistent with any desired conception of the public interest. As regulation goes global, persistent questions have to be asked not only of its effectiveness in delivering improvements in audit practice, but also of the democratic nature of global regulatory regimes, the interests they serve and the policies they develop.

Finally, it could be argued that, as a subject, both auditing and its regulation need to break free from what can be quite conservative shackles. The typical aftermath of a major set of financial scandals is the introduction of a set of regulatory reforms which end up giving auditors, those professionals whose work had been called into question by the scandals, more things to check, monitor and control. Auditors may not like the regulations, they may constrain practice or make the auditing job less attractive to high flying graduates, but they will tend to deliver increased revenues for audit firms that are able to pass on the costs of the extra work as being necessary to meet today's more exacting auditing standards. What prospects are there for regulatory provisions or developments that really do challenge the essential construction of an independent, external auditor appointed to report on the truth and fairness of corporate accounting information? What would the world of auditing look like if regulators were able or prepared to act differently and were, for instance, somehow prepared to countenance quite different forms of audit functions or even the absence of an audit function? For instance, what prospect would there be for an audit function explicitly accountable to stakeholder groups beyond shareholders? Or one that concretely rules out accountability beyond that to shareholders and firmly caps liability but demands much more detailed, public reporting by both internal and external auditors? What about an audit approach that focuses much more on corporate social and environmental responsibilities and actions? Or one that countenances the mandatory rotation of audit firms or an approach to auditing that requires the auditor to get ever closer to the client and allows for a relaxation of the need to comply with a whole range of stipulations on independence?

We are not seeking to make an explicit case for any of these alternative audit functions or regulatory approaches but to provide a reminder of the value, but also the real difficulty, of thinking differently and more deeply about auditing and audit regulation. It is intriguing in an era when we are supposed to have greater freedoms and choice – and a much heralded capacity to do many different things in different ways, with developments in internet and mobile telephone technology having revolutionized many aspects of daily life – that talk of experimentation and difference in auditing regulation can sound rather unusual, if not odd. Difference in regulation is quickly transformed into notions of competition – and regulators will generally say that competition among regulators is harmful as it will inevitably generate 'a race to the bottom', wherein corporations seek to register in regimes that have adopted the lightest touch approach to regulation. It is also said that regulators need to cooperate to ensure that they are capable of adequately monitoring corporate practices and transactions that are inherently global in nature. There is a certain irony in regulators charged with the task of facilitating the global spread of financial markets apparently not believing (for their own field of operation) in the forces of competition that underpin such markets. Not surprisingly, cases have been made economically that regulatory competition will establish optimal, rather than minimal, levels of regulation – arguments with which some regulators now appear to be familiar in speaking of an alternative regulatory 'race to the top' (e.g. Tafara 2006). However, it is very clear that there are now real constraints on or boundaries around what is deemed legitimate or appropriate regulation. For instance, as exemplified in the above speech by the SEC's Director of the Office of International Affairs, the legitimacy of Sarbanes-Oxley as a regulatory regime is now being defended on the grounds that other countries have also adopted various similar provisions. How willingly such adoptions have been undertaken is not addressed, even though it is clear that the coercive institutional pressures of global capital markets (particularly the extra-territorial powers embodied in Sarbanes-Oxley) have influenced or helped to shape regulatory responses outside the US.

Ultimately, in understanding auditing regulation, it is important to draw distinctions between evidenced-based analysis of regulatory practice and the rhetoric associated with battles for regulatory legitimacy, driven in large part by the need for regulators to justify the costs of ever-expansive regulatory regimes. The real test of any regulatory regime will be how it fares in the midst of a major corporate crisis. The Sarbanes-Oxley and Revised Eighth Directive eras are currently operating in virgin mode. Their prospects of longer-term survival, however, can only be aided by the establishment of a sound knowledge base as to how such systems operate in practice, coupled with a regulatory willingness to adapt, develop and innovate as conditions and experience dictate. A world committed to harmonization is also one that has to learn from difference and to consider (and invest appropriately in) new ideas and approaches. In this respect, it is crucial to understand that the Achilles' heel of any regulatory system is not likely to be a lack of oversight but a lack of foresight!

References

Carrera, N., Gomez-Aguilar, N., Humphrey, C. and Ruiz-Barbadillo, E. (2006) 'Mandatory Audit Firm Rotation in Spain: A Policy That Was Never Applied', working paper, Instituto de Empresa Business School, Madrid.

Downes, D. (2005) 'Progress on Eighth Company Law Directive', *Accountancy Ireland*, 37(6, December): 27–9.

Evers, L. (2002) 'European View of UK Accountancy – Do They Really Mean Us?', *Accountancy*, 130 (1310, October): 16.

Financial Reporting Council (FRC) (2006) *Transparency Reporting by Auditors of Public Interest Entities*, A Consultation Document on the Implementation of Article 40 of the Eighth Company Law Directive on the Statutory Audit of Annual Accounts, Professional Oversight Board, FRC, London.

Giovanoli, M. (2000) 'A New Architecture for the Global Financial Market: Legal Aspects of International Financial Standard Setting', in M. Giovanoli (ed.) *International Monetary Law: Issues for the New Millennium*, Oxford: Oxford University Press, pp. 30–1.

Humphrey, C., Moizer, P. and Turley, S. (2006) 'Independence and Competence', *Advances in Public Interest Accounting*, forthcoming.

Lemieux, P. (2004) 'The Public Choice Revolution', *Regulation*, 27(3, Fall): 22–6.

Loft, A., Humphrey, C. and Turley, S. (2006) 'In Pursuit of Global Regulation: Changing Governance and Accountability Structures at the International Federation of Accountants (IFAC)', *Accounting, Auditing and Accountability Journal*, 19(3): 428–51.

McCreevy, C. (2006) 'EU Audit Regulation and International Cooperation', Speech/06/592, *FEE Conference on Audit Regulation*, Brussels, 12 October 2006.

Online. Available at: <http://www.iasplus.com/europe/0610mccreevyaudit.pdf> (accessed 21 February 2007).

Oxera (2006) *Competition and Choice in the UK Audit Market*, Oxera Consulting Ltd, 40/41 Park End Street, Oxford OX1 1JD.

Stigler, G. (1971) 'The Theory of Economic Regulation', *Bell Journal of Economics and Management Sciences*, 2(1): 3–21.

Tafara, E. (2006) 'Statement by SEC Staff: A Race to the Top: International Regulatory Reform Post Sarbanes-Oxley', *International Financial Law Review*, September. Online. Available at: <http://www.sec.gov/news/speech/2006/ spch091106et.htm> (accessed 21 February 2007).

Uche, C.U. (2001) 'The Theory of Regulation: A Review Article', *Journal of Financial Regulation and Compliance*, 9(1, February): 67–80.

Index